Micro, Small, and Medium Enterprises in Vietnam

UNU World Institute for Development Economics Research (UNU-WIDER) was established by the United Nations University as its first research and training centre and started work in Helsinki, Finland, in 1985. The mandate of the institute is to undertake applied research and policy analysis on structural changes affecting developing and transitional economies, to provide a forum for the advocacy of policies leading to robust, equitable, and environmentally sustainable growth, and to promote capacity strengthening and training in the field of economic and social policy-making. Its work is carried out by staff researchers and visiting scholars in Helsinki and via networks of collaborating scholars and institutions around the world.

United Nations University World Institute for Development Economics Research (UNU-WIDER)
Katajanokanlaituri 6B, 00160 Helsinki, Finland
www.wider.unu.edu

Micro, Small, and Medium Enterprises in Vietnam

Edited by

JOHN RAND AND FINN TARP

A study prepared by the United Nations University World Institute for Development Economics Research (UNU-WIDER)

OXFORD
UNIVERSITY PRESS

OXFORD
UNIVERSITY PRESS

Great Clarendon Street, Oxford, OX2 6DP,
United Kingdom

Oxford University Press is a department of the University of Oxford.
It furthers the University's objective of excellence in research, scholarship,
and education by publishing worldwide. Oxford is a registered trade mark of
Oxford University Press in the UK and in certain other countries

World Institute for Development Economics Research of the United Nations University (UNU-WIDER),
Katajanokanlaituri 6B, 00160 Helsinki, Finland

First Edition published in 2020

Impression: 1

Published in the United States of America by Oxford University Press
198 Madison Avenue, New York, NY 10016, United States of America

British Library Cataloguing in Publication Data
Data available

Library of Congress Control Number: 2019946154

ISBN 978–0–19–885118–9

DOI: 10.1093/oso/9780198851189.003.0001

Printed and bound in Great Britain by
Clays Ltd, Elcograf S.p.A.

Foreword

Small and medium enterprises (SMEs) have been at the heart of Vietnam's structural transition following the *doi moi* reform process in the mid-1980s. The unprecedented economic growth and poverty reduction that quickly followed promoted the country from a low-income to a middle-income economy over a relatively short timeframe, which in turn resulted in an impressive lowering of poverty levels and increased prosperity and general wellbeing of the population. The much-improved social indicators sparked serious enquiry into the poverty-reducing impact of Vietnam's SMEs, which is the origins of this book. The research looks at enterprises within the private manufacturing sector—urban and rural, formal and informal—using rich data from surveys since 2005 and every two years covering some 2,500 enterprises across ten provinces.

John Rand and Finn Tarp, the editors of this book, have been heavily involved from the beginning—crafting the surveys, gathering and interpreting the wealth of survey data. I heartily thank them for the steady direction of the research work, their analytical skills and authorship which are brought together here for us to read and contemplate the process of economic development and social progress at the country level.

Danida, Denmark's International Development Agency, provided considerable support to the survey work. UNU-WIDER gratefully acknowledges the support and financial contributions to its research programme by the governments of Finland, Sweden, and the United Kingdom. Without this vital funding our research and policy analysis work would be impossible.

Kunal Sen
Director, UNU-WIDER
Helsinki, November 2019

Acknowledgements

The intention of putting together this volume on the development of small and medium enterprises (SMEs) in Vietnam developed gradually over a period of more than a decade, after we first arrived in Vietnam in late 2000. A significant number of people have worked together with us in many capacities during the planning, implementation and analysis of the SME surveys underlying the volume. While we will try—in what follows—to do justice to their many vital contributions, we apologize up-front for any omissions. The list is long and a complete inventory is simply not feasible for reasons of space.[1]

A profound debt is owed to senior colleagues in Vietnam, including the former Presidents of CIEM, Dr Le Dang Doanh, Dr Dinh Van An, and Associate Professor Le Xuan Ba, as well as the current CIEM President Dr Nguyen Dinh Cung. Together with the present and former Director General of ILSSA Dr Dao Quang Vinh and Associate Professor Dr Nguyen Thi Lan Huong, they worked with us in guiding the SME project from beginning to end of the six survey rounds. We have come to appreciate the key leadership qualities that have helped promote effective collaboration between all partners in the SME survey. These top-level colleagues, including Trinh Duc Chieu, contributed as well in critical ways to the very many seminars and conferences that have been an integral part of the SME process, and which are fully documented at CIEM's website.

Financial support from Danida under its various programmes over the period in reference is acknowledged with sincere gratitude. A particular thanks is due to the former Danish Ambassador in Vietnam, H.E. the late Peter Lysholt Hansen. Peter was—with his never-failing sense of strategic priorities—highly instrumental in the early stages of setting up the SME survey, and without his support, the SME project would never have seen the light of day. This book is dedicated to his memory with sincere gratitude.

Ambassador John Nielsen followed up in his effective ways and supported the research effort throughout its various stages to its end.

[1] For full details on background and contributions please see the six cross-section reports covering each of the SME rounds available at the following website: http://web.econ.ku.dk/ftarp/publications.html#. In each of these reports we have for the past 10–15 years carefully recorded our acknowledgments to the many colleagues and friends with whom we have worked in pursuing the SME survey in Vietnam. Reference can also be made to the detailed questionnaires and the data available on the UNU-WIDER and DERG websites. We explicitly acknowledge that the following colleagues have in various ways contributed as co-authors of the cross-sectional reports: Kasper Brandt, Smriti Sharma, Neda Trifković, Marie Skibsted, Benedikte Bjerge, Nina Torm, Simon McCoy, Patricia Silva, Theo Larsen, and Theo Talbot.

Our work would not have been possible without continuous professional and administrative interaction, advice and encouragement from a large number of individuals at CIEM and ILSSA. Among many others, we would like to highlight our gratitude to the former CIEM Vice-President, Mrs Vu Xuan Nguyet Hong and present Vice-President Dr Nguyen Thi Tue Anh as well as Dr Dang Thi Thu Hoai who have been close collaborators from the very beginning. The same goes for Mr Bui Van Dung and Mr Nguyen Thanh Tam, who were active members of the research team as were in the early years Dr Tran Tien Cuong and Mr Trinh Duc Chieu. Moreover, we are most grateful to Project Assistants Ms Do Hong Giang and Ms Bui Phuong Lien. Without their tireless support in the organization of numerous project activities, including the publication of countless reports and studies during a decade of project work the present volume would have been impossible.

Turning to the essential, highly productive, and stimulating collaboration with the data collection and management teams from ILSSA, they were effectively coordinated by the present Director General Dr Dao Quang Vinh, the former Directors General Dr Nguyen Huu Dzung and Associate Professor Dr Nguyen Thi Lan Huong, Vice Directors General, Mr Le Ngu Binh, Mr Luu Quang Tuan, and their immediate daily colleagues including Dr Chu Thi Lan, Ms Nguyen Hai Ninh, Ms Nguyen Phuong Tra Mi, Ms Hoang Thi Minh, Ms Le Quynh Huong, Mr Le Hoang Dzung, Mr Nguyen Tien Quyet, Mr Nguyen Van Du, and Ms Tran Thu Hang. The survey would not have taken off without the efforts of these and many other ILSSA staff too numerous to name here in compiling the questionnaires, training enumerators, implementing the survey in the field, and cleaning the data.

A particular thanks is also extended for the effective and most helpful assistance provided by all administrative levels in Vietnam from the centre in Hanoi and all the way out to the provincial, district and commune officials and people who helped organizing numerous field trips and pilots over more than decade of work. Without these crucial efforts neither we personally nor the international collaborators in general would have been in a position to even begin comprehending the realities and challenges of SME development in Vietnam. We hope all we learnt comes out clearly.

Importantly, we would like to express our deepest sense of appreciation for the valuable time the several thousand small and medium enterprises throughout Vietnam made available to us in 2005, 2007, 2009, 2011, 2013, and 2015 during the interviews carried out as part of this study. It was a humbling and thought-provoking experience to see the openness and eagerness with which they welcomed and engaged with us all and the many enumerator enumerator teams. We sincerely hope that the present volume will prove useful in the shared search for effective policies geared towards improving their daily struggle in the market place promoting their enterprises. This is in the final analysis the overarching goal of this work, and our own personal ambition.

To the many staff at the Danish Embassy, who have supported us under the guidance of the ambassadors mentioned, we would like to acknowledge the efforts of former Deputy Heads of Mission Dr Tove Degnbol and Ms Lis Rosenholm, alongside Ms Mimi Groenbech, Henrik Vistisen, and Cathrine Dolleris. A very particular set of thanks goes to Ms Vu Huong Mai, who together with many others provided much of the essential administrative support and oversight required from the Danish Embassy.

Each SME round involved careful preparation, implementation, analysis, and discussion of results in a wide range of workshops and launching events with a total number of participants of more than 1,000. The present volume benefitted from the specific insights and helpful comments made by numerous colleagues to whom we are most grateful.

We would also like to express our most sincere gratitude to the chapter authors of this volume for their willingness to participate in this project and for their many insightful contributions. Warm thanks are also due to UNU-WIDER and the University of Copenhagen for institutional support and never failing collaboration. We wish in particular to thank Lorraine Telfer-Taivainen, UNU-WIDER Editorial and Publishing Associate, for advice, hard work and making the collaboration with Oxford University Press run smoothly. Adam Swallow, Economics and Finance Commissioning Editor at Oxford University Press, and his colleagues provided expert guidance with the publication process, and we do wish to acknowledge the anonymous referee reports that helped sharpen our focus. Finally, a word of thanks to the donors of UNU-WIDER, Finland, Sweden, and the United Kingdom, as well as Danida in the early rounds of the SME survey for their core support to the work programme of UNU-WIDER without which this volume would not have been possible.

John Rand and Finn Tarp
Copenhagen, November 2019

Contents

PART III. CERTIFICATION, WORKING CONDITIONS, AND UNION MEMBERSHIP

List of Figures

List of Tables

List of Abbreviations

ALC	Amended Labor Code
BRC	Business Registration Certificate
CBAs	collective bargaining agreements
CC	Central Committee
CCPs	cooperatives/collectives/partnerships
CIEM	Central Institute of Economic Management
CLUR	Certificate of Land Use Right
CPV	Communist Party of Vietnam
DANIDA	Danish International Development Agency
DERG	Development Economics Research Group
DIAL	Développement, Institutions et Mondialisation
ECN	Enterprise Code Number
EO	entrepreneurial orientation
FDI	foreign direct investment
FE	fixed effects
GDP	gross domestic product
GMM-Sys	System Generalized Method of Moments estimator
GSO	General Statistical Office
HCMC	Ho Chi Minh City
HH	household
HLP	High-Level Panel
ICA	Investment Climate Assessment
IHBs	Informal Household Businesses
ILO	International Labour Organisation
ILSSA	Institute of Labour Science and Social Affairs
IPO	initial public offering
IRD	French Research Institute for Sustainable Development
ISIC	International Standard Industrial Classification of All Economic Activities
ISO	International Organization for Standardization
IV	instrumental variable
IZA	Institute of Labor Economics
MC	managerial capital
MCA	multiple correspondence analysis
MOLISA	Ministry of Labour, Invalids and Social Affairs
MPI	Ministry of Planning and Investment
MRPK	marginal revenue product of capital
MSMEs	micro, small, and medium enterprises
NATSEM	National Social and Economic Modelling Centre

NEU	National Economics University
NSOE	non-state-owned enterprise
NUL	new Union Law
OECD	Organisation for Economic Co-operation and Development
OID	overidentifying restrictions
OLS	ordinary least squares
OSH	occupational safety and health
PC	People's Council
PCI	Provincial Competitiveness Index
PCOM	People's Committee
PDTS	potential debt tax shield
RE	random effect
RIF	Recentered Influence Function
ROA	return on assets
SCOLI	spatial cost of living index
SDGs	Sustainable Development Goals
SME	small and medium enterprises
SPCBs	state-owned commercial banks
SOE	state-owned enterprise
TFP	total factor productivity
UCPH	University of Copenhagen
UNU-WIDER	United Nations University Institute for Development Economics Research
UQR	unconditional quantile regressions
USAID	US Agency for International Development
VA	value added
VCCI	Vietnam Chamber of Commerce and Industry
VGCL	Vietnam General Confederation of Labour
VHLSS	Vietnam Household Living Standard Survey
VND	Vietnam Dong
VSME	Vietnam Small and Medium Enterprise
WBES	World Business Environment Survey
WC	working conditions

Notes on Contributors

Hanna Berkel is a PhD candidate at the Department of Economics, University of Copenhagen. Her research focusses on enterprises in the Global South and applying mixed methods. She holds a Bachelor's in European Studies and a Master's in Global Development, and has worked as a research assistant at the University of Copenhagen and UNU-WIDER.

Axel Demenet is the Economic and Financial Counsellor at the Embassy of France in Madrid, on account of the French Ministry for the Economy and Finance. He has worked as a consultant for various institutions. His research interests included the vulnerability and resilience of informal microenterprises, especially in the context of Vietnam; the micro-economic analysis of firm-level corruption, as well as the efficiency of national research systems. He graduated from the Ecole Normale Supérieure, and the Ecole Nationale de la Statistique.

Quynh Hoang holds a PhD in development economics and is currently an affiliated researcher at DIAL, a research unit of the French Research Institute for Development, and the University of Paris Dauphine. During her PhD, she studied the ethnic inequalities and ethnic poverty in Vietnam along three axes: effects of community participation in poverty reduction programmes, earnings gaps by gender and ethnicity, and the formation of social networks by ethnic affiliation. She also extends her research to enterprises' performance.

Christina Kinghan is an economist at the Central Bank of Ireland. She completed her PhD in development economics at Trinity College Dublin, with a specific focus on household and enterprise behaviour in Vietnam. Her current work focuses on macroprudential policy and household finance.

Hai Anh La is a senior research fellow at the National Social and Economic Modelling Centre (NATSEM) at the University of Canberra. Her main research areas are household welfare, social protection, poverty, and migration in developing countries. She is also interested in policy modelling and evaluation using microsimulation techniques, focusing on the Australian and Vietnamese tax-transfer system. She has published in journals such as *Journal of Development Studies, Journal of International Financial Markets, Institutions and Money, Journal of Asian Economics,* and *Emerging Market Finance and Trade.*

Carol Newman is a professor in economics at the Department of Economics, Trinity College Dublin. Her research is the microeconomics of development with a focus on both household and enterprise behaviour. She has published widely in the fields of development economics and agricultural economics, in particular in the area of enterprise dynamics and performance in developing countries.

Tam Thanh Nguyen is a researcher at the Central Institute for Economic Management in Vietnam. He obtained his master's degree in business economics from the University of Queensland, Australia, in 2011. Currently, he is a PhD candidate and a research assistant at University of Queensland Business School. His research interests cover innovation, human resources, firm internationalization, strategy, and corporate governance with specific focus on Vietnam and Australia.

Christophe J. Nordman is senior researcher at the French Research Institute for Sustainable Development (IRD), is affiliated as Research Fellow at the Institute of Labor Economics (IZA), and is currently assigned to the French Institute of Pondicherry (India) and the mixed research unit DIAL (IRD, University Paris-Dauphine). He has published extensively on the various dimensions of labour in developing countries (including Africa, South Asia, Vietnam), as well as the formation of earnings, skills and social networks, discrimination, employment and household vulnerabilities, and the labour consequences of migrations.

Conor O'Toole is a Senior Research Officer at the Economic and Social Research Institute, and an Adjunct Associate Professor at Trinity College Dublin. He was formerly a Senior Economist in the Central Bank of Ireland. His research expertise covers a number of fields including corporate and SME finance, macroprudential policy, and household finance. His work has been published extensively in a number of leading academic journals, including the *Review of Finance, Journal of Banking and Finance, Journal of Financial Stability,* and the *Journal of Corporate Finance.*

John Rand is a professor at the Department of Economics, University of Copenhagen. He is also Non-Resident Research Fellow with UNU-WIDER. His research centres around the microeconomics of development with a focus on enterprise behaviour and dynamics. He has published widely in the fields of development economics and industrial policy in developing countries.

Enrico Santarelli is a professor of economic policy at the Department of Economics, University of Bologna. He has published widely in the fields of entrepreneurship, industrial economics and innovation in high-impact academic journals. His current research is concerned with the interaction of institutions, entrepreneurship, and productivity in both advanced and transition countries. He is Editor of *Small Business Economics*, a leading journal in the field of entrepreneurship studies.

Smriti Sharma is a lecturer (assistant professor) in economics at Newcastle University Business School, United Kingdom. Her fields of interest are development economics, behavioural economics and labour economics. She has published extensively on micro-enterprises in India and Vietnam as well as on caste and gender-based discrimination in labour markets in India and Bangladesh.

Finn Tarp is Professor at the University of Copenhagen (UCPH) and Coordinator of the UCPH Development Economics Research Group (DERG). He was Director of UNU-WIDER from 2009–18, and is now a Non-Resident Senior Fellow of UNU-WIDER. Professor Tarp is a leading international expert on development strategy and foreign aid, with an interest in poverty, income distribution and growth, micro- and macroeconomic policy and modelling, agricultural sector policy and planning, household/enterprise development, and economic adjustment and reform as well as climate change, sustainability, and natural resources. He has published widely in leading economics and development journals and books by international academic publishers.

Hien Thu Tran is an associate professor at the Telfer School of Management, University of Ottawa, in the area of strategy and entrepreneurship. She has published widely on entrepreneurship, management, and industrial economics in high-impact academic journals. Her current research is concerned with the interaction of institutions, innovation, and entrepreneurship, and how this interaction facilitates the process of knowledge spillover among entrepreneurs and organizations in transition countries.

Thi Bich Tran is an associate professor at the Faculty of Statistics, the National Economics University (NEU) of Vietnam. Her research is development economics and policy issues with a particular focus on labour market, firm productivity, and institutions in Vietnam. She has published widely in the field of economic development and public administration, in particular the area of informality, firm productivity, and governance.

Neda Trifković is a post-doc at the Department of Economics, University of Copenhagen. Her research interests are focused on agricultural and development economics, in particular certification, corporate social responsibility, contract farming, transformation of global value chains, labour and working conditions in small and medium enterprises, extreme weather events, and violence against women. She has published articles in all of these areas.

Chieu Duc Trinh is a senior researcher at the Central Institute for Economic Management in Vietnam. He obtained his bachelor's degree in development economics in 1998, and his master's degree in applied econometrics in 2008. His main research interest is enterprise reform and development, especially state-owned enterprise (SOE) reform and small and medium enterprise (SME) development. He has contributed to drafting numerous regulations and policies of the government for SOE reform on SME development, as well as published widely in these fields.

Nina Torm is an assistant professor at the Department of Social Sciences and Business at Roskilde University, Denmark. Her research interests revolve around labour market issues including regulatory frameworks, job creation, social protection and informality in developing countries, with a particular focus on East Asia and East Africa. Her work has been published in the field of development economics and labour studies, mostly in the area of enterprise and worker dynamics. Moreover, she regularly consults for various international organizations, especially the International Labour Organization.

1
Introduction

John Rand and Finn Tarp

Over the past 30 years, Vietnam has experienced unprecedented growth and poverty reduction, turning the country into a middle-income economy over a relatively short time span. Most of this growth came from structural change, where a significant proportion of the labour force moved swiftly from the agricultural sector to manufacturing. During the pre-industrial transition stage in the late 1980s, agriculture accounted for more than 40 per cent of GDP and 75 per cent of employment (Malesky and London 2014). Three decades later the share of workers registered within agriculture has more than halved, with labour having shifted towards both industry and services—a process that is still ongoing (McCaig and Pavcnik 2016; McCaig and Pavcnik 2018a; Tarp 2018). Moreover, this change has so far happened without worrying trends as regards income inequality, especially within urban areas, where change has gone hand-in-hand with higher salaries in manufacturing and services and increased wage-job opportunities in those sectors (Benjamin et al. 2017).

Private small and medium enterprises (SMEs) have been key for the structural transition in Vietnam that followed the initiation of the Doi Moi reform process in 1986. A leading global expert on Vietnam uses the term 'gradualist' when describing the nature of the policy-making process underlying the impressive Vietnamese development performance (Rama 2008). By this Rama refers to the fact that Vietnam adopted early on a dual-track approach, and that policy makers allowed firms to expand alongside the state sector as long as they fulfilled their quotas at state-given prices (Malesky and London 2014). Also important for the development of a thriving private SME sector has been the innate reform design and willingness to experiment combined with the decentralized nature of the reform process. The government tried out larger scale reforms in selected provinces, before deciding whether to implement a given initiative at the national level. As such, experimentation and quality governance were crucial for the success of nationwide reform initiatives taking place in parallel with the policy to promote private SMEs. These initiatives included state-owned enterprise (SOE) reform, FDI and industrial zone policies, and business-related administrative initiatives, such as the introduction of one-stop shops (Rama 2008; Malesky and London 2014).

John Rand and Finn Tarp, *Introduction* In: *Micro, Small, and Medium Enterprises in Vietnam*. Edited by: John Rand and Finn Tarp, Oxford University Press (2020). © United Nations University World Institute for Development Economics Research (UNU-WIDER).
DOI: 10.1093/oso/9780198851189.003.0001

Although Vietnam has throughout the reform process experimented with and allowed for an increased influence of the private sector, significant state influence remains a core feature of the Vietnamese development strategy. Large state-owned enterprises (SOEs) continue to receive government protection and highly favourable conditions compared to smaller domestic and foreign firms. This is so in spite of the observation that this may be detrimental to economic growth, as it discourages investment in skills for those without connections within the state apparatus (Phan and Coxhead 2013). This preferential treatment of SOEs in key industries has influenced the development of private industrial SMEs, as resource allocation for the most productive firms has been 'politically constrained'.

The Vietnamese government has throughout acknowledged that especially industrial SOEs need to improve their efficiency, and though they have struggled to do so, it remains a key policy priority of the government to ensure significant state influence in key areas of the industrial sector. At present the SOE share in GDP continues to be about the same as it was in 1990 (approximately 30 per cent). In contrast, private SMEs account for around 95 per cent of all firms, about half of the workforce and approximately 40 per cent of GDP (GSO 2018). The large number of SMEs embodies a significant potential for dynamic and inclusive economic growth. This is so because SMEs can be a dynamic force in generating labour-intensive growth; in increasing competition in local markets; and in generating much needed savings and innovation. Moreover, structural transformation—the movement of workers from low-productivity to high-productivity activities and sectors—requires SME expansion and is as already noted an essential feature of rapid and sustained growth and development.

However, SMEs also represent a series of policy challenges for future economic development in Vietnam and elsewhere. Many small firms continue to operate as household enterprises at the border between formality and informality. They often remain credit rationed and/or constrained, with negative repercussions for an optimal allocation of scarce resources, productivity and the welfare of employers and employees. In addition, the potential and significance of SMEs normally stand in stark contrast with the widespread lack of understanding of the characteristics, dynamics and constraints faced by smaller firms. We conceived this volume to help promote a better understanding of what drives SME growth and develop insights into the underlying behaviour of SME owners, managers, and employees. We see this as an essential task and necessary for both the development profession and policy makers at large as they strive to address the objective of promoting sustainable private sector development—with a view to achieving key aims among the Sustainable Development Goals (SDGs) launched by the UN in 2015. Importantly, SMEs are central—not only in promoting inclusive and sustainable economic growth, employment, and decent work for all (SDG8); SMEs also promote sustainable industrialization and foster innovation (Goal 9) and can help reduce income inequalities (SDG10) if they receive support to provide good-quality jobs.

Finally, they can support achieving gender equality (SDG5) and women's empowerment through female entrepreneurship.

In Vietnam, SMEs have (as already noted) been at the very core of the government strategy for inclusive growth and economic transformation. Yet, although Vietnam has seen a rapid increase in the number of registered enterprises, evidence also shows that only a small fraction of smaller household businesses have become registered during the past three decades. This means that the official statistics do not capture well some 30 million employees even if they form a critically important part of the SME dynamics, both in terms of job and income creation. It is therefore apparent that studying the dynamics and growth process of smaller (both formal and informal) firms is key for disentangling our understanding of Vietnam's economic success story.

The roots of this volume grow from the time when the first Danida-supported SME survey of Vietnamese non-state manufacturing enterprises covering more than 2,500 firms in ten provinces began in 2005.[1] We focused from the start on the private manufacturing sector, and we included rural and urban as well as formal and informal enterprises. The success of the 2005 SME survey inspired the Central Institute of Economic Management (CIEM) of the Ministry of Planning and Investment (MPI) in Hanoi, the Institute of Labour Science and Social Affairs (ILSSA) of the Ministry of Labour, Invalids and Social Affairs (MOLISA), the Development Economics Research Group (DERG) of the University of Copenhagen and UNU-WIDER, together with Danida, to plan and carry out an ambitious series of SME panel surveys. Since 2005, we implemented the survey of these enterprises every two years, and it is on this extraordinary foundation that the present volume builds.

Importantly, since the survey tracked the same SMEs over time, the SME database is by now a very strong tool for gaining detailed and policy-relevant information about private sector firm dynamics and enterprise development in Vietnam from 2005–15. During this decade, the number of registered non-state SME manufacturing firms more than tripled and so did their labour force. The overall performance of the smaller firms shows a clear and promising trend of consistent growth, but the process is taking place in what remains a constrained environment that often results in a non-optimal allocation of resources. For example, while some companies face credit constraints, other challenges are the rigidities of the regulatory environment or institutional weaknesses. Understanding the circumstances under which both formal and informal SMEs operate and the constraints and opportunities they face is a key input into evidence-based

[1] We acknowledge inspiration from the 1991 survey by Ronnås (1992), and note that the ten provinces include Ha Noi, Ha Tay (now part of Ha Noi), Hai Phong, Ho Chi Min City, Phu Tho, Nghe An, Quang Nam, Khanh Hoa, Lam Dong, and Long An. Further details on the data are available in Chapter 2.

policy-making for the future of businesses, the overall economy, and the welfare of the Vietnamese people in both urban and rural areas.

While six detailed descriptive cross-section reports for each of the SME survey years are available,[2] capturing change from one survey to the next, the present volume presents for the first time a comprehensive set of detailed analytical studies, which rely throughout on the complete and coherent data from more than 2,500 SMEs in ten provinces. Attention is on the time dimension rather than on individual cross-section information and descriptions. We carefully selected these papers from a UNU-WIDER call for research proposals, and we reviewed and discussed all papers in a joint workshop in November 2017 in Hanoi. Thus, all chapters in the volume—including this framework-setting introduction and the concluding chapter by the editors—rely extensively on the SME panel; owners, managers, and employees in the firms included in this panel have all lived through and experienced a critical period in Vietnam's economic development process while managing their daily private and productive lives. How the firms coped and ended up performing in a highly dynamic macroeconomic environment under a complex set of constraints is key in what the research work tries to uncover.

ILSSA carried out the wide range of tasks related to the planning and implementation of the SME survey in the field and UNU-WIDER and DERG collaborated with CIEM in all aspects of survey design and data analysis. A full package of capacity-building activities by DERG—and later on UNU-WIDER staff—including both formal courses, on-the-job training and a wealth of seminars, were conducted in Vietnam and elsewhere throughout this process under ongoing institutional twinning arrangements. The shared scholarly aim was to ensure that the SME project developed both the data required to deliver policy-relevant research to decision makers and the research capacity within Vietnamese institutions to take advantage of that data.

We did not foresee in 2005—when we launched the SME panel survey—that the report of the UN Secretary General's High-level Panel of Eminent persons on the Post-2015 Development Agenda (HLP), would call—more than ten years later—for a data revolution for sustainable development post-2015 as follows:[3]

> We also call for a data revolution for sustainable development, with a new international initiative to improve the quality of statistics and information available to citizens. We should actively take advantage of new technology, crowd sourcing, and improved connectivity to empower people with information on the progress towards the targets.
>
> (Chapter 4, Implementation, Accountability and Building Consensus, p. 21.)

[2] See http://web.econ.ku.dk/ftarp/publications.html#++++.

[3] See https://www.un.org/sg/en/management/beyond2015.shtml.

The HLP call for a data revolution is most pertinent, and it forms the rationale for the UNU-WIDER project on structural transformation and inclusive growth in Vietnam under which we pursued the SME panel surveys over the years.[4] While substantial improvements in statistical systems took place in many developing countries over the past decades, performance remains poor in far too many sectors and countries. The call for 'increased support for strengthening data collection and capacity-building in Member States' was rightly reiterated in the Sustainable Development Goals (SDGs). It is this background—and recalling UNU-WIDER's long-standing expertise in innovation in data collection and analysis—that leads us to believe that data will be at the epicentre of development action in the coming decades. At the same time, while the logic of a concerted push towards a data revolution is compelling, these calls are often somewhat 'fluffy'—and it is not entirely clear from ongoing debates that it is widely understood what such a revolution actually demands and means in concrete practice.

We developed the aims of this volume with these concerns in mind using Vietnam as a fascinating case due to the concrete and unique, and coincidental, availability of the SME experience and panel dataset. Furthermore, Vietnam's contemporary similarities to a large number of developing economies, including its strong private sector performance after the Doi Moi reforms, make its experience and policy recommendations, based on analysis of microeconomic data, highly relevant for many regional and extra-regional stakeholders. In fact, Vietnam provides an exceptionally informative environment in which to observe and consider the importance of key factors and mechanisms influencing SME performance and development, including:

- credit access and management practices;
- political connections, institutional quality, and innovation; and
- certification, working conditions, and union membership.

These dimensions therefore make up the three core-components of this volume, and the associated Chapters 3–11 identify throughout the policy challenges in each area. They follow this scene-setting introduction and a detailed description of the data in Chapter 2; and we conclude by drawing up a series of policy implications in Chapter 12.

In sum, the aims of this volume are to:

- Provide an in-depth evaluation of the development of private sector formal and informal manufacturing SMEs in a developing country—Vietnam in this case—over the past decade, combining a unique primary source of panel data with the best analytical tools available.

[4] See https://www.wider.unu.edu/project/structural-transformation-and-inclusive-growth-viet-nam.

- Generate a comprehensive understanding of the impact of business risks, credit access, and institutional characteristics, on the one hand, and government policies on SME growth performance at the enterprise level, on the other, including the importance of working conditions, informality, and union membership.
- Serve as a lens through which other countries, and the international development community at large, may wish to approach the massive task of pursuing a meaningful data revolution as an integral element of the SDG development agenda.
- Make available a comprehensive set of materials and studies of use to academics, students, and development practitioners interested in an integrated approach to the study of growth, private sector development, and the microeconomic analysis of SME development in a fascinating developing country.

Finally, we hope that the volume can provide a comprehensive analytic contribution to a crucial topic within the discipline of development economics based on some fifteen years of continued efforts. In addition, we wish to help persuade national and international policy makers (including donors) of the need to take the call for a data revolution seriously, not only in rhetoric, but also in concrete plans and budget allocations, and in the necessary sustained action at country level. This is where inclusive socioeconomic development takes place and benefit poor and discriminated people who are struggling to make ends meet; and private sector progress is fundamental in this effort.

Focusing next on the specific context of the individual chapters, and relating to selected literature in the field rather than going in chronological order, one of the most significant challenges encountered by private industrial SMEs in Vietnam in developing their potential is restricted access to credit. This topic is of particular importance, and has led to a variety of papers on the topic over the years using different data sources. As an example, Rand (2007) used the pilot data of the data utilized in this book volume to analyse the extent to which borrowing constraints restrict firm access to credit. Based on information from 1,106 Vietnamese manufacturing SMEs, his paper suggested that approximately 25 per cent of enterprises are credit constrained, and that these small firms would increase their debt demand by 115 per cent if borrowing constraints were relaxed. His analysis also suggested that informal credit markets in Vietnam play an important role especially for fast growing firms, as successful entrepreneurs do not have the time to go through the administrative difficulties faced in the formal credit system. Another contribution by Malesky and Taussig (2009a) analyses the dynamics of relationship-based lending in the country's financial system. Using data from the Vietnam Provincial Competitiveness Index (PCI) initiative, covering around 6,400 firms in all provinces in Vietnam, they assess the extent to which firm owners' political connections are determinants of bank loans. The results show that these connections increase the likelihood of accessing loans by 4 per cent. Their paper moreover finds that political connections have a distortive impact on capital allocation mechanisms and that the most profitable private firms actually opt out of the formal financial system, and choose to use informal means to access credit.[5]

Three chapters in this book volume extend and deepen this literature. First, Christina Kinghan, Carol Newman, and Conor O'Toole look in Chapter 3 at capital allocation and credit access for SME growth, and find that capital allocation in Vietnam is sub-optimal. Firms with higher returns to capital are less likely to access formal finance, confirming on a much stronger data set the results in Rand (2007). Enrico Santarelli and Hien Thu Tran address in turn in Chapter 4 the interaction between human capital and institutional quality in determining the dynamics of capital structure. The authors find that it is very hard for non-state firms to access formal financing, and the ones capable of doing so rely on their influence, using tax benefits against financial distress. At the same time, whilst human capital encourages more loans, its interaction with institutional quality favours other financial resources over debt financing, again consistent with the early results in Rand (2007). Chapter 6 by John Rand links to the issue of credit allocation by studying the effect of political connectedness on credit constraints. Controlling for unobserved time-invariant firm-level heterogeneity, as well as self-selection and access to alternative credit markets, his chapter shows that political connections decrease the likelihood of SMEs being credit constrained by 4 per centage points, basically confirming the findings in Malesky and Taussig (2009a) using different analytical approaches.

While work on assessing the relevance of political and economic institutions in influencing a sound and stable business and investment environment has been a core research topic for decades, the direction of causality has remained a challenge, and this is also so in the context of Vietnam (Malesky 2010). Yet, since the early 1990s, business/government relations in Vietnam have been highly decentralized towards the province level. Exploiting this variation across different provinces Malesky et al. (2015a) utilize the Annual Enterprise Survey published by the General Statistical Office (GSO) in combination with data from the Provincial Competitiveness Index (PCI) to determine the extent to which local institutions affect the environment for firm investment. They identify transparency—i.e., making available provincial planning documents—as the most robust predictor

[5] This is in line with the analysis by Steer and Sen (2010), who find that informal institutions in Vietnam have contributed to expanding the private sector, in particular given the absence in this process of complete and trustworthy formal institutions. Using primary data from 305 firms collected in 2004, the authors show how informal institutions such as social networks, friends and families have helped Vietnamese firms gather information on their trading partners in the absence of formal means to access this information.

of private firm investment in Vietnam, and more relevant than property rights, contracting institutions, and corruption. This effect is particularly significant for small domestic private firms (SMEs). Another element affecting the quality of the investment environment is corruption. Rand and Tarp (2012) used two rounds of the data underpinning this book volume to develop a better understanding of the nature, evolution, and potential impact of bribe-paying behaviour. Based on data for 1,659 manufacturing SMEs in the ten provinces they show that bribe incidence is highly associated with firm-level differences in visibility, sunk costs, and ability to pay. Formality correlates positively with bribe incidence, so 'visibility' in this sense seems to dominate the 'bribes-to-hide' effect in determining corruption.

Chapter 6 as well as Chapter 8 in this volume follow directly in the footsteps of the work about institutional quality and investment behaviour. We already commented on Chapter 6, and Tam Thanh Nguyen and Chieu Duc Trinh look in Chapter 8 at how slack resources affect investments in innovation for Vietnamese SMEs, and find that whilst financial slack hinders innovation, human capital slack stimulates innovation in the direction of new business processes or products. Moreover, firms located in more favourable business environments experience less positive effects from human capital slack, and lesser negative effects of financial capital slack. Chapter 9 by Neda Trifković links indirectly to the discussion of institutional quality and corruption by looking at the role of international private standards in reducing business risks, defined as financial loss or physical damage related to business activities. As the chapter shows, international standards have the potential to increase productivity for Vietnamese SMEs, as international certification correlates with lower risk of temporary closure, informal payments, and customer risk.

The institutional context not only matters for firm access to credit and investments. Institutions play a key role in a firm's decision to formally register and pay taxes. In the case of Vietnam, Malesky and Taussig (2009b) argue that improvements in institutions have a strong impact on the likelihood of SMEs registering formally from the very commencement of their activities. At the same time, they reduce the amount of time informal firms choose to remain informal. Informality affects state-revenue. It also affects the health and safety of firm employees, as they lack access to a number of non-wage benefits, such as contributions for pension, paid holidays, right to minimum wages and to a maximum number of weekly working hours. Many do not have access to a written contract. This weakens the conditions of the institutional structure, which in turn encourages more informality. To address the problem of endogeneity in the relation between formality and quality of institutions, Malesky and Taussig (2009b) rely on a two-stage instrumental variable approach, using the experience of the Vietnam War as an exogenous determinant of today's institutions. The results support a causal relation going from institutions to formalization. Moreover, in a disaggregated analysis it emerges that property rights are the most relevant institution in Vietnam when it comes to drivers of formalization, more important than regulatory frameworks and contract enforcement work.

Rand and Torm (2012a) also offer evidence on the benefits of formality. They found that being formal increases profits for Vietnamese SMEs by about 10 per cent, once they control for firm size, firm location, workforce and owners characteristics. These results also hold for informal firms in 2007 that formalized by 2009, and which saw their profits increase by 16 per cent. The Rand and Torm study finds evidence as well for formalization leading to higher capital stocks, and a more empowered workforce, where workers' rights and duties are set out in formal contracts. Combining qualitative with quantitative evidence, the authors show as well that informality is often the result of lack of awareness of the benefits of formality. Most informal SMEs are only aware of the financial costs of formalization. Furthermore, Rand and Torm (2012b) find that formalization brings forward salaries that are between 10 and 20 per cent higher for formal workers compared to informal firms, a result driven mostly by observed characteristics, such as firm size, workforce characteristics, and location of the firms.[6]

McCaig and Pavcnik (2018b) is another study of the financial benefits of formalization, and they use data from three rounds of the Vietnam Household Living Standard Survey (VHLSS). They show that registration does not bring about particular benefits for Vietnamese SMEs, which is contrary to the findings in Rand and Torm (2012a). McCaig and Pavcnik (2018b) utilize data that enables them to observe whether firms that choose to formalize are significantly different in terms of growth rates *prior* to formalization compared to firms that choose not to formalize. Moreover, they document that very few firms formalize to hire more paid employees. They rather choose to employ unpaid family-members. These results are partly in line with those of Cling et al. (2017), who find that many household businesses do not perceive any growth benefits of formalization. They state that procedures are complicated, and they are unable to determine how taxes are calculated, reinforcing the perception of taxation as an arbitrary process.

Finally, some scholars argue that informality is the consequence of *lack of information* on behalf of SMEs and blurry regulations in place in relation to registration. In fact, as Cling et al. (2017) argue, informality is the result of complex and unclear registration procedures, rather than an intention to evade taxation. To support their argument, the authors use first-hand data from a survey implemented in Ho Chi Min City and Hanoi, combined with qualitative interviews from a sub-sample of the survey. The evidence shows that almost all informal SMEs are generally unaware of regulations, though they appear to be aware of the fact that they would be less subject to corruption if they registered. In addition, the Cling et al. paper finds that the incentives beyond the setting up of

[6] For a detailed discussion of Vietnamese formal/informal wage gaps at worker-level, see Nguyen et al. (2013).

the business are quite important when it comes to formalization: if the business has been set up because of an independent choice and not in response to the lack of any other viable alternative, the likelihood is higher that is it registered. The location of business premises also matters, as businesses with fixed premises are more likely to be registered. Whether institutions, information or trade affect informality in Vietnam, the accumulated evidence seems to point to the notion that the benefits of formality have to be more clearly communicated and understood by SMEs.

Informality can also exist at the employee level (within a formal firm). This is so even if registration should be compulsory for all formal workers. Accordingly, not many employees enjoy social insurance as present, as a vast majority of them tends to collect their benefits upon termination of employment. This means that very few meet the requirement of twenty or more years of contributions necessary for claiming a pension at a later stage. Salaries for employees also tend to be underreported to reduce contributions from employers, and employees often agree to receive slightly higher salaries on the condition of remaining unregistered (Castel and Pick 2018). This is problematic as formality and employee registration bring forward a number of other benefits for both firms and employees, including stable wages, decrease in casual labour, better access to less expensive credit, higher profits, and increase in customer demand. Formal firms are much more productive than informal firms partly due to higher levels of education recorded amongst formal firm owners (La Porta and Shleifer 2014).

Three chapters are directly relevant to these reflections about firm informality and labour conditions. In Chapter 7, Thi Bich Tran and Hai Anh La address the reasons that push household businesses to remain informal. They find that informality amongst top-tier firms results from household businesses perceiving the tax cost of formalization to be larger than the benefits of formalization. As government officials do not promote formalization amongst this category of firms, the authors hypothesize that corruptive behaviour between top tier firms and government officials may perpetuate the former's condition of informality. Turning to Christophe J. Nordman and Smriti Sharma in Chapter 10, they look at economic returns derived from working conditions and shows that no mechanism is in place in Vietnam to compensate labourers working in unfavourable conditions and lacking a formal contract. In addition, employees hired through formal procedures, and lacking a formal contract, earn less than similar employees hired relying on social network channels. Finally, Nina Torm deals in Chapter 11 with the benefits of trade union membership. She finds that, controlling for firm and worker characteristics, the wages of unionized workers are between 9 and 22 per cent higher than wages of non-unionized workers, with gains increasing progressively towards the upper end of the distribution. Axel Demenet and Quynh Hoang in Chapter 5 also touch upon informality, though indirectly. They study the degree of informality and firm performance looking at the importance of management practices for

SMEs productivity; and they show a positive and significant association between managerial capital and firm productivity, particularly relevant for micro (informal) and small enterprises, as opposed to more formal firms of medium size.

In sum, we reiterate that the Vietnamese economy has undergone dramatic changes in the last thirty years or so since Doi Moi began in 1986. Whilst the country has on the one hand opened up to the global economy, a number of wide ranging domestic changes have also taken place, which have contributed to increasing the general wellbeing of the population. Structural reallocations of the labour force from agriculture to manufacturing has increased the number of domestic firms; combined with an increase in the number of foreign firms and foreign direct investment. The introduction of the Enterprise Law in 2000 played a key role in this, in particular for small and micro-enterprises, easing the procedures for firm registration. Nonetheless, these procedures remain rather complex and ambiguous, especially when it comes to smaller firms, which do not need to register fully, depending on the size of their turnover and the location of their premises.

Arguably, the blurred lines between formality and informality have negative consequences for the future of the Vietnamese economy, especially as evidence demonstrates that small informal firms have lower levels of total factor productivity, are more credit constrained, and the wages of their employees are significantly lower than the wages of their formal counterparts. However, formalization encounters a number of obstacles. Going forward it seems policy makers will have to promote SME-formalization, whilst at the same time improving the institutional environment for formalization. In the meantime, SMEs must adapt to the changing character of the Vietnamese economy. Highly relevant success stories from the early stages of privatization and transition show that those Vietnamese SMEs that were capable of adapting their strategy to the needs of the export-oriented and labour-intensive manufacturing sector are those that managed to achieve sustainable growth (Taussig 2013). Yet, as seen above, the process of adaptation, renewal and growth remains paved with challenges. We try in this book to shed further light on the nature of these challenges and suggest new perspectives on how to tackle them.

Acknowledgements

We thank Daniela Espro for excellent research assistance.

References

Benjamin, D., L. Brandt, and B. McCaig (2017). Growth with equity: Income inequality in Vietnam 2002–2014, *Journal of Economic Inequality,* 15: 25–46.

Castel, P., and A. Pick (2018). Increasing social insurance coverage in Vietnam's SMEs, Paris: OECD Development Policy Papers No. 13.

Cling, J., M. Razafindrakoto, and F. Roubaud (2017). Explanatory factors behind formalizing non-farm household businesses in Vietnam, HAL Id: hal-01664202.

General Statistics Office of Vietnam (2018). *Results of the 2017 Economic Census*, Statistical Publishing House. https://www.gso.gov.vn/default_en.aspx?tabid=515&idmid=5&ItemID=18974 (accessed 17 February 2019).

La Porta, R., and A. Shleifer (2014). Informality and development, *Journal of Economic Perspectives*, 28(3): 109–26.

Malesky, E. (2010). Straight ahead on red: How foreign direct investment empowers sub-national leaders, *Journal of Politics*, 70(1): 97–119.

Malesky, E., and M. Taussig (2009a). Where is credit due? Legal institutions, connections, and efficiency of bank lending in Vietnam, *Journal of Law, Economics and Organizations*, 25(2): 535–58.

Malesky E., and M. Taussig (2009b). Out of the gray: The impact of provincial institutions on business formalization in Vietnam, *Journal of East Asian Studies*, 9: 249–90.

Malesky E., and J. London (2014). The political economy of development in China and Vietnam, *Annual Review of Political Science*, 17: 395–419.

Malesky E., N. McCulloch, and D. N. Nguyen (2015a). The impact of governance and transparency on firm investment in Vietnam, *Economics of Transition*, 0(0): 1–39.

McCaig, B., and N. Pavcnik (2016). Moving out of agriculture: Structural change in Vietnam. In M. MacMillan, D. Rodrik, and C. Sepulveda (eds), *Structural Change, Fundamentals and Growth. A Framework and Case Studies*. Washington DC: International Food Policy and Research Institute.

McCaig, B., and N. Pavcnik (2018a). Export markets and labor allocation in a low-income country, *American Economic Review*, 108(7): 1899–1941.

McCaig, B., and N. Pavcnik (2018b). Business formalization in Vietnam, LCERPA Working Paper, No.2018/7.

Nguyen, H. C., C. J. Nordman, and F. Roubaud (2013). Who suffers the penalty? A panel data analysis of earning gaps in Vietnam, *Journal of Development Studies*, 49(12): 1694–1710.

Phan, D., and I. Coxhead (2013). Long-run costs of piecemeal reforms: Wage inequality and return to education in Vietnam, *Journal of Comparative Economics*, 41: 1106–22.

Rama, M. (2008). Making Difficult Choices: Vietnam in Transition. Working Paper 40. Washington, DC: Commission on Growth and Development, World Bank.

Rand, J. (2007). Credit Constraints and Determinants of the Cost of Capital in Vietnamese Manufacturing. *Small Business Economics*, 29 (1–2): 1–13.

Rand, J., and N. Torm (2012a). The benefits of formalization: Evidence from Vietnamese manufacturing SMEs, *World Development*, 40(5): 983–98.

Rand J. and N. Torm (2012b). The informal sector wage gap among Vietnamese microfirms, *Journal of the Asia Pacific Economy,* 17(4): 560–77.

Rand, J. and F. Tarp (2012). Firm-level corruption in Vietnam, *Economic Development and Cultural Change*, 60(3): 571–95.

Ronnås, P. (1992). *Employment Generation through Private Entrepreneurship in Vietnam.* ILO and SIDA: Geneva.

Steer, L., and K. Sen (2010). Formal and informal institutions in a transition economy: The case of Vietnam, *World Development,* 38(11): 1603–15.

Tarp, F. (2018). Viet Nam: The dragon that rose from the ashes, Helsinki: WIDER Working Paper 2018/126.

Taussig M., (2013). The neglected need for strategic renewal in emerging markets: Lessons from Vietnam in transition, *Business Horizons,* 56: 465–71.

2

The Vietnam SME Data, 2005–15

Hanna Berkel, John Rand, Finn Tarp, and Neda Trifković

2.1 Delving into the Vietnam SME Data

This chapter sheds light on the Vietnam SME database. It covers six survey rounds during the period 2005–15 and represents the basis for the analytical work in all subsequent chapters. We start by outlining the overall purpose behind collecting the SME data and continue to describe the data, including sample design, firm and owner characteristics and attrition. Section 2.2 compares the SME data with the characteristics of Vietnam's overall enterprise population as provided by the General Statistics Office of Vietnam (GSO) to evaluate the representativeness of the former.

2.1.1 Purpose

Since the initiation of the Doi Moi reforms in 1986, it is widely believed that SMEs have critical characteristics that contribute to Vietnam's economic and social development. Specifically, SMEs represent a source of growth, savings, employment creation, and increased competition. Despite their vast potential, general knowledge on their characteristics, as well as the opportunities and constraints they were facing was lacking at the beginning of the twenty-first century. Accordingly, it was difficult for researchers to formulate evidence-based policy recommendations and for the government to assist this sector. This led the Institute of Labour Science and Social Affairs (ILSSA) of the Ministry of Labour, Invalids and Social Affairs (MOLISA) jointly with the Central Institute of Economic Management (CIEM) to implement a representative survey of non-state manufacturing enterprises in 2005. Technical collaboration came forward from the Development Economics Research Group (DERG) at the Department of Economics at the University of Copenhagen and funding was provided by Danida (CIEM 2007). The chosen firms were located in ten different provinces,[1] as shown in Figure 2.1: Ha Noi, Phu

[1] In 2009, Ha Tay province became part of Ha Noi such that Ha Tay does not appear as a separate province in Figure 2.1. In our dataset, we maintain Ha Tay as a separate province because it facilitates the comparability with previous years.

Hanna Berkel, John Rand, Finn Tarp, and Neda Trifković, *The Vietnam SME Data, 2005–15* In: *Micro, Small, and Medium Enterprises in Vietnam*. Edited by: John Rand and Finn Tarp, Oxford University Press (2020).

DOI: 10.1093/oso/9780198851189.003.0002

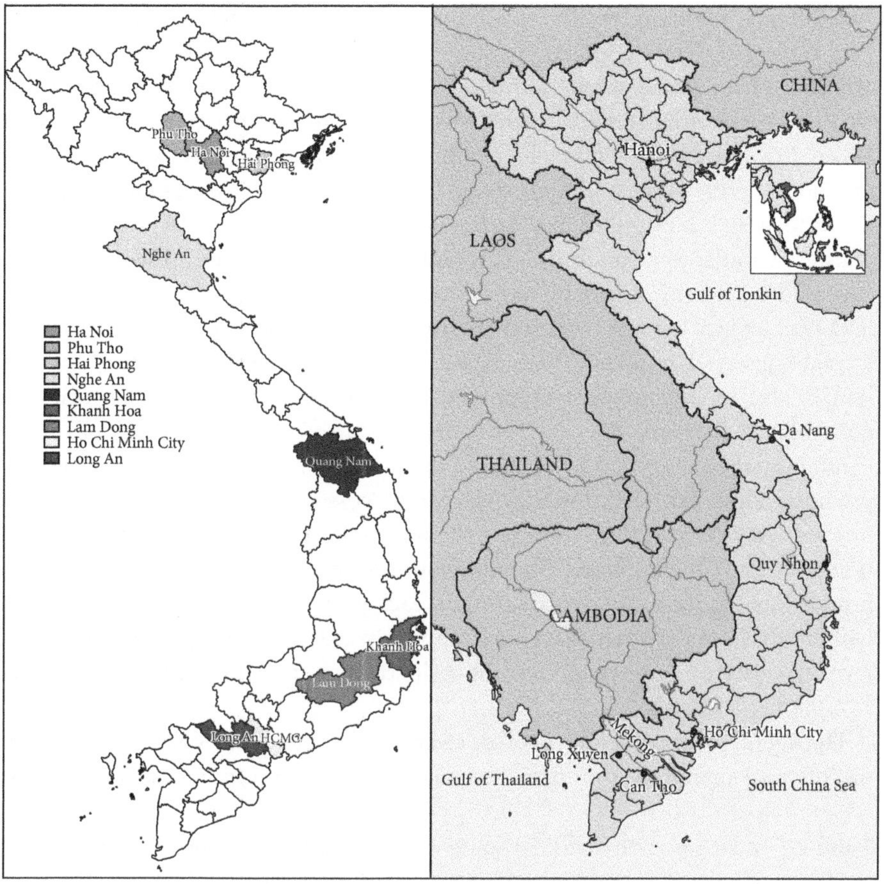

Figure 2.1 Location of the sampled provinces and map of Vietnam

Source: igismap.com for Vietnam shapefile used for the left-hand map created in Stata by the authors, and Tarp (2017: 28) for the right-hand map.

Tho, Ha Tay, Hai Phong, Nghe An, Quang Nam, Khanh Hoa, Lam Dong, Ho Chi Minh City, and Long An. Subsequently, five more survey rounds took place biannually until 2015, supported from 2011 by UNU-WIDER. The overall aim was to follow the same enterprises over time to understand their long-term development and to analyse the business environment in which they operate (Brandt et al. 2016; Rand et al. 2014, 2008; Rand and Tarp 2012, 2010).

2.1.2 Sample Design

In Vietnam, non-state manufacturing enterprises register as private, collective, partnerships, limited liability or joint stock companies with foreign capital.

Accordingly, the sampling frame we aimed for does not include state-owned or FDI enterprises. The population frame of non-state manufacturing enterprises originated from two datasets from GSO and additional on-site screening of firms by the enumerators. First, the 2002 Establishment Census (GSO 2004), from which the number of non-state registered household business establishments that do not satisfy the conditions stated in the Enterprise Law was taken. Second, the Industrial Survey (GSO 2007), from which the number of enterprises formally registered under the Enterprise Law, was obtained. Our ten provinces jointly covered 30 per cent of the country's overall non-state manufacturing population in 2005. As we wanted to ensure representativeness at the province level for formal/registered non-state manufacturing firms, we aimed at estimating the sample size for the smallest group (in this case Lam Dong) and subsequently determine the sample sizes for the remaining provinces. For reasons of implementation, the survey had to be limited to a select number of districts within each province. Thus, firm selection took place in a two-step sampling procedure. In the first step, districts within each province were selected using probability proportional to size (PPS) sampling. The number of selected districts in each province is proportional to the number of districts in each province. In the second step, firms within a selected district were randomly selected from the population list of formal/registered non-state and household manufacturing firms (including 164,468 firms), as shown in Table 2.1.

During the pilot surveys, it became clear that we could only collect information on informal manufacturing firms through snowballing techniques. Accordingly,

Table 2.1 Vietnam's non-state and household manufacturing: population by province in 2005

Province	Householdenterprises	Non-stateenterprises	Total
Ha Noi	16,588	2,429	19,017
Phu Tho	17,042	127	17,169
Ha Tay*	23,890	201	24,091
Hai Phong	12,811	363	13,174
Nghe An	22,695	237	22,932
Quang Nam	10,509	111	10,620
Khanh Hoa*	5,603	256	5,859
Lam Dong	5,268	160	5,428
HCMC	34,241	3,682	37,923
Long An	8,050	205	8,255
Total	156,697	7,771	164,468

Notes: Includes only non-state manufacturing enterprises. Figures for Ha Tay have been downward adjusted and Khanh Hoa upwards adjusted after a series of consultations with both central and local government officials.

Source: The Real Situation of Enterprises (GSO 2005) and Results of Establishment Census of Vietnam (GSO 2004).

within each district, we selected firms not represented in the 'formal' sampling frame, yet visually present for interview (on-site identification). Within each district, we asked the enumerators to find as many additional informal firms as possible within each chosen site (block enumeration). The results of this stratified 2-step sampling approach and resulting number of informal firms are in Table 2.2, where we for each survey year have reported data by province and by legal status.[2] Analysts can calculate the corresponding sampling weights for formal/registered firms based on the information provided in Table 2.1.

Over the years, the survey team re-interviewed surviving firms in a tracer survey. Questionnaires are comparable across all survey rounds, and we randomly replaced exit firms using two criteria. First, holding a constant level of household enterprises from the 2002 Establishment Census (GSO, 2004). Second, the updated population of firms registered under the Enterprises Law in the years in which the surveys took place. We note that our data do not necessarily correspond exactly with what was happening in Vietnam's overall SME population during 2005–15 (for more details see Section 2.2.2). However, our data is unique in the sense that it follows the same SMEs (both formal and informal) and their employees over time.

2.1.3 Characteristics of the Sample

The core variables used in subsequent chapters are firm size (number of employees), location, sector, ownership, and formality status. Appendix Tables A2.1 and A2.2 provide additional details on the characteristics of the firms followed over a decade. We measure firm size based on the number of employees and classify firms in three size categories following World Bank suggestions: Micro enterprises are composed of fewer than ten employees, while small-sized firms have between 10 and 49 workers and medium companies from 50 up to 300 employees.[3] Due to our focus on SMEs, we exclude large enterprises with more than 300 workers. In our sample, the average number of workers per firm decreased from 19 in 2005 to 16 in 2015. In 2005, 63 per cent of the sample's enterprises were micro sized, 29 per cent small and 8 per cent medium sized. These shares changed to 70, 23, and 7 per cent in 2015, respectively. Figure 2.2 breaks these numbers down by legal status. In 2005, the share of firms that were of micro size and informal (36 per cent) was higher than the share of formal micro enterprises (27 per cent). In 2015, many informal firms had formalized such that more micro enterprises were formal (60 per cent) than informal (10 per cent) in our sample.

More than half of the sampled firms are household enterprises. This implies that the 2000 Vietnam enterprise law does not recognize them. The share of

[2] An enterprise is legally formal when it has a tax code.

[3] There were no large firms in the initial sample, but some have become large over time.

Table 2.2 Number of interviewed enterprises by year: province and formality status

	2005		2007		2009		2011		2013		2015	
	F	Inf	F	Inf	F	Inf	F	Inf	F	Inf	F	Inf
Ha Noi	222	75	226	54	236	48	239	36	228	55	275	18
Phu Tho	32	245	49	194	74	185	79	174	76	180	197	55
Ha Tay*	114	281	99	283	106	271	139	206	174	171	305	62
Hai Phong	137	64	121	74	148	62	175	29	156	26	195	23
Nghe An	109	279	99	250	145	209	166	181	162	173	272	66
Quang Nam	81	91	79	76	101	57	107	54	112	55	156	10
Khanh Hoa	98	4	84	2	92	3	96	1	89	1	90	7
Lam Dong	68	21	75	7	57	13	70	11	74	14	86	4
HCMC	652	43	589	20	599	19	566	8	600	12	642	9
Long An	82	47	90	36	100	27	106	18	108	27	122	9
Sample size	1,595	1,151	1,511	996	1,658	894	1,743	718	1,799	714	2,340	263

Note: *In 2009, Ha Tay province became part of Ha Noi. However, in this dataset Ha Tay is maintained as a separate province because it facilitates the comparability with previous years.

Source: Authors' calculations based on SME data.

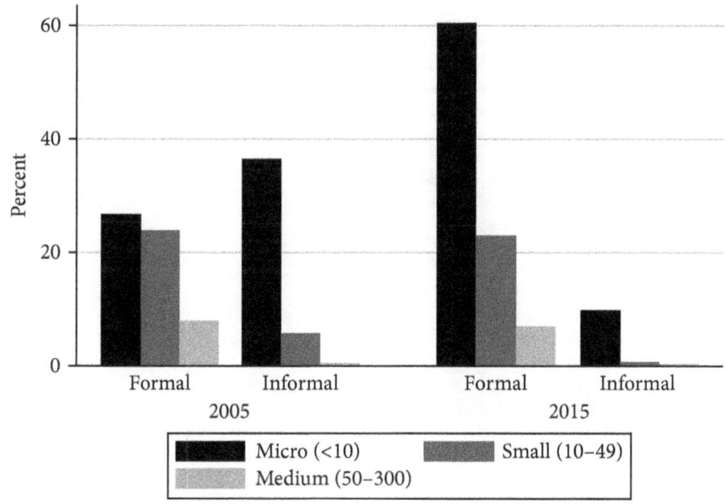

Figure 2.2 SME sample by firm size and formality status
Source: Authors' calculations based on SME data.

limited liability companies in the sample increased from 16 to 24 per cent and the percentage of joint stock companies without state capital grew from 2 to 4 per cent during the 2005–15 period. During the same period, sole proprietorships decreased from 10 to 6 per cent, while partnerships, collectives and cooperatives jointly shrank from 4 to 2 per cent. As can be seen from Figure 2.2, the formality rate increased sharply from 57 per cent in 2005 to almost 90 per cent in 2015; and around 40 per cent of the sampled businesses maintained written accounts over the whole period.

Figure 2.3 illustrates the composition of the sample's manufacturing industries based on standard ISIC-codes in 2005 and 2015, respectively. Food and beverages represent the biggest industry, as 30 per cent of the firms belong to it. Fabricated metal products (17 per cent), wood (11 per cent), furniture (8 per cent), rubber (5 per cent), and non-metallic mineral products (5 per cent) follow suit. Each of the remaining industries includes less than 5 per cent of the enterprises. The composition of industries has changed over time in that there are relatively more enterprises in the food and beverages, fabricated metal, wood and apparel industries, and fewer in furniture, non-metallic mineral products, textiles, and electronic machinery.

2.1.4 Sample Attrition

Attrition related to firms closing operations, refusing to participate in the survey, changing their location or not found by the enumerator, often raise analytical

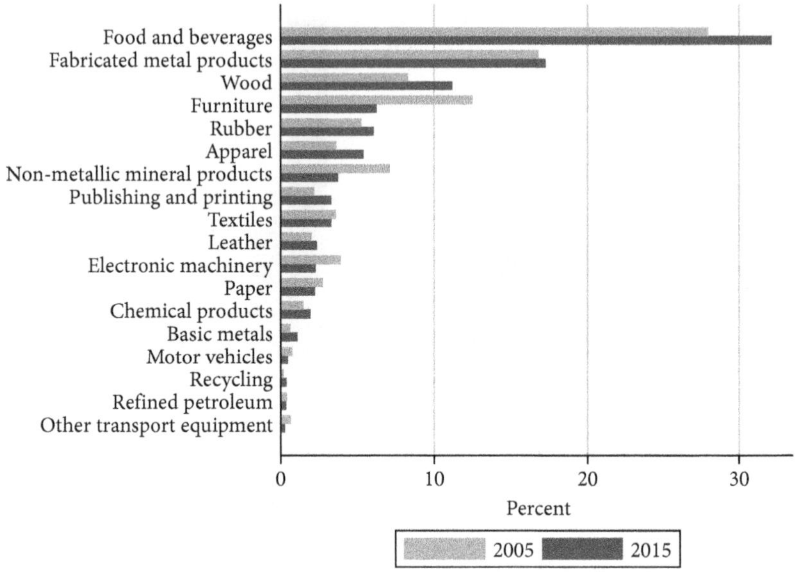

Figure 2.3 SME sample by manufacturing industries
Source: Authors' calculations based on SME data.

concerns. However, as the survey design allowed us to follow exiting firms (or the previous owners of closed down firms) we can for most years conclude that the majority of firms not found were in deed 'real' closures and not attrition due to refusal to participate or mobility related reasons. As presented in Table 2.3, we interviewed 2,746 enterprises in 2005. In 2015, only 982 of these same enterprises remained active. The recoded attrition rate varies by survey year and lies between 15 to 21 per cent, whereas the ten-year attrition rate is 64 per cent. This gives an annual 'death' rate between 9 and 10 per cent.

Table 2.3 compares the characteristics of the attrited enterprises with the non-attrited firms to establish whether any particular features supported the non-attrited ones in keeping their business running for such a long period. The table first examines whether there exists a difference in firm size between attrited and non-attrited businesses. It appears that attrited firms were significantly larger than non-attrited ones in the three survey rounds: 2007, 2009, and 2013. It therefore seems, at least in some years, that larger SMEs may have faced more challenges to survive than smaller ones. Regarding the location of the attrited and non-attrited enterprises, we look at the share of firms that operated in the two biggest cities, Ha Noi and Ho Chi Minh. The firms that did not survive in the first three survey rounds were significantly more likely to be located in these two cities than the firms that kept operating. This could be due to more competition in the country's largest cities such that it is more difficult for businesses to survive there than in other parts/cities of the country.

Table 2.3 Extent of attrition and comparison of enterprises by attrition status

	Sample size	Number attrited between *t-1* and *t*	Mean: attrited	Mean: non-attrited	Difference (t-test)
Firm size					
2005	2,746				
2005–7 panel	2,182	564	25	18	***
2005–7–9 panel	1,787	395	29	15	***
2005–7–9–11 panel	1,415	372	17	15	
2005–7–9–11–13 panel	1,159	256	18	14	*
2005–7–9–11–13–15 panel	982	177	13	14	
Firms in Ha Noi and HCMC (%)					
2005	2,746				
2005–7 panel	2,182	564	46	34	***
2005–7–9 panel	1,787	395	44	31	***
2005–7–9–11 panel	1,415	372	43	28	***
2005–7–9–11–13 panel	1,159	256	30	28	
2005–7–9–11–13–15 panel	982	177	30	27	
Firms in five biggest industries (%)					
2005	2,746				
2005–7 panel	2,182	564	66	72	***
2005–7–9 panel	1,787	395	64	73	***
2005–7–9–11 panel	1,415	372	67	75	***
2005–7–9–11–13 panel	1,159	256	69	76	***
2005–7–9–11–13–15 panel	982	177	75	76	
HH enterprises share (%)					
2005	2,746				
2005–7 panel	2,182	564	62	69	***
2005–7–9 panel	1,787	395	62	71	***
2005–7–9–11 panel	1,415	372	69	71	
2005–7–9–11–13 panel	1,159	256	64	73	***
2005–7–9–11–13–15 panel	982	177	67	74	*
Informal firms (no tax cod, %e)					
2005	2,746				
2005–7 panel	2,182	564	34	35	
2005–7–9 panel	1,787	395	34	35	
2005–7–9–11 panel	1,415	372	38	34	
2005–7–9–11–13 panel	1,159	256	34	35	
2005–7–9–11–13–15 panel	982	177	41	33	*

Note: [1]Food and beverages, fabricated metal products, wood, furniture, rubber.

Source: Authors' calculations based on SME data.

Concerning household enterprises, the samples were statistically different in 2005, 2007, 2013 and 2015. Specifically, the share of household firms was higher in the non-attrited than in the attrited sample. This is consistent with the trends observed for firm size: attrited enterprises were generally larger than non-attrited enterprises and larger firms are less likely to be household enterprises. However,

Table 2.4 Comparison of balanced and unbalanced panel by firm size, location, sector, and ownership type

	2005		2007		2009		2011		2013		2015	
Frequencies												
Full sample	2,746		2,507		2,552		2,461		2,493		2,603	
New entrants	1,764		325		521		451		464		502	
Incumbent firms not new entrants	0		1,200		1,049		1,028		1,047		1,119	
Balanced panel	982		982		982		982		982		982	
Firm Size	Mean	SD	Mean	SD	Mean	SD	Mean	SD	Mean	SD	Mean	SD
Full sample	19.19	53.74	19.19	49.97	18.77	62.55	15.97	32.65	15.19	44.58	15.61	37.09
New entrants	21.70	64.06	18.58	35.69	19.37	32.59	16.52	34.57	16.69	33.91	17.04	40.13
Incumbent firms not new entrants	–	–	21.87	63.86	17.60	39.64	16.21	29.79	16.15	58.90	16.80	41.65
Balanced panel	14.66	25.93	16.11	30.88	19.71	89.05	15.47	34.57	13.46	28.34	13.52	29.03
Share of firms in Hanoi and HCMC	Mean		Mean		Mean		Mean		Mean		Mean	
Full sample	36.13		35.46		35.34		34.50		35.90		36.27	
New entrants	40.99		48.92		45.11		45.23		43.75		42.03	
Incumbent firms not new entrants	–		38.42		37.94		36.58		40.40		41.47	
Balanced panel	27.39		27.39		27.39		27.39		27.39		27.39	
Share of firms in five biggest sectors[1]												
Full sample	70.76		69.57		70.45		71.11		72.08		72.88	
New entrants	67.12		64.62		65.64		64.52		67.46		71.31	
Incumbent firms not new entrants	–		66.42		68.26		69.55		69.72		70.33	
Balanced panel	77.29		75.05		75.35		75.76		76.78		76.57	
Share of household firms												
Full sample	68.90		69.17		66.42		65.01		63.62		63.35	
New entrants	65.36		63.69		48.37		61.20		55.60		57.17	
Incumbent firms not new entrants	–		66.00		67.49		58.95		60.27		59.25	
Balanced panel	75.25		74.85		74.85		73.12		70.98		71.18	
Share of informal firms (no tax code)												
Full sample	41.92		39.73		35.03		29.18		28.64		10.10	
New entrants	38.95		32.92		27.83		26.39		31.68		40.24	
Incumbent firms not new entrants	–		38.67		35.37		27.14		25.98		2.41	
Balanced panel	47.25		43.28		38.49		32.59		30.04		3.46	

Note: [1]Food and beverages, fabricated metal products, wood, furniture, rubber.

Source: Authors' calculations based on SME data.

attrited firms are no more likely to be formal, i.e. to have a tax code, than businesses that survived in all survey rounds except for the last one in 2015. Here 61 per cent of the enterprises that did not survive were formal compared to 77 per cent in the non-attrited sample. In 2015, the share of informal firms was higher among the attrited than the non-attrited businesses, signalling that it may be more challenging now to operate an informal firm due to different initiatives of the government to formalize the Vietnamese economy. In sum, attrited SMEs in Vietnam are more likely to be larger, located in Ha Noi or Ho Chi Minh City, and to operate a household enterprise in 'smaller'/less concentrated industries.

Table 2.4 compares the firms in the full sample, new entrants, incumbent firms, and those in the balanced panel by year. The 982 firms that survived the whole period of 2005–15 were, on average, smaller than new entrants and incumbent firms except for in 2009. Moreover, a smaller share of the balanced panel was located in the two biggest cities, Ha Noi and Ho Chi Minh, than new entrants and incumbent firms. Regarding the different manufacturing industries, the balanced panel had a higher share of enterprises operating in the five biggest industries than the other two groups, except for 2013 and 2015. This fits well the previous observations that enterprises that survived were, on average, smaller, less likely to be located in the two largest cities, and more likely to operate in one of the five largest industries. Further, the 982 survivors included a higher share of firms that were household enterprises and were more likely to be informal in most years. However, in 2015, almost none of the firms in the balanced panel were informal anymore, perhaps because the government succeeded in its formalization efforts. As we wanted to continue examining informal enterprises, the share of informal firms among the new entrants remained around 40 per cent, which is quite high.

2.1.5 SCOLI

Costs of living are likely to change at varying pace across both space and time. Thus, it is crucial to take into account spatial price variations. Therefore, the studies in this volume rely on a spatial cost of living index (SCOLI) which is interpreted as the minimum cost of buying a given level of utility at given prices in each of Vietnam's provinces (Kakwani and Hill 2002).

2.2 Considering the Representativeness of the Vietnam SME Data

Tables A2.3 to A2.8 show that Vietnam's enterprise population has been increasing at a steady pace over the ten years in focus here. It is therefore of interest to evaluate the representativeness of the SME data by comparing it to the country's total enterprise population as given by GSO.[4] While the GSO data contain information on all types of legal ownership, i.e. state-owned (SOE), non-state (NSOE), FDI and household (HH) enterprises,[5] as well as on all sectors, we focus in this volume on NSOE and HH enterprises from the manufacturing sector. Table A2.3 shows that in Vietnam, the overall enterprise population (SOE, NSOE, FDI, HH) increased from 2.7 million in 2005 to 5.1 million in 2015 (row 1), whereas the manufacturing enterprise population grew from around 680,000 to almost 900,000 in these ten years (row 5). Manufacturing NSOEs and manufacturing HHs increased from 17,000 and 660,000, respectively, to 56,000 and 800,000 in the same period (rows 6 and 7). The SME sample analysed in this book consisted of 0.4 per cent of Vietnam's total manufacturing enterprise population (SOE, NSOE, FDI, HH) in 2005 and 0.3 per cent in the subsequent years.

Our SME data stem as noted from 10 of Vietnam's 63 provinces, and they host approximately 55 per cent of the country's manufacturing NSOEs and around 25 per cent of its manufacturing households. In 2005, the SME sample covered around 10 per cent of the manufacturing NSOEs located in the selected provinces and 1 per cent of their manufacturing household firms. Due to the large growth-rate of the manufacturing sector, these shares decreased to 3 per cent for manufacturing NSOEs and 0.8 per cent for manufacturing households in 2015.

Tables A2.4 and A2.5 compare the GSO and SME firms by province, ownership type, and manufacturing sector. Ho Chi Minh City and Ha Noi are the two cities with the biggest populations of manufacturing NSOEs and HHs. In 2005, Ho Chi Minh City had 4,600 manufacturing NSOEs and 34,000 manufacturing households, which changed to 18,000 and 29,000 in 2015, respectively. In the same period, Ha Noi's non-state manufacturing enterprises grew from 2,400 to 11,000, while its manufacturing households grew strongly from 17,000 to 85,000. These two cities were also the ones with the highest numbers of firms interviewed in the SME survey rounds. Overall, the manufacturing enterprises in the SME data represented, depending on the year, between 7 and 2 per cent of Ho Chi Minh's manufacturing NSOEs, while the SME data on households covered around 1 per cent of the manufacturing households in this city. Lam Dong is one of the ten provinces where the enterprise population is smallest and increased most slowly over time. In 2015, the SME sample captured 7 per cent of Lam Dong's manufacturing NSOEs and 1 per cent of its manufacturing households.

GSO data show that 97 per cent of firms in Vietnam are household enterprises and their number almost doubled from 2.7 to 4.7 million in 2005–15 (row 4 in Table A2.3). In the SME data, more than 60 per cent of the interviewed firms are

[4] GSO provided the original dataset on enterprises, which we compared to our sample's enterprises, while the numbers for households are taken from GSO reports on non-farm individual establishments (GSO, 2015, 2014, 2010a, 2004).

[5] GSO uses the term 'non-farm individual business establishments', which is equivalent to 'household enterprises' in this book

household enterprises and these were about 0.3 per cent of all of Vietnam's manufacturing households in 2005 (see Table A2.6). Overall, the SME data captured 5 per cent of Vietnam's manufacturing non-state enterprises in 2005 and 2 per cent in 2015. These shares became smaller over time because the country's manufacturing enterprise population grew, while the sample size only changed slightly every year. Limited liability companies form the biggest subgroup of non-state manufacturing enterprises in Vietnam, followed by private enterprises in 2005 (6,000) and by joint stock companies without state capital in 2015 (9,000). In 2005, the country had almost 9,000 limited liability companies in the manufacturing sector, which increased to 30,000 in 2011 and 39,000 in 2015. In 2005, the SME data included 5 per cent of Vietnam's manufacturing limited liability companies and 2 per cent of the same in 2015. Vietnamese manufacturing cooperatives and partnerships increased only slightly from 1,000 to 1,500 in the ten-year period. In our SME sample, between 3 and 9 per cent of the interviewed firms are cooperatives or partnerships (see Table A2.6).

In terms of the manufacturing industries, Table A2.7 shows that in 2005, one-fifth of Vietnam's manufacturing NSOEs were in the food and beverages industry, followed by fabricated metal products (11 per cent), non-metallic mineral products (8 per cent), wood (8 per cent), and furniture (8 per cent). The first two also represented the two largest industries in the SME survey.[6] The third largest industry in the SME data, rubber and plastics, was overrepresented, as it ranks seventh in the population. In 2005, the share of interviewed SMEs in Vietnam's manufacturing NSOEs was 5 per cent. The SME sample held 14 per cent of Vietnam's NSOEs in the coke and refined petroleum industry, 9 per cent of the rubber industry, and 8 per cent of firms in the paper industry. These shares are relatively large due to, among other factors, the small size of these industries: only 14 NSOEs existed in the coke and refined petroleum industry.

In 2015, fabricated metal products (17 per cent in NSOE population), and food and beverages (14 per cent in NSOE population) remained the largest industries in both the manufacturing NSOE population and SME data (excluding households). Yet, they had swapped places. Wearing apparel was Vietnam's third biggest manufacturing industry (9 per cent) and followed suit as number four in the SME data. As in 2005, the rubber and plastic industry was overrepresented as number three in the SME data, while it was only the sixth largest among the manufacturing NSOEs (6 per cent) in Vietnam. Publishing and printing (8 per cent) rose to fourth place in the manufacturing NSOE population, while it was the sixth biggest in the SME survey. The fifth largest industry was the wood industry in both the population (8 per cent) and the SME survey (see Table A2.7).

[6] We do not have any information on household enterprises by manufacturing industry. Therefore, Table A2.7 only compares NSOE with SME-data, excluding households.

Table A2.8 compares Vietnam's HH enterprises and SME HHs by year. We do not have sufficient information on the manufacturing industries of Vietnam's HH enterprises such that we cannot compare Vietnam's HH population with SME HHs by manufacturing industry.

2.3 Conclusion

Our SME data represent both the dynamics and evolution of registered formal non-state manufacturing firms in the ten selected provinces in Vietnam over the period 2005 to 2015. However, as reliable information on the characteristics of the enterprise population of the informal manufacturing does not exist, we cannot establish appropriate weights for this group of firms. Moreover, given that our sample of informal household businesses was identified at locations where several registered entities operate means that our sample of informal household businesses is unlikely to be strictly representative of informal SMEs in Vietnam. The informal firms we capture are in all likelihood more established and productive informal entities. Being able to follow firms over a ten-year period offers many advantages of analytical nature. At the same time, when referring to the informal firms, the reader must keep the above characteristic of the data in mind throughout the following chapters.

Appendix

Table A2.1 Firm, owner, and worker characteristics by year

	2005	2007	2009	2011	2013	2015
Firm characteristics						
Firm size (number of employees)	19.19	19.19	18.77	15.97	15.19	15.61
Firm age	11.53	13.53	14.63	13.45	15.53	16.54
Household	68.90	69.17	66.42	65.01	63.62	63.35
Private/sole proprietorship	10.16	7.70	7.84	7.92	8.10	6.34
Partnership/Collective/ Cooperative	3.50	3.99	2.86	2.72	2.17	2.04
Limited liability company	15.70	17.35	19.51	20.52	21.86	23.86
Joint stock company (without state capital)	1.75	1.79	3.37	3.82	4.25	4.42
Food and beverages	27.93	27.72	29.19	30.39	31.09	32.12
Tobacco	0.00	0.32	0.12	0.00	0.00	0.04
Textiles	3.61	4.59	4.94	4.39	4.01	3.30
Apparel	3.64	4.19	4.23	4.96	4.89	5.42
Leather	2.00	2.07	1.88	1.99	2.13	2.34
Wood	8.27	11.89	12.03	10.28	10.19	11.18
Paper	2.73	2.75	2.74	2.72	2.97	2.23

Publishing and printing	2.18	2.35	2.94	2.44	2.61	3.30
Refined petroleum	0.40	0.00	0.39	0.28	0.32	0.35
Chemical products	1.40	1.83	1.57	1.58	2.09	1.92
Rubber	5.28	5.31	5.56	4.71	5.54	6.07
Non-metallic mineral products	7.10	6.02	5.29	4.79	4.13	3.76
Basic metals	0.62	1.12	1.37	1.46	1.08	1.08
Fabricated metal products	16.79	16.83	16.93	17.76	17.17	17.25
Electronic machinery	3.93	3.31	2.74	3.01	2.61	2.27
Motor vehicles	0.73	1.20	0.94	0.69	0.48	0.46
Other transport equipment	0.66	0.28	0.27	0.33	0.36	0.27
Furniture	12.49	7.82	6.74	7.96	8.10	6.26
Recycling	0.18	0.40	0.12	0.24	0.24	0.38
High-tech firms	17.81	12.60	10.70	11.99	11.55	9.26
Export firms	6.37	5.66	5.84	6.04	6.30	6.95
Internat. certification (Yes = 1)	3.53	4.27	5.68	6.70	7.34	4.19
Urban	64.64	64.62	63.99	62.62	63.18	63.35
Formal credit access (Yes = 1)	22.72	35.14	36.79	27.55	23.79	23.67
Credit constrained	25.27	24.05	26.61	28.02	30.84	20.73
Bookkeeping	36.53	35.54	40.60	38.60	38.79	38.99
Technology innovation (Yes = 1 if introduction of new product or improvement of product or new process/ technology or all)	66.72	48.15	45.02	44.09	19.66	33.88
Formal (= have a BRC)	57.03	58.05	62.88	68.25	68.56	88.98
Observations	2,746	2,507	2,552	2,461	2,493	2,603

Source: Authors' calculations based on SME data.

Table A2.2 Firm, owner, and worker characteristics by year

	2005	2007	2009	2011	2013	2015
Financial information						
Real revenue (VND)	6,271,785	5,020,016	5,048,084	9,892,408	4,429,981	8,217,846
Profit/revenue share	20.00	21.40	21.60	19.50	22.40	23.60
Assets/revenue share	1535.73	309.34	239.63	306.42	238.23	185.29
Debt/revenue share	12.60	12.60	12.70	10.40	9.70	9.30
Have debt (Yes=1)	57.48	53.06	58.05	48.72	49.22	35.51
Owner characteristics						
Age	44.67	45.31	45.71	45.76	46.18	46.44
Female owners	0.3063	0.3303	0.3413	0.3690	0.3995	0.4072
Primary or below	10.52	13.12	13.01	10.00	5.98	6.57
Lower secondary	32.08	31.95	28.72	28.40	24.59	20.94
Upper secondary or above	57.39	54.93	58.27	61.60	69.43	72.49
Member of Communist Party	8.85	7.38	7.09	9.43	9.23	7.26
Workforce Characteristics						
Manager	NA	25.69	26.82	29.20	31.96	35.04
Professional	NA	0.03	0.03	0.03	0.04	0.03
Production worker	NA	65.95	65.07	62.01	59.64	57.34
Female workers	35.63	36.99	37.62	36.98	38.54	38.16
Trade union in firm	9.25	9.65	8.54	8.37	9.55	12.45
Observations	2,746	2,507	2,552	2,461	2,493	2,603

Source: Authors' calculations based on SME data.

Table A2.3 Overview: Vietnam's enterprise population

	2005	2007	2009	2011	2013	2015
Vietnam's enterprise population						
1 OVERALL ENTERPRISE POPULATION (=Enterprises (SOE, NSOE, FDI) & household (HH) enterprises) (2+4)	2,711,096	3,429,084	4,074,429	4,464,197	4,984,751	5,085,525
2 Enterprises (SOE, NSOE, FDI)	91,755	129,379	205,689	339,217	359,866	414,186
3 Non-state enterprises (NSOE)	84,003	120,380	196,776	325,771	347,795	401,186
4 Household (HH) enterprises	2,619,341	3,299,705	3,868,740	4,124,980	4,624,885	4,671,339
Vietnam's manufacturing enterprise population						
5 OVERALL MANUFACTURING ENTERPRISE POPULATION (SOE, NSOE, FDI, HH)	678,499	836,154	869,379	888,340	912,873	894,552
6 Non-state manufacturing enterprises	16,958	22,342	33,893	47,027	50,322	55,966
7 Manufacturing households	657,968	809,948	830,576	835,469	856,634	832,290
Manufacturing enterprise population in the 10 provinces of SME data						
8 OVERALL MANUFACTURING ENTERPRISE POPULATION (SOE, NSOE, FDI, HH)	167,332	NA	245,496	252,301	250,408	249,111
9 Non-state manufacturing enterprises	8,971	11,813	19,030	26,932	29,177	33,644
10 Manufacturing households	156,697	NA	224,548	223,180	219,060	213,183

Note: Since the SME data was collected in the year before the publishing year, we compare the SME data with the enterprise population of the previous year as well, e.g. the 2007 survey round is compared to Vietnam's enterprise population in 2006 because the SME data was collected in 2006; the 2015 survey round is compared to Vietnam's 2014 enterprise population because the SME data was collected in 2014.

Source: GSO data on enterprises from 2014, 2012, 2010, 2008, 2006, 2004; for households: GSO, 2015, 2014, 2010a, 2004.

Table A2.4 Vietnam's non-state manufacturing enterprises and SME data by provinces

	2005			2007			2009		
	Vietnam's NSOE Population	SME Data	Share	Vietnam's NSOE Population	SME Data	Share	Vietnam's NSOE Population	SME Data	Share
Ha Noi	2,373	173	0.0729	2,966	161	0.0543	5,273	176	0.0334
Phu Tho	128	29	0.2266	174	21	0.1207	239	35	0.1464
Ha Tay	415	61	0.1470	NA	70	0.0000	NA	68	NA
Hai Phong	540	93	0.1722	670	103	0.1537	811	92	0.1134
Nghe An	148	90	0.6081	185	61	0.3297	381	75	0.1969
Quang Nam	101	21	0.2079	166	24	0.1446	272	36	0.1324
Khan Hoa	256	36	0.1406	363	30	0.0826	517	36	0.0696
Lam Dong	107	18	0.1682	164	17	0.1037	247	16	0.0648
HCMC	4,637	309	0.0666	6,721	257	0.0382	10,660	295	0.0277
Long An	266	24	0.0902	404	29	0.0718	630	28	0.0444
Total 10 provinces	8,971	854	0.0952	11,813	773	0.0654	19,030	857	0.0450
Other 53 provinces	7,987	0	0.0000	10,529	0	0.0000	14,863	0	0.000
Total Vietnam/Sample	16,958	854	0.0503	22,342	773	0.0346	33,893	857	0.0253

	2011			2013			2015		
	Vietnam's NSOE Population	SME Data	Share	Vietnam's NSOE Population	SME Data	Share	Vietnam's NSOE Population	SME Data	Share
Ha Noi	8,452	181	0.0214	9,501	163	0.0172	10,825	173	0.0160
Phu Tho	393	34	0.0865	450	33	0.0733	444	31	0.0698
Ha Tay	NA	61	0.0000	NA	71	0.0000	NA	64	NA
Hai Phong	1,095	100	0.0913	1,176	100	0.0850	1,147	111	0.0968

Continued

Table A2.4 *Continued*

	2011			2013			2015		
	Vietnam's NSOE Population	SME Data	Share	Vietnam's NSOE Population	SME Data	Share	Vietnam's NSOE Population	SME Data	Share
Nghe An	543	74	0.1363	571	85	0.1489	613	71	0.1158
Quang Nam	463	32	0.0000	482	42	0.0871	556	38	0.0683
Khan Hoa	521	35	0.0672	605	35	0.0579	588	40	0.0680
Lam Dong	284	20	0.0704	336	24	0.0714	386	28	0.0725
HCMC	14,288	289	0.0000	16,218	323	0.0199	17,988	364	0.0202
Long An	893	35	0.0392	1,117	31	0.0278	1,097	34	0.0310
Total 10 provinces	26,932	861	0.0320	30,456	907	0.0298	33,644	954	0.0284
Other 53 provinces	20,095	0	0.0000	23,891	0	0.0000	22,322	0	0.0000
Total	47,027	861	0.0183	53,867	907	0.0168	55,966	954	0.0170

Note: Since the SME data was collected in the year before the publishing year, we compare the SME data with the enterprise population of the previous year as well, e.g. the 2007 survey round is compared to Vietnam's enterprise population in 2006 because the SME data was collected in 2006; the 2015 survey round is compared to Vietnam's 2014 enterprise population because the SME data was collected in 2014.

Source: GSO data on enterprises from 2014, 2012, 2010, 2008, 2006, 2004; for households: GSO, 2015, 2014, 2010a, 2004; authors' calculations based on SME data.

Table A2.5 Vietnam's manufacturing HH population and manufacturing households in SME data by province

	2005			2007			2009		
	Vietnam's Manufacturing HH Population	SME Data	Share	Vietnam's Manufacturing HH Population	SME Data	Share	Vietnam's Manufacturing HH Population	SME Data	Share
Ha Noi	16,588	124	0.0075	NA	119	NA	92,566	108	0.0012
Phu Tho	17,042	248	0.0146	NA	222	NA	20,238	224	0.0111
Ha Tay	23,890	334	0.0140	NA	312	NA	NA	309	NA
Hai Phong	12,811	108	0.0084	NA	92	NA	10,832	118	0.0109
Nghe An	22,695	298	0.0131	NA	288	NA	29,938	279	0.0093
Quang Nam	20,509	141	0.0069	NA	131	NA	14,124	122	0.0086
Khan Hoa	5,603	66	0.0118	NA	56	NA	6,408	59	0.0092
Lam Dong	5,268	71	0.0135	NA	65	NA	7,797	54	0.0069
HCMC	34,241	386	0.0112	NA	352	NA	32,285	323	0.0100
Long An	8,050	105	0.0130	NA	97	NA	10,370	99	0.0095
Total 10 provinces	156,697	1,892	0.0121	NA	1,734	NA	224,549	1,695	0.0075
Other 53 provinces	543,612	0	0	NA	0	0	606,028	0	0
Total	657,968	1,892	0.0029	NA	1,734	NA	830,576	1,695	0.0020

	2011			2013			2015		
	Vietnam's Manufacturing HH Population	SME Data	Share	Vietnam's Manufacturing HH Population	SME Data	Share	Vietnam's Manufacturing HH Population	SME Data	Share
Ha Noi	91,110	94	0.0010	90,262	120	0.0013	85,213	120	0.0014
Phu Tho	19,063	219	0.0115	20,071	223	0.0111	18,074	221	0.0122
Ha Tay	0	284	NA	0	274	NA	0	303	NA
Hai Phong	11,411	104	0.0091	11,108	82	0.0074	11,600	107	0.0092

Continued

Table A2.5 *Continued*

	2011			2013			2015		
	Vietnam's Manufacturing HH Population	SME Data	Share	Vietnam's Manufacturing HH Population	SME Data	Share	Vietnam's Manufacturing HH Population	SME Data	Share
Nghe An	29,966	273	0.0091	31,944	150	0.0047	31,626	267	0.0084
Quang Nam	14,846	129	0.0087	15,733	125	0.0079	15,955	128	0.0080
Khan Hoa	6,042	62	0.0103	5,895	55	0.0093	5,591	57	0.0102
Lam Dong	7,389	61	0.0083	7,563	64	0.0085	8,013	62	0.0077
HCMC	33,000	285	0.0086	28,905	289	0.0099	29,400	287	0.0098
Long An	10,353	89	0.0086	7,579	104	0.0137	7,711	97	0.0126
Total 10 provinces	223,180	1,600	0.0072	219,060	1,586	0.0072	213,183	1,649	0.0077
Other 53 provinces	612,289	0	0	637,574	0	0	619,107	0	0
Total	835,469	1,600	0.0019	856,634	1,586	0.0019	832,290	1,649	0.0198

Source: GSO, 2015, 2014, 2010a, 2010b, 2008, 2007, 2004; authors' calculations based on SME data; authors' calculations based on SME data.

Table A2.6 Vietnam's manufacturing enterprise population and SME data by ownership type and year

	2005			2007			2009		
	Vietnam's SME Population	SME Data	Share	Vietnam's SME Population	SME Data	Share	Vietnam's SME Population	SME Data	Share
State-owned enterprises	1,247	0	0.0000	859	0	0.0000	948	0	0.0000
FDI enterprises	2,326	0	0.0000	3,005	0	0.0000	3,962	0	0.0000
Non-state enterprises	16,958	854	0.0504	22,342	773	0.0346	33,893	857	0.0253
Private	5,838	279	0.0478	6,770	193	0.0285	8,450	200	0.0237
Collectives & Cooperatives & Partnership	1,117	96	0.0859	981	100	0.1019	1,223	73	0.0597
Limited Liability	8,621	431	0.0500	12,059	435	0.0360	19,354	498	0.0257
Joint stock without state capital	1,094	49	0.0448	2,102	45	0.0214	4,290	86	0.0200
Joint stock with state capital	815	0	0.0000	1,337	0	0.0000	576	0	0.0000
Total	20,531	854	0.0416	22,342	773	0.0346	33,893	857	0.0253
Household enterprises	657,968	1,892	0.0029	809,948	1,734	0.0021	830,576	1,695	0.0000
Total	678,499	2,746	0.0040	832,290	2,507	0.0030	864,469	2,552	0.0030

	2011			2013			2015		
	Vietnam's SME Population	SME Data	Share	Vietnam's SME Population	SME Data	Share	Vietnam's SME Population	SME Data	Share
State-owned enterprises	653	0	0.0000	202	0	0.0000	190	0	0.0000
FDI enterprises	5,191	0	0.0000	5,715	0	0.0000	6,470	0	0.0000
Non-state enterprises	47,027	861	0.0183	50,322	907	0.0180	55,966	954	0.0170
Private	7,628	195	0.0256	7,395	202	0.0273	6,574	165	0,0251
Collectives & Cooperatives	1,287	67	0.0521	1,696	54	0.0318	1,584	53	0.0334

Continued

Table A2.6 *Continued*

	2011			2013			2015		
	Vietnam's SME Population	SME Data	Share	Vietnam's SME Population	SME Data	Share	Vietnam's SME Population	SME Data	Share
Limited Liability	29,997	505	0.0168	33,008	545	0.0165	38,518	621	0.0161
Joint stock without state capital	7,570	94	0.0124	8,223	106	0.0129	9,290	115	0.0124
Joint stock with state capital	545	0	0.0000	NA	0	0.0000	NA	0	0.0000
Total	47,027	861	0.0183	56,239	907	0.0161	62,626	954	0.0152
Household enterprises	835,469	1,600	0.0019	856,634	1,586	0.0019	832,290	1,649	0.0020
Total	882,496	2,461	0.0028	912,873	2,493	0.0027	894,916	2,603	0.0029

Note: Since the SME data was collected in the year before the publishing year, we compare the SME data with the enterprise population of the previous year as well, e.g. the 2007 survey round is compared to Vietnam's enterprise population in 2006 because the SME data was collected in 2006; the 2015 survey round is compared to Vietnam's 2014 enterprise population because the SME data was collected in 2014.

Source: GSO data on enterprises from 2014, 2012, 2010, 2008, 2006, 2004; for households: GSO, 2015, 2014, 2010a, 2004; authors' calculations based on SME data.

Table A2.7 Vietnam's NSOEs and SME data by manufacturing sector and year

	2005			2007			2009		
	Vietnam's Population	SME Data	Share of interviewed SMEs in Population	Vietnam's SME Population	SME Data	Share of interviewed SMEs in Population	Vietnam's SME Population	SME Data	Share of interviewed SMEs in Population
Manufacturing Total	16,958	854	0.0504	22,342	773	0.0346	33,893	857	0.0253
Food and beverages	4,018	138	0.0343	4,916	125	0.0254	6,529	131	0.0201
Tobacco	6	0	0.0000	4	2	0.5000	6	2	0.3333
Textiles	646	33	0.0511	914	46	0.0503	1,259	53	0.0421
Wearing apparel	1,156	53	0.0458	1,544	58	0.0376	2,668	62	0.0232
Leather	315	10	0.0317	398	13	0.0327	611	14	0.0229
Wood	1,356	64	0.0472	1,747	66	0.0378	2,984	71	0.0238
Paper and paper products	726	57	0.0785	976	48	0.0492	1,532	57	0.0372
Publishing, printing etc.	882	34	0.0385	1,547	38	0.0246	2,192	53	0.0242
Coke and refined petroleum	14	2	0.1429	26	0	0.0000	52	3	0.0577
Chemicals and chemical products	665	27	0.0406	934	23	0.0246	1,387	28	0.0201
Rubber and plastic	946	88	0.0930	1,307	82	0.0627	1,908	96	0.0503
Non-metallic mineral products	1,366	42	0.0307	1,644	34	0.0207	2,330	43	0.0185
Basic metals	278	11	0.0396	402	15	0.0373	663	16	0.0241
Fabricated metal products	1,869	129	0.0690	2,665	106	0.0398	4,397	121	0.0275
Machinery and equipment	860	54	0.0628	1,094	45	0.0411	1,641	41	0.0250
Motor vehicles and trailers	217	13	0.0599	152	11	0.0724	258	16	0.0620
Other transport equipment	320	11	0.0344	401	6	0.0150	575	4	0.0070
Furniture	1,284	87	0.0678	1,608	54	0.0336	2,803	45	0.0161
Recycling	34	1	0.0294	63	1	0.0159	98	1	0.0102
Other manufacturing	0	0	0.0000	0	0	0.0000	0	0	0.0000

Continued

Table A2.7 *Continued*

	2011			2013			2015		
	Vietnam's SME Population	SME Data	Share of interviewed SMEs in Population	Vietnam's SME Population	SME Data	Share	Vietnam's SME Population	SME Data	Share of interviewed SMEs in Population
Manufacturing Total	47,027	861	0.0183	53,867	907	0.0168	55,966	954	0.0170
Food and beverages	7,115	138	0.0194	7,570	144	0.0190	8,033	138	0.0172
Tobacco	6	0	0.0000	9	0	0.0000	7	0	0.0000
Textiles	1,872	43	0.0230	2,181	35	0.0160	2,259	36	0.0159
Wearing apparel	4,023	66	0.0164	4,879	71	0.0146	4,970	81	0.0163
Leather	991	16	0.0000	1,299	18	0.0000	1,185	23	0.0194
Wood	4,082	54	0.0132	3,965	70	0,0177	4,346	76	0.0175
Paper and paper products	1,756	56	0.0319	1,947	62	0.0318	1,988	48	0.0241
Publishing, printing etc.	3,392	40	0.0000	4,097	47	0.0000	4,747	70	0.0147
Coke and refined petroleum	79	2	0.0253	91	2	0.0220	91	3	0.0330
Chemicals and chemical products	2,014	30	0.0149	2,586	37	0.0143	2,777	36	0.0130
Rubber and plastic	2,908	76	0.0000	3,545	94	0.0000	3,560	100	0.0281
Non-metallic mineral products	3,454	51	0.0148	3,567	46	0.0129	3,685	45	0.0122
Basic metals	861	20	0.0232	985	15	0.0152	922	13	0.0141
Fabricated metal products	7,741	139	0.0180	8,876	145	0.0163	9,488	167	0.0176
Machinery and equipment	2,261	50	0.0000	3,024	48	0.0000	2,715	45	0.0166
Motor vehicles and trailers	178	13	0.0730	349	8	0.0229	206	7	0.0340
Other transport equipment	424	5	0.0118	520	5	0.0096	420	4	0.0095
Furniture	2,942	61	0.0207	3,199	59	0.0184	3,220	47	0.0146
Recycling	NA	1	0.0000	0	1	0.0000	0	5	0.0000
Other manufacturing	927	0	0.0000	1,178	0	0.0000	1,347	0	0.0000

Note: Since the SME data was collected in the year before the publishing year, we compare the SME data with the enterprise population of the previous year as well, e.g. the 2007 survey round is compared to Vietnam's enterprise population in 2006 because the SME data was collected in 2006; the 2015 survey round is compared to Vietnam's 2014 enterprise population because the SME data was collected in 2014.

Source: GSO data on enterprises from 2014, 2012, 2010, 2008, 2006, 2004; authors' calculations based on SME data.

Table A2.8 Vietnam's HH enterprises and SME households by year

	2005			2007			2009		
	Vietnam'sHH Enterprise Population	SMEData	Share	Vietnam'sHH Enterprise Population	SMEData	Share	Vietnam'sHH Enterprise Population	SMEData	Share
Manufacturing HHs	700,309	1,892	0.0027	NA	1,734	NA	830,576	2,552	0.0031
Total HHs	2,619,341	1,892	0.0007	3,299,705	1,734	0.0005	3,868,740	2,552	0.0007
	2011			**2013**			**2015**		
	Vietnam'sHH Enterprise Population	SMEData	Share	Vietnam'sHH Enterprise Population	SMEData	Share	Vietnam'sHH Enterprise Population	SMEData	Share
Manufacturing HHs	835,469	1,600	0.0019	856,634	1,586	0.0019	832,290	1,649	0.0020
Total HHs	4,124,980	1,600	0.0004	4,624,885	1,586	0.0003	4,671,339	1,649	0.0004

Source: GSO, 2015, 2014, 2010a, 2010b, 2008, 2007, 2004; authors' calculations based on SME data

References

Brandt, K., J. Rand, S. Sharma, F. Tarp, and N. Trifković (2016). Characteristics of the Vietnamese business environment: Evidence from a SME survey in 2015. Helsinki: UNU-WIDER.

GSO (2004). *Results of Establishment Census of Vietnam 2002.* Hanoi: Statistical Publishing House.

GSO (2007). *The Situation of Enterprises through the Results of Surveys conducted in 2004, 2005, 2006.* Hanoi: Statistical Publishing House

GSO (2008). *The Situation of Enterprises through the Results of Surveys Conducted in 2005, 2006, 2007.* Hanoi: GSO.

GSO (2010a). *Results of a Survey on Non-farm Individual Business Establishments 2010.* Hanoi: Statistical Publishing House.

GSO (2010b). *Statistical Yearbook of Vietnam 2010. Enterprise and Individual Business Establishment.* Hanoi: Statistical Publishing House

GSO (2014). *Results of a Survey on Non-farm Individual Business Establishments 2014.* Hanoi: Statistical Publishing House.

GSO (2015). *Statistical Yearbook of Vietnam 2015: Enterprise, Cooperative and Non-farm Individual Business Establishment.* Hanoi: Statistical Publishing House.

Kakwani, N., and R. J. Hill (2002). Economic theory of spatial cost of living indices with application to Thailand. *J. Public Econ.*, 86: 71–97.

Rand, John (2007). *Characteristics of the Vietnamese Business Environment. Evidence from a SME Survey in 2005.* Central Institute of Economic Management. Hanoi: Central Institute for Economic Management.

Rand, J., and F. Tarp (2010). *Characteristics of the Vietnamese Business Environment. Evidence from a SME Survey in 2009.* Hanoi: Central Institute for Economic Management.

Rand, J., and F. Tarp (2012). *Characteristics of the Vietnamese Business Environment. Evidence from a SME Survey in 2011.* Central Institute for Economic Management (CIEM), Hanoi.

Rand, J., F. Tarp, P. Castro da Silva, C. T. Tran, and T. Thanh (2008). *Characteristics of the Vietnamese Business Environment. Evidence from a SME Survey in 2007.* Hanoi. Hanoi: Central Institute for Economic Management.

Rand, J., F. Tarp, and N. Trifković (2014). *Characteristics of the Vietnamese Business Environment. Evidence from a SME Survey in 2013.* Hanoi: Central Institute for Economic Management.

PART I
CREDIT ACCESS AND MANAGEMENT PRACTICES

3

Capital Allocation, Credit Access, and Firm Growth

Christina Kinghan, Carol Newman, and Conor O'Toole

3.1 Introduction

Since the original *Doi Moi* economic reforms, Vietnam has undergone considerable economic transformation. Living standards have risen and the economy has been reoriented away from central planning towards a more market-based economic structure. The development of private sector businesses, as well as foreign direct investment, have played an important role in this transformation. Understanding the catalysts for such rapid economic development can shed important light for policy makers and academics looking to decompose the sources of growth in a developing country context.

One sector of the Vietnamese economy that has experienced rapid reform is the financial sector. While initially Vietnam was slow to embrace capital and banking market liberalization, a series of policy initiatives throughout the 1990s and into the 2000s laid the foundations for rapid change in financial markets. Kovsted et al. (2003) note that financial reform initially took place in two phases: (1) initial banking reforms between 1988 and 1997 which split the commercial state lending from the Central Bank, State Bank of Vietnam, as well as allowing joint stock commercial banks and foreign branches; (2) the banking law of 1998 which removed administrative control over interest rates and strengthened the independence of the Central Bank. These changes—along with a multitude of other reforms—led to a rapid financial deepening of the economy and high levels of credit growth. Private sector credit to GDP increased considerably between 1995 and 2015. Recent research has found that this process of financial development has led to a reduction in credit constraints and fostered higher investment amongst Vietnamese companies (O'Toole and Newman 2017).

However, much of the existing research has focused on large companies or has been aggregate in nature. Fewer research papers have considered the role that financial reform has played in the development of small and medium sized companies, Rand (2007) being a notable exception. Indeed, where these issues have been considered, the efficiency of capital allocation has not been factored

Christina Kinghan, Carol Newman, and Conor O'Toole, *Capital Allocation, Credit Access, and Firm Growth*
In: *Micro, Small, and Medium Enterprises in Vietnam*. Edited by: John Rand and Finn Tarp, Oxford University Press (2020).
DOI: 10.1093/oso/9780198851189.003.0003

into the discussion. In an economy with perfect credit markets, we expect funds to flow to firms with the highest marginal revenue product of capital until marginal revenue equals the marginal cost on average. However, as many imperfections exist in credit markets, exploring their allocative efficiency in relation to their impact on firm growth is an important research area. A focus on the financing of SMEs is of particular importance given the extensive international evidence that these companies are most likely to suffer credit access difficulties due to informational asymmetries, a lack of collateral or other financial market failures (Berger and Udell 2006.

To address this gap in the literature, we use a detailed panel dataset on a cohort of micro, small and medium-sized enterprises operating in Vietnam to explore the relationship between capital allocation efficiency, credit access and firm growth. We approach our analysis in two steps. In the first step, using data on approximately 2,600 firms over the period 2005–15, we explore the relationship between credit access and capital efficiency for Vietnamese SMEs. More specifically, we examine the extent to which financing is allocative efficient by considering the relationship between credit constraints, credit demand and the marginal value of additional capital for firms. This sheds important light on whether the financial system is functioning in an efficient manner by allocating finance to those with the highest marginal returns. If credit is demanded by lower-productivity firms, this may suggest a selection effect which leads to an inefficient credit structure. If credit constraints are higher for more efficient firms, this may suggest that the financial system is not channelling funds to their most efficient use. As such, we also directly examine whether higher-efficiency firms have access to formal financing.

In the second step, we explore the impacts of misallocation on firm growth. If higher efficiency firms have restricted access to finance, we should find their investment and employment reduced to a greater extent by credit constraints. To explore this issue, we estimate investment and employment equations and explore whether these sources of firm growth are affected by credit constraints, a key channel through which financing impacts the real economy. We then identify the relationship between firm growth and the efficiency of capital allocation by considering whether credit constraints are limiting investment for those firms with the highest marginal returns. If we find evidence that high-return investors (with a high marginal revenue product of capital) are more likely to have their investment and employment impacted by credit constraints, then we can conclude that finance is not being allocated to its most beneficial use in the Vietnamese economy.

Our contributions to the literature are as follows. First, we extend the existing literature to explore how access to finance is linked to capital efficiency. By separately considering credit demand and credit supply indicators, we provide new insights into these channels. Second, we are the first study to our knowledge to link credit constraints to investment and employment controlling for the efficiency of capital. Third, we provide new empirical evidence on the link between credit constraints and capital misallocation for a unique panel of micro, small, and medium-size firms and in a developing country context, distinguishing between formal and informal credit channels. Finally, our chapter provides new insights for Vietnam on the potential role that easing credit access could have on firm growth through a discussion of capital allocation efficiency and its links to investment and employment.

A number of findings emerge from our analysis. First, we find that high-return investors, with the greatest marginal return on capital, have a lower likelihood of having formal finance (loans outstanding with formal credit institutions). In contrast, we find that informal finance is not related to returns to capital. We consider two possible underlying mechanisms. First, it could be that formal credit markets are not allocating finance to the highest-return firms and that informal credit markets are filling this gap. Second, it could also be the case that firms with formal credit have already successfully invested these funds reducing the marginal benefit of an additional unit of capital. The former is suggestive of inefficiencies in the financial market while the latter may simply reflect a dynamic adjustment process. Understanding which channel is in operation is important.

Decomposing credit access into the demand for credit and the supply of credit, we find that firms with the highest return on capital are associated with lower demand for credit. We also find some evidence that efficient firms are more likely to be discouraged borrowers and are less likely to be credit-rationed, suggesting that credit supply constraints are affecting the choices of efficient enterprises in relation to accessing formal finance. In relation to firm growth, we find evidence that rejected credit applications are limiting investment activity, particularly for high-return firms, i.e. the firms with higher investment efficiency are more affected by credit constraints.

The rest of this chapter is structured as follows. Section 3.2 discusses related literature. Section 3.3 describes the data and the empirical approach. Section 3.4 documents the empirical findings and Section 3.5 concludes.

3.2 Related Literature

Our research is related to four broad strands of existing empirical literature. First, this work is linked to the general literature on access to credit and firm performance. Second, our research is related to the broader literature on investment, employment, and credit access in the context of financial sector development. Third, our chapter speaks to the recent literature that attempts to identify distortions in the economy that prevent the efficient allocation of resources across firms. Fourth, our chapter is closely linked to studies focusing on credit access, financial markets, and Vietnamese small firms. Understanding the specificities of the Vietnamese case is important to identify the role that changes to financial markets can play in the development of the SME sector in emerging economies.

The first strand of literature that we speak to explores the determinants and impacts of credit constraints in developed and developing economies. This is a vast literature and so here we provide a short description of the studies that are most closely related to ours to demonstrate the channels through which credit constraints can impact the real economy as a means of guiding our empirical analysis.

Financial market imperfections, which distort the efficient allocation of capital, arise for a number of reasons. In their seminal work, Stiglitz and Weiss (1981) define credit rationing as cases where either: (a) identical firms receive different credit outcomes; or (b) some firms cannot access financing at any interest rate. This can be due to a number of potential market imperfections such as: (a) moral hazard and principal agency problems; (b) adverse credit selection; (c) monitoring difficulties; (d) informational asymmetries; (e) and legal enforcement (Lawless et al. 2017). A large number of papers have documented that small and young firms are more likely to be affected by such difficulties (Berger and Udell 2006; Beck and Demirguc-Kunt 2006 and as such credit market policies have been devised globally to address credit constraints particularly for small and medium-sized firms.

A large number of studies have focused on credit market constraints in developing country contexts and in particular the characteristics associated with constrained firms. Byiers et al. (2010) find that firm size, ownership, and managerial capacity affect credit access using a manufacturing survey for Mozambique. Hansen and Rand (2014) explore differences in access to credit across gender for a sample of 16 sub-Saharan African economies. Beck et al. (2008) find that institutional and financial development alleviates SME access to finance constraints and supports their contribution to economic growth. While these studies address a range of factors that influence SME access to finance, to our knowledge, ours is the first study that addresses the relationship between credit access and the efficiency of capital for the SME sector (formal and informal) in a developing country context.

The second strand of relevant literature links investment financing, employment growth, and access to credit. This literature generally finds that financing constraints lower investment activity for enterprises thus preventing firms from growing (Chirinko 1993 Bond and Söderbom 2013; Fazzari et al. 1988; Campello et al. 2010). Such financing constraints—which come about due to market imperfections—therefore lead to a lower rate of economic growth as the capital stock is less than the optimal level.

A key focus of our chapter is the relationship between credit access and firm growth. Two measures of firm growth often used in the literature are investment and employment. The relationship between investment and access to credit has been found to vary, depending on the degree of development of the financial system as well as the banking market structure and institutional set-up. This is an important consideration in the Vietnamese context, given how the economy has developed financially in terms of credit deepening in recent years. Ryan et al. (2014) find that banking competition increases SME financing constraints and the effects are greatest in countries with bank-dependent financial systems. Love (2003) and O'Toole and Newman (2017) find that credit constraints are lower where credit markets are deeper and more market-oriented. Beck et al. (2006b) note that institutional set-up and legal protections also matter for access to finance. In terms of employment growth, a number of studies has also been found to reduce firm employment growth (Gerlach-Kristen et al. 2015; Spaliara 2009). Chodorow-Reich (2014) also finds that credit market disruptions had a large impact on employment after the recent financial crisis in the US. However, these papers do not consider whether the effects of constraints differ depending on the efficiency of capital of the firm, which is what we explore directly in this chapter.

Third, this chapter examines credit constraints as a source of capital market inefficiency and so contributes to the emerging literature examining the link between credit market distortions and resource misallocation pioneered by Hsieh and Klenow (2009.[1] Examples in an Asian context include Brandt et al. (2013) who explore the extent to which TFP losses in China's non-agricultural sectors between 1985 and 2007 were associated with factor market distortions. They find evidence that the reversal in TFP growth can be attributed for the most part to capital misallocation due to capital market distortions that favoured investment in the state sector rather than more productive sectors of the economy. In the case of Japan, Caballero et al. (2008) find evidence for inefficient resource allocations resulting from the extension of credit to insolvent borrowers. Industries with greater numbers of insolvent borrowers had lower levels of job creation and lower levels of productivity.[2] There is a notable dearth in the literature of papers which examine the role of financial frictions and capital market misallocation in other developing country contexts such as Vietnam. Moreover, to our knowledge there is no empirical evidence specifically focusing on micro, small, and medium-sized firms which examines the interplay between formal and informal credit.

The final literature that complements our research addresses credit access and firms in Vietnam. There are a number of papers of particular relevance. Rand

[1] See Restuccia and Rogerson (2017) for an overview of the recent literature on this topic.

[2] See also Caggese and Cuñat (2013) for evidence from Italy that links credit constraints to misallocation through an exporting channel and Gopinath et al. (2015) for evidence of the link between size-dependent financial frictions and capital misallocation in an EU context.

(2007) uses a survey of SMEs in the manufacturing industry to explore the determinants of credit constraints, credit demand and the cost of capital for small firms in Vietnam. Drawing on a cross-sectional study covering approximately 1,000 SMEs across four provinces (Ha Tay, Long An, Quang Nam, Phu Tho) and three of the largest cities (Ho Chi Minh, Ha Noi, and Hai Phong), the study used direct indicators of credit rejections to explore which firms were constrained. The results indicate that between 14 and 25 per cent of SMEs were constrained and that these companies would increase their debt by between 40 and 115 per cent if constraints were loosened. The research also finds an important role for informal financing for those firms who are fast growing. Rand et al. (2009) also explore survey data on SME access to financing in Vietnam. They find that the formal financial sector is just about keeping up with growth.

There has been a notable increase in the degree of financial development in Vietnam since the mid-1990s as private sector credit has soared and reforms have been implemented in financial markets. To explore how this has impacted companies on the ground, O'Toole and Newman (2017) use the Vietnamese national enterprise survey to test the impact of financial development in Vietnam on investment credit constraints for both large firms and SMEs. Using a standard Tobin's Q investment model, they separate financial development into three specific aspects: overall financial depth, the state-owned enterprise use of finance, and the degree of market-oriented bank lending. They develop indicators of financial development along these channels at the province level in Vietnam. A number of findings emerge from their research. They find that financial development reduces external financing constraints for firms, thus facilitating higher investment activity. Financing constraints are decreasing in credit to the private sector, increasing in the use of finance by SOEs and decreasing in the degree to which finance is allocated on market-terms by commercial banks.

CAO Thi Khanh (2016) explores the factors that determine access to formal credit in Vietnam as well as considering whether firms are satisfied with the financing process. Using a survey of Vietnamese SMEs conducted over 2005–13, the findings indicate that banking relationships and the business environment were important factors when applying for formal credit as well as in credit obtainment. However, positive measures of firms' performance, such as high return on assets scores and sales growth, did not have a significant influence on whether firms obtained credit. Furthermore, Vietnamese formal financial institutions were found to depend too much on collateral assets in assessing whether to supply credit.

A final study that provides important context for this chapter is Kovsted et al. (2003) who document the financial development process in Vietnam up to 2003. Their research provides insight into the overall process of financial reform that occurred in Vietnam, the changing structure of the financial sector and its lending agents, an overview of the regulatory and central banking operations, and the many policy initiatives that were undertaken in the phase of reform up to 2003. Our study is complementary in that we review access to finance issues and developments in lending in the period following the initial reforms.

3.3 Data and Empirical Approach

3.3.1 Data Overview

This chapter uses a firm-level panel dataset, gathered using the Survey of Small and Medium Scale Manufacturing Enterprises (SMEs) in Vietnam. The SME survey is conducted every two years on over 2,500 enterprises across ten provinces with a large proportion of the firms surveyed across all years of the survey. The population of non-state manufacturing enterprises in the ten selected provinces is based on two data sources from the General Statistics Office of Vietnam. These are the Establishment Census and the Industrial Survey. This panel is compiled from surveys conducted in Vietnam in 2005, 2007, 2009, 2011, 2013, and 2015. The provinces surveyed included the cities, Ha Noi, Ho Chi Minh City (HCMC) and Hai Phong, and the provinces of Ha Tay, Long An, Phu Tho, Quang Nam, Nghe An, Khanh Hoa, and Lam Dong.

For the purposes of our analysis, the survey captures a range of questions on applications for finance, the types of credit the firms apply for as well as the success of credit applications. Importantly, the data also captures the range of other balance-sheet and profit and loss controls that are needed to undertake standard assessment of investment as well as accurately control for credit risk and firm quality.

3.3.2 Empirical Approach

Understanding the relationship between access to finance and capital efficiency

The first part of our empirical assessment links the marginal revenue product of capital (our proxy for firm capital efficiency) to broadly defined indicators of access to finance. We then separately focus on considering the association between credit demand and credit supply and capital allocation. It is important to split out supply and demand effects to understand whether capital efficiency in the economy is affected by the credit markets provision of financing or to selection effects due to the type of enterprise that is seeking credit. Table 3.1 presents the main indicators that we use in our empirical methodology.

We use the marginal revenue product of capital (MRPK) as our measure of capital efficiency and our measure is based on the underlying model of Hsieh and

Table 3.1 Indicators of access to finance, credit demand, and credit supply

Indicator	Definition
Formal credit access	Variable = 1 if firm has a formal loan or line of credit and 0 otherwise
Informal credit access	Variable = 1 if firm has an informal loan or line of credit and 0 otherwise
Credit demand: applied loan	Variable = 1 if firm applied for a loan to a formal financial institution and 0 otherwise
Credit demand: requires loan	Variable = 1 if the firm indicated it needs a loan to undertake its activities and 0 otherwise
Credit supply: credit rationed	Variable = 1 if firm has been rejected for a formal loan and 0 otherwise
Credit supply: discouraged borrowers	Variable = 1 if firm did not apply for a loan due to (a) possible rejection, (b) the process was too difficult, or (c) theinterest rates were too high and 0 otherwise
Credit supply: credit constrained	This variable is a composite of credit rationed and discouraged borrowers

Source: Authors' esimates.

Klenow (2009) whose focus was on the extent of resource misallocation in both labour and capital markets. Our firm-specific measure of MRPK is given by:

$$MRPK_{si} = \alpha_S \frac{\sigma - 1}{\sigma} \frac{P_{si} Y_{si}}{K_{si}} \tag{3.1}$$

where α_S is the sector level (2-digit) elasticity of capital with respect to output and is computed as one minus the share of labour costs in total value added of the sector, sigma is the elasticity of substitution and is set conservatively at a value of 3, $P_{si}Y_{si}$ is nominal value added of the firm, and K_{si} is the capital stock of the firm measured as total assets.

If all resources are allocated efficiently then the MRPK will be equalized across firms. Firms with higher than average MRPK face disincentives (such as credit constraints) for investing in capital, while those with below-average MRPK benefit from more favourable investment conditions (such as access to credit).

To measure formal credit access, we use an indicator which captures whether or not the firm has a formal loan or line of credit with a financial institution. This should give a broad indication of access to finance in the formal financial system. To measure informal access to credit, we use an indicator which captures whether the firm has an informal loan outstanding.

The above indicators measure usage of credit and do not disentangle credit demand and supply factors. To identify these two channels separately, we use two indicators for credit demand and two for credit supply. On the demand side, the indicators capture: (a) whether the firm applied for formal credit; and (b) whether the firm reports that it needs a loan. On the supply side, we use two traditional indicators of credit constraints to capture: (a) rejection rates for loan applications (credit rationing); and (b) discouraged borrowers. These are standard measures in the literature (see Casey and O'Toole (2014 for a discussion).

Our main research objective is to empirically test for a relationship between credit access (as defined above) and capital efficiency. We therefore estimate the following equation which links each of the indicators above to a proxy for the firm's marginal revenue product of capital, controlling for firm profitability, size, age, and a range of fixed effects. Controlling for both firm profitability and marginal returns should ensure that credit market selection effects due to profitability are absorbed in the profit variable and that the capital efficiency measure captures allocation effects.

$$Pr(I=1)_{it} = \beta_0 + \beta_1 ln\, MRPK_{it} + \beta_2 ln\, profit_{it} + \beta_3 age_{it} + \beta_4 ln\, emp_{it} + \alpha_i + \tau_t + s_s + \pi_p + e_{it} \quad (3.2)$$

I represents, in turn, each of the binary indicator variables noted above, ln *MRPK* is the log of the marginal revenue product of capital, *ln profit* is the log of the profits of the firm, *age* is the age of the firm and *ln emp* is the number of employees, used to capture firm size. We saturate the model with fixed effects for sector, time, and province to ensure that time-invariant confounding factors are removed at these levels of variation. The model is estimated using a linear probability approach with and without a within-group transformation to remove firm-fixed effects. Standard errors are clustered at the sectoral level. Subscript i refers to firm i in the panel, α_i are firm-specific, time-invariant effects, π_p are province dummies, τ_t are year dummies, s_s are sector dummies, and e_{it} is an *i.i.d.* error term. These notations are carried through Equations (3.3) and (3.4).

Exploring the impacts on firm growth

First, we consider the association between access to finance and firm capital efficiency focusing on both credit supply and credit demand. This provides us with some tentative conclusions as to how high investment-return firms interact with the Vietnamese credit market.

Second, we focus on the credit supply side and test whether there is any evidence that credit supply constraints are limiting firm growth for high-return investors. If this is the case, it would provide evidence that capital allocation is not efficient and the policy conclusions can be directly linked to potential supply-side distortions. To measure firm growth, we focus on investment and employment which are two channels used extensively in the literature.

For many small firms, investment is often lumpy and infrequent. They may make a large investment in a specific year and then not invest again for a period of time. To capture these dynamics, we focus on both the extensive and the intensive margin of investment. We define a variable for whether or not firms invest in capital (measured as fixed or intangible assets) which is binary. To capture the intensive margin, we take the log of total expenditure on investment for investors only. To measure employment growth, we take the log of the total number of employees in the enterprise. To test for the impact of credit constraints, and their interaction with capital efficiency, we estimate the following investment equation:

$$\begin{aligned} \ln Inv_{it} = {} & \beta_0 + \beta_1 rev\_gr_{it-1} + \beta_2 \ln profit_{it-1} + \beta_3 age_{it-1} + \beta_4 age^2{}_{it-1} \\ & + \beta_5 \ln emp_{it-1} + \theta_1 CC_{it-1} + \theta_2 \ln MRPK_{it-1} + \theta_3 CC_{it-1} \times \ln MRPK_{it-1} \\ & + \alpha_i + \tau_t + s_s + \pi_p + e_{it} \end{aligned} \tag{3.3}$$

The key variables of interest are *CC* which measures credit constraints and ln *MRPK*. As control variables, we include *rev_gr*, which is the growth in revenue between period t–1 and period t, and lagged profitability to capture firm fundamentals. We control for the age of the firm and its square. We also include the lagged number of employees as a control for firm size. Lags are included to avoid simultaneity problems. As above, we saturate the model with fixed effects for sector, time, and province to ensure that time-invariant confounding factors are removed at these levels of variation. The model is estimated using a within-group transformation to remove firm-fixed effects. Standard errors are clustered at the sectoral level.

If credit constraints are limiting investment, then we expect $\theta_1 < 0$. If the credit market is not efficiently allocating capital, then we would expect $\theta_3 < 0$ indicating that the effect of credit constraints is greater for more efficient firms. For the extensive margin binary model, we estimate a linear probability model with the same set of covariates. For employment, we use a similar specification with the addition of a control to proxy for the marginal revenue product of labour.

3.3.3 Summary Statistics

To motivate our empirical analysis, we present a number of summary charts which contextualize our research. Figure 3.1 presents trends in the credit supply and demand variables to gain insight into how firms' access to finance has evolved over the survey period. Both indicators of credit demand suggest that it has been in decline since 2007 suggesting firms are lowering their requirements for new credit over time in Vietnam. In terms of credit supply, the share of discouraged borrowers appears to have risen over the period 2007–13 but has fallen back in 2015. The loan rejection rate (Credit Rationing) appears relatively steady over the period but has fallen somewhat between 2011 and 2015.

Figure 3.2 illustrates how firms in our sample grow in terms of employment and investment over time. Employment growth has generally been falling over the

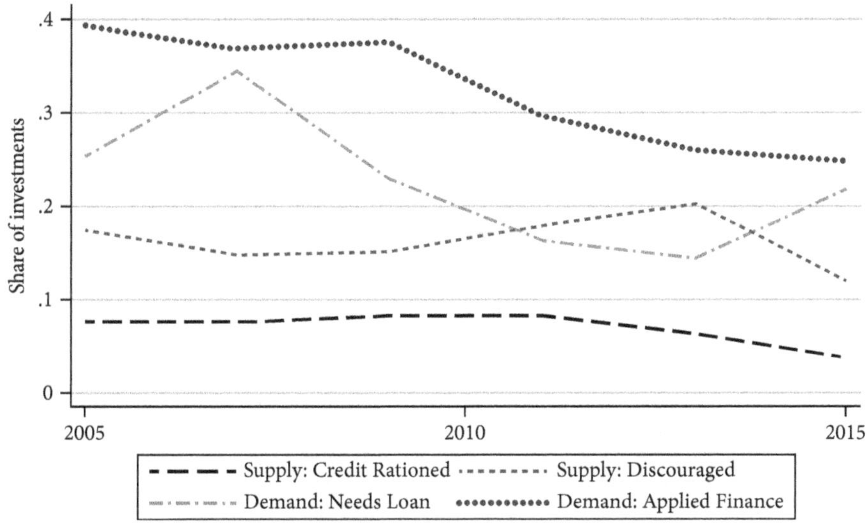

Figure 3.1 Access to credit indicators
Source: Authors' calculations using Vietnam SME survey.

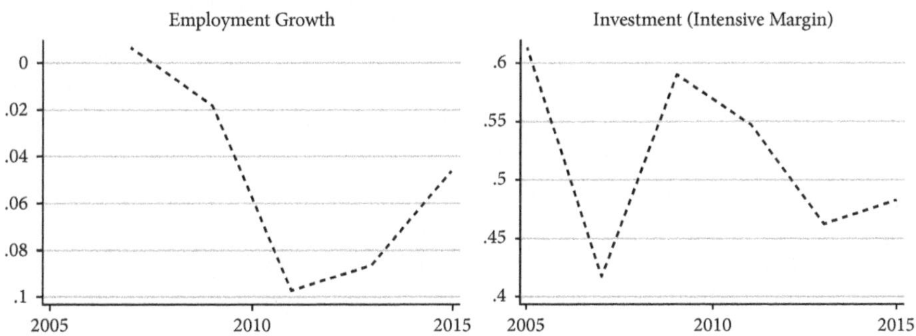

Figure 3.2 Illustrative measures of firm growth
Source: Authors' calculations using Vietnam SME survey.

sample period suggesting SME firms in Vietnam are getting smaller. In more recent years, however, the rate of decline in employment has moderated somewhat. In terms of investment activity, also illustrated in Figure 3.2, we see that the proportion of firms investing every year has also fallen over the sample period, from over 60 per cent in 2005 to around 48 per cent in 2015. The biggest fall in investment rates was between 2005 and 2007 but it increased again between 2007 and 2009. A further decline in the number of firms investing occurred between 2009 and 2013, which is not surprising given the financial crisis, recovering marginally between 2013 and 2015.

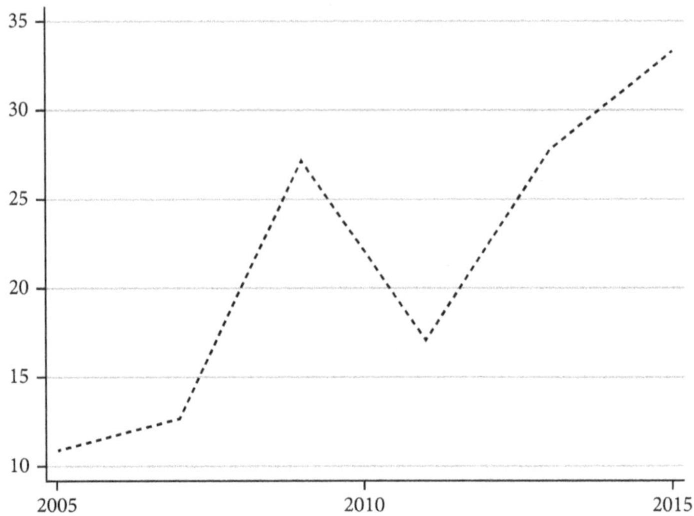

Figure 3.3 Marginal revenue product of capital
Source: Authors' calculations using Vietnam SME survey.

The average marginal revenue product of capital is presented in Figure 3.3. The figure is an average across all firms in each survey wave. The data suggest that marginal returns increased during the early period, fell back coinciding with the global financial crisis, but rebounded in more recent times. Given that the Vietnamese economy has undergone a considerable transformation, including a broadening of the financial sector, it is surprising that the marginal product of capital has been very volatile. In an economy which is transitioning to a market-orientation, it is not unsurprising that during this transition, more efficient firms could be replaced by inefficient firms which raises overall marginal products. Indeed, O'Toole and Newman (2017) show that this market re-alignment coincided with a re-orientation of the financial sector away from the state-owned enterprises and towards an improved allocation of finance. This would suggest that the firms with higher levels of efficiency are not those to whom the credit market is channelling funds. Furthermore, it may be that lending institutions are focusing on informal signals for the allocation of formal finance rather than key firm performance indicators. Indeed, Malesky and Taussig (2008) found that banks in Vietnam placed a greater emphasis on connections rather than performance indicators in the allocation of credit.

Table 3.2 presents summary statistics on the key indicators of access to finance, credit demand and credit supply for each year of our analysis. Approximately 25 per cent of firms were constrained in each year of the survey; however, this figure declined to 16 per cent in 2015. Between 25 per cent and 40 per cent of firms obtained access to formal finance and over 60 per cent of firms accessed informal

Table 3.2 Summary statistics on access to finance, credit demand, and credit supply

Year	2005	2007	2009	2011	2013	2015
Sample size	**2,823**	**2,635**	**2,657**	**2,537**	**2,575**	**2,648**
Credit constrained	25	22	23	26	26	16
Formal credit access	37	36	37	28	24	24
Informal credit access	71	61	70	64	63	65
Requires loan	25	34	23	16	14	22
Discouraged borrower	17	15	15	18	20	12
Credit rationed	8	8	8	8	6	4
Applied loan	39	37	38	29	26	25

Source: Authors' calculation using Vietnam SME Survey.

Table 3.3 Summary statistics on main continuous variables (millions VND)

Variable	Obs.	Mean	Std. Dev.	Min	Max
Total investment	8,230	820	2,045	0	19,103
Revenue	15,494	3,534	8,174	27	75,179
Gross profit	15,493	498	1,086	−14	10,500
Firm age	15,775	14	10	2	77
Total labour	15,811	18	50	1	2,561
Total assets	15,494	3,920	7,533	24	68,244

Note: Outliers removed at 1st and 99th percentile.
Source: Authors' calculation using Vietnam SME Survey.

finance. Less than 10 per cent of firms in each survey year are considered to be credit rationed.

Table 3.3 presents summary statistics on the main continuous variables of interest in our analysis. The average age of firms in the dataset was 14 years and the average number of employees was 18. The average investment made by firms was approximately 820 Million VND and the average profit was 479 Million VND.

3.4 Results

In this section, we present the main results of our empirical estimations. We first document the findings in relation to access to finance and capital efficiency, separating out supply and demand side factors. Second, we explore the relationship between capital efficiency, credit constraints and investment. Finally, we examine the relationship between credit constraints, efficiency and employment.

3.4.1 Financing and Capital Efficiency

The use of financing and capital efficiency

Our empirical exploration begins by testing the relationship between access to formal and informal finance and capital efficiency. The regression results from the estimation of Equation (3.2) using a linear probability models are presented in Table 3.4. We estimate each specification using both simple OLS techniques and a linear fixed-effects estimator (FE). As the fixed effects transformations remove firm-specific unobserved heterogeneity that could bias the estimates, our preferred specification is the FE. If there is a discrepancy between OLS and FE findings, the FE should take priority. Province, sector, and time-fixed effects are included in all specifications and standard errors are clustered at the sector level.

As illustrated in columns (1) and (2), we find a negative correlation between the MRPK and the likelihood of having a formal loan. This suggests that firms with a higher marginal revenue product of capital have a lower likelihood of having formal finance. On face value, this result suggests that capital allocation is not efficient as the firms with higher returns on capital are not the ones to which the credit market is channelling funds. However, it could also be the case that the

Table 3.4 Relationship between capital efficiency, formal, and informal credit

	(1)	(2)	(3)	(4)
	Formal finance OLS	**Formal finance FE**	**Informal finance OLS**	**Informal finance FE**
Ln MRPK	−0.029***	−0.020***	0.006	0.007
	(0.004)	(0.005)	(0.003)	(0.006)
Constant	−0.390***	−0.214	0.650***	1.943***
	(0.049)	(0.132)	(0.027)	(0.123)
Province FE	Y	Y	Y	Y
Sector FE	Y	Y	Y	Y
Time FE	Y	Y	Y	Y
Other controls	Y	Y	Y	Y
Observations	15,062	15,062	15,072	15,072
R-squared	0.188	0.042	0.031	0.014
Number of firm ID		5,012		5,014

Notes: Robust standard errors clustered at sector level are included in parentheses. *** $p<0.01$, ** $p<0.05$, * $p<0.1$.

Note (1): OLS regression refers to pooled cross sectional estimation of the data. Fixed effect (FE) estimation uses a simple within-group mean removal technique.

Note (2): As specified in Equation (3.2) other controls included are firm profitability, firm age, and firm size. Results are not presented here but are available on request.

Source: Authors' estimates using WIDER Vietnam SME survey data.

firms that have access to formal finance have already undertaken productive investments lowering their MRPK in which case the negative correlation here is simply picking up a dynamic adjustment process. We will explore this possibility when we consider the impact of access to credit on firm growth below.

In contrast to the results for formal financing, we find a positive correlation between MRPK and informal financing, in columns (3) and (4), although the magnitude is small and is not well-determined. This suggests that the efficiency of capital is not an important consideration in the allocation of informal financing.

Identifying credit demand and supply effects

In the section above, we found some tentative evidence that the formal financing market is not allocating financing efficiently. We delve deeper into this issue by trying to understand whether this is coming through demand or supply effects in these markets. In this section, we test the relationship between formal credit demand, formal credit supply, and capital efficiency.

The regressions exploring the relationship between credit demand and efficiency, estimated using a linear probability model and the same specification as for the regressions presented in Table 3.4, are presented in Table 3.5.

Table 3.5 Relationship between capital efficiency and credit demand

VARIABLES	(1)	(2)	(3)	(4)
	Applied loan OLS	Applied loan FE	Requires loan OLS	Requires loan FE
Ln MRPK	−0.028***	−0.020***	−0.016***	−0.013***
	(0.004)	(0.005)	(0.002)	(0.003)
Constant	−0.379***	−0.302**	−0.213***	0.614***
	(0.052)	(0.125)	(0.022)	(0.143)
Province FE	Y	Y	Y	Y
Sector FE	Y	Y	Y	Y
Time FE	Y	Y	Y	Y
Other controls	Y	Y	Y	Y
Observations	15,071	15,071	15,075	15,075
R-squared	0.183	0.041	0.133	0.046
Number of firm ID		5,013		5,014

Notes: Robust standard errors clustered at sector level are included in parentheses. *** $p<0.01$, ** $p<0.05$, * $p<0.1$.

Note (1): OLS regression refers to pooled cross sectional estimation of the data. Fixed effect (FE) estimation uses a simple within-group mean removal technique.

Note (2): As specified in Equation (3.2) other controls included are firm profitability, firm age, and firm size. Results are not presented here but are available on request.

Source: Authors' estimates using WIDER Vietnam SME Survey data.

A number of findings emerge. Across all specifications, it appears that credit demand is negatively associated with the marginal revenue product of capital. As firms have a higher level of capital efficiency, their demand for credit falls. This is a surprising result as these firms are potentially the ones to gain most from taking on credit and increasing investment.

We also explore the relationship between credit supply and capital efficiency using the same specification. The results are presented in Table 3.6. We find that marginal returns to capital are negatively correlated with the probability of being credit-rationed and positively correlated with the probability of being a discouraged borrower, although in both cases the results are not well determined. It does provide, however, some suggestive evidence that being turned down for a loan (credit rationing) may well be justified on efficiency grounds as these firms have indeed lower returns to capital. On the other hand, firms who choose not to apply for a loan for fear of being rejected—the process being too difficult or the rate of interest being too high—are likely to be the ones that would yield high returns on that investment. Caution, however, should be exercised in this interpretation given that the results are not statistically well-determined.

Table 3.6 Relationship between capital efficiency and credit supply

	(1)	(2)	(3)	(4)
	Credit rationed OLS	**Credit rationed FE**	**Discouraged OLS**	**Discouraged FE**
Ln MRPK	−0.002	−0.004*	0.024***	0.009
	(0.001)	(0.002)	(0.005)	(0.006)
Constant	0.029*	0.052	0.405***	0.693***
	(0.014)	(0.113)	(0.051)	(0.072)
Province FE	Y	Y	Y	Y
Sector FE	Y	Y	Y	Y
Time FE	Y	Y	Y	Y
Other controls	Y	Y	Y	Y
Observations	15,075	15,075	15,075	15,075
R-squared	0.034	0.011	0.036	0.014
Number of firm ID		5,014		5,014

Notes: Robust standard errors clustered at sector level are included in parentheses. *** $p<0.01$, ** $p<0.05$, * $p<0.1$.

Note (1): OLS regression refers to pooled cross sectional estimation of the data. Fixed effect (FE) estimation uses a simple within-group mean removal technique.

Note (2): As specified in Equation (3.2) other controls included are firm profitability, firm age, and firm size. Results are not presented here but are available on request.

Source: Authors' estimates using WIDER Vietnam SME Survey data.

3.4.2 Do Financing Constraints Affect Firm Growth for Efficient Firms?

Financing and investment

To this point, we have explored the relationship between capital efficiency and access to finance. We find some tentative evidence that capital allocation may not be optimal as firms with higher marginal returns are less likely to have formal finance. In this section, we undertake a more direct test, which asks whether firm growth has been limited by credit allocation problems. To test this hypothesis, we explore whether credit constraints impact investment and employment and if the effect is larger for higher return firms. This is a more direct test of whether credit supply is limiting the efficient allocation of capital.

Table 3.7 presents the results for the specification exploring the relationship between credit constraints, the efficiency of capital, and investment as given in Equation (3.3). We present the results for both the intensive and extensive margin. All independent variables are lagged to avoid simultaneity issues and in each case the model is estimated including firm-fixed effects. We separately test the effects on all constrained firms and on credit-rationed firms and discouraged borrowers. In each case we interact MRPK and credit constraints to examine whether there is an impact on investment.

On the intensive margin, we find a negative interaction between the marginal product of capital and credit rejections (column 4). This suggests that as efficiency increases (higher marginal product firms), credit constraints lower the level of investment that firms undertake. That we find this channel specifically for the intensive margin and not the extensive margin, may reflect the fact that those firms with high marginal products may have internal resources that they will use to undertake *at least some* investment even if they are credit-constrained. They will not invest the optimal level but they will appear in the measure for the extensive margin as having some positive level of investment. More generally, this finding suggests that credit allocation may be the allocation of investment in the Vietnamese economy.

Financing and employment

The second measure of firm growth that we consider is employment. We test the relationship between employment, credit constraints, and capital efficiency using the same specification as above. The channel through which access to finance impacts employment is not as direct as investment, as the latter requires potentially larger amounts of funds at a particular point in time while expanding the work force could be done incrementally. It may be the case, however, that employment growth is slowed if firms cannot access sufficient working capital to manage wage bills or—if firms forego investments—they may operate at a lower than optimal capital output ratio thus lowering employment growth.

Table 3.7 Testing the effect of credit constraints and capital efficiency on investment

	(1)	(2)	(3)	(4)	(5)	(6)
	Extensive	**Intensive**	**Extensive**	**Intensive**	**Extensive**	**Intensive**
Lag Ln MRPK* Lag Credit Constraints	−0.010	−0.086				
	(0.011)	(0.061)				
Lag Ln MRPK	−0.004	0.093*	−0.006	0.077*	−0.004	0.080*
	(0.007)	(0.047)	(0.005)	(0.038)	(0.006)	(0.044)
Lag credit constraints	−0.027	−0.230				
	(0.038)	(0.153)				
Lag Ln MRPK* Lag credit rationed			0.004	−0.093*		
			(0.019)	(0.050)		
Lag credit rationed			−0.031	−0.328***		
			(0.054)	(0.104)		
Lag Ln MRPK* Lag discouraged Borrower					−0.014	−0.063
					(0.010)	(0.075)
Lag discouraged borrower					−0.019	−0.114
					(0.031)	(0.192)
Constant	−0.742***	2.923***	−0.381**	3.225***	−0.745***	3.245***
	(0.137)	(0.490)	(0.136)	(0.446)	(0.138)	(0.479)
Controls	Y	Y	Y	Y	Y	Y
Province FE	Y	Y	Y	Y	Y	Y
Sector FE	Y	Y	Y	Y	Y	Y
Time FE	Y	Y	Y	Y	Y	Y
Firm FE	Y	Y	Y	Y	Y	Y
Observations	10,040	5,022	10,040	5,022	10,040	5,022
R-squared	0.037	0.061	0.037	0.061	0.037	0.061
Number of firm ID	3,621	2,522	3,621	2,522	3,621	2,522

Notes: Robust standard errors clustered at sector level are included in parentheses. *** $p<0.01$, ** $p<0.05$, * $p<0.1$.

Note (1): As specified in Equation (3.3) other controls include revenue growth, firm age and age squared, lagged profitability in logs, and lagged number of employees in logs.

Source: Authors' estimates using WIDER Vietnam SME Survey data.

Table 3.8 Testing the effect of credit constraints, credit allocation and employment

	(1)	(2)	(3)
Lag Ln MRPK* Lag Credit Constraints	0.005		
	(0.015)		
Lag credit constraints	0.018		
	(0.040)		
Lag Ln MRPK	−0.002	−0.003	0.000
	(0.011)	(0.009)	(0.011)
Lag Ln MRPL	−0.065**	−0.065**	−0.065**
	(0.026)	(0.026)	(0.026)
Lag Ln MRPK* Lag credit rationed		0.030	
		(0.037)	
Lag credit rationed		0.078	
		(0.087)	
Lag Ln MRPK * Lag discouraged borrower			−0.008
			(0.014)
Lag discouraged borrower			−0.015
			(0.043)
Constant	1.383***	1.379***	1.391***
	(0.284)	(0.280)	(0.285)
Controls	Y	Y	Y
Province FE	Y	Y	Y
Sector FE	Y	Y	Y
Time FE	Y	Y	Y
Firm FE	Y	Y	Y
Observations	8,145	8,145	8,145
R-squared	0.072	0.073	0.072
Number of firm ID	3,152	3,152	3,152

Notes: Robust standard errors in parentheses. *** $p<0.01$, ** $p<0.05$, * $p<0.1$

Note (1): Controls include: revenue growth, firm age and age squared, lagged profitability in logs, lagged number of employees in logs, and the lag of the log of the firm's marginal revenue product of labour.

Source: Authors' estimates using WIDER Vietnam SME Survey data.

The results using the same specification as for Table 3.7, with the addition of a control for the marginal revenue product of labour, are presented in Table 3.8. We do not find any statistically significant interactions between the marginal products and credit constraints in the employment specifications. This suggests that the negative effect of credit on capital efficiency and firm growth is running through the investment channel and not the employment channel.

3.5 Conclusions and Policy Implications

This chapter explores the impact of credit access on firm growth by examining whether credit is flowing to firms with the highest return on capital. Standard neoclassical economic models would suggest that an efficient capital market should intermediate financing to firms with the highest returns on investment allowing them to invest and grow. For the case of Vietnam—a country that is transitioning to a more market-oriented economy—we find evidence that financial markets are not necessarily intermediating finance to its highest return in the case of SMEs, and this is limiting investment at the firm level.

More specifically, we find that high-return investors, with the greatest marginal return on capital, have a lower likelihood of having formal finance (loans outstanding with formal credit institutions). Marginal returns on capital do not seem to impact on informal financing. This could be suggestive evidence that formal credit markets are not allocating finance to the highest return and that informal credit markets are filling a void to address this gap.

Directly testing whether credit supply is the limiting channel, we find evidence that rejected credit applications are limiting investment activity but not employment, particularly for firms with higher investment efficiency. The effects are found to be running through the credit-rationing channel on the intensive margin of investment.

Our results provide a number of insights for policy. Having formal credit in Vietnam is associated with lower marginal returns on capital. While this might be suggestive of good credit allocation (as firms with formal credit have been able to make investments), the fact that credit constraints are found to limit investment for high marginal return firms would indicate otherwise. We find suggestive evidence that borrower discouragement may be an important credit constraint in Vietnam. More efficient firms appear to be more discouraged. Since these borrowers often do not interface with a formal financial institution (as compared with rejected borrowers who make an application), targeted credit policies, such as guarantee schemes, for example, are less likely to be effective in addressing this market failure. Improving awareness amongst firms, and increasing information about the formal credit process, might prove to be the more effective policy response.

References

Beck, T., and A. Demirguc-Kunt (2006). Small and medium-size enterprises: Access to finance as a growth constraint, *Journal of Banking and Finance,* 30: 2931–43.

Beck, T., A. Demirguc-Kunt, and V. Maksimovic (2008). Financing patterns around the world: Are small firms different?, *Journal of Financial Economics,* 89: 467–87.

Beck, T., A. Demirguc-Kunt, L. Laeven, and V. Maksimovic (2006). The determinants of financing obstacles, *Journal of International Money and Finance,* 25: 932–52.

Berger, A., and G. Udell (2006). A more complete conceptual framework for SME finance, *Journal of Banking and Finance,* 30: 2945–66.

Bond, S. R., and Söderbom, M. (2013). Conditional investment-cash flow sensitivities and investment, *Journal of the European Economic Association*, 11: 112–36.

Brandt, L., Tombe, T., and Zhu, X. (2013), Factor market distortions across time, space, and sectors in China, *Review of Economic Dynamics*, 16(1): 39–58.

Byiers, B., Rand, J., Tarp, F., and Bentzen, J. (2010). Credit demand in Mozambican manufacturing, *Journal of International Development*, 22: 37–55.

Caballero, R. J., Hoshi, T., and Kashyap, A. K. (2008). Zombie lending and depressed restructuring in Japan, *American Economic Review*, 98(5): 1943–77.

Caggese, A., and Cuñat, V. (2013). Financing constraints, firm dynamics, export decisions, and aggregate productivity, *Review of Economic Dynamics*, 16(1), 177–93.

Campello, M., Graham, J. R., and Harvey, C. (2010). The real effects of financial constraints: Evidence from a financial crisis, *Journal of Financial Economics*, 97: 470–87.

CAO Thi Khanh, N. (2016). What Factors Determine whether SMEs Obtain Credit from Formal Credit Market? The Case of Vietnam. APIR Discussion Paper Series, Asia Pacific Institute of Research.

Casey, E., and O'Toole, C. (2014). Bank lending constraints, trade credit and alternative financing during the financial crisis: Evidence from European SMEs, *Journal of Corporate Finance*, 27: 173–93.

Chirinko, B. (1993). Business fixed investment spending: Modeling strategies, empirical results, and policy implications, *Journal of Economic Literature*, 31: 1875–1911.

Chodorow-Reich, G. (2014). The employment effects of credit market disruptions: Firm-level evidence from the 2008–9 financial crisis, *The Quarterly Journal of Economics*, 129: 1–59.

Fazzari, S., Hubbard, R. G., and Petersen, B. (1988). Financing constraints and corporate investment, *Brookings Papers on Economic Activity*, 19: 141–206.

Gerlach-Kristen, P., O'Connell, B., and O'Toole, C. (2015). Do credit constraints affect SME investment and employment?, *The Economic and Social Review*, 46: 51–86.

Gopinath, G., Kalemli-Ozcan, S., Karabarbounis, L., and Villegas-Sanchez, C. (2015). Capital Allocation and Productivity in South Europe. NBER Working Paper No 21453. Cambridge, MA: National Bureau of Economic Research.

Hsieh, C.-T., and Klenow, P. (2009). Misallocation and manufacturing TFP in China and India, *The Quarterly Journal of Economics*, 124: 1403–48.

Kovsted, J., Rand, J., Tarp, F., Nguyen, D. T., Nguyen, V. H., and Thao, T. M. (2003). Financial Sector Reforms in Vietnam: Selected Issues and Problems. MPRA Paper. Munich: University Library of Munich.

Lawless, M., O'Toole, C., and Slaymaker, R. (2017). Measuring the Investment Gap and Its Financing Requirements for Irish SMEs. Tech. rep.Dublin: Economic and Social Research Institute.

Love, I. (2003). Financial development and financing constraints: International evidence from the structural investment model, *Review of Financial Studies*, 16: 765–91.

Malesky, E. J. and Taussig, M. (2008). Where is credit due? Legal institutions, connections, and the efficiency of bank lending in Vietnam, *The Journal of Law, Economics and Organization*, 25(2): 535–78.

O'Toole, C., & Newman, C. (2016). Investment financing and financial development: Evidence from Viet Nam. *Review of Finance, 21*(4), 1639–74. Rand, J. (2007). Credit constraints and determinants of the cost of capital in Vietnamese manufacturing, *Small Business Economics*, 29: 1–13.

Rand, J., Tarp, F., Coung, T. T., and Nguyen, T. (2009). SME Access to Credit. MPRA Paper Munich: University Library of Munich.

Restuccia, D. and Rogerson, R. (2017). The causes and costs of misallocation, *Journal of Economic Perspectives*, 31(3): 151–74.

Ryan, R., Conor, M., and McCann, F. (2014). Does bank market power affect SME financing constraints?, *Journal of Banking and Finance,* 49: 495–505.

Spaliara, M.-E. (2009). Do financial factors affect the capital-labour ratio? Evidence from UK firm-level data, *Journal of Banking and Finance,* 33: 1932–47.

Stiglitz, J., and A. Weiss (1981). Credit rationing in markets with imperfect information, *American Economic Review,* 71: 393–410.

4
The Interaction of Institutional Quality and Human Capital in Shaping the Dynamics of Capital Structure

Enrico Santarelli and Hien Thu Tran

4.1 Introduction

Firms are financed through various means: internal capital, debt, equity, or any hybrid forms. The combination of different sources of finance is often referred to as the 'capital structure puzzle' initially proposed by Myers (1984). The choice of capital structure is one of the most important strategic decisions that managers face in today's increasingly volatile and hypercompetitive market. But what do we know about the capital structure of small businesses in a transition economic setting? The answer is 'not much' as almost all the existing empirical literature on capital structure has so far mostly focused on established firms, especially market-listed companies in advanced countries. Ignoring the peculiarities of small enterprises, which represent the majority of the firm population and account for a remarkable part of gross domestic product (GDP) and employment in most countries, especially in transition and developing countries, extant studies tend therefore to underestimate an important aspect of the capital structure puzzle. In Vietnam, for example, there are only around 1,000 firms that issue publicly traded securities, yet according to the General Statistics Office (GSO 2016) they contribute up to 65 per cent of GDP and hold 23 per cent of the whole national capital investment. However, there are around 56,000 small firms with total assets of less than 10 billion Vietnam Dong (VND), accounting for 93.8 per cent of the whole firm population, and contributing to nearly 30 per cent of GDP. The latter create more than half a million new jobs and employ more than 51 per cent of the labour force.

So far, the three most influential theories of capital structure—trade-off theory, pecking order theory, and market-timing theory—offer several predictions regarding firm-specific factors affecting firm capital structure. Under trade-off theory, the firm seeks to balance the tax benefits from using debt against the costs of financial distress that rise at an increasing rate with the use of leverage. Hence, this theory predicts an 'optimal' ratio of debt to equity, where the tax benefits of

Enrico Santarelli and Hien Thu Tran, *The Interaction of Institutional Quality and Human Capital in Shaping the Dynamics of Capital Structure* In: *Micro, Small, and Medium Enterprises in Vietnam*. Edited by: John Rand and Finn Tarp, Oxford University Press (2020). DOI: 10.1093/oso/9780198851189.003.0004 deductible interest are just offset by the costs of financial distress (Miller 1977). The theory predicts that larger firms, in general, and firms with more tangible assets and characterized by higher profitability could enjoy greater tax benefits of debt and hence should have higher leverage. The pecking order theory (Myers 1984; Myers and Majluf 1984) relies upon the concept of asymmetric information between managers and investors that guides managers in their preference for raising funds. According to this theory, firms stick to a 'pecking order' in their search for funding, first using internally generated funds (primarily retained earnings) with the lowest degrees of asymmetric information, then tapping private debt (primarily in the form of loans from financial institutions), and seeking equity from outside sources as a last resort. Based on this, the theory predicts that more profitable firms can rely on internal funds and hence have lower leverage. As a consequence, there is no 'optimal' ratio of debt to equity. Finally, the market-timing theory of capital structure is the most recent addition to the theories of capital structure, emerging from a study by Baker and Wurgler (2002) that considers how the efforts of management to 'time' the issuance of equity relate to the firm's capital structure. Of these three major competing theories explaining capital structure decisions, only the first two are relevant for small firms that do not issue publicly traded securities. There has been no consensus about which theory best explains small firms' capital structure decisions (Serrasqueiro and Caetano 2015).

Further, while developed countries tend to have an advanced institutional environment and a developed capital market such that capital-constrained firms can easily access different sources of finance to optimize their capital structure (Rajan and Zingales 1995; Wald 1999), very little is known about how firms in transition countries determine their capital structure and how this decision is influenced by the local institutional quality, which is normally characterized by distinctive characteristics such as inefficient markets, active government involvement, weak financial market, and high uncertainty (Booth et al. 2001; Chang et al. 2014). These transition settings challenge the efficacy of existing business models and theories, and thus provide a useful context to explore how firms facing radical external institutional and market changes of the transition develop a relevant capital structure to bring about required organizational changes. As a transition country, Vietnam presents an interesting and highly relevant context to explore the wider applicability of the capital structure literature. With the implementation of the *doimoi* policy over the past 30 years driving the centrally planned economy towards more market-driven arrangements, Vietnam has experienced substantial changes in virtually every aspect of its society and economy (Tran and Santarelli 2017).

Our chapter contributes to the literature as follows. First, we explore what determines the evolution of capital structure over time. In this connection, we address the question of 'which capital structure theory—trade-off or pecking order—best explains the capital structure decisions of non-state firms during the post-transition process in Vietnam?'. We classify the determinants into three categories—individual-level, firm-level, and regional-level categories—in order to provide a comprehensive insight into firms' capital structure black boxes. Second, since the financial market is relatively underdeveloped in Vietnam, and non-state firms are constrained by a complex credit-rationing process, the use of formal external financing directly from the market is very limited, and hence we predict that informal sources of debt will be more important than formal ones. Thus, we study how informality in the financing market is associated with firms' leverage decisions. Finally, we identify that an optimal capital structure or a beneficial leverage level in small firms will depend significantly on their entrepreneurs' human capital and the local institutional environment. In particular, the extent to which firms can access formal loans or may need to exploit informal loans instead is contingent on the combination of their owners' education, experience and transparent and fair credit rationing rules in a high-quality institution. We look into the dynamic relationship between environmental institutional quality and firms' changing leveraging decisions, taking into account the interaction effect of entrepreneurs' human capital and local institutions.

For empirical evidence, we use a unique database provided by the CIEM-DANIDA (Central Institute for Economic Management and Danish International Development Agency) project covering around 2,000 micro, small and medium-sized enterprises in Vietnam for each year from 2003–14. We estimate our empirical models by employing the System Generalized Method of Moments estimator (GMM-Sys) (Blundell and Bond 1998). The structure of the chapter is as follows. We review the related literature on capital structure theories, determinants of capital structure, and how capital structure influences firm survival, and develop our hypothesis in Section 4.2. Section 4.3 discusses our data, their descriptive statistics, and pair-wise correlation. Section 4.4 presents variable construction and estimation models. Section 4.5 discusses the main results and provides interpretation. Finally, Section 4.6 concludes.

4.2 Literature Discussion

4.2.1 Trade-off Theory versus Pecking Order Theory

In theory, firm capital structure is optimal in efficient markets (Rubinstein 2003). However, in practice, the financial market is never efficient. Subsequent theoretical work has taken into account the imperfections of financial markets and has shown that firms establish their capital structure depending on firm-specific attributes and macroeconomic factors that determine the various costs and benefits associated with debt and equity financing (Frank and Goyal 2009).

Our empirical analysis is motivated by two strands of the capital structure literature which are directly relevant to non-state small and medium-sized enterprises (SMEs).

The trade-off strand states that optimal capital structure is determined by firms balancing tax savings from debt against deadweight bankruptcy costs. Classic arguments for this trade-off theory are based on bankruptcy costs in a situation of excessive debt, tax deductibility of interest expenses, and agency costs of equity derived from excess free cash flows (Jensen and Meckling 1976). It is therefore suggested that there is an optimal level of debt where the marginal benefit equals the marginal cost of an additional unit of debt (Bradley et al. 1984). The pecking order theory argues that a pecking order in financing exists if there is information asymmetry in companies between the insiders, either shareholders or managers, and outsiders, mainly investors. There is thus a preference hierarchy of financing sources: firms prefer to use retained earnings as their first financing source, followed by debt and, lastly, by equity. Equity is less attractive to firms given that it entails larger information asymmetry costs (Baskin 1989), or managerial optimism (Heaton 2002), making its issuance more expensive relative to other funding sources.

Empirically, these two theories have often been placed in opposition when seeking to identify which offers the best explanation regarding capital structure decisions. In the empirical studies, some of the findings are consistent with the trade-off theory while others are consistent with the pecking order theory.[1] A large number of these empirical studies have focused on the debt determinants of large and listed companies, whereas capital structure decisions of SMEs have only recently gained interest (Sogorb-Mira 2005; Serrasqueiro and Caetano 2015). The serious lack of capital and existence of information asymmetry prevent SMEs from accessing external financing sources and thus being able to peg with a hierarchical order of selection. However, to balance debt tax shield benefits and deadweight bankruptcy costs associated with debt financing, they need a high level of financial literacy around debt and tax systems, which appears to be far beyond their ability. While various empirical studies support a particular theory in explaining SMEs' capital structure decisions (for instance, the pecking order theory in Ou and Haynes 2006; Ramalho and Silva 2009), Serrasqueiro and Caetano (2015) conclude that the pecking order theory and trade-off theory are not mutually exclusive, i.e. when SMEs adopt a financing behaviour, following one theory does not imply a distance from the other theory. In what follows, we will review the (contradictory) predictions of the two theories regarding the key determinants of capital structure such as profitability, growth opportunities, asset tangibility, income volatility, firm size, and tax shield benefits.

[1] For a review, see Köksal and Orman (2014).

According to trade-off theory, profitability is positively associated with leverage for three reasons (Bonfim and Antão 2012). First, as profitability increases, bankruptcy costs decrease, pushing firms to higher levels of leverage. Second, facing higher expected tax rates than less or non-profitable firms, more profitable firms should borrow to shield income from taxation. This asymmetric taxation of profits and losses drives profitable firms to higher levels of debt as they benefit more from the resulting tax benefits of debt (DeAngelo and Masulis 1980). Third, in the agency theoretical framework, profitable firms tend to have severe free cash-flow problems, that is, more excess earnings over profitable investments, thus also requiring higher leverage to restrain management discretion. However, the pecking order theory suggests a negative relationship between profitability and leverage level since profitable firms have internal funds (retained earnings) to support investments and are less likely to seek debt financing.

The two theories also disagree with respect to the relationship between leverage and growth opportunities. While trade-off theory predicts a negative relationship between leverage and firm growth, the pecking order theory predicts a positive relationship. Supporting the agency theoretical framework, trade-off proponents suggest that firms with high-growth opportunities tend to have few free cash-flow problems but high financial distress costs of debt due to significant conflicts of interest between shareholders and debt holders. Thus, high-growth firms should use less debt. However, pecking-order theorists claim that high growth is likely to put a strain on retained earnings since internal funds are unlikely to be sufficient to support emerging investment opportunities, and it therefore pushes capital-constrained firms into debt financing. This supports a positive relationship between debt and growth opportunities once internal retained earnings have been fully exhausted.

Asset tangibility is normally a proxy for the availability of collateral, and thus firms with considerable tangible assets tend to have low expected distress costs and few debt-related agency problems. Trade-off theory asserts that firm leverage increases with tangibility of assets (Rajan and Zingales 1995; Frank and Goyal 2009). This is because tangible assets are easier to collateralize and they suffer a smaller loss in value when firms go into distress. In addition, since firms tend to match the maturity of assets with that of liabilities, tangibility should be positively correlated with long-term leverage. However, according to pecking order theory, firms with high tangibility can have low leverage because they tend to have low information asymmetry, making the issuance of equity less costly (Harris and Raviv 1991).

According to trade-off theory, the value of interest tax shields incentivizes firms to hold high levels of debt when facing high tax rates. The effect of taxes on debt ratios, however, has been difficult to clearly identify in the data, and the available evidence is rather mixed and weak (see, for example, Antoniou et al. 2008; Frank and Goyal 2009). This may be because non-state firms face severe constraints in accessing external financing, there is uncertainty about what would constitute a good proxy for tax effects, and transaction costs make it difficult to identify tax effects even when they are an element of a firm's problems. Thus, in practice, researchers normally analyse non-debt tax shields, such as depreciation deductions, depletion allowances, and investment tax credits, which can be a substitute for the interest expenses and consequently can reduce the need to carry debt (DeAngelo and Masulis 1980). These shields can be considered as substitutes for the corporate tax benefits of debt financing. Therefore, while tax shields make it attractive to secure additional financing using debt, trade-off theory predicts a negative relationship between leverage and non-debt tax shields. More often than not, empirical studies produce results that are supportive of this trade-off theory prediction (Köksal and Orman 2014). Nevertheless, the pecking order theory, with the underpinning principle that a company follows a certain 'pecking order' in its capital structure choices (internal funds first, then debt, and equity) does not, however, provide an explicit explanation for the relationship between non-debt tax shields and leverage.

Large firms tend to be diversified and have stable cash flow, so their probability of bankruptcy is smaller than that of SMEs. Trade-off theory asserts that large firms have higher leverage compared with small firms. However, since large firms also tend to have less asymmetric information and lower adverse selection, pecking order theory suggests that large firms can more easily issue equity compared to small firms, and thus prefer equity to debt, resulting in lower leverage.

Although the two theories are in contradiction as far as the prediction of the impact of profitability, growth opportunities, and firm size on leverage are concerned, they agree on the impact of volatility (or firm risk) on leverage ratios. Risky firms tend to have volatile cash flows and high costs of financial distress. Under trade-off theory, the impact of volatility on debt financing is negative as debt increases bankruptcy costs. In addition, the probability of wasting interest tax shields increases when earnings are less than tax shields (Frank and Goyal 2009). Bankruptcy risks and tax shields both work to reduce leverage. Under pecking order theory, business risk exacerbates the adverse selection between firms and creditors. Thus, firms with more volatile cash flows are less likely to be indebted to lower the possibility that they will have to issue new risky securities or forego future profitable investments when cash flows are low.

4.2.2 Institutional Effects in Transition Countries

Institutions are recognized as being fundamental to economic growth and development because they provide the basic rules of human interaction for people in their use of scarce resources. More recent international studies pay particular attention to how institutional differences across countries shape capital structure decisions (Öztekin 2015). Institutional characteristics affect not only the costs and benefits of operating at various leverage ratios, but also the speed at which a firm converges to its long-term capital structure. If a province's institutional characteristics make debt and equity financing more costly, firms in that province will exhibit slower adjustment speeds.

With the collapse of the Soviet bloc in the late 1980s, firms in post-socialist countries had to readjust their working principles to be competitive in the open market. This also created a wave of new-born enterprises. These countries underwent severe economic reforms during the 1990s to produce significant changes to their institutional settings as well as their macroeconomic indicators. All these major changes were expected to have an impact on the capital structure of firms from transition countries (De Haas and Peeters 2006; Decoure 2007). Cross-country studies have shown that firms in these countries tend to use short-term debt rather than long-term debt (Demirguc-Kunt and Maksimovic 1999).

Since at least the mid-1990s, there have been a growing number of studies that explore the determinants of capital structure in individual transition countries,[2] including Vietnam.[3] The ideologies of the centrally planned mechanism prioritize state ownership in controlling the capital market. By introducing a monobank system—a system consisting of the central bank and various specialized state-owned banks (an investment bank, a foreign trade bank, an agricultural bank, etc.), which are regulated directly by instructions from the central bank—the central planning board can control all funds and cash flows. A large proportion of these funds is for state investment in state-owned enterprises and public services. However, the newly developed market institutions have not been supported by an effective system of legalization and legal practices in which private transactions are enforced, fair competition, free entry and orderly ways of exit are maintained, and the rights of debtors and creditors are secured. As a result, this substantially limits firms' financing choices, especially those of private firms. Evidence suggests that private firms in China are denied access to bank loans and often must resort to expensive trade credits (Brandt and Li 2003; Cull et al. 2009), while informal and short-term loans are preferred by new business founders in Vietnam (Rand 2007). Many private entrepreneurs in Vietnam with experience of doing business in informal markets in the past mainly use their savings rather than bank credits to finance their businesses (Tran and Santarelli 2014).

[2] See, for example, Wiwattanakantang (1999), Deesomsak et al. (2004) for Thailand; Pandey (2004) for Malaysia; Huang and Song (2006), Qian et al. (2009), Chang et al. (2014) for China; Correa et al. (2007) for Brazil; Qureshi (2009) for Pakistan; Espinosa et al. (2012) for Chile; and Sbeti and Moosa (2012) for Kuwait.

[3] Almost all the studies of the capital structure in Vietnam (for instance Nguyen 2010; Nguyen et al. 2012; Vo 2017) focus solely on listed firms and limit exploring whether determinants of capital structure of the country are comparable to those of advanced countries.

4.2.3 Hypothesis

Vietnam is currently one of the fastest emerging markets undergoing transition to a market economy. Its rapidly expanding capital market is gradually opening up to global investors and international firms. This suggests that some of the trade-off theory's predictions are more appropriate for the case of Vietnam than those of the pecking order theory. First, there are so many profit opportunities in the country that entrepreneurs are always in need of loans to finance their start-ups and operations. The underdevelopment of the Vietnamese financial market, however, limits their access to formal loans and prioritizes loans from informal sources. Second, large size, profitability, and high growth are key indicators in the credit-rationing criteria of formal creditors. Thus, large, profitable, and high-growth firms will attempt to obtain more loans, especially from formal sources to finance their activities. Third, since SMEs find it difficult to obtain formal financing due to difficulties in proving their creditworthiness, small cash flows, inadequate credit history, high risk premiums, underdeveloped bank–borrower relationships, and high transaction costs (Tran and Santarelli 2014), collateral is essential for them to obtain loans. Thus asset tangibility, a good proxy for collateral availability, stimulates firms to adopt more debt financing. Finally, income volatility indicates high firm risk and instable cash flows. As a consequence, firms with volatile income will be less likely to obtain loans since debt financing may exacerbate their bankruptcy risks. Thus, we propose the following hypothesis:

Hypothesis: The leverage decisions of firms in Vietnam follow trade-off theory predictions, rather than those of pecking order theory.

Nevertheless, modern Vietnam, during the transition to a market economy, still suffers many institutional constraints with complex administrative regulation, excessive bureaucracy, and frequent changes in 'red tape' increasing the risk and cost of doing business for private entrepreneurs (Glewwe and Dang 2011; de Jong et al. 2012). As a consequence, although the government has recognized entrepreneurial activities as an essential driver of economic growth, there is a lack of an established system of entrepreneurial finance. Since the early 1990s, shortage of capital was at the top of the list of constraints identified by Vietnamese entrepreneurs in almost every survey of private small firms in the country (Tran and Santarelli 2014). Until recently, state-owned commercial banks still relied on political connections to determine loan access as a credit source for private enterprises regardless of their profitability or growth (Malesky and Taussig 2009). In fact, recent research indicates that SMEs in transition economies may experience highly constrained pecking orders, given the significant institutional biases they face in accessing debt from the formal financial sector (Newman et al. 2012). Rand (2007) suggests that formal loans are relatively unimportant for new business founders compared to informal loans and personal savings due to collateral requirements from the formal financial system. Thus, we realize that SMEs in Vietnam may passively follow a pecking-order strategy in financing their businesses.

On one hand, social capital from membership of business networks plays an important role in gaining support and accessing external resources, including financial capital (Santarelli and Tran 2013). However, our data show that only 7.5 per cent of firms were members of business associations in 2015. On the other hand, human capital helps entrepreneurs to acquire financial resources, as it is one of the factors that investors and banks rely on to evaluate credit applications. Tran and Santarelli (2014) suggest that human capital helps family firms to relax their capital constraints since they have a greater knowledge of financing alternatives. However, we observe from our data that around 80 per cent of respondents have low levels of educations (unskilled/technical training with no certificate/vocational education). This once again supports the passively adopted pecking-order strategy of relying mainly on internal funding, since even when SMEs try to apply for loans, they are unlikely to obtain them.

4.3 Data Description

The dataset used in our empirical investigation is a 12-year panel of Vietnamese small and medium private manufacturing enterprises covering the period from 2003 to 2014. The dataset is extracted from five waves of the Danish International Development Agency (DANIDA) surveys (carried out in 2005, 2007, 2009, 2011, 2013, and 2015), providing highly detailed information on various aspects of entrepreneurs and their firms. These SME surveys stemmed from the collaboration of the Central Institute for Economic Management (CIEM) in Hanoi, Vietnam and the Ministry of Labour, Invalids and Social Affairs of Vietnam, the Department of Economics of the University of Copenhagen, and the Royal Embassy of Denmark in Vietnam. The surveys are designed with the objective of collecting and analysing data representative of the private sector as a whole in Vietnam. This means that, as well as interviewing large or formally registered enterprises, a substantial number of non-registered businesses are also studied in order to gain a comprehensive understanding of SME dynamics in Vietnam.

The sample we use for our analysis was extracted from the master dataset based on the following criteria: (i) firms' sales, total assets and/or labour force are non-zero; (ii) state-owned firms and joint ventures are excluded; and (iii) unregistered (informal) businesses who do not pay tax are excluded. The final sample consists of 24,640 observations covering 4,458 firms, of which up to 73 per cent (3,273) obtained some type of loan. Among these indebted firms, nearly 52 per cent (1,698) applied for loans from formal sources, 72 per cent (2,360) applied for loans from informal sources, and 36 per cent (1,181) applied for loans from both sources. The average leverage ratio (debt to total asset) of our sampled firms is comparatively low and stable, varying between 9 per cent and 14 per cent from 2003 to 2008, and then reducing to less than 9 per cent from 2009 onwards when transitional measures brought positive changes to the macro institutional environment.

The tabulation of legal ownership types by provinces shows that only 55 per cent of the sampled firms are household enterprises compared to around 90 per cent in the firm population (CIEM et al. 2011). Many households operate informally (unregistered) and thus are excluded from the analysis. The location–sector split of our sample suggests that the three largest sectors in terms of number of enterprises are food and beverages, fabricated metal products, and manufacturing of wood products. Finally, some 67 per cent of small and medium firms are registered as limited liability companies, compared to 33 per cent of micro firms. Moreover, up to 90 per cent of all micro firms are household establishments. Only 26 per cent of the joint stock firms are found in the medium firm category, and almost 21 per cent with this legal structure are found in the micro category; see Santarelli and Tran (2018: tables 1–3).

The second dataset that we use for our analysis is the provincial competitiveness index (PCI) data, which was first created for a sample of regions in 2005 and then for all 63 provinces and municipal cities from 2006 onwards. The survey is a product of the collaboration between the Vietnam Chamber of Commerce and Industry (VCCI) and the US Agency for International Development (USAID). PCI is a provincial institutional index, a weighted average of the nine sub-indices, each measuring a different aspect of local formal or informal governance.[4]

4.4 Estimation Methods

4.4.1 Variables

Dependent variable

There are several different leverage measures used in capital structure studies. Following Köksal and Orman (2014), we consider three different measures of leverage: formal, informal, and total debt over total assets.[5] It is important to

[4] For the data and information about the methodology of the PCI index, see PCI (n.d.).

[5] Formal loans come from weak relationships: banks, venture capital funds, social funds, etc., while informal loans are from strong networks such as families, relatives, friends, private creditors, etc. They are specified from the most important (in value terms) current formal and informal loan respectively.

distinguish between formal and informal leverage since formal debt and informal debt inherently carry different implications for the outcome of the business. As mentioned earlier, firms in transition countries tend to employ more informal forms of financing, reflecting the greater dependence of these firms on families and friends. While these informal sources enable firms to have less pressure from interest rates, they can, however, erode the necessary entrepreneurial efforts to maintain firm survival and growth.

Independent variables

(i) Profitability is the ratio of before-tax profit to total assets (return on assets (ROA)). While trade-off theory expects a positive impact of profitability on leverage, pecking order theory suggests a negative impact.

(ii) Growth opportunities are reflected by the growth of sales as in Schoubben and Van Hulle (2004), Frank and Goyal (2009), and Köksal and Orman (2014). While trade-off theory predicts a negative impact of firm growth on leverage ratios, pecking order theory predicts a positive impact.

(iii) Following Rajan and Zingales (1995) and Demirguc-Kunt and Maksimovic (1999), we define asset tangibility as the ratio of tangible fixed assets to total assets. Trade-off theory predicts a positive relationship between leverage and tangibility, while pecking order theory generally predicts a negative relationship between leverage and tangibility.

(iv) Following Titman and Wessels (1988) and Rajan and Zingales (1995), firm size consists of labour size (natural logarithm of total number of employees) and economic size (natural logarithm of total assets). Trade-off theory asserts that large firms have higher leverage compared with small firms but, according to pecking order theory, large firms prefer equity to debt, and thus have lower leverage.

(v) While tax shields make it more attractive to secure additional financing using debt, trade-off theory predicts a negative relationship between leverage and non-debt tax shields. Nevertheless, pecking order theory does not provide an explicit explanation of the impact of tax on leverage. Rather than including corporate taxes and non-debt tax shields separately in our analyses following Köksal and Orman (2014), we use a single indicator called the 'potential debt tax shield' (PDTS) proposed by Shuetrim et al. (1993), which simultaneously takes account of the presence of both effects. Whether a firm actually enjoys a positive tax advantage for debt financing depends on the trade-off between these two effects.

$$PDTS = \begin{cases} I_{it} + \dfrac{T_{it}}{\tau_t} & if\ T_{it} > 0 \\ 0 & if\ T_{it} = 0 \end{cases},$$

where I_{it} and T_{it} denote, respectively, interest payments and tax payments by firm i at time t, and τ_t denotes the statutory corporate tax rate at time t.[6]

(vi) Firm risk or volatility is measured by the standard deviation of operating income over total assets as in de Jong et al. (2008). Both the trade-off and the pecking order theories predict a negative relationship between leverage and business risk.

(vii) Institutional barriers are measured by the PCI, which is designed to assess the ease of doing business, economic governance, and administrative reform efforts by Vietnam's provincial and city governments in order to promote private sector development. The overall PCI index score comprises ten sub-indices reflecting economic governance areas that affect private sector development. The higher a province's PCI index, the higher the quality of the institutions in that province. In particular, that province is considered to perform well if it has: (1) low entry costs for business start-up; (2) easy access to land and security of business premises; (3) a transparent business environment and equitable business information; (4) minimal informal charges; (5) limited time requirements for bureaucratic procedures and inspections; (6) minimal crowding out of private activity from policy bias toward state, foreign, or connected firms; (7) proactive and creative provincial leadership in solving problems for enterprises; (8) developed and high-quality business support services; (9) sound labour training policies; and (10) fair and effective legal procedures for dispute resolution.[7]

Control variables

(i) Education and experience of firm owners; (ii) firm ownership types: households, private firms, cooperatives, limited liability firms, and joint-stock companies; (iii) firm age; (iv) export firms; and (v) regional dummies. Table 4.1 presents the measurement of all adopted variables.

Table 4.2 provides basic summary statistics. Although up to 70 per cent of our sampled firms obtained some type of loans, loans make up just under 10 per cent of the firm's total assets, of which 7 per cent are from formal sources and 3 per cent from informal sources. Exploring this further, around 60 per cent to 70 per cent of formal loans are from state-owned commercial banks, and the same proportion applies to informal loans obtained from family and friends. When comparing the debt ratios to statistics reported in other studies (such as Gannetti 2003; Li et al. 2009), it is clear that Vietnamese firms have much lower levels of leverage in their capital structures than firms in other countries. Given the fact that a significant number of firms report 'lack of capital' as one of their three

[6] Shuetrim et al. (1993, in Köksal and Orman, 2014) show that it is equal to the sum of interest paid and taxable income after all non-debt tax deductions have been made.

[7] For the methodology, sampling method, questionnaire, and annual report on PCI, see PCI (n.d.).

Table 4.1 Measurement of variables

Variables	Proxies	Measures
Dependent variables	Total debt ratio	The ratio of total debt over total assets
	Total formal debt ratio	The ratio of debt from formal sources over total assets[a]
	Total informal debt ratio	The ratio of debt from informal sources over total assets[a]
Independent variables	Firm profitability	Return on assets (ROA): the ratio of before-tax profit to total assets
	Growth opportunities	Growth of sales: $\frac{(Sales_t - Sales_{t-1})}{Sales_{t-1}}$
	Asset tangibility	The ratio of tangible fixed assets to total assets
	Firm size	Labour size: natural logarithm of total number of employees of the firm
		Economic size: natural logarithm of total assets of the firm
	Tax shields	Potential debt tax shield (PDTS), I_{it} and T_{it} denote, respectively, interest payments and tax payments by firm i at time t, and τ_t denotes the statutory corporate tax rate at time t. $PDTS = \begin{cases} I_{it} + \frac{T_{it}}{\tau_t} & if\ T_{it} > 0 \\ 0 & if\ T_{it} = 0 \end{cases}$
	Firm risk/volatility	The standard deviation of operating income over total assets
	Institutional barriers	The provincial competitiveness index (PCI) comprises ten sub-indices reflecting economic governance areas that affect private sector development. For the methodology, see PCI (n.d.).
Individual-level control variables	Education	A dummy attains 1 if the firm owner has high level of education (college and university degrees), and zero otherwise
	Experience	The sum of three types of experience: self-employment experience (the likelihood of previously being self-employed), industry experience (the likelihood of previously working in the same line of business), and management experience (the likelihood of previously working as a manager)
Firm-level control variables	Firm age	Number of years that a firm is in operation
	Export firms	A dummy attains 1 if the firm produces products/services for exporting
	Ownership types	1. Household; 2. Collective/cooperative/partnership; 3. Private firms; 4. Limited liability; 5. Joint stock
Province-level control variables	Regional dummies	1. Ha Noi; 2. Phu Tho; 3. Ha Tay; 4. Hai Phong; 5. Nghe An; 6. Quang Nam; 7. Khanh Hoa; 8. Lam Dong; 9. Ho Chi Minh city; 10. Long An

[a] Formal loans come from weak relationships: banks, venture capital funds, social funds, etc., while informal loans are from strong networks such as families, relatives, friends, private creditors, etc. They are specified from the most important (in value terms) current formal and informal loans respectively.

Source: Authors' calculations.

biggest challenges in firms' establishment and operations (Tran and Santarelli 2014), the actual low (formal/informal) leverage ratios reflect the underdeveloped and weak financial market in Vietnam, which fails to address capital constraint issues. There is significant variation in age across our sampled firms. The average firm age is 12 years, and the standard deviation of firm age is 9.73. On average, almost 75 per cent of firms' assets are tangible assets. Only 7 per cent of the sampled firms are involved in export activities.

The correlation matrix in Table 4.2 indicates that there are high correlations of 0.71 and 0.52 between the overall leverage level and the formal/informal debt ratios respectively, reflecting the fact that formal and informal loans are equally important to Vietnamese firms in financing their investments. There is a trivial correlation of 0.04 between formal debt ratio and informal debt ratio, which indicates that firms mainly rely on one loan source at a particular point of time, rather than using both at the same time. Firm size is significantly and negatively correlated with firms' ROA: smaller firms are more profitable. Profitability is positively associated with all measures of leverage, whereas asset tangibility is negatively associated with these measures. Export firms appear to be more leveraged than their counterparts. We also find a significantly positive correlation between the entrepreneur's human capital variables and leverage ratios. Finally, PCI index is negatively associated with all measures of human capital and leverage ratios. This indicates that firms are less financially constrained in provinces with high-quality institutions. However, these provinces are also attractive repositories of highly educated and richly experienced entrepreneurs, suggesting some possible interactions between institutional quality and the entrepreneur's human capital.

4.4.2 Methodology

We estimate a dynamic panel model that estimates the unobserved leverage ratio, *t*, from the past leverage ratio, *t−1* and other explanatory variables.

$$LEV_{i,t} = \alpha LEV_{i,t-1} + \beta X_{i,t} + \gamma PCI_{i,t} + \delta_{i,t}, \qquad (4.1)$$

where $LEV_{i,t}$ is firm *i*'s debt ratio in year *t*, $LEV_{i,t-1}$ is firm *i*'s debt ratio in year *t−1*, α is the adjustment parameter, β and γ are the coefficients to be estimated. $X_{i,t}$ are observable firm and province characteristics, and $PCI_{i,t}$ is institutional quality index of the province where firm *i* is located.

Equation (4.1) contains the endogenous lagged dependent variable and the short panel bias (Blundell and Bond 1998; Huang and Ritter 2009). We therefore use the system GMM technique to estimate Equation (4.1), and we control for the potential endogeneity of the explanatory variables, including the lagged dependent variable, by using lags of the same variables as instruments. According to Wintoki et al. (2012), the system GMM procedure can both take advantage of the panel

Table 4.2 Descriptive statistics and pair-wise correlation matrix

Var	Mean	Std	Min	Max	(1)	(2)	(3)	(4)	(5)	(6)	(7)	(8)	(9)	(10)	(11)	(12)	(13)	(14)	(15)	(16)	(17)
(1)	0.099	0.29	0	13.3	1.00																
(2)	0.07	0.24	0	12.5	0.71*	1.00															
(3)	0.03	0.15	0	9.8	0.52*	0.04*	1.00														
(4)	11.82	9.73	0	76	−.06*	−.05*	−.05*	1.00													
(5)	14.09	1.72	4.59	20.8	0.02*	0.03*	−.04*	−.04*	1.00												
(6)	2.07	1.14	0	7.56	0.16*	0.15*	0.09*	−.13*	0.64*	1.00											
(7)	0.35	3.35	−1.3	406	0.03*	0.03*	0.02*	−.02*	−.08*	−.00	1.00										
(8)	18.2	1,496	−1	196,001	0.00	0.01	0.00	−.00	0.01	0.01	−0.00	1.00									
(9)	0.22	0.91	0	60.1	0.04*	0.04*	0.03*	−.03*	−.09*	0.01	0.71*	−0.00	1.00								
(10)	0.75	0.30	0	1	−.07*	−.12*	−.14*	0.04*	0.07*	−.01	−.02*	0.00	−.01	1.00							
(11)	817,525	149*10^5	0	178*10^7	0.03*	0.03*	0.00	−0.00	0.09*	0.10*	0.00	−0.00	0.00	−.03*	1.00						
(12)	0.074	0.26	0	1	0.09*	0.08*	0.05*	−.04*	0.25*	0.38*	0.00	−0.00	0.01	−.04*	0.05*	1.00					
(13)	0.27	0.44	0	1	0.11*	0.09*	0.08*	−.14*	0.36*	0.43*	−0.01	−0.00	0.01	−.05*	0.06*	0.20*	1.00				
(14)	0.26	0.44	0	1	0.01	0.00	−.01	.01	−.02*	−.06*	0.01	−0.01	−.00	0.03*	−0.01	−.04*	−.15*	1.00			
(15)	0.062	0.24	0	1	0.04*	0.03*	0.03*	−.06*	0.09*	0.16*	−0.01	−0.00	−.00	0.03*	−0.00	0.09*	−.16*	−0.01	1.00		
(16)	0.114	0.32	0	1	0.05*	0.03*	0.03*	−.09*	−.14*	−0.01	0.00	0.00	−.01	−0.01	−.06*	−.01	−.02*	−.05*	0.04*	1.00	
(17)	57.9	4.09	47.7	67.1	−.04*	−.03*	−.04*	−.06*	0.15*	0.05*	−0.00	0.04*	−.00	0.03*	−.15*	0.02*	0.05*	0.05*	−.01	0.01	1.00

Note: * significant at 1 per cent level. (1) debt ratio; (2) formal debt ratio; (3) informal debt ratio; (4) firm age; (5) economic size; (6) labour size; (7) return on assets (ROA); (8) growth of sales; (9) firm volatility; (10) firm tangibility; (11) potential debt tax shield (PDTS); (12) export firm; (13) education; (14) self-employment experience; (15) management experience; (16) industry experience (17) provincial competitiveness index (PCI).

Source: Authors' calculations.

structure of our dataset and account for the frequently ignored methodological concerns that are common to corporate finance studies, such as dynamic endogeneity.

4.5 Estimation Results

We estimate three equations in which the overall debt ratio, the formal debt ratio, and the informal debt ratio take turns to be the dependent variable. The results are presented in Table 4.3. For each equation, we provide three treatments: columns (1), (4), and (7) examine the relationship between capital structure determinants and the three leverage ratios; columns (2), (5), and (8) add provincial institutional quality index into the estimation; and columns (3), (6), and (9) look into the interaction between institutional quality and the entrepreneur's human capital variables. We will now look at the effect of individual capital structure determinants to explore if our hypothesis is supported.

The results show that firm size is a reliable factor for all sources of leverage. This seems to be driven more by countries with weak institutional settings, in which the liability of newness and smallness represents a key challenge to start-up firms. While labour size has a significant and positive relationship with leverage ratios, which supports the trade-off theory's assertion that large firms have higher leverage compared with small firms, economic size is negatively associated with debt financing. Firms with large asset pools are able to leverage their assets to various means to create stable cash in-flows without debt obligations.

Profitability has a significantly positive impact on overall and formal leverage. As profitability increases, the higher are the expected tax rates and the lower the bankruptcy risk, which pushes firms to obtain more (formal) loans to capitalize abundant growth opportunities in a transitional economic setting, as well as to shield their income from taxation. This again supports the trade-off theory. Furthermore, high profitability also improves firms' credit ratings to obtain formal loans, so they rely less on informal loan sources when it comes to further investments. However, sales growth does not exert a significant impact on leverage, which fails to support either the trade-off theory or pecking order theory.

We also find that asset tangibility reflects the availability of collateral for acquiring loans. Nevertheless, we find a significant and negative relationship between firms' asset tangibility and leverage ratios, which supports the pecking order theory. Given the underdevelopment of the financial market and the importance of informal loans in Vietnam, access to formal loans is challenging, and thus rather than obtaining credits, firms will try to bootstrap by all means such as by leasing or renting their land or factories, to create stable income from their large fixed assets. However, we do support both the trade-off theory and pecking order theory in finding a significant and negative relationship between

Table 4.3 Determinants of total leverage, formal leverage, and informal leverage

Variable	Total leverage			Formal leverage			Informal leverage		
	(1)	(2)	(3)	(4)	(5)	(6)	(7)	(8)	(9)
Debt ratio, *t–1*	0.391**(0.008)	0.136**(0.009)	0.129**(0.008)	0.516**(0.009)	0.202**(0.007)	0.191**(0.007)	0.496**(0.008)	0.128**(0.006)	0.128**(0.006)
Firm age	0.001*(0.000)	0.000(0.000)	0.000(0.000)	0.000(0.000)	−0.001*(0.000)	−0.001*(0.000)	0.000(0.000)	−0.000*(0.000)	−0.000*(0.000)
Labour size	0.007(0.007)	0.014*(0.006)	0.014*(0.005)	0.011*(0.005)	0.015**(0.004)	0.016**(0.004)	0.001(0.003)	0.003(0.002)	0.003(0.002)
Economic size	−0.026**(0.004)	−0.017**(0.004)	−0.019**(0.003)	−0.021**(0.003)	−0.016**(0.002)	−0.016**(0.002)	−0.010**(0.002)	−0.013**(0.001)	−0.013**(0.001)
Profitability	0.007*(0.003)	0.008*(0.004)	0.005(0.004)	0.006**(0.002)	0.008**(0.003)	0.008**(0.003)	0.001(0.002)	0.000(0.001)	0.000(0.001)
Growth opportunities	−0.000(0.000)	−0.000(0.000)	−0.000(0.000)	0.000(0.000)	0.000(0.000)	0.000(0.000)	0.000(0.000)	−0.000(0.000)	−0.000(0.000)
Income volatility	−0.577**(0.162)	−1.308**(0.151)	−1.252**(0.141)	−11.162**(0.596)	2.404**(0.154)	2.250**(0.154)	−0.897**(0.062)	−0.216**(0.021)	−0.217**(0.021)
Asset tangibility	−0.149**(0.022)	−0.154**(0.021)	−0.140**(0.019)	−0.086**(0.016)	−0.122**(0.013)	−0.119**(0.013)	−0.074**(0.010)	−0.062**(0.007)	−0.062**(0.007)
Debt tax shield (PDTS)	0.000**(0.000)	0.000**(0.000)	0.000**(0.000)	0.000**(0.000)	0.000*(0.000)	0.000*(0.000*)	0.000(0.000)	0.000(0.000)	0.000(0.000)
Export firm	0.010(0.020)	0.011(0.019)	0.005(0.018)	0.004(0.014)	0.002(0.012)	0.000(0.012)	0.013(0.009)	0.019**(0.006)	0.019**(0.007)
Professional education	0.062**(0.011)	0.038**(0.009)	0.229**(0.072)	0.037**(0.007)	0.016**(0.006)	0.047(0.048)	0.009*(0.004)	0.002(0.003)	0.000(0.027)
Self-employment experience	0.041**(0.008)	0.038**(0.007)	1.345**(0.039)	0.016**(0.005)	0.011*(0.005)	0.224**(0.026)	0.006(0.004)	0.001(0.002)	0.027*(0.015)
Management experience	−0.032*(0.014)	0.005(0.016)	1.332**(0.041)	−0.023*(0.010)	0.017*(0.009)	0.233**(0.028)	−0.003(0.007)	0.004(0.005)	0.031(0.016)
Industry experience	0.073**(0.011)	0.159**(0.016)	1.352**(0.039)	0.000(0.008)	0.015(0.011)	0.214**(0.026)	0.010*(0.005)	0.004(0.006)	0.027*(0.015)
PCI index		−0.002**(0.000)	−0.006**(0.001)		0.000(0.000)	0.001**(0.000)		0.000(0.000)	0.000(0.000)
PCI * education			−0.004**(0.001)			−0.001(0.001)			−0.000(0.000)
PCI * experience			−0.022**(0.001)			−0.004**(0.000)			−0.000*(0.000)
Private firm	−0.025(0.021)	−0.023(0.022)	−0.031(0.021)	−0.022(0.015)	−0.016(0.014)	−0.017(0.014)	−0.012(0.009)	−0.037**(0.008)	−0.036**(0.008)
Cooperative/partnership firm	0.029(0.044)	0.029(0.044)	0.023(0.041)	0.018(0.031)	−0.017(0.028)	−0.016(0.027)	0.015(0.020)	0.028*(0.016)	0.029*(0.016)
Limited liability firm	0.021(0.025)	0.032(0.024)	0.029(0.023)	0.011(0.018)	−0.022(0.015)	−0.023(0.015)	0.008(0.011)	0.007(0.008)	0.007(0.008)
Joint stock firm	−0.039(0.043)	−0.064(0.039)	−0.045(0.036)	−0.006(0.031)	−0.042*(0.024)	−0.041*(0.024)	−0.018(0.019)	−0.032*(0.014)	−0.033*(0.014)
Provincial dummies	$\chi^2(8)=230$**	$\chi^2(8)=513$**	$\chi^2(8)=513$**	$\chi^2(8)=228$**	$\chi^2(8)=698$**	$\chi^2(8)=699$**	$\chi^2(8)=584$**	$\chi^2(8)=1337$**	$\chi^2(8)=1332$**
Intercept	1.129**(0.165)	0.027(0.139)	0.672**(0.132)	18.404**(1.156)	9.183**(0.310)	8.909**(0.311)	-2.868**(0.233)	−0.886**(0.067)	−0.889**(0.068)
Wald χ^2 test	3244**	1751**	3028**	6957**	9007**	9170**	6722**	7039**	7045**
Observations	18,358	16,309	16,309	16,098	14,049	14,049	16,098	14,049	14,049

Source: Authors' calculations.

firm risk (volatility) and leverage. The volatility of firms' incomes indicates the instability of returns to entrepreneurs and a higher risk of bankruptcy, but also a large potential magnitude of profit. Thus, although a higher risk of returns is correlated with lower debt ratios, the magnitude of the correlation is weaker with informal debt ratios. Given its open policy for the last three decades, Vietnam is characterized by a generation of young, ambitious, and dynamic entrepreneurs who are willing to take advantage of every opportunity that comes their way. Unable to obtain loans from formal sources due to volatile cash flows, they renegotiate terms with family and friends to obtain informal financial support.

Finally, potential debt tax shields are significantly and positively associated with leverage. These tax shields act as powerful substitutes for corporate tax benefits of debt financing, and thus firms with higher amounts of debt tax shields should choose to have lower levels of debt according to the trade-off theory. However, we fail to support this theory for the case of Vietnam. We claim that these tax shield benefits, such as depreciation deductions, depletion allowances, and investment tax credits, make it more attractive to secure additional financing. Nevertheless, these tax shield benefits are strongly available when we consider the overall and formal leverage ratios of firms. They gradually lose their significance, and become insignificant and irrelevant for informal leverage sources. Obviously, loans acquired from informal sources, such as families and friends, are considered as internal/own capital, and thus are not applicable for any tax exemption or shield benefits.

Overall, our findings support the trade-off theory with respect to the effects of profitability, volatility, and firm size, while supporting the pecking order theory with respect to asset tangibility. Therefore, overall, we cannot strongly support our hypothesis, and contend that the leverage decisions of firms in Vietnam follow the explanations of both the pecking order theory and the trade-off theory. They work in a complementary rather than mutually exclusive manner in explaining the capital structure decisions of firms in a transition economic setting.

With regard to the effects of control variables, firm and individual characteristics that explain total debt decisions appear to play a similar role in formal and informal debt decisions, although the statistical significance may differ. Export firms in particular are slightly more indebted, but their loans are mainly from informal sources. As expected, the entrepreneur's human capital is a crucial determinant of a firm's capital structure. We find a consistent positive impact of professional education on the overall and the formal leverage ratios. Keeping other factors constant, entrepreneurs with high education levels (college and university degrees) are more likely to have 6.2 per cent higher financial leverage. Since education level is always one of the most important screening criteria for banks and venture capital funds to make investment decisions, it is plausible that highly educated entrepreneurs find it easier to obtain formal loans. Surprisingly, while self-employment and industry experience are important for obtaining loans, especially formal ones, management experience plays the exact opposite role. An entrepreneur who has owned/started up a firm previously or has worked in the same line of business gives a positive signal to formal creditors when they evaluate the risks and returns of investments into a firm. This valuable entrepreneurial experience is also found to exert a significantly positive effect on various measures of entrepreneurial performance in Vietnam (Santarelli and Tran 2013). However, management experience is more meaningful to wage employment opportunities (Carbonara et al. 2019). As expected, we consistently find an insignificant effect of human capital variables on the informal debt ratio.

Importantly, disparities in regional institutional development matter for firms' leverage decisions. Our variable of interest, provincial institutional quality, is negatively associated with the overall leverage ratio. Firms residing in provinces with high-quality institutions are found to have lower leverage levels than their counterparts in low-quality institutions. Advanced market institutions require banks to apply strict screening criteria to monitor loan financing, and, thus, firms with bad credit in well-developed provinces cannot obtain loans or cannot borrow as much as they want. However, a developed institutional environment also favours the emergence and development of alternative financing instruments such as equity and, as a result, local firms reduce their reliance on debt financing (Li et al. 2009). The significant and positive effect of PCI on the formal debt ratio indicates that better legal rules and better protection of creditors in high-quality institutions also encourage more formal debt financing (supporting Demirguc-Kunt and Maksimovic 1999). But it is worth noting that our measure of institutional development across regions (PCI) in Vietnam is much broader than the creditor protection measure typically used in prior work.

While higher professional education is positively associated with leverage ratios, institutional quality has a negative impact on debt financing. Further, better developed provinces are attractive destinations for highly educated entrepreneurs and workers in general. These inconclusive pair-wise correlations suggest the need to study the interaction effects of human capital and institutional quality on capital structure decisions. We present the estimation results of these interactions in columns (3), (6), and (9) for the overall debt ratio, formal debt ratio, and informal debt ratio respectively. Interestingly, although human capital motivates and enables entrepreneurs to adopt debt financing, highly educated and experienced entrepreneurs residing in high-quality institutions do not find loans attractive as other sources of finance. Being exposed to various sources of finance in a well-developed province with an advanced financial market, they acquire fewer loans and move toward more sophisticated financial sources (such as venture capital). The single effect of education becomes insignificant when we add its interaction term with PCI in the estimation. This again affirms the crucial role of the institutional environment in obtaining loans in particular and capital structure decisions in general. No matter how well educated entrepreneurs are, they fail to access debt financing if they are located in a province with low-quality institutions. In summary, we show that human capital and institutional development interact in important ways to affect capital structure decisions: the role of human capital in firms' capital structure decisions is strengthened in more developed provinces. As suggested by Carbonara et al. (2016), advanced institutional quality not only facilitates the development of an efficient financial market that eases access to formal loans and other more attractive sources of finance, but it also promotes entrepreneurial start-up activities in different economic settings.

4.6 Discussion and Conclusion

Employing a unique database on Vietnamese firms, this chapter addresses the questions: 'Which capital structure theory—trade-off or pecking-order—best explains the capital structure decisions of non-state and non-listed firms during the post-transition process in Vietnam?' and 'How do human capital and provincial institutional quality as well as their interaction influence these decisions?' We classify the determinants into three categories: individual-level, firm-level, and regional-level categories and find that the leverage decisions of Vietnamese firms generally follow the explanation of both the trade-off theory with respect to the effects of profitability, volatility, and firm size, and pecking order theory with respect to the effect of asset tangibility. Although many studies favour either the trade-off theory or pecking order theory over the other to describe the capital structures of firms (Köksal and Orman 2014), we claim that this is not necessarily the case for young and dynamic entrepreneurs in a transition country. Both theories work in a complementary manner to explain the financing choices of private firms in Vietnam. Since the financial market is underdeveloped and state-controlled in Vietnam and non-state firms are constrained by a complex credit-rationing process, accessing formal sources of loans is extremely tough for young and non-state firms. However, Vietnam is a land full of opportunity where entrepreneurs always have new opportunities to begin again after failed business attempts, with the support of their family and friends (Carbonara et al. 2019). Thus, given their liability of newness and smallness, bootstrapping skills and informal sources of finance are far more essential to their financial decisions. It is therefore not possible to explain this informality characteristic of firms' capital structure in transition countries in general, and Vietnam in particular, by relying on only one particular standard capital structure theory.

Given the widespread prevalence of informal loans, we study how informality in the financing market is associated with the leverage decisions of firms. We find a rather consistent pattern of estimation results in terms of effect direction across all sources of loans. Nevertheless, profitability and debt tax shields are no longer significantly important when entrepreneurs adopt informal debt financing.

Finally, identifying an optimal capital structure or a beneficial leverage level depends significantly on the local institutional environment. We study the effect of provincial institutions on firms' leverage levels and find that high-quality institutions with transparent and fair credit rationing rules, legal protection of creditors, and efficient government involvement enables firms to reduce their reliance on debt financing and to adopt other more appropriate sources of financing.

Inspection of individual characteristics reveals that the human capital of entrepreneurs is an important factor in determining their capital structure. Generally, educated and experienced entrepreneurs are more likely to take loans to finance their investments. However, when entrepreneurs reside in a high-quality institutional province, education and experience may respond adversely to leveraging decisions. They all use fewer loans and switch to other more attractive financial sources that become available and accessible when institutional quality is improved.

Our results are relevant for policy makers and managers of firms in transition economies. The evidence supports the well-studied consensus that obtaining external formal financing is extremely difficult for firms in these countries. As a result, they mostly rely on internally generated funds or informal financing sources to support their investment activities and growth (Mateev et al. 2013). We claim that institutional quality plays a crucial role in easing access to formal debt financing, and thus extending financing choices for non-state firms.

Nevertheless, the situation has improved since the enactment of the new Law on State Bank and Law on Credit Institutions in December 1997. State-owned commercial banks were restructured toward stock holding institutions and the State Bank of Vietnam was reformed toward specializing in monetary policy and supervising the banking system. Credit institutions, regardless of ownership, are growing in terms of quantity and quality, which provides firms with easier access to various sources of financing in a more market-oriented manner (World Bank 2005).

References

Antoniou, A., G. Yilmaz, and P. Krishna (2008). The determinants of capital structure: Capital market-oriented versus bank-oriented institutions, *Journal of Financial and Quantitative Analysis*, 43(1): 59–92.

Baker, M., and J. Wurgler (2002). Market timing and capital structure, *Journal of Finance*, 57(1): 1–32.

Baskin, J. B. (1989). An empirical investigation of the pecking order hypothesis, *Financial Management*, 18(1): 26–35.

Blundell, R. W., and S. R. Bond (1998). Initial conditions and moment restrictions in dynamic panel data models, *Journal of Econometrics*, 87(1): 115–43.

Bonfim, D., and P. Antão (2012). The Dynamics of Capital Structure Decisions. Banco De Portugal Working Paper Series No.6. Lisbon: Economics and Research Department, Banco de Portugal.

Booth, L., V. Aivazian, A. Demirguc-Kunt, and V. Maksimovic (2001). Capital structures in developing countries, *The Journal of Finance*, 56(1): 87–130.

Bradley, M., A. J. Gregg, and E. H. Kim (1984). On the existence of an optimal capital structure: Theory and evidence, *Journal of Finance*, 39(3): 857–78.

Brandt, L., and H. Li (2003). Bank discrimination in transition economies: Ideology, information, and incentives?, *Journal of Comparative Economics*, 31(3): 387–413.

Carbonara, E., E. Santarelli, and H. T. Tran (2016). De jure determinants of new firm formation: How the pillars of constitutions influence entrepreneurship, *Small Business Economics*, 47(1): 139–62.

Carbonara, E., H. T. Tran, and E. Santarelli (2019). Determinants of novice, portfolio and serial entrepreneurship: An occupational choice approach, *Small Business Economics*, forthcoming, DOI: https://doi.org/10.1007/s11187-019-00138-9.

Chang, C., X. Chen, and G. Liao (2014). What are the reliably important determinants of capital structure in China?', *Pacific Basin Finance Journal*, 30(1): 87–113.

CIEM, DoE, ILSSA, and UNU-WIDER (2011). Characteristics of the Vietnamese Business Environment: Evidence from a SME Survey in 2011. Available at: https://www.wider.unu.edu/sites/default/files/Report-Characteristics%20of%20the%20Vietnamese%20Business%20Environment-Eng.pdf (accessed 8 February 2017).

Correa, C., L. C. Basso, and W. T. Nakamura (2007). What Determines the Capital Structure of the Largest Brazilian Firms? An Empirical Analysis Using Panel Data. Available at: http://dx.doi.org/10.2139/ssrn.989047 (accessed 15 February 2017).

Cull, R., L. C. Xu, and Z. Tian (2009). Formal finance and trade credit during China's transition, *Journal of Financial Intermediation*, 18(2): 173–92.

DeAngelo, H., and R. W. Masulis (1980). Optimal capital structure under corporate and personal taxation, *Journal of Financial Economics*, 8(1): 3–29.

Decoure, N. (2007) The determinants of capital structure in transition economies, *International Review of Economics and Finance*, 16: 400–15.

Deesomsak, R., K. Paudyal, and G. Pescetto (2004). The determinants of capital structure: Evidence from the Asia Pacific region, *Journal of Multinational Financial Management*, 14: 387–405.

De Haas, R., and M. Peeters (2006). The dynamic adjustment towards target capital structures of firms in transition economies, *Economics of Transition*, 14(1): 133–69.

de Jong, A., R. Kabir, and T. T. Nguyen (2008). Capital structure around the world: The roles of firm- and country-specific determinants, *Journal of Banking & Finance*, 32 (9): 1954–69.

de Jong, A., M. Verbeek, and P. Verwijmeren (2012). Does financial flexibility reduce investment distortions?, *Journal of Financial Research*, 35(2): 243–59.

Demirguc-Kun, A., and V. Maksimovic (1999). 'Institutions, financial markets and firm debt maturity', *Journal of Financial Economics*, 54: 295–336.

Espinosa, C. M., C. V. Maquieira, J. P. Vieito, and M. A. Gonzalez (2012). Capital structures in developing economies: The Latin American case, *Investigacion Economica*, 71(282): 35–54.

Frank, M. Z., and V. K. Goyal (2009). Capital structure decisions: Which factors are reliably important?, *Financial Management*, 38(1): 1–37.

Gannetti, R. T. (2003). Bowling ninepins in Tocqueville's township, *American Political Science Review*, 97(1): 1–16.

Glewwe, P., and H. A. H. Dang (2011). Was Vietnam's economic growth in the 1990s pro-poor? An analysis of panel data from Vietnam, *Economic Development and Cultural Change*, 59(3): 583–608.

GSO (General Statistics Office of Vietnam) (2016). *Statistic Yearbook 2016*. Hanoi: Statistical Publisher.

Harris, M., and A. Raviv (1991). The theory of capital structure, *Journal of Finance*, 46(1): 297–355.

Heaton, J. B. (2002). Managerial optimism and corporate finance, *Financial Management*, 31(2): 33–45.

Huang, R., and J. R. Ritter (2009). Testing theories of capital structure and estimating the speed of adjustment, *Journal of Financial and Quantitative Analysis*, 44(2): 237–71.

Huang, S. G. H., and F. M. Song (2006). The determinants of capital structure: Evidence from China, *China Economic Review*, 17(1): 14–35.

Jensen, M., and W. H. Meckling (1976). Can the Corporation Survive? Center for Research in Government Policy and Business Working Paper PPS 76-4. Rochester, NY: University of Rochester.

Köksal, B., and C. Orman (2014). Determinants of capital structure: Evidence from a major developing economy, *Small Business Economics*, 44(2): 255–82.

Li, K., H. Yue, and L. Zhao (2009). Ownership, institutions, and capital structure: Evidence from China, *Journal of Comparative Economics*, 37(3): 471–90.

Malesky, E. J., and M. Taussig (2009). Where is credit due? Legal institutions, connections and the efficiency of bank lending in Vietnam, *Journal of Law, Economics and Organization*, 25(2): 535–78.

Mateev, M., P. Poutziouris, and K. Ivanov (2013). On the determinant of SME capital structure in Central and Eastern Europe. A dynamic panel analysis, *Research in International Business and Finance*, 27(1): 28–51.

Miller, M. H. (1977). Debt and taxes, *Journal of Finance*, 32(4): 261–75.

Myers, S. C. (1984). The capital structure puzzle, *Journal of Finance*, 39(3): 575–92.

Myers, S. C., and N. S. Majluf (1984). Corporate financing and investment decision when firms have information that investors do not have, *Journal of Financial Economics*, 13(2): 187–221.

Newman, A., S. Gunessee, and B. Hilton (2012). Applicability of financial theories of capital structure to the Chinese cultural context: A study of privately-owned SMEs, *International Small Business Journal*, 30(1), 65–83.

Nguyen, D. T., I. Diaz-Rainey, and A. Gregoriou (2012). Financial Development and the Determinants of Capital Structure in Vietnam. Available at: http://dx.doi.org/10.2139/ssrn.2014834 (accessed 15 February 2017).

Nguyen, X. T. (2010). The Determinants of Capital Structure: An Empirical Study of Listed Firms on the Vietnamese Stock Exchange. Finance and Corporate Governance Conference 2011 Paper. Available at: http://ssrn.com/abstract=1725710 (accessed 15 February 2017).

Ou, C., and G. W. Haynes (2006). Acquisition of additional equity capital by small firms: Findings from the National Survey of Small Business Finance, *Small Business Economics*, 27(2): 157–68.

Öztekin, O. (2015). Capital structure decisions around the world: Which factors are reliably important?, *Journal of Financial and Quantitative Analysis*, 50(3): 301–23.

Pandey, I. M. (2004). Capital structure, profitability and market structure: Evidence from Malaysia, *Asia Pacific Journal of Economics & Business*, 8(2): 78–91.

PCI (n.d.). The Provincial Competitiveness Index (PCI). Available at: http://eng.pcivietnam.org/index.php and http://eng.pcivietnam.org/about/pci-methodology/ (accessed 8 February 2017).

Qian, Y., T. Yao, and T. S. Wirjanto (2009). Do Chinese publicly listed companies adjust their capital structure toward a target level?, *China Economic Review*, 20(4): 662–76.

Qureshi, M. (2009). Does pecking order theory explain leverage behavior in Pakistan?, *Applied Financial Economics*, 19(17): 1365–70.

Rajan, R. G., and L. Zingales (1995). What do we know about capital structure? Some evidence from international data, *The Journal of Finance*, 50(5): 1421–60.

Ramalho, J., and J. Silva (2009). A two-part fractional regression model for the financial leverage decisions of micro, small, medium and large firms, *Quantitative Finance*, 9(5): 621–36.

Rand, J. (2007). Credit constraints and determinants of the cost of capital in Vietnamese manufacturing, *Small Business Economics*, 29(1–2): 1–13.

Rubinstein, M. (2003). Great moments in financial economics: II. Modigliani–Miller theorem, *Journal of Investment Management*, 1(2): 7–13.

Santarelli, E., and H. T. Tran (2018). The Interaction of Institutional Quality and Human Capital in Shaping the Dynamics of Capital Structure in Vietnam. WIDER Working Paper 2018/66. Available at: https://www.wider.unu.edu/sites/default/files/Publications/Working-paper/PDF/wp2018-66.pdf (accessed 1 March 2019).

Santarelli, E., and H. T. Tran (2013). The interplay of human and social capital in shaping entrepreneurial performance: The case of Vietnam, *Small Business Economics*, 40 (2): 435–58.

Sbeti, W. M., and I. Moosa (2012). 'Firm-specific factors as determinants of capital structure in the absence of taxes, *Journal of Applied Financial Economics*, 22(3): 209–13.

Schoubben, F., and C. Van Hulle (2004). The determinants of leverage: Differences between quoted and non quoted firms, *Tijdschrift voor Economie en Management* Vol. XLIX (4): 589–621.

Serrasqueiro, Z., and A. Caetano (2015). Trade-off theory versus pecking order theory: Capital structure decisions in a peripheral region of Portugal, *Journal of Business Economics and Management*, 16(2): 445–66.

Shuetrim, G., P. Lowe, and S. Morling (1993). The Determinants of Corporate Leverage: A Panel Data Analysis. Reserve Bank of Australia Working Paper 9313. Available at: https://www.rba.gov.au/publications/rdp/1993/pdf/rdp9313.pdf (accessed 1 March 2017).

Sogorb-Mira, F. (2005). 'How SME uniqueness affects capital structure: Evidence from a 1994–1998 Spanish data panel, *Small Business Economics*, 25(5): 447–57.

Titman, S., and R. Wessels (1988). The determinants of capital structure choice, *The Journal of Finance*, 43(1): 1–19.

Tran, H. T., E. Carbonara, and E. Santarelli (2017). Determinants of Novice, Portfolio and Serial Entrepreneurship: An Occupational Choice Approach. GLO Discussion Paper 74. Available at: https://www.econstor.eu/bitstream/10419/158030/1/GLO_DP_0074.pdf (accessed 8 February 2017).

Tran, H. T., and E. Santarelli (2014). Capital constraints and the performance of entrepreneurial firms in Vietnam, *Industrial and Corporate Change*, 23(3): 827–64.

Tran, H. T., and E. Santarelli (2017). Spatial heterogeneity, industry heterogeneity, and entrepreneurship, *Annals of Regional Science*, 59(1): 69–100.

Vo, X. V. (2017). Determinants of capital structure in emerging markets: Evidence from Vietnam, *Research in International Business and Finance*, 40(C): 105–13.

Wald, J. (1999). How firm characteristics affect capital structure: An international comparison, *The Journal of Financial Research*, 22(2): 161–87.

Wintoki, M. B., J. S. Linck, and J. M. Netter (2012). Endogeneity and the dynamics of internal corporate governance, *Journal of Financial Economics*, 105(3): 581–606.

Wiwatttanakantang, Y. (1999). An empirical study on the determinants of capital structure of Thai firms, *Pacific-Basin Finance Journal*, 7(3–4): 371–403.

World Bank (2005). *Vietna Managing Public Expenditure for Poverty Reduction and Growth*. Washington DC: World Bank.

5

How Important Are Management Practices for the Productivity of Small and Medium Enterprises?

Axel Demenet and Quynh Hoang

Neither husband nor wife knew how to read—a slight defect of education, which did not prevent them from ciphering admirably and doing a most flourishing business. [...] To relieve himself of the necessity of keeping books and accounts, he bought and sold for cash only.

Balzac, *Le Curé de Village*, 1841

5.1 Introduction

Few will question the relevance of a multinational manufacturing corporation's expenditure on advertising.* However, eyebrows may be raised if the same question is asked about a single, informal worker producing rubber sandals. The purpose of this chapter is to investigate the matter, in a comparative manner: does managerial capital (MC) have the same effect on productivity among micro, small, and medium firms? While past and ongoing research in management studies and economics has proved the relevance of MC for large or medium enterprises, the population of micro and small enterprises has largely been ignored.

Given the weight of micro, small, and medium enterprises (MSMEs) in total employment, and because the long-awaited development process is occurring

* The authors wish to thank all participants from the Vietnamese Central Institute for Economic Management, the Ministry of Planning and Investment of Vietnam, the Development Economics Research Group (DERG) of the University of Copenhagen, and UNU-WIDER, involved in the design, collection, and cleaning of the survey data on which this chapter is built. Special thanks are due to John Rand. Previous versions of this work were meaningfully enriched by comments received at the 84th ACFAS conference, Montreal; the STBI seminar at the University of Economics of Ho Chi Minh City, and the 7th Vietnam Economist Annual Meeting, Ho Chi Minh City. The views expressed are the authors' own.

Axel Demenet and Quynh Hoang, *How Important Are Management Practices for the Productivity of Small and Medium Enterprises?* In: *Micro, Small, and Medium Enterprises in Vietnam*. Edited by: John Rand and Finn Tarp, Oxford University Press (2020). © United Nations University World Institute for Development Economics Research (UNU-WIDER). DOI: 10.1093/oso/9780198851189.003.0005 through productivity gains, there is value in understanding the mechanisms that foster (or limit) their expansion. Several types of constraints to expansion have already been put forward, with access to savings (Dupas and Robinson 2013), access to finance (de Mel et al. 2008), and human capital (Hsieh and Klenow 2009) being among the more documented ones. The lack of MC, by contrast, has only recently emerged as a constraint (Bruhn et al. 2010).

In the developing world, MSMEs rarely use what are considered to be elementary business practices in industrialized countries. The majority do not keep basic written accounts, and they compete mostly with other local household businesses. Yet, micro entrepreneurs themselves mention factors such as 'keeping and interpreting financial records' or 'promoting products' as being important for business success (Bradford 2007). However, some enterprises do display high organizational and managerial abilities. This heterogeneity in MC endowment can enter the production function as an additional efficiency factor; it could be argued that even among micro firms, managerial inputs can improve the productivity of other inputs. Competing more aggressively, advertising products, incentivizing wage determination or innovating could lead to higher value added.

Proving a causal relationship between productivity and MC is challenging, as the latter does not offer exogenous variations. It is, rather, part of the often-blamed (and always unobserved) 'ability' of the firm's operator, and any relation found to productivity can be attributed to some other unobserved factor. Our approach is therefore not to argue that the results are fully causal, which observational data would struggle to back up. Instead, it measures the effect of changes in firms' MC on productivity and mark-up and compares this relationship by firm size. To do this, we use a synthetic indicator of MC and consistent productivity and mark-up estimates. We aim to show that MC matters for micro and small firms, and to identify which dimension of MC is the most influential.

We rely on a panel of Vietnamese MSMEs which includes proxies for several aspects of MC. We start by estimating the productivity and mark-up of firms, controlling for simultaneity and input price bias. We propose a multidimensional measure of MC based on five axes used to compute a weighted score. We then investigate the effect of MC on firm-level productivity and mark-up, controlling for unvarying heterogeneity. We find that changes in MC are associated with large positive effects on productivity, but they do not enhance firms' market power. We also test for heterogeneity of the effect by firm size category. While larger firms are found to be more productive than smaller ones, on average, we find that the effect of MC is still significant—and of comparable magnitude—among the smallest firms. Micro and small firms that have higher levels of managerial ability are indeed more efficient than others—and they are *as much* more efficient as medium-size firms. We further investigate the separated effect of the MC indicators and find the effect to be mainly driven by firms' ability to advertise and compete aggressively.

Section 5.2 reviews the literature, Section 5.3 provides the empirical measures of productivity and MC; Section 5.4 presents the estimation results of the link between MC and productivity, and Section 5.5 presents the robustness test. Section 5.6 concludes.

5.2 Literature Review: What Do We Know about the Managerial Capital of Micro and Small Enterprises?

What exactly constitutes managerial capital (MC)? The notion has no widely accepted definition and borrows from several fields of studies, which have complementary definitions. As Syverson puts it (2011), 'Managers are conductors of an input orchestra.' Defining MC then amounts to measuring the length of the conductor's baton, but it could also relate to the conductor's attitude and psychological traits. In the related development economics literature that has recently surged, MC is persistently proxied by business practices (and among micro and small firms, by elementary business skills). Management studies, in which the focus has long been on the influence of managers, additional features of MC relate to the entrepreneurial spirit. Taken broadly, MC thus refers to all *practices* and *traits* of an enterprise operator that potentially have an influence on the firm's efficiency. This can include formal book-keeping, inventory management, financial or strategic planning, and pricing strategy, as well as innovativeness or self-confidence.

There is general consensus on what are considered to be 'good practices' for large enterprises and the effects of these practices on productivity are well known (Bloom, Mahajan, et al. 2010; Syverson 2011; Bloom, Eifert, et al. 2013; Bloom, Schankerman, et al. 2013). The picture is fuzzier in the case of household micro and small firms. This section starts by reviewing the literature to determine which skills, practices, or characteristics can proxy managerial capital among micro and small firms, and to what extent their influence on performance is established.

5.2.1 Business Practices: Mixed Evidence from Business Training Programmes

Numerous programmes have been launched around the developing world to improve the business skills of microenterprises, and this has led to a substantial body of literature evaluating the impact of these programmes. The content of these programmes gives insights into what economists consider to be important business skills for this population. They are often elementary, compared to those of larger firms, and frequently include book-keeping, separating household and business budgets, elaborating growth strategies, financial planning, pricing and cost calculation, marketing, inventory management, savings, and debt management.

These programmes differ in content and in terms of target population, scale, means, and implementation schemes, which makes it difficult to draw clear conclusions. However, two recent papers have presented their results. McKenzie and Woodruff (2014) reviewed 20 studies (including 16 randomized control trials), of which only two had sufficient statistical power to show significant impacts from these programmes. These two studies found that training had an impact on short-term profits and sales: Berge et al. (2014), by combining survey data and lab experiment, and De Mel et al. (2014), by evaluating a combination of training and grants. The other studies they reviewed lacked statistical power, and long-term profits were not significantly affected. This led McKenzie and Woodruff (2014) to conclude that 'there is little evidence to help guide policy makers as to whether any impacts found come from [...] productivity improvements, and little evidence to guide the development of the provision of training'. In addition to this review, Cho and Honorati (2013) conducted a meta-analysis using 37 impact evaluation studies—with some overlap with the studies reviewed by McKenzie and Woodruff (2014). They obtained constrasting results showing little effect of training programmes on labour outcomes, although there was clearer evidence of improvement in business practices. More importantly perhaps, they suggest that a combination of interventions is likely to yield better results than each intervention being applied separately.

5.2.2 Entrepreneurial Orientation and the Managerial Performance of Micro Enterprises

The traits and attitudes of managers may matter as much as business practices. The analysis of attitudes and psychological factors is another topic covered by some business training, which, unsurprisingly, has been more popular in managerial studies than in economics.

Making business owners more proactive and perseverant seems to increase their performance (Glaub and Frese 2011). This finding echoes a second and complementary strand of literature on the link between management and the performance of microenterprises. The concept of entrepreneurial orientation (EO) is a potential proxy for unobserved managerial ability related to attitudes (Miller 1983; Covin and Slevin 1989). EO can be measured at the firm level along five dimensions: proactiveness, innovativeness, risk-taking, competitive aggressiveness, and autonomy of workers (Lumpkin and Dess 1996).

A recent set of papers aimed at providing empirical evidence on the link between EO and the performance of microenterprises found a positive association between EO and performance in the case of Mexico, Argentina, Malaysia, and the Philippines (Campos et al. 2013; Berrone et al. 2014; Lindsay et al. 2014; Munoz et al. 2015). While their results converge, these studies, however, share numerous and substantial methodological shortcomings. First, the samples are small, ranging from 151 to 735 observations (with a 46 per cent response rate for the latter) and generally non-random—with on-site or administrative identification of respondents, which likely results in sampling errors. Second, the questionnaires are often self-administered or mailed. Consequently, accurate measures of performance are beyond the reach of these surveys, and all of the cited papers rely on self-reported evaluations of performance, the consistency of which is highly questionable.[1] Further meta-analysis, as carried out by Rauch et al. (2009), is also problematic. Among the 53 samples used, the average sample size is just under 270 respondents and only seven papers use a dependent variable that is not 'perceived performance'.

Findings from the evaluation of training programmes aimed at improving business practices have shown few significant improvements in performance. Similarly, the empirical investigations into the role of EO (which approximates the part of managerial ability related to attitudes) among microenterprises suffer from too many methodological shortcomings to provide convincing evidence. There is thus room for a closer look at the link between MC (understood as practices and traits) and productivity and at the potential heterogeneity of this link across firm size. The only contribution in this regard is by McKenzie and Woodruff (2016), who looked at the influence on productivity of business practices in marketing, stock-keeping, record-keeping, and financial planning. Their results, which to some extent contradict the lack of impact of business training, show that these practices explain as much variation in outcomes in microenterprises as in large firms. Notwithstanding the importance of this contribution to the literature on the MC of microenterprises, their data do not allow consistent productivity levels to be estimated.

Against this backdrop, the present work relies on a rich panel data of MSMEs, covering mostly micro and small informal firms, and several indicators of both business practices and entrepreneurial attitudes. The estimation of consistent firm-level productivity is a necessary, and complex, first step, as unbiased estimation of production functions is an ongoing topic in empirical economics. Using an MC index, we then estimate its influence on productivity, removing fixed observed and unobserved heterogeneity and, more importantly, we test the heterogeneity of this influence by firm size.

[1] In general, relying on self-reported perception is problematic for comparison purposes. In some cases, the questions used are beyond the reporting capacity of many micro-entrepreneurs, e.g. 'return on capital employed' or 'growth of the company's value' (Campos et al. 2013; Munoz et al. 2015).

5.3 Empirical Strategy

This empirical analysis relies on a panel of household firms surveyed between 2007 and 2013,[2] with 8,864 observations of 2,901 unique firms. The sample is primarily made up of micro firms, which consistently represent around 70 per cent of observations, depending on the year. Informal household firms, defined as having no business registration certificate, represent 26 to 34 per cent of firms per year. The average firm size is around 14 workers. Fewer than 35 per cent of firms operate in premises that are dedicated to production only, which means that the majority operate at home or in shared spaces.

If MC does have an influence on productivity, it should enable firms to reach a similar level of output with less inputs—or conversely to increase output while inputs are kept constant. This may reflect firms being more efficient in their production processes, but it may also signal increased market power. In order to evaluate this link and to further test its relevance by firm size, the necessary first step is to estimate firm-level productivity and mark-up. Sections 5.4.1 and 5.4.2 provide details of these estimations, which have to overcome a number of endogeneity concerns. Section 5.4.3 describes the proxy variables for managerial capital and the construction of the index, which is based on business practices (formal accounts, advertising, wage determination) and entrepreneurial traits (innovation, aggressive competition).

5.3.1 Estimating Firm-level Productivity

Empirical study of the link between MC and firm-level productivity can only be as good as the first-stage estimations of this productivity. The correct identification of the production functions is among the oldest challenge in the empirical economic literature and is still evolving. Essentially, true productivity levels remain unobserved and so are productivity shocks to which firms may react differently. As long as input levels are chosen in relation to these unobserved determinants, ordinary least squares (OLS) estimations will be biased.

Specifying a Cobb–Douglas value added function:

$$VA_{it} = \beta_0 + \beta_1 l_{it} + \beta_2 k_{it} + \omega_{it} + \epsilon_{it}, \tag{5.1}$$

where VA_{it} is the value added of firm i at time t. l and k, are respectively the labour and capital inputs. All variables are transformed in natural logarithm. The error

[2] The SME survey has been conducted nine times, most recently in 2005, 2007, 2009, 2011, 2013, and 2015. As the proxy indicators of MC changed substantially in the 2005 and 2015 survey rounds, we restrict our sample to the 2007 to 2013 rounds. The sample size for each survey was initially around 2,500 firms, from which observations present in only one year were dropped.

term has two components, ω_{it} and ϵ_{it}, the former being correlated with inputs. The size and direction of the bias of the OLS coefficient on capital will depend on the correlation between inputs and productivity shocks, and more crucially on whether this correlation varies with time. If it does not, the inclusion of firm-level fixed-effects will yield consistent coefficients. Provided firm exit is also determined by this unobserved but unvarying productivity, then fixed effects will also solve potential selection bias due to endogenous exits. The unvarying nature of the unobserved productivity could, however, be a rather strong hypothesis, especially when using long-term panels. Other approaches allow for inputs to be endogenous with respect to a time-varying unobservable. Three contributions largely frame the empirical literature in this regard: Olley and Pakes (1996), Levinsohn and Petrin (2003), and Ackerberg et al. (2015) (henceforth OP, LP, and ACF respectively). The first two rely on the relationship between some intermediate input entering the production function and the unobserved productivity:

$$m_{it} = f_t(k_{it}, \omega_{it}). \tag{5.2}$$

This function can be inverted, assuming in particular a monotonic increase in ω_{it} so that the productivity is a function of two *observed* inputs:

$$\omega_{it} = g_t(k_{it}, m_{it}). \tag{5.3}$$

OP build on the idea that firms change investment (conditional on capital stock) in response to productivity shocks and provide a non-parametric representation of this inverse function to estimate production functions in two stages. However, investment may not react strongly to productivity shocks—or at least, not monotonically—and the adjustments may take place at other levels. LP suggest using, instead, a more varying intermediate input demand function such as material expenditure or energy costs. ACF highlight a functional dependence problem with the specifications of both OP and LP, whereby labour can be a deterministic function of the variables on which the first stage is conditioned. They propose an alternative (though quite related) estimation strategy, where inverted input demand functions are conditional on the choice of labour input. Wooldridge (2009) additionally proposes a stacked version of LP's moments, estimated by generalized method of moments (GMM) with efficiency gains, again based on unconditional input demands.[3] As well as being more efficient than the two-step estimators, this procedure can also correct for serial correlation (Van Beveren 2010).

[3] Comprehensive reviews of production function estimation techniques include Eberhardt and Helmers (2010) and Van Beveren (2010).

We rely on a combination of FE, LP, and Wooldridge's (2009) estimations of production function in addition to the benchmark OLS regressions.

OLS estimation of the firm-level value added function hence follows Equation (5.1), including a time trend. Assuming that the unobserved productivity is mostly fixed in time, we estimate the same equation with firm-level fixed effects:

$$VA_{it} = \beta_0 + \beta_l l_{it} + \beta_k k_{it} + \omega_i + \epsilon_{it}. \tag{5.4}$$

From both regressions, we can predict the productivity levels by taking:

$$\hat{\omega} = (\epsilon_{it} - \hat{\beta}_l l_{it} - \hat{\beta}_k k_{it}). \tag{5.5}$$

Further controlling for the simultaneity of inputs using LP, OP, or ACF requires additional hypothesis on the evolution of productivity and on the timing of firms' choices. As investment only concerns 45.5 per cent of firms across years (only 33.7 per cent among firms with one or two workers), it cannot be used as a proxy without introducing selection bias. Among the available non-parametric corrections, the LP procedure thus makes more sense and electricity costs are used as intermediate input proxy in the core of the analysis. Productivity is then typically assumed to follow a first-order Markov process: $\omega_{it} = E(\omega_{it}|\omega_{it-1}) + \xi_{it}$ where ξ_{it} is uncorrelated with k_{it} but can depend on l_{it}. The LP procedure then assumes that given $k_{it}$the firm will decide on l_{it}, and then determine m_{it} accordingly. The rearrangement of Equation (5.1) is thus:

$$VA_{it} = \beta_l l_{it} + \varphi_{it}(k_{it}, m_{it}) + \epsilon_{it}, \tag{5.6}$$

where:

$$\varphi_{it}(k_{it}, m_{it}) = \beta_0 + \beta_k k_{it} + g_t(k_{it}, m_{it}) \tag{5.7}$$

and

$$E(\epsilon_{it}|l_{it}, k_{it}, m_{it}) = 0 \tag{5.8}$$

The ACF critique essentially states that l_t and m_t are instead chosen simultaneously, which plagues the identification of β_l in the first stage. Following Wooldridge (2009), the last and preferred specification of productivity estimation in this analysis consists in estimating β_k and β_l directly by GMM.

Assuming:

$$E(\omega_{it}|l_{it}, k_{it}, m_{it}, l_{it-1}, k_{it-1}, m_{it-1},\ldots, l_{i1}, k_{i1}, m_{i1}) = 0 \tag{5.9}$$

and restricting the dynamics of productivity shocks:

$$E(\omega_{it}|k_{it}, l_{it-1}, k_{it-1}, m_{it-1}, \ldots) = E(\omega_{it}|\omega_{it-1}) = j(\omega_{it-1}) = j(g(l_{it-1}, k_{it-1})). \tag{5.10}$$

We can write $\omega_{it} = j(\omega_{it-1}) + a_{it}$ with $E(a_{it}|k_{it}, l_{it-1}, k_{it-1}, m_{it-1}, \ldots) = 0$. In other words, inputs l_{it} and m_{it} are correlated with productivity innovations a_{it}; whereas k_{it}, which is set at the previous period, is not. Neither are all past values of l_{it}, k_{it} and m_{it}. They provide a set of instruments to identify β_l and β_k.

We estimate the four models (OLS, FE, LP, and Wooldridge) of value added function from the unbalanced panel of firms.[4] We use the log of deflated value added as outcome, the log of total employment at year n, and the log of real capital value at the end of the previous year as inputs. The LP model further includes the log of real electricity expenditures from the last period as proxy. Wooldridge's estimations of productivity rely on lagged values of l_i and exponential functions of log inputs and intermediate input.

Concerns about input prices bias, the endogenous exit of firms, and industry-specific effects may remain. Indeed, if firms face different input demand functions (and/or operate at different points of the curves), the correction introduced by the proxy intermediate input variable will further bias the results. Electricity costs are, however, arguably similar across firms, and should not introduce further differences. Material expenditures are used as robustness checks to estimate alternative productivity measures (available upon request). Next, to the extent less productive firms are more likely to exit the sample, it is still possible that the productivity estimations will suffer from endogenous exit. The only method that directly corrects for this is the OP estimation, and, in practice, the corrections for firm exit are very small.[5] Lastly, a common practice—challenged, among others, by Bernard et al. (2009)—consists in estimating production function separated by industry. Given the high concentration of our sample firms within a few sectors, industry-specific estimates would require grouping arbitrarily sectors where few observations exist, and would result in introducing additional noise rather than separating heterogeneous manufacturing firms. Productivity is thus estimated on the full sample of firms.

Table 5.1 presents the coefficient estimates of the firm-level production function on the whole population of firms, using the unbalanced panel. Column 1 corresponds to OLS estimation of Equation (5.1) with an additional time trend, column 2 further introduces fixed effects to estimate Equation (5.4), column 3 applies

[4] On implementing production function estimators in Stata, see Yasar et al. (2008), Petrin (n.d.) and Petrin et al. (2004).

[5] Such is the case for Newman et al. (2015) using Vietnamese data on larger firms.

Table 5.1 Production function estimations

	OLS	FE	LP	Wooldrige
Log of labour	0.967***	0.686***	0.892***	0.941***
	(0.011)	(0.020)	(0.013)	(0.020)
Log of capital	0.226***	0.150***	0.143***	0.154***
	(0.008)	(0.010)	(0.012)	(0.010)
year=2009	0.091***			
	(0.017)			
year=2011	0.234***			
	(0.019)			
year=2013	0.275***			
	(0.020)			
Constant	7.306***	9.239***		0.210
	(0.095)	(0.137)		(2.533)
Observations	8,759	8,759	5,822	5,797

Note: *** p<0.01, ** p<0.05, * p<0.1. Clustered standard errors. by firms in models 1, 2, and 4, bootstrapped with 250 replications for LP estimates.

Source: Authors' calculations.

the LP procedure with electricity costs as intermediate input, and column 4 implements Wooldridge's GMM estimation. Values of inputs, output, and value added are all deflated using the regional price deflator for the 2005–15 periods. Past values of inputs are limited to one lag in order to prevent losing years of observations. Values of inputs in 2007 are only used as past values in the LP and Wooldrige specifications. The LP and Wooldrige results also use fewer observations due to missing information on intermediate input variables. Looking at excluded firms did not reveal any specific pattern. In particular, excluded firms were not concentrated among the smallest microenterprises, which could have been using proportionally less electricity.

Compared to the benchmark and expectedly biased OLS estimations, all corrections consistently reduce the estimated returns to capital, which is consistent with the simultaneity bias (more productive firms choosing more capital). The reduction in the labour coefficient is less marked; heterogeneity in productivity levels may arguably allow employing more workers altogether, or producing the same output with less workers. Fixed effects estimations overcorrect the bias for both inputs and find lower returns (and overall decreasing returns to scale). Correcting for fixed and varying simultaneity, both models find returns to capital of nearly 15 per cent at the mean, and the preferred Wooldridge specification yields high average returns to labour, close to the OLS estimates. One explanation may lie in the proportion of micro firms in the sample for which more productive firms are those who can employ an additional worker.

5.3.2 Estimating Mark-ups

Two key aspects of firm performance have been emphasized in the literature—technical efficiency in production and market power. If the market is perfectly competitive, price is equal to marginal cost and, then, product efficiency is a sufficient measure. However, perfect competition is hardly ever found. A firm that takes advantage of the price–cost margin, may earn higher profits while not necessarily improving its technical efficiency. Thus, in addition to firm productivity, we estimate mark-ups as another measure of firm performance to distinguish different channels by which MC may have any effect on firms.

The literature on mark-up estimation is quite extensive, starting with Hall's (1986, 1988, 1990) approach, and then Klette (1999). We focus on the empirical framework developed by De Loecker and Warzynski (2012) (hereafter DLW), covering firm-specific mark-up estimation. Their empirical model is based on the assumption that a firm minimizes its cost for a variable input that can be adjusted freely. Holding other inputs constant, a competitive firm will expand its use of one input (material in our case) until the revenue share of materials equals the output elasticity, which reduces as materials input increases. However, a firm may choose not to increase this input to the equality point, but to produce a lower quantity and raise the output price instead. In this case, it indicates that the firm is able to exercise market power by charging a price above marginal cost. The mark-ups expression is given by:

$$\mu_{it} = \theta_{it}^{X}(a_{it}^{X})^{-1}, \tag{5.11}$$

whereμ_{it} is the mark-up or price-marginal cost fraction of firm i at time t; $\theta_{\text{it}}^{\text{X}}$ is the output elasticity of an input X; and $\alpha_{\text{it}}^{\text{X}}$is the expenditure share of the input X in the total sales. This variable input could be either labour or intermediate materials. However, in our data, many firms are household businesses that do not pay wages (approximately 1,600 observation), making us unable to calculate the expenditure share of labour in the total shares. Thus, we estimate mark-ups using materials as our variable input. It can be seen that while the revenue share of materials can be directly obtained from the data, the estimation of output elasticity is more challenging. Indeed, we need to estimate the gross output production function in order to find output elasticity of materials.[6] The gross output translog production function is given by:

[6] See DLW (2012) for the GMM procedures to identify the output elasticity of materials followed in this paper.

$$Output_{it} = \beta_l l_{it} + \beta_k k_{it} + \beta_m m_{it} + \beta_{ll} l_{it}^2 + \beta_{kk} k_{it}^2 + \beta_{mm} m_{it}^2 + \beta_{lk} l_{it} k_{it} + \beta_{lm} l_{it} m_{it} + \beta_{km} k_{it} m_{it} + \beta_{lkm} l_{it} k_{it} m_{it} + \omega_i + \epsilon_{it}. \quad (5.12)$$

The output elasticity for an input free of adjustment cost (materials) is then estimated as:

$$\hat{\theta}_{it} M = \hat{\beta}_m + 2\hat{\beta}_{mm} m_{it} + \hat{\beta}_{ml} l_{it} + \hat{\beta}_{mk} k_{it} + \hat{\beta}_{lmk} l_{it} k_{it}. \quad (5.13)$$

After estimating the output elasticity of materials (and the share of materials in the total output), we can calculate the firm's mark-ups. Our estimated mark-ups based on the Cobb–Douglas production function is 1.92 at the mean and 1.30 for the median, while the estimation is 1.14 and 0.83, respectively, under a translog production function. Our estimated mark-ups under translog specifications are slightly lower than DLW's (2012) estimations for firms in Slovenia and mark-ups reported by Rand (2017) who use the same survey but at different periods of time. The gap would be due to the differences in the nature of the dataset between a survey and a census (Rand 2017) in the case of DLW (2012) and due to the differences in approach, between estimations based on output elasticity of labour and elasticity of materials. We will use the preferred translog specification in examining the link between MC and firm performance in Section 5.

5.3.3 A Multidimensional Measure of Managerial Capital

Managerial capital (MC), as shown in Section 5.2, relates to all the practices and traits of business operators that have the potential to influence firms' efficiency. A major advantage of the SME survey in this regard is that it not only provides indicators linked with business practices, but also proxies of entrepreneurial attitudes. In this study we use a multidimensional measure of MC, based on five proxy variables that are found (and are consistent) in all rounds of the survey. The incidence of each indicator by firm size is provided in Table 5.2.

First, book-keeping is indicated by whether the respondent does 'maintain a formal accounting book'. Thirty-eight per cent of firms across years do keep formal accounts, and the proportion strongly increases with firm size. It should be stressed that this variable captures the existence of a complete set of accounts; a negative answer may not indicate the total absence of books, as many microenterprises may keep simple records through personal notes. Second, a binary indication of marketing efforts is based on a positive answer to the question 'do you advertise your products?', and includes all practices from door-to-door information to radio or TV spots. Advertising is almost inexistent among micro firms (4 per cent), but is less rare among medium firms (26 per cent). A third indication of business practices is the method of wage determination, indicating whether wages are determined by following other sectors' rates, following local competitors' rates, by individual negotiations, by the paying capacity of the firm, or by none of these methods (which is the case for almost 15 per cent of firms that have no employees). The most common method for determining wages in all firms is individual negotiations, while micro firms, even among those paying wages, predominantly report no fixed method for determining wages (29 per cent). The last two indicators proxy dimensions of firms' entrepreneurial orientation. Innovation is used as the third axis, and covers all forms of innovation from 'introducing new products' or 'new processes or technologies', to the 'improvement of existing products'. On average, more than 55 per cent of MSMEs in Vietnam have at least one kind of innovation—the bigger they are, the higher their level of innovation.

Finally, we construct an indicator of competitive aggressiveness combining two variables: firms that report 'fixing prices lower than competitors', and firms that report 'bribes to gain new markets'. The latter is probably less consensual, but while bribes in general have a negative impact on many outcomes, firm-level corruption restricted to 'non-extortive' bribes can have a positive impact (Vial and Hanoteau 2010). Only 7 per cent of small and medium firms and 3 per cent

Table 5.2 Proxies of managerial capital: incidence by firm size

	Formal accounts	**Advertising**	**Innovation**	**Aggressive competition**
Micro	0.20	0.04	0.47	0.03
Small	0.79	0.26	0.72	0.08
Medium	0.99	0.49	0.80	0.07
Total	0.38	0.12	0.55	0.05
	Workers' management (wage determination)			
	None	*Follow local private rates*	*Follow state enterprises*	*Set by authorities*
Micro	0.29	0.11	0.01	0.01
Small	0.00	0.19	0.03	0.04
Medium	0.01	0.23	0.22	0.08
Total	0.21	0.14	0.01	0.02
	Workers' management (wage determination)			
	Follow rates in agriculture	*Individual negotiations*	*Paying capacity*	*Other*
Micro	0.01	0.38	0.16	0.01
Small	0.01	0.43	0.27	0.02
Medium	0.01	0.35	0.28	0.02
Total	0.01	0.39	0.19	0.02

Source: Authors' calculations.

of micro firms show some degree of aggressive competitive behaviour. The discriminating power of most of the MC proxies is high, with few firms reporting 'good' business practices or entrepreneurial behaviours.

A synthetic indicator of MC is built using multiple correspondence analysis (MCA) for each year, and is used in estimating the effect of MC on productivity (before using each indicator separately). All variables except wage determination are binary. Wage determination is kept flexible in MCA as there is no indication of one method being a priori superior to the other. MCA builds a binary indicator matrix that shows the incidence of each axis by firm, which is used to obtain weights from the factorial axis. A firm's MC score is thus calculated by the weighted sum of its responses, and can be noted as:

$$MC_i = \sum_{j=1,..,5} D_{ij} W_j,$$

where MC_i is the i-th observation's managerial capital score, D_{ij} the response of unit i to dimension j, and W_j the MCA weight for the first axis applied to category j.

The distribution of the MC normalized score by firm size is plotted in Figure 5.1. The score values can be compared between firms, rather than directly interpreted in levels. Units with a higher score display a mix of more frequent business practices (keeping written accounts, advertising, fixing wages in line with the state authorities' rate or relatively to local competitors) and more entrepreneurial traits (competing aggressively, innovating through products or technologies). As expected, the smaller the firm, the lower the MC: micro firms are concentrated in the lowest score values, and almost none show high levels of MC score.

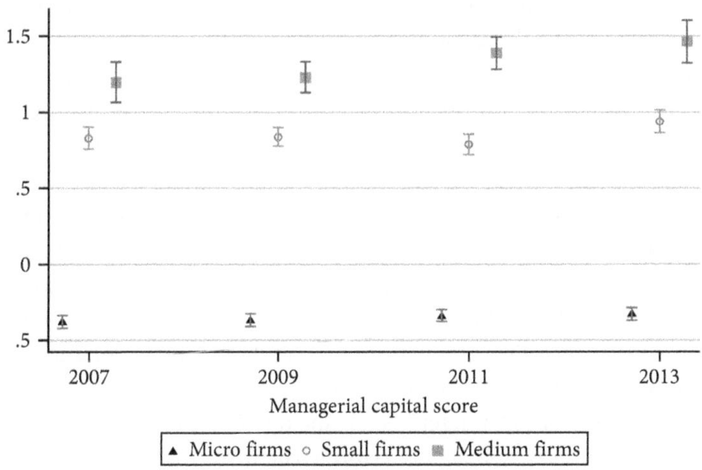

Figure 5.1 Managerial capital normalized score by year and firm size

Source: Authors' calculations.

5.4 The Link between Managerial Capital and Firm Performance

This section investigates the link between managerial capital (MC) and productivity, and tests whether this link depends on firm size. OLS regressions of MC on productivity are likely to be biased by the exclusion of variables positively associated with both MC and productivity, even when both variables are measured convincingly. As MC essentially aims at measuring owners' abilities, any proxy can only capture part of this. Our strategy is to get as close to causal inference as possible using the whole population of firms, and then to test whether these associations are similar across firm size. The assumption is that even though some varying heterogeneity could plague the estimation of the MC-productivity link, these potential biases can be constant by firm size, and comparing the significance and size of the effects is hence feasible.

In order to control for all fixed determinants of MC and productivity, whether observed or not, all estimates use firm-level fixed effects. The outcome variable is the total factor productivity estimated in Section 5.4. Specifically, we use the standardized productivity estimates of the preferred specification (Wooldridge 2009). The baseline specification is thus:

$$\Omega_{it} = \beta_0 + \beta_1 MC_{it} + \beta_2 S_{it} + \gamma C + \omega_i + \epsilon_{it}, \tag{5.14}$$

where Ω_{it} represents firm-level productivity estimated by Wooldridge's (2009) GMM, MC_{it} is the managerial capital score of firm i at time t, S_{it} is the firm size category, and C is a vector of controls for trends. This set of control variables aims to remove potentially differentiated evolutions by years, sectors, or regions (and finally with time*regions). As neither the productivity levels nor the MC scores can be directly interpreted in levels, all results are provided as standardized variations. The results of this baseline estimation are provided in the first column of Table 4.3. We find that a standard deviation in MC score results in an 8 per cent increase in productivity, on average, among the MSME sample, significant at 1 per cent. This average effect is net of the influence of firm size.

A further concern regarding bias arises from the limited indicators of managerial capital available in the data. As other practices and traits that could serve as additional proxies are not available in our data, part of the manager's ability remains unobserved by our MC score. We introduce a set of controls to proxy individual ability, which shows some variation across year (firm owner does change in some cases). Gender, education (higher secondary or more), and age are controlled for in the following model (included in the X vector). An additional set of time-varying firm characteristics is included: informality (being registered or not), type of premises, and access to infrastructures (road, in this case). We also add a set of social networks, measured by the number of contacts in the same business sector, different sector, banking officials, and politicians/civil officials. All can vary during the time period considered and may influence productivity. These additional controls have little influence on the MC coefficient, which tends to indicate that fixed-effects estimates removed most of the existing bias.

Looking at the description of MC score by size, we know that larger firms have both better business practices and more entrepreneurial attitudes. We also know from Section 5.4.1 estimates that productivity levels strongly and constantly increase with firm size. The results provided in Table 4.3 are net of this firm size effect, but the coefficient of MC score can nevertheless have different slopes depending on the size category if its influence on microenterprises is lower than in small and medium firms. A third model includes interactions between MC index and size categories to test for a differentiated effect of MC depending on the category. In Table 5.3, we report a Wald test for joint significance of the interaction term.

Table 5.3 Managerial capital and productivity

	(1)	(2)	(3)	(4)	(5)	(6)
Standardized values of (MC)	0.083***	0.089***	0.115***	0.114***	0.117***	0.111***
	(0.010)	(0.010)	(0.012)	(0.012)	(0.012)	(0.012)
Small size (11–50)	0.562***	0.545***	0.601***	0.600***	0.595***	0.516***
	(0.022)	(0.022)	(0.026)	(0.026)	(0.026)	(0.026)
Medium (51–300)	1.177***	1.144***	1.149***	1.147***	1.147***	1.025***
	(0.051)	(0.051)	(0.060)	(0.060)	(0.063)	(0.059)
(Small)*MC				−0.099***	−0.101***	−0.085***
				(0.019)	(0.019)	(0.018)
(Medium)*MC				−0.057*	−0.057	−0.043
				(0.035)	(0.035)	(0.033)
Log of mark-ups						0.338***
						(0.041)
Controls (ability)	No	Yes	Yes	Yes	Yes	Yes
Controls (social networks)	No	No	Yes	Yes	Yes	Yes
Time dummies	No	Yes	Yes	Yes	Yes	Yes
Sector dummies	No	Yes	Yes	Yes	Yes	Yes
Region dummies	No	Yes	Yes	Yes	No	No
Time*region interaction	No	Yes	Yes	Yes	No	No
District dummies	No	No	No	No	Yes	Yes
Time*District interactions	No	No	No	No	Yes	Yes
Constant	−0.179***	−0.308**	−0.289**	−0.359***	−0.244	−0.112
	(0.006)	(0.120)	(0.119)	(0.123)	(0.165)	(0.153)
Observations	5,893	5,893	5,893	5,893	5,893	5,843
R-squared	0.281	0.314	0.320	0.323	0.380	0.447
Number of id	2,782	2,782	2,782	2,782	2,782	2,767

Note: Testparm interactions (column 5): F (2, 2,781) = 11.55. Prob > F = 0.000. *** p<0.01, ** p<0.05, * p<0.1.

Source: Authors' calculations.

MC and productivity levels do depend on firm size. However, *the extent to which MC does influence productivity* does not: MC is as important among micro firms as it is among medium ones.[7] The MC indicators, although more scarcely found among micro firms, discriminate equally or more in this population between productive firms and subsistence businesses. The effect of business practices and EO on productivity is thus as large as among larger enterprises.

We continue our analysis of the association between MC and mark-ups by re-running all the above estimations using log of mark-ups as the outcome (Table 5.4). Firm size has a strong association with mark-ups but our variable of interest, MC, does not have a consistent significant effect on mark-ups. Since

Table 5.4 Managerial capital and firms' mark-ups

Log of mark-ups	**(1)**	**(2)**	**(3)**	**(4)**	**(5)**
Standardized values of (MC)	0.009	0.012	0.017	0.017	0.018*
	(0.009)	(0.009)	(0.011)	(0.011)	(0.011)
Small size (11–50)	0.191***	0.204***	0.213***	0.213***	0.223***
	(0.025)	(0.024)	(0.026)	(0.026)	(0.025)
Medium (51–300)	0.282***	0.307***	0.338***	0.339***	0.333***
	(0.037)	(0.037)	(0.048)	(0.048)	(0.057)
(Small)*MC			−0.015	−0.014	−0.019
			(0.022)	(0.022)	(0.021)
(Medium)*MC			−0.033	−0.032	−0.025
			(0.023)	(0.023)	(0.028)
Controls (ability)	No	Yes	Yes	Yes	Yes
Controls (social networks)	No	No	Yes	Yes	Yes
Time dummies	No	Yes	Yes	Yes	Yes
Sector dummies	No	Yes	Yes	Yes	Yes
Region dummies	No	Yes	Yes	Yes	No
Time*region interaction	No	Yes	Yes	Yes	No
District dummies	No	No	No	No	Yes
Time*District interactions	No	No	No	No	Yes
Constant	−0.177***	−0.212***	−0.211***	−0.186**	−0.319***
	(0.007)	(0.073)	(0.073)	(0.075)	(0.103)
Observations	5,901	5,901	5,901	5,901	5,901
R-squared	0.033	0.078	0.078	0.080	0.180
Number of id	2,773	2,773	2,773	2,773	2,773

Note: *** p<0.01, ** p<0.05, * p<0.1.
Source: Authors' calculations.

[7] The marginal effects of MC by size category and significance levels are available upon request, and confirm this finding.

mark-ups reflect firms' market power, the insignificant results mean that the market could be highly competitive and higher MC would not play a role in increasing the firm's mark-ups. We then use log of mark-ups as a control for our estimation on MC and productivity. The results are shown in column 6 of Table 4.3. We find that mark-ups have a positive association with firms' productivity but our coefficient of MC on productivity does not change. This suggests that the role of MC lies mainly in technical efficiency.

These results provide a global picture of the relationship between MC and productivity by firm size. They show that when every other factor (except some possibly remaining time-varying heterogeneity) is controlled for, including the same levels of inputs, firms with a higher MC generate more output because they are technically more efficient. However, they say little about the relative importance of our indicators of MC. Different types of business practices or entrepreneurial attitudes have different types of impact. Formal written accounts or wage determination may influence the labour or capital productivity (as each additional worker or capital unit may be more effective). On the other hand, marketing, aggressive competition, or innovation might directly increase the value added for given levels of inputs. A first indication lies in the individual contributions of each variable to the MC score, where advertising, accounts, and competition seem to be the most discriminating factors. An alternative possibility is to regress all indicators separately on productivity.

Table 5.5 provides the coefficients of the separate indicators. As they conceptually represent different parts of a single variable, including all the indicators jointly could result in multi-collinearity. It is nevertheless possible to gain an insight into which has the largest influence. The wage determination variable is transformed into a binary indication: autonomy in wage setting if a firm determines wages based on local private rates, state-owned enterprises' (SOEs) or authority's rates (these three methods are found to be the most weighted in the MC score).

Entrepreneurial orientation, measured by innovation, and business practices, measured by autonomy in wage determination aggressiveness, turn out to be the most influential factors in all models. The absence of significant effects of other dimensions should not lead to the conclusion that they are irrelevant dimensions of MC; the joint influence of all factors is proven above; it is rather the intensity of each variable that is jointly evaluated here.

5.5 Robustness

Most of the previous analysis relies on the firm-level productivity estimated in the first stage. A remaining bias in these estimates would cast doubt on the results of the second stage, in particular if the bias is somehow also correlated with MC. The

Table 5.5 Managerial capital indicators and productivity

	(1)	(2)	(3)	(4)
Advertising	0.049**	0.024	0.027	0.032*
	(0.024)	(0.018)	(0.018)	(0.018)
Innovation	0.052***	0.035***	0.029***	0.027**
	(0.012)	(0.010)	(0.011)	(0.011)
Competition	0.047*	0.018	0.023	0.031
	(0.029)	(0.024)	(0.025)	(0.025)
Accounts	0.051*	0.026	0.023	0.035
	(0.026)	(0.022)	(0.022)	(0.022)
Wage determination	0.026	0.026**	0.025*	0.021
	(0.016)	(0.013)	(0.013)	(0.013)
Size categories	No	Yes	Yes	Yes
Controls	No	No	Yes	Yes
Time and regions dummies	No	No	Yes	No
Time and district dummies	No	No	No	Yes
Constant	−0.058***	−0.219***	−0.401***	−0.266
	(0.012)	(0.012)	(0.127)	(0.169)
Observations				
R-squared	5,893	5,893	5,893	5,893
Number of id	0.011	0.267	0.300	0.358

Note: Clustered standard errors in parentheses. *** $p<0.01$, ** $p<0.05$, * $p<0.1$.
Source: Authors' calculations.

results were re-obtained using an alternative estimation of productivity, based on a different correction for simultaneity using material expenditures.[8]

Returns to capital and labour go through overall comparable corrections when using this alternative proxy of material expenditures, although the coefficients of capital of the LP and Wooldridge estimators are higher (and the returns to labour are lower). Firm-level productivity is then used as outcome variable and the results of similar regressions to those in Section 5.5 are provided in Table 5.6. The effect of MC is consistent and still yields a 10 per cent increase in productivity per standard deviation. The heterogeneity of the coefficient by firm size is, again, impossible to back up: MC does matter among small firms, at least as much as it does for medium-size ones. Finally, productivity estimates using corrections other than the preferred Wooldridge specification (fixed effects and LP) were used with similar results.

5.6 Conclusion and Discussion

This chapter provides a straightforward answer to an open question of growing importance. It uses rich panel data consisting of 8,864 observations of 2,901

[8] Results of the production function estimations are available upon request.

Table 5.6 Managerial capital and alternative measures of productivity

	(1)	(2)	(3)	(4)	(5)
Standardized values of (MC)	0.071***	0.079***	0.101***	0.100***	0.100***
	(0.010)	(0.010)	(0.012)	(0.012)	(0.012)
Small size (11–50)	0.528***	0.507***	0.554***	0.554***	0.551***
	(0.022)	(0.021)	(0.025)	(0.025)	(0.024)
Medium (51–300)	1.090***	1.052***	1.056***	1.056***	1.050***
	(0.052)	(0.051)	(0.058)	(0.059)	(0.061)
(Small)*MC				–0.083***	–0.084***
				(0.019)	(0.019)
(Medium)*MC				–0.048	–0.048
				(0.035)	(0.035)
Log of mark-ups					
Controls (ability)	No	Yes	Yes	Yes	Yes
Controls (social networks)	No	No	Yes	Yes	Yes
Time dummies	No	Yes	Yes	Yes	Yes
Sector dummies	No	Yes	Yes	Yes	Yes
Region dummies	No	Yes	Yes	Yes	No
Time*region interaction	No	Yes	Yes	Yes	No
District dummies	No	No	No	No	Yes
Time*District interactions	No	No	No	No	Yes
Constant	-0.167***	-0.259**	-0.244*	-0.313**	-0.216
	(0.006)	(0.127)	(0.125)	(0.130)	(0.172)
Observations	5,913	5,913	5,913	5,913	5,913
R-squared	0.253	0.300	0.305	0.308	0.364
Number of id	2,775	2,775	2,775	2,775	2,775

Note: Testparm interactions (column 5): F (2, 2,774) = 9.4. Prob > F = 0.000. p<0.01, ** p<0.05, * p<0.1.
Source: Authors' calculations.

unique firms surveyed between 2007–13, in which a set of MC indicators is available and consistent across years. One original feature is that these indicators enable combining standard indicators of business practices and less frequent indicators of firms' EO into a single score of MC. The results of consistent firm-level productivity and mark-up estimates are regressed on this score. A variation of one standard deviation in the MC score is associated with an 8 to 11 per cent significant increase in productivity. The interaction terms with firm size category are significant, as confirmed by further marginal results. However, we do not find a significant association with firms' market power.[9]

Even though a large number of biases are technically controlled for, variations in MC remain unexplained. Rather, the statement is that MC does matter among

[9] A useful comparison for challenging the validity of these results is the paper of McKenzie and Woodruff (2016), in which the effect of business practices on profits is large (22 per cent at the mean for a one standard deviation in MC).

micro and small firms, at least as much as it matters among medium ones. The results of low estimated mark-ups and insignificant association between mark-ups and MC can be interpreted as follows: in highly competitive markets (concentrated in some specific sectors such as food and beverages, fabricated metal production, etc.), MC is important for firms to gain technical efficiency rather than to acquire greater market power. It is further shown that the part of MC score related to entrepreneurial attitude (innovation) is the more significant factor when considering all indicators separately rather than when combined.

The implications of these results are, however, not straightforward. By using observational data we are able to employ a more complex measure of MC, including elements that one cannot exogenously change with a training programme. But a key preliminary question would be to determine whether MC, and in particular its EO component, is teachable at all. If the observed variations find no explanation, one would be left with the frustrating justification of unobserved individual talent (as Balzac attributes to *Monsieur Graslin*, whose education level plays no part in explaining entrepreneurial talent). A rough indication is given by regressing MC scores on the set of available individual characteristics with OLS to provide some insights into its variation. Around 30 per cent of the variance of the MC score is explained by the (limited number of) individual characteristics. Yet, besides younger individuals having higher MC scores, education has by far the largest influence. The little variance explained can be interpreted as proof of the relevance of the MC index—which indicates more than the differences in education.

References

Ackerberg, D. A., K. Caves, and G. Frazer (2015). Identification properties of recent production function estimator, *Econometrica*, 83(6), 2411–51.

Berge, L. I. O., K. Bjorvatn, and B. Tungodden (2014). Human and financial capital for microenterprise development: Evidence from a field and lab experiment, *Management Science*, 61(4), 707–22.

Bernard, A. B., S. Redding, and P. K. Schott (2009). Products and productivity, *Scandinavian Journal of Economics*, 111(4), 681–709.

Berrone, P., H. Gertel, R. Giuliodori., L. Bernard, and E. Meiners (2014). Determinants of performance in microenterprises: preliminary evidence from Argentina, *Journal of Small Business Management*, 52(3): 477–500.

Bloom, N., B. Eifert, A. Mahajan, D. McKenzie, and J. Roberts (2013). Does management matter? Evidence from India, *The Quarterly Journal of Economics*, 128(1): 1–51.

Bloom, N., A. Mahajan, D. McKenzie, and J. Roberts (2010). Why do firms in developing countries have low productivity?, *American Economic Review: Papers & Proceedings*, 100(2): 619–23.

Bloom, N., M. Schankerman, and J. Van Reenen (2013). Identifying technology spillovers and product market rivalry, *Econometrica*, 81(4): 1347–93.

Bradford, W. D. (2007). Distinguishing economically from legally formal firms: Targeting business support to entrepreneurs in South Africa's townships, *Journal of Small Business Management*, 45(1): 94–115.

Bruhn, M., D. Karlan, and A. Schoar (2010). 'What capital is missing in developing countries?, *American Economic Review: Papers & Proceedings*, 100(2): 629–33.

Campos, H. M., L. S. A. Acuña, J. P. N. de la Parra, and F. A. A. Valenzuela (2013). Entrepreneurial orientation in Mexican microenterprises, *Journal of Entrepreneurship. Management and Innovation*, 9(3): 5–20.

Cho, Y., and M. Honorati (2013). Entrepreneurship Programs in Developing Countries: A Meta Regression Analysis. Policy Research Working Paper 6402. Washington, DC: The World Bank.

Covin, J. G., and D. P. Slevin (1989). Strategic management of small firms in hostile and benign environments, *Strategic Management Journal*, 10: 75–87.

De Loecker, J., and F. Warzynski (2012). Mark-ups and firm-level export status, *The American Economic Review*, 102(6): 2437–71.

De Mel, S., D. McKenzie, and C. Woodruff (2008). Returns to capital in microenterprises: Evidence from a field experiment. *Quarterly Journal of Economics*, 123(4), 1329–72.

De Mel, S., D. McKenzie, and C. Woodruff (2014). Business training and female enterprise start-up, growth, and dynamics: Experimental evidence from Sri Lanka, *Journal of Development Economics*, 106: 199–210.

Dupas, P., and J. Robinson (2013). Savings constraints and microenterprise development: evidence from a field experiment in Kenya, *American Economic Journal: Applied Economics*, 5(1): 163–92.

Eberhardt, M., and C. Helmers (2010). Untested Assumptions and Data Slicing: A Critical Review of Firm-level Production Function Estimators. Economics Series Working Paper 513. Oxford: Department of Economics, University of Oxford.

Glaub, M., and M. Frese (2011). A critical review of the effects of entrepreneurship training in developing countries, *Enterprise Development and Microfinance*, 22(4).

Hall, R. E. (1986). Market structure and macroeconomic fluctuations, *Brookings Papers on Economic Activity*, 2, 285–322.

Hall, R. E. (1988). The relation between price and marginal cost in US industry, *Journal of Political Economy*, 96(5): 921–47.

Hall, R. E. (1990). Invariance properties of Solow's productivity residual. In P. Diamond (ed.), *Growth-Productivity-Unemployment: Essays to Celebrate Bob Solow's Birthday*. Cambridge, MA: MIT Press.

Hsieh, C-T., and P. J. Klenow (2009). Misallocation and manufacturing TFP in China and India, *Quarterly Journal of Economics*, 124(4): 1403–46.

Klette, T. J. (1999). Market power, scale economies and productivity: Estimates from a panel of establishment data, *The Journal of Industrial Economics*, 47(4): 451–76.

Levinsohn, J., and A. Petrin (2003). Estimating production functions using inputs to control for unobservables, *The Review of Economic Studies*, 70: 317–41.

Lindsay, V., N. Ashill, B. Roxas, and A. Victorio (2014). Entrepreneurial orientation and performance of microenterprises in an emerging economy, *Journal of Strategic Marketing*, 22(7): 631–56.

Lumpkin, G. T., and G. Dess (1996). Clarifying the entrepreneurial orientation construct and linking it to performance, *Academy of Management Review*, 21(1): 135–72.

McKenzie, D., and C. Woodruff (2014). What are we learning from business training and entrepreneurship evaluations around the developing world?, *World Bank Research Observer*, 29(1): 48–82.

McKenzie, D., and C. Woodruff (2016). Business practices in small firms in developing countries, *Management Science*, 63(9): 2773–3145.

Miller, D. (1983). The correlates of entrepreneurship in three types of firms, *Management Science*, 29(7): 770–92.

Munoz, J. M., D. H. B. Welsh, S. H. Chan, and P. V. Raven (2015). Microenterprises in Malaysia: A preliminary study of the factors for management success, *International Entrepreneurship and Management Journal*, 11: 673–94.

Newman, C., J. Rand, T. Talbot, and F. Tarp (2015). Technology transfers, foreign investment and productivity spillovers, *European Economic Review*, 76: 168–87.

Olley, S., and A. Pakes (1996). The dynamics of productivity in the telecommunications equipment industry, *Econometrica*, 64: 1263–98.

Petrin, A. (n.d.). Amil Petrin Website. Available at: https://sites.google.com/a/umn.edu/amil-petrin/home/Available-Programs (accessed on 26 June 2018).

Petrin, A., B. P. Poi, and J. Levinsohn (2004). Production function estimation in stata using inputs to control for unobservables, *Stata Journal*, 4(2): 113–23.

Rand, J. (2017). Comparing Estimated and Self-reported Mark-ups for Formal and Informal Firms in an Emerging Market Context. WIDER Working Paper 2017/160. Helsinki: UNU-WIDER.

Rauch, A., J. Wiklund, G. T. Lumpkin, and M. Frese (2009). Entrepreneurial orientation and business performance: Cumulative empirical evidence, *Entrepreneurship Theory and Practice*, 33(3): 761–88.

Syverson, C. (2011). What determines productivity?, *Journal of Economic Literature*, 49(2): 326–65.

UNU-WIDER (n.d.). The Small and Medium Enterprise (SME) Survey. Available at: https://www.wider.unu.edu/project/small-and-medium-enterprise-sme-survey (accessed on 19 June 2018).

Van Beveren, I. (2010). Total factor productivity estimation: A practical review, *Journal of Economic Surveys*, 26(1): 98–128.

Vial, V., and J. Hanoteau (2010). Corruption, manufacturing plant growth, and the Asian paradox: Indonesian evidence, *World Development*, 38(5): 693–705.

Wooldridge, J. M. (2009). On estimating firm-level production functions using proxy variables to control for unobservables, *Economics Letters*, 104: 112–14.

Yasar, M., R. Raciborski, and B. P. Poi (2008). Production function estimation in stata using the Olley and Pakes method, *Stata Journal*, 8(2): 1–11.

PART II

POLITICAL CONNECTIONS, INSTITUTIONAL QUALITY, AND INNOVATION

6
Are Politically Connected Firms Less Constrained in Credit Markets?

John Rand

6.1 Setting the Scene

A wide range of outcomes related to political connections of firms has been researched. These include (i) the influence on choice of dispute settlement, (ii) quality of corporate governance, (iii) initial public offering (IPO) firm value, (iv) effective tax rates paid by the company, (v) firm performance, (vi) societal cost, etc. (among others: Ang and Jia 2014; Fan et al. 2007; Adhikari et al. 2006; Faccio 2006; Claessens et al. 2008). Within this literature, some focus especially on the impact of firm-level political connections on access to formal finance. The heterogeneity in results is striking, as some studies conclude that lenders, especially in developing countries, do favor politically connected firms (e.g., Mian and Khwaja 2005; Claessens et al. 2008; Boubakri et al. 2012), while others have questioned such generalizations (Jackowicz et al. 2014; Siegel 2007), emphasizing that there are significant costs of being politically connected as well. This chapter addresses the question to what extent political connections influence firm-level access to formal finance of small and medium enterprises (SMEs) in Vietnam, taking into account that there may be heterogeneity in firm-level access to cheaper informal credit options.

The literature studying the benefits of political connectedness often takes point of departure in the resource dependency theory, which studies how external resources affect organizational behaviour. Resources form the basis of power, which is relational and situational, and can be mutual between actors within a network (Pfeffer and Salancik 1978). Using this perspective, political connections facilitate relatively easier access to relevant resources (such as access to finance) and increase the likelihood of receiving government contracts. Assuming that there is only a limited amount of political capital available for private firms to acquire, and that political ties lead to preferential access to resources (bank lending), inequality of political capital across locations is one key determinant of the benefit a firm can derive from acquiring such capital. The underlying rationale then becomes that the more political capital there is available, the smaller the returns to acquiring such capital will become.

John Rand, *Are Politically Connected Firms Less Constrained in Credit Markets?* In: *Micro, Small, and Medium Enterprises in Vietnam*. Edited by: John Rand and Finn Tarp, Oxford University Press (2020).
DOI: 10.1093/oso/9780198851189.003.0006

Using the resource perspective Leuz and Oberholzer-Gee (2006) find, in the case of Indonesia, that political connections help to attain preferential local financing, but work at the expense of a dynamic integration into global financial markets. However, cross-country evidence by Richter (2010) shows that political connections help improve a company's access to finance *beyond* the domestic debt markets. It is further suggested that political connections hereby are a firm-level substitute for strong national property rights that can therefore reduce the perceived risk of connected firms in an environment with low rule of law. Studying the lending behaviour of Pakistani firms between 1996 and 2002, Mian and Khwaja (2005) observe that politically connected firms borrow more than unconnected firms, and have a remarkable 50 per cent higher default rate on their liabilities. The analysis further reveals that the political status is the sole driver thereof, and that the benefits increase according to the political importance of the respective connection. Interestingly, their findings are not robust for private lenders, which indicates that political connections only facilitate access to credit from state-influenced financial institutions. Given that two-thirds of formal financing to the Vietnamese SMEs considered in our sample come from State Owned Commercial Banks (SOCBs), this result may be of particular importance in the context of Vietnam.

Another argument is that government ties can help overcome market/state imperfection such as red-tape, low enforcement of property rights, heavy government regulations or 'extra-legal fees' (Chen et al. 2011). This is in accordance with the argument that 'Chinese managers rely perhaps more heavily on the cultivation of personal relationships to cope with the exigencies of their situation' (Child 1994: 150). Li et al. (2008) examine how membership of the communist party affects performance of Chinese private firms in an environment of continued ideological discrimination against private ownership. The authors observe a positive effect conditional on firm-specific variables, and attribute most of the effect to lower cost-of-capital facing political connected firms. Interestingly, the influence is stronger in regions with weaker institutions and legal protection (Li et al. 2008). Studying how the cost of equity capital correlates with being politically connected, Boubakri et al. (2012) confirm this observation in a cross-country study addressing possible endogeneity concerns, where the authors find that political connections lower the cost-of-capital, especially for older and larger firms and for firms operating in weaker institutional environments.

When examining the disadvantages of being politically connected, point of departure can be taken in the argument that government bureaucrats tend to be more interested in rent seeking and political objectives than longer-term corporate and industry efficiency (Shleifer and Vishny 1998). Political connections can therefore be seen as unfavourable, because of the concomitant increased exposure to government actors. In a politically unstable environment (Poland) Jackowicz et al. (2014) show how the operational performance of non-listed firms is negatively affected by political connections, and that this negative influence on firm performance is intensified as the number of connections rises. Supportive evidence in Siegel (2007) analyses how South Korean firms shape cross-border alliances based on connections to socio-political networks. Network connections to political enemies of the respective current regime in power are found to substantially slow the rate at which cross-border strategic alliances are established. As such, overall industry dynamics are distorted, harming both politically connected and unconnected firms in the economy. Finally, in a study in France, Bertrand et al. (2018) find that political connections impose significant economic costs on firms, as firm managers and owners grant political favours to local government in the form of generating employment opportunities around election time. Moreover, politically connected firms have a lower operating profit due to relatively higher labour cost (per unit efficiency). Furthermore, Fan et al. (2007) show how political connections can negatively influence companies' performance, as the connections tend to harm the board of directors' corporate governance.

In an effort to reconcile such contrasting findings on the costs and benefits of political connectedness, several studies take a contingency perspective that identifies ownership, the enterprise's stage of development, and/or the quality of the political connections as underlying cause of the ambiguous outcomes (e.g., Du and Girma 2010; Peng and Luo 2000; Chen et al. 2011). As an example, Du and Girma (2010) use a panel of over 106,000 Chinese private start up enterprises between 1999 and 2004 and they find that political connections do enhance firm survival. However, conditional on firm survival, productivity growth is higher in firms that operate without political connections while politically connected firms are more focused on job creation. Furthermore, the benefits of political affiliation are stronger in capital-intensive industries and in cases where the firm is connected to local, rather than prefecture-level authorities. The authors also conclude that in terms of overall efficiency, political connections lead to a suboptimal allocation of resources, and especially credit, by interfering with traditional market forces. A similar argument has been brought forward by Chen et al. (2011) who observe that firms are more likely to establish political connections where market orientation of the local economy is low and where the government's discretion in allocation of economic resources is high. Thereby, incentives for officials to engage in rent-seeking motivate private firms to seek political connections in order to protect themselves from such behaviour, which relates to Shleifer and Vishny's (1998) notion of the state as a 'grabbing hand'.

To summarize, the existing literature relies on the resource dependency of firms and the grabbing hand of a rent-seeking state to motivate arguments for positive or negative firm outcomes of political connections. While ambiguous outcomes are observed, contingency perspectives try to understand how and why outcomes differ, and highlight that the impact of political connections is highly context-specific. To our knowledge there is only limited firm-level evidence regarding the impact of political connections in Vietnam, and the fact that most of existing research stems from countries with more volatile political environments, raises the question to which extent existing research applies to Vietnam. We know of one study for Vietnam at the firm level studying the impact of political connections on credit access (Malesky and Taussig 2009). Using data from 6,400 firms across all provinces in 2006 it is observed that one additional political connection increases the probability of obtaining a loan by 4 per cent. During a subsequent test of the impact of credit access on firm performance, the authors however observe that political connections do not influence profit or investment growth. These results challenge the assertion that relationship-based lending is an effective substitute for legal institutions. Rather, they indicate that political connections are ineffective in channelling bank credit to the most profitable investors. However, this study (given its cross-sectional nature) is subject to concerns of individual heterogeneity being a simultaneous driver of both access to finance and political connectedness.

This chapter instead utilizes a panel of small and medium enterprises (SMEs) observed biannually between 2005 and 2015. Controlling for unobserved time-invariant firm-level heterogeneity as well as differences in productivity between firms (to indirectly control for self-selection of the most productive firms into being politically connected) and having access to informal credit markets, we show that firm owner membership of the Communist Party of Vietnam (CPV) (all else equal) decreases the likelihood of being constrained in formal financial markets by 4 percentage points. In addition, when accessing formal credit, politically connected firms face 2–5 per cent lower cost-of-capital than non-connected SMEs. Finally, we document that political connections are especially valuable during periods of financial distress both in terms of credit access and cost-of-capital when obtaining loans from formal financial institutions, whereas these benefits are less prevalent during business cycle upswings.

6.2 Defining Credit Constraints and Political Connectedness

Data to analyse the relationship between politically connected firms and access to finance and credit constraints come from the Vietnam Small and Medium Enterprise (VSME) tracer panel survey carried out biannually between 2005 and 2015 in the following nine provinces in Vietnam: Ha Noi (including Ha Tay), Hai Phong, Ho Chi Minh City, Phu Tho, Nghe An, Quang Nam, Khanh Hoa, Lam Dong, and Long An (CIEM 2006, 2008, 2010, 2012, 2014, and 2016).[1] It should be noted that although the survey focuses on SMEs, the tracer dimension of the data

[1] Provinces were not chosen randomly. It was decided that the surveys should cover the main urban cities as well as selected rural areas. The choice of rural provinces was driven by funding related issues (each selected province was either a Danida or Sida focus province at the time).

allows to track and interview firms with more than 300 employees, if they have been previously interviewed. The data are based on face-to-face interviews with owners/managers of businesses and are collected in the months of June–August. The sampling frame of the tracer survey was established in 2005, where the population of listed non-state manufacturing enterprises in the selected provinces was established based on two data sources from the General Statistics Office of Vietnam (GSO); the Establishment Census from 2002 and the Industrial Survey of 2002–04.[2] Additional details on the sampling can be found in CIEM (2006).

One important aspect of the data needs attention. The majority of firms considered are smaller household businesses. Some of these are administratively listed firms (sampled appropriately using census data information), and others are non-listed household businesses (obtained through on-site 'block' identification) operating alongside the formal entities. Thus, while the group of listed firms well represents the 'formal' manufacturing sector in the ten selected provinces, our sample of informal household businesses may not be representative of 'non-listed' manufacturing firms in Vietnam, as they may represent the more established and productive informal entities. The distinction between formal and informal enterprises may be important when analysing credit access. On the one hand, informal businesses will not be eligible for formal loans in the company name, but have to rely on formal financing obtained based on personal wealth records without reliance on firm assets as collateral. On the other hand, since the data at hand (for the majority part) are smaller household businesses, informality will not necessarily matter that much for the relative probability of obtaining formal financing. Results reveal that using a control for being a household business and/or being an informal business did not change the results. We therefore in the following only report results from distinguishing between household and non-household enterprises.

6.2.1 Defining Political Connectedness

Vietnam is by and large a one-party nation with four formal political structures making up the regime: (i) the CPV, (ii) the people's armed forces, (iii) the Vietnam Fatherland Front and (iv) the state bureaucracy. Through the National Party Congress, the CPV elects the Central Committee (CC), which again elects the Politburo. Most political power is entrusted in these two government entities. The CPV sets the policy direction, which is implemented through different sub-levels of government (national, provincial, district, commune). At the sub-national level,

[2] The population of individual business establishments that do not satisfy the conditions stated in the Law on Enterprises of Vietnam (also referred to as household enterprises) is obtained from the Establishment Census. This information is combined with data on enterprises formally registered under the Law on Enterprises from the Industrial Survey; see CIEM (2006) for details.

the People's Council (PC) is the highest legislative institution, and it selects the People's Committee (PCOM) to serve as the executive institution at each respective local governmental level. PC members, who in most cases are members of the Communist Party (Malesky et al. 2014), are selected through voter elections. Members of local PCOMs are also elected, but by PC members only, and their choice needs the consent of the PCOM at the next higher level (Kerkvliet and Marr 2004).[3] As such, membership of the Communist Party seems to a necessary first step for closer ties to local legislative and executive government bodies. Before the 12th National Congress of the CPV it was estimated that over 4.5 million members were represented. This indicates that only around 5 per cent of the population are members of the CPV.

As alluded to in the introduction, being politically connected may bring both benefits and costs, which is also illustrated in Gainsborough (2010) in the case of Vietnam. In Vietnam, new private entrepreneurs continued to have relatively strong political ties after the initiation of the Vietnamese Doi Moi reform process. Some of these new entrepreneurs even stayed directly politically involved in local government matters, and a non-negligible batch of younger private sector entrepreneurs were children of the political elite. Gainsborough (2010) even states that to succeed in business, private companies are reliant on local governments; a statement clearly signalling the potential benefits of being politically connected. One mechanism highlighted in Gainsborough (2010) goes through easier access to formal finance, which is the focus of this paper. However, there is also evidence signalling that the benefits of being politically connected at the local level in Vietnam may be limited. Local government have generally been more accountable toward higher levels of government than toward local populations and businesses (Markussen and Tarp 2014), and public funding has generally prioritized infrastructure, health and education, and offered relatively little support to private businesses (Malesky et al. 2014).

In this chapter, we use an indicator variable taking the value 1 if the firm owner is member of the CPV, and zero otherwise, as proxy for political connectedness. In Tables 5. 1A and 1B we document summary statistics, by political connectedness and by year, for all variables subsequently used in the analysis of the impact of political connections on the probability of being financially constrained. Related to our definition, we see that 8.1 per cent of the sample are politically connected, ranging from 7.1 in 2007 to 9.4 in 2011. Note that variation exists even when only considering the balanced panel; a variation that we are utilizing below for identification. Moreover, Table 6.1A shows that differences exist between politically connected firms and non-connected firms along observable characteristics. Politically connected firms are larger, have higher debt-ratios, lower profit shares and are more formal (less likely to be a household firm).

[3] Further details on Vietnamese election processes can be found in Malesky and Schuler (2011).

Table 6.1A Summary statistics, by connectedness

	All	Politically connected	Not Connected	
Politically connected	0.081	1.000	0.000	*
Credit constrained (Yes=1)	0.258	0.241	0.260	
Have informal loans (Yes=1)	0.578	0.597	0.577	
Number of employees (log)	1.736	1.965	1.716	*
Revenue (log)	13.465	13.637	13.450	*
Capital stock (log)	13.647	13.854	13.629	*
Intermediate Inputs (log)	13.003	13.169	12.988	*
Debt ratio	0.077	0.102	0.074	*
Have debt (Yes=1)	0.504	0.560	0.500	*
Profit share	0.652	0.621	0.654	*
Household business (Yes==1)	0.692	0.568	0.703	*
Number of observations	13,819	1,117	12,702	

Table 6.1B Summary statistics, by year

	2005	2007	2009	2011	2013	2015
Politically connected	0.085	0.071	0.073	0.094	0.091	0.071
Credit constrained (Yes=1)	0.253	0.241	0.266	0.280	0.308	0.207
Have informal loans (Yes=1)	..	0.596	0.695	0.640	0.624	0.340
Number of employees (log)	1.904	1.832	1.778	1.697	1.615	1.574
Revenue (log)	13.379	13.449	13.567	13.490	13.436	13.471
Capital stock (log)	13.499	13.699	13.738	13.886	13.628	13.450
Intermediate inputs (log)	12.917	12.978	13.136	13.018	12.987	12.982
Debt ratio	0.092	0.084	0.081	0.064	0.064	0.072
Have debt (Yes=1)	0.575	0.531	0.581	0.487	0.492	0.355
Profit share	0.634	0.670	0.659	0.662	0.648	0.639
Household business (Yes==1)	0.720	0.716	0.689	0.681	0.673	0.668
Number of observations	2,446	2,324	2,341	2,227	2,166	2,315

Note: * indicates differences in means tested at the 5% significance level.
Source: author's calculations.

6.2.2 Defining Credit-Constrained Firms

Defining firm-level credit constraints has been discussed intensively in the small and medium size enterprise (SME) literature over the last couple of decades. Beck and Demirgüç-Kunt (2006) use the World Business Environment Survey (WBES) data and utilize a perception-based approach were firms are asked whether they perceive themselves as financially constrained and whether this is creating an obstacle to their firm growth. Hansen and Rand (2014a) show that using Investment Climate Assessment (ICA) surveys almost 50 per cent of the firms perceive lack of access to credit to be a serious or very serious constraint to firm growth.

Moreover, in the context of Vietnam, Rand (2007) shows that more than 50 per cent of SMEs perceive access to finance as the most severe obstacle to firm growth.

As also emphasized in Hansen and Rand (2014b), perceptions about being financially constrained does not imply that the firms are in fact credit-constrained. Boulier and Goldfarb (1998) summarize the discussion about how (and if) surveys should be used for analysis of economic inference. They conclude that the reliability of these different types of survey data information can be ranked, and according to their analysis, the most reliable information is obtained through simple direct questions (i) related to an action taken in relation to a given activity and (ii) easily verifiable through a 'third party'. As such, perception-based questions are not seen as a reliable source of information.

Focusing on credit-related questions, the recommendations in Boulier and Goldfarb (1998) would rank a question such as 'Has your firm during the past two years applied for a bank loan?' as more reliable than a subjective/perception-based question such as 'Do you think that the access to credit presents any obstacle to the current operations of your establishment?' In the following we therefore base our credit constraint definition only on questions that would rank highly in a Boulier and Goldfarb (1998) reliability classification.

In addition, our measure of credit constraints needs to ensure that constrained firms are only classified for firms having credit demand. Here we address this form of selection bias following Bigsten et al. (2003), Rand (2007), Bentzen et al. (2010) and Hansen and Rand (2014a, 2014b) in (i) first identifying firms with demand for credit, and (ii) conditional on credit demand, identifying credit-constrained firms. Following the reliability criteria described above, we in this chapter apply the following question to distinguish between firms with and without credit demand: 'no need for a loan – firm has sufficient capital'.

As in previous literature cited above, we classify a firm as credit-constrained if it (i) applied for and was denied credit or (ii) did not apply for credit due to reasons such as 'application procedures too complex', 'collateral requirements unattainable', or 'possible loan size and maturity insufficient'. Firms not applying for a loan and responding 'interest rates too high' or 'did not think it would be approved' as reasons for not applying are still labelled as being financially constrained as these answers may reflect that the investment project applied for is not competitive at going interest rates.

Tables 5.1A and 1B report that 25.8 per cent of the sample can be classified as financially constrained. This number reflects a steady increase from 2005–13 (from 25.3–30.8 per cent), accompanied by a significant drop in 2015 to only 20.7 per cent being credit-constrained (in formal financial markets). Moreover, this significant drop in credit-constrained firms in 2015 is accompanied by a significant reduction in the number of firms having informal loans, but is also reflecting that only one-third of firms in 2015 have debt as compared to around half of the firms in the other survey years. As such, the 2015 decline in credit-constrained firms may be reflecting a general decline in debt demand. Note also from Table 6.1A, that no apparent difference in credit access (formal or informal) is found between politically connected and non-connected firms. This apparent lack of relationship between being politically connected and being financially constrained is what we put under deeper scrutiny in the next sections.

6.3 Empirical Approach and Results

We operate with several different specifications for analysing the relationship between the probability of being credit-constrained and political connectedness. First, we rely on the following simple pooled non-linear (probit) model:

$$c_{it} = 1[\beta_0 + \beta_1 member_{it} + \acute{x}_{it}\sigma + \epsilon_{it} > 0], \tag{6.1}$$

where c is an indicator variable taking the value of one if the firm is defined as credit-constrained and zero otherwise, *member* = 1 if the firm owner is a member of the communist party and zero otherwise, x contains proxies for credit access, and ϵ is a firm-specific error term.

However, the above specification does not utilize the dynamics observed in political connectedness over time. We therefore also estimate the following pooled non-linear (logit) model:

$$P(c_{it} = 1) = \frac{exp[\gamma_0 + \gamma_1 entry_{it} + \gamma_2 always_{it} + \acute{x}_{it}\sigma + \epsilon_{it}]}{1 + exp[\gamma_0 + \gamma_1 entry_{it} + \gamma_2 always_{it} + \acute{x}_{it}\sigma + \epsilon_{it}]}, \tag{6.2}$$

where *entry* = 1 if the firm owner goes from not being politically connected in period t−1 to becoming connected in period t (and zero otherwise), and *always* = 1 if the firm owner is politically connected throughout the 2005–15 period. The coefficient on γ_1 measures the difference in credit constraints for political 'switchers' as compared to firms staying politically unconnected throughout the period under study. The coefficient γ_2 measures a similar difference in the probability of being credit-constrained between politically unconnected firms to firms who are connected throughout the period under study.

As the above specification does not fully control for the individual fixed effects affecting the probability of being credit-constrained we as a robustness check also run the following conditional fixed-effects logit model:

$$P(c_{it} = 1) = \frac{exp[\gamma_0 + \gamma_1 member_{it} + a_i + \acute{x}_{it}\sigma + \epsilon_{it}]}{1 + exp[\gamma_0 + \gamma_1 member_{it} + a_i + \acute{x}_{it}\sigma + \epsilon_{it}]}, \tag{6.3}$$

where a_i represents the firm-specific fixed effect.

Finally, we have to acknowledge that the relatively vibrant informal sector credit market may influence credit constraint determinants in formal credit markets, especially for smaller household businesses. In order to take into account the interaction of formal and informal financial markets, we will model the determination of credit access in the two sectors jointly using a non-linear biprobit model, which utilizes the fact that the propensity to have a loan in formal and informal financial markets may not be independent:

$$c_{it} = 1[\beta_{10} + \beta_{11} member_{it} + \acute{x}_{1it}\sigma + \epsilon_{1it} > 0] \tag{6.4}$$

$$i_{it} = 1[\beta_{20} + \beta_{21} member_{it} + \acute{x}_{2it}\sigma + \epsilon_{2it} > 0],$$

where $\epsilon_{1it}$and ϵ_{2it} have mean zero and unit variance, such that $(\epsilon_{1it}, \epsilon_{2it}) \sim binorm(0, 0, 1, 1, \rho)$ and $\rho$is the coefficient of correlation.

Table 6.2 reports the results from specification (1). Column 1 only includes time-fixed effects in addition to the reported variables, whereas column 2 also include both location- and sector-fixed effects. Column 3 adds additional variables (described in Tables 5.1 and 5.2) likely to influence credit market access. Finally, in columns 4 and 5 we do the analysis separately for household business and non-HH firm entities. We consistently find that politically connected firm owners are less likely to be constrained in formal credit markets. Controlling for location- and sector-fixed effects we consistently find that membership of the communist party lowers the probability of being financially constrained by 4 percentage points.

Table 6.3 reports results from specification (2) for the full sample (column 1), household firms only (column 2) and non-HH enterprises (column 3), respectively. It should be noted that this specification excludes firms that lost or did not state precisely the nature of their political connections, which reduces the sample by approximately 1,100 observations (8 per cent). We find that firms that are politically connected throughout the survey and firms switching into connectedness are significantly less likely to be constrained in formal credit markets, confirming the overall results in Table 6.2. Coefficient estimates for the full sample in panel A, column 1 are equivalent to marginal effect estimates of -0.055 (always) and −0.062 (entry), respectively. This means that excluding firm owners who lose their membership (mostly due to change of owner) or who did not precisely state the nature of their political connection (party membership or local cadre member) increases the marginal effects as compared to results in Table 6.2. Moreover, it should be noted that the effect is larger in non-HH enterprises. Panel B of Table 6.3 reports results from estimating specification (3). Allowing for individual fixed effects strengthens the conclusion, leading to the result that political connections reduce the probability of being credit-constrained, especially for non-HH enterprises.

Finally, in Panel A of Table 6.4 we report results from the bivariate probit model (specification (4)). The reported test for independence between the equations shows that the null hypothesis of independence is rejected and in Panel B of

Table 6.2 Credit constraint determinants

	1		2		3		4		5	
	All		All		All		Household firms		Non-HH firms	
Politically connected	**−0.030***	**(1.96)**	**−0.040*****	(2.71)	**−0.042*****	(2.83)	**−0.046****	(2.49)	*	(1.66)
Number of employees (log)	0.025***	(4.14)	0.019***	(2.94)	0.000	(0.01)	0.013	(1.26)	−0.009	(0.73)
Capital stock (log)	−0.016***	(4.55)	−0.021***	(5.84)	−0.019***	(5.12)	−0.017***	(4.06)	−0.023***	(2.93)
Intermediate Inputs (log)	0.024***	(5.78)	0.023***	(5.46)	0.023***	(5.23)	0.019***	(3.76)	0.021***	(2.34)
Time-fixed effects	Yes		Yes		Yes		Yes		Yes	
Province-fixed effects	No		Yes		Yes		Yes		Yes	
Sector-fixed effects	No		Yes		Yes		Yes		Yes	
Additional controls	No		No		Yes		Yes		Yes	
Observations	13,819		13,819		13,819		9,561		4,258	
Pseudo R-sq	0.014		0.033		0.036		0.036		0.033	

Note: t-stats (in parentheses) clustered at the firm level. *** indicates significance at the 1% level, ** at the 5% level, and * at the 10% level.

Source: author's calculations.

Table 6.3 Always connected versus getting connected

PANEL A: Pooled logit						
	1		2		3	
	All		Household firms		Non-HH firms	
Always connected	**−0.318****	(2.17)	−0.308	(1.56)	**−0.388***	(1.81)
Entry (getting connected)	**−0.362****	(2.12)	−0.257	(1.21)	**−0.577****	(2.22)
Production function controls	Yes		Yes		Yes	
Time-fixed effects	Yes		Yes		Yes	
Province-fixed effects	Yes		Yes		Yes	
Sector-fixed effects	Yes		Yes		Yes	
Additional controls	Yes		Yes		Yes	
Observations	12,696		8,920		3,776	
Pseudo R-sq	0.036		0.035		0.037	

PANEL B: Conditional fixed effects Logit						
	1		2		3	
	All		Household firms		Non-HH firms	
Entry (getting connected)	**−0.592*****	(2.61)	−0.308	(1.06)	**−0.989****	(2.40)
Time-fixed effects	Yes		Yes		Yes	
Production function controls	Yes		Yes		Yes	
Additional controls	Yes		Yes		Yes	
Observations	7,241		4,939		1,967	
Firms	1,726		1,153		551	

Note: t-stats (in parentheses) clustered at the firm level. *** indicates significance at the 1% level, ** at the 5% level, and * at the 10% level.

Source: author's calculations.

Table 6.4 we also confirm that the likelihood of being constrained in formal credit markets is significantly related to having obtained an informal loan (if a firm has an informal loan the probability of being financially constrained in formal credit markets is 15 per cent higher than if the firm does not have informal loans). The results of the bivariate probit model therefore suggests that the informal credit market is a (good) substitute for the formal credit market, especially for smaller household enterprises (not reported). In addition, we see from column 2, that conditioning on having access to informal credit, the well-determined effect of politically connections on reducing the probability of being constrained in formal financial markets is only maintained by newly connected firms.

Table 6.4 Formal versus informal lending

PANEL A: Biprobit—constrained and informal lender				
	Constrained	Informal	Constrained	Informal
Politically connected	**−0.096***	**−0.120****		
	(1.83)	**(2.39)**		
Always connected			**−0.135**	**−0.278*****
			(1.47)	**(3.25)**
Entry (getting connected)			**−0.203****	**−0.009**
			(2.06)	**(0.11)**
Time-fixed effects	Yes		Yes	
Province-fixed effects	Yes		Yes	
Sector-fixed effects	Yes		Yes	
Additional controls	Yes		Yes	
Observations	11,373		10,452	
Rho	0.307	17.00	0.311	16.53
Wald test (p-value)	0.000		0.000	

PANEL B: Pooled logit—constrained with informal lender control				
	1		2	
	All		All	
Politically connected	**−0.114**	(1.29)		
Always connected			**−0.119**	(0.77)
Entry (getting connected)			**−0.345****	(2.00)
Informal	**0.871*****	(16.86)	**0.882*****	(16.36)
Time-fixed effects	Yes		Yes	
Province-fixed effects	Yes		Yes	
Sector-fixed effects	Yes		Yes	
Additional controls	Yes		Yes	
Observations	11,373		10,452	
Pseudo R-sq	0.059		0.060	

Note: t-stats (in parentheses) clustered at the firm level. *** indicates significance at the 1% level, ** at the 5% level, and * at the 10% level.

Source: author's calculations.

Overall, we therefore conclude that we find a well-determined relationship between becoming politically connected and having easier access to formal financial markets. And this reduced probability of being credit-constrained in formal markets does not reduce the firm's probability of obtaining informal financing.

Table 6.5 documents simple loan characteristics for formal and informal loans respectively. Looking at formal loans in Panel A, we see that two-thirds of formal loans are obtained from State Owned Commercial Banks (SOCBs), most loans require collateral, and both of these seem independent of whether the firm owner is politically connected or not. Moreover, interest rates do not seem to differ along

Table 6.5 Formal versus informal loan characteristics

Panel A: Formal loans	1A All	2A Connected	3A All with informal	4A Connected with informal
State bank	0.667	0.672	0.675	0.627
Interest rate (%/month)	1.120	1.112	1.144	1.123
Collateral needed	0.922	0.892	0.931	0.881
Panel B: Informal loans	**1B All**	**2B Connected**	**3B All with formal**	**4B Connected with formal**
Friends and family	0.615	0.554	0.584	0.559
Interest rate (%/month)	0.678	0.821	0.827	0.844
Loans with no interest (share of total)	0.559	0.432	0.479	0.407
Collateral needed	0.082	0.071	0.099	0.102

Source: author's calculations.

the connectedness dimension, and formal loan characteristics do not seem to differ conditioning on having access to informal loans (columns 3 and 4). In Panel B of Table 6.5, we document the characteristics of the informal loans obtained by firms. Almost two-thirds of these loans are from friends and family and many of these loans are obtained without having to pay interest. In addition, few informal loans require collateral. In our sample of almost 14,000 SME observations we on average find that informal loans are smaller, easier to obtain and cheaper. As such, informal lending markets seem to be a competitive alternative to formal financing among smaller SMEs. Interestingly, it also looks as if politically connected firms face higher cost of informal capital than their non-connected counterparts do.

Given the differences in attributes between politically connected SMEs and non-connected firms, in Table 6.6 we run simple cost-of-capital regressions for formal loans, controlling for the observable heterogeneity between the two groups. Column (1) only includes production function and credit access controls in addition to year-fixed effects. Column (2) adds a control for access to SOCBs. Being politically connected may facilitate easier (and maybe cheaper) access to SOCB finance, but it may also create a negative lock-in effect (negative network externalities may force politically connected firms to obtain finance from a specific SOCB, maybe even at a higher cost than the alternative financial opportunities available—weakness of strong ties argument). Column (3) adds location- and sector-fixed effects, whereas column (4) tests whether there has been cost-of-capital changes over time for politically connected firms.

First, we see that the cost of formal capital is lower for politically connected firms. Being politically connected lowers interest rates on formal loans with between 0.025 and 0.057 percentage points, equivalent to a 2.2–5.1 per cent

Table 6.6 Cost of capital and political connectedness

	1	2	3	4
	Formal loan	Formal loan	Formal loan	Formal loan
Politically connected	−0.034**	−0.037**	−0.025*	−0.057***
	(1.99)	(2.36)	(1.68)	(2.67)
Loan from SOCB		0.164***	0.160***	0.160***
		(14.23)	(13.70)	(13.67)
Connected#2007				−0.004
				(0.14)
Connected#2009				0.066
				(1.49)
Connected#2011				−0.002
				(0.03)
Connected#2013				0.097**
				(2.00)
Connected#2015				0.078**
				(2.33)
Production function controls	Yes	Yes	Yes	Yes
Time-fixed effects	Yes	Yes	Yes	Yes
Additional controls	Yes	Yes	Yes	Yes
Location-fixed effects	No	No	Yes	Yes
Sector-fixed effects	No	No	Yes	Yes
Observations	3,522	3,522	3,522	3,522
R-sq	0.314	0.367	0.418	0.419

Note: t-stats (in parentheses) clustered at the firm level. *** indicates significance at the 1% level, ** at the 5% level, and * at the 10% level.

Source: author's calculations.

lower cost-of-capital than non-connected SMEs. We also see that obtaining a loan from a SOCB is relatively more expensive than receiving external finance from a formal private bank (about 0.016 percentage points difference in interest rates). However, this is not explaining the difference in interest payments between connected and non-connected firms (column 2), and controlling for location and sector only reduces the coefficient on party membership but the estimate remains well-determined at the 10 per cent level. Finally, column 4 shows that the favourable cost-of-capital conditions for politically connected firms has diminished in recent years, and in fact in 2013 and 2015, we find no differential cost-of-capital effect along the connectedness dimension.

Having documented that politically connected firms over the period 2005–2015 are less credit constrained and had more favourable loan conditions (at least in the earlier years) when obtaining external finance, makes it interesting to do a back-of-the-envelope estimate of the differences in the desired level of debt for politically connected and unconnected firms, respectively. Following the approach by Rand (2007), we use a two-step sample selection model, recording whether enterprises with positive debt holdings are credit-constrained and conditional on being a credit-constrained firm, holding positive debt, and estimate the desired level of debt of the individual firm.

The estimation problem is that the desired debt level of a firm is only observed if the firm has positive debt and the firm cannot be labelled as being financially constrained. Direct estimation of the demand for formal external financing using all firms will be therefore biased if the same variables determining whether a firm has debt or is credit-constrained, also affect the level of observed debt. Therefore, inverse Mills ratios from estimating a (i) debt probability model and (ii) credit constraint probability model, have to be obtained, and thereafter the demand for debt can be modelled as:

$$d_i = \beta_1 x_i + \beta_2 \frac{\varphi(c_i)}{F(c_i)} + \beta_3 \frac{\varphi(b_i)}{F(b_i)}, \tag{6.5}$$

where $\frac{\varphi(c_i)}{F(c_i)}$ and $\frac{\varphi(b_i)}{F(b_i)}$ are the inverse Mill's ratios for being credit-constrained and having debt, respectively, and $\varphi(*)$ and $F(*)$ are the probability and cumulative distribution functions, respectively. Having estimated determinants for demand of external finance using (6.5) (not reported) we inquire how much SMEs would increase their debt burden if all credit constraints were removed and their desire for external finance was fully met. This we do for the (i) full sample, (ii) political connected firms and (iii) non-connected firms. Based on these estimates the so-called credit gap can be calculated using the approach in Rand (2007) as:

$$GAP = d_c \frac{f_c}{f} + d_{uc} \frac{f_{uc}}{f} - d_a = \beta_1 x_c \frac{f_c}{f} + d_{uc} \frac{f_{uc}}{f} - d_a, \tag{6.6}$$

where d_c and d_{uc} are desired debt for constrained and unconstrained firms, respectively; f_c and f_{uc} are the number of constrained and unconstrained firms respectively, and d_a is the average actual debt. Means of observables for the constrained firms are represented by x_c and β_1 are the estimates obtained from (6.5).

Table 6.7 shows that the average debt burden lies between 1.7 (in 2007) and 4.7 (in 2013) per cent. Given that the number of credit-constrained firms is between 20.7 (in 2015) and 30.8 (in 2013) per cent of the sample, this signals (using equation (6)) that Vietnamese SMEs would increase their debt burden by 20.4 (2007) to 72.2 (2013) per cent if all credit constraints were removed. Looking at the trend, unfulfilled credit demand is as expected increasing from 2007–2013 during the period of financial distress, but sharply declining in 2015. Moreover, we note that especially during the crisis period (2007–11) politically connected firms have much less unfulfilled credit demand than non-connected SMEs. These back-off-the-envelope calculations therefore suggest that political connections are especially valuable in terms of access to formal external finance during periods of financial distress (both in terms of credit access, non-rationing and cost-of-capital), whereas these benefits are less prevalent during more financially favourable periods.

Table 6.7 Credit gap by year and connectedness

		2007	2009	2011	2013	2015
All	Loanable funds need	1.7	3.2	2.7	4.7	3.2
	Constrained firms demand	20.4	38.6	42.3	72.2	43.6
Politically connected	Loanable funds need	0.1	3.4	−1,3	5.9	2.7
	Constrained firms demand	0.4	32.1	−14,7	70.5	26.4
Unconnected	Loanable funds need	1.9	3.2	2.8	4.7	3.2
	Constrained firms demand	22.9	40.7	46.2	75.5	46.4

Source: author's calculations.

6.4 Conclusion

In the context of SMEs in Vietnam this paper asked the simple questions: Are politically connected firms (i) more likely to get formal credit and (ii) if obtaining finance, do they receive cheaper loans. Results reveal—controlling for unobserved time-invariant firm-level heterogeneity, productivity self-selection concerns, and access to alternative credit markets—that having a firm owner that is (or becomes) a member of the Communist Party of Vietnam is linked with a lower likelihood of being constrained in formal financial markets. In addition, politically connected firms obtaining formal finance face on average lower cost-of-capital than non-connected SMEs. However, results also indicate that the impact of political connections is most valuable during periods of financial distress. Whether this preferential treatment in formal credit markets of politically connected firms is a causally dominating mechanism with respect to the overall impact on firm performance is a question going beyond this chapter.

References

Adhikari, A., C. Derashid, and H. Zhang (2006). Public policy, political connections, and effective tax rates: Longitudinal evidence from Malaysia, *Journal of Accounting and Public Policy*, 25(5): 574–59.

Ang, Y. Y., and N. Jia (2014). Perverse complementarity: Political connections and the use of courts among private firms in China, *The Journal of Politics*, 76(2): 318–32.

Beck, T., and A. Demirgüç-Kunt (2006). Small and medium size enterprises: Access to finance as a growth constraint. *Journal of Banking and Finance*, 30(11): 2931–43.

Bentzen, J., Byiers, B., Rand, J., and Tarp, F. (2010). Credit demand in Mozambican manufacturing, *Journal of International Development*, 22: 37–55.

Bertrand, M., F. Kramarz, A. Schoar, and A. Thesmar (2007). The Cost of Political Connections. *Review of Finance,* 22(3): 849–876.

Bigsten, A., Collier, P., Dercon, S., Fafchamps, M., Gauthier, B., Gunning, J. W., Oduro, A., Oostendrop, R., Patillo, C., Söderbom, M., Teal, F., and Zeufack, A. (2003). Credit constraints in manufacturing enterprises in Africa, *Journal of African Economies,* 12: 104–25.

Boubakri, N., Guedhami, O., Mishra, D., and Saffar, W. 2012. Political connections and the cost of equity capital, *Journal of Corporate Finance* 18(3): 541–59.

Boulier, B. L. and Goldfarb, R. S. (1998). The use and non-use of surveys in economics, *Journal of Economic Methodology,* 5(1), 1–21.

Chen, C. J. P., Li, Z., Su, X., and Sun, Z. 2011. Rent-seeking incentives, corporate political connections, and the control structure of private firms: Chinese evidence, *Journal of Corporate Finance* 17(2): 229–43.

Child, J. 1994. *Management in China during the Age of Reform.* Cambridge: Cambridge University Press.

CIEM (2006–2016). Characteristics of the Vietnamese Business Environment: Evidence from a Survey from 2005 2007 2009 2011 2013 2015. Latest report available at https://www.wider.unu.edu/publication/characteristics-vietnamese-business-environment (accessed on 21 November 2017).

Claessens, S., Feijen, E., and Laeven, L. 2008. Political connections and preferential access to finance: The role of campaign contributions, *Journal of Financial Economics* 88(3): 554–80.

Du, J. and Girma, S. 2010. Red capitalists: Political connections and firm performance in China, *KYKLOS* 63(4): 530–45.

Faccio, M. 2006. Politically connected firms, *American Economic Review,* 96(1): 369–86.

Fan, J. P. H., T. J. Wong, and T. Zhang (2007). Politically connected CEOs, corporate governance, and post-IPO performance of China's newly partially privatized firms, *Journal of Financial Economics,* 84(2): 330–57.

Gainsborough, M. (2010). *Vietnam: Rethinking the State.* London: Zed Books.

Hansen, H. and Rand, J. (2014a). The myth of female credit discrimination in African manufacturing, *Journal of Development Studies,* 50(1): 81–96.

Hansen, H. and Rand, J. (2014b). Estimates of gender differences in firm's access to credit in Sub-Saharan Africa, *Economics Letters,* 123: 374–7.

Jackowicz, K., Kozowski, L., and Mielcarz, P. 2014. Political connections and operational performance of non-financial firms: New evidence from Poland, *Emerging Markets Review* 20: 109–35.

Kerkvliet, B. J. and Marr, D. G. 2004. *Beyond Hanoi: Local Government in Vietnam.* Copenhagen: NIAS Press.

Leuz, C. and Oberholzer-Gee, F. 2006. Political relationships, global financing and corporate transparency: Evidence from Indonesia, *Journal of Financial Economics* 81(2): 411–39.

Li, H., Meng, L., Wang, Q., and Zhou, L. A. 2008. Political connections, financing and firm performance: Evidence from Chinese private firms, *Journal of Development Economics*, 87(2), 283–99.

Malesky, E., Nguyen, C. V., and Tran, Anh. 2014. The impact of recentralization on public services: A difference-in-differences analysis of the abolition of elected councils in Vietnam, *American Political Science Review*, 108(1), 144–68.

Malesky, E. and Schuler, P. 2011. The single-party dictator's dilemma: Information in elections without opposition, *Legislative Studies Quarterly*, 36(4), 491–530.

Malesky, E. and Taussig, M. (2009). Where is credit due? Legal institutions, connections and the efficiency of bank lending in Vietnam, *The Journal of Law, Economics and Organisation*, 25(2): 535–578.

Markussen, T. and F. Tarp (2014). Political connections and land-related investment in rural Vietnam, *Journal of Development Economics*, 110: 291–302.

Mian, A. R. and Khwaja, A. J. 2005. Do lenders favor politically connected firms? Rent provision in an emerging financial market, *Quarterly Journal of Economics*, 120(4), 1371–1411.

Peng, M., and Y. Luo (2000). Managerial ties and firm performance in a transition economy: The nature of a micro–macro link, *Academy of Management Journal* 43(3): 486–501.

Pfeffer, J., and G. R. Salancik (1978). *The External Control of Organizations: A Resource Dependence Perspective*. New York: Harper & Row.

Rand, J. (2007). Credit constraints and determinants of the cost of capital in Vietnamese manufacturing, *Small Business Economics*, 29: 1–13.

Richter, B. K. (2010). The Role Political Connections Play in Access to Finance: Evidence from Cross-listing. Available at SSRN: http://ssrn.com/abstract=1503542 or http://dx.doi.org/10.2139/ssrn.1503542 (accessed on 21 November 2017).

Schleifer, A., and R. W. Vishny (1998). *The Grabbing Hand: Government Pathologies and Their Cures*. Cambridge: Harvard University Press.

Siegel, J. (2007). Contingent political capital and international alliances: Evidence from South Korea, *Administrative Science Quarterly*, 52(4): 621–66.

7

Why Do Household Businesses Stay Informal?

Thi Bich Tran and Hai Anh La

7.1 Introduction

In spite of the benefits of formalization such as the improvement in firms' profits and customer base, better access to infrastructure and other public goods, and protection from corruption (Boly 2018; Cling et al. 2012; Demenet et al. 2016; Fajnzylber et al. 2011; McKenzie and Sakho 2010; Rand and Torm 2012a), the informal sector remains large (La Porta and Shleifer 2014; Williams et al. 2016). This sector is observed with a heterogenous structure which is composed of lower tiers of vulnerable workers with low levels of education and upper tiers of high earnings and skilled employers. The informal sector is also perceived as a weakness in economic development (Loayza 1996; C. Nguyen et al. 2013) with tax erosion (Dabla-Norris et al. 2008), the unequal playing field for firms which comply with regulations (Tenev et al. 2003), and the disadvantages for employees working without social security. Therefore, the identification of the factors associated with informality and formalization becomes a desirable policy goal.

Theories explaining the existence of the informal sector can be classified into two categories. The first strand of the literature attributes burdens of regulations as a catalyst for the prevalence of informal activity among lower tiers of the sector (Rauch 1991; Loayza 1996; Marcouiller and Young 1995; Azuma and Grosman 2002). Avoiding heavy regulatory burdens—including tax, labour regulations, and entry costs—is therefore recommended (Nelson and De Bruijn 2005; T. Nguyen, Verreynne, and Steen 2014). However, there may be another primary reason: informal employers are too weak to have incentives to formalize (Cunningham and Maloney 2001; Fajnzylber et al. 2011; Günther and Launov 2012).

The second strand of the literature focuses on the quality of the legal system as one of the determinants which induce informality (Tenev et al. 2003; Dabla-Norris et al. 2008; Fajnzylber et al. 2009; Soto 1989). Among them, Dabla-Norris et al. (2008) find different effects of regulatory burdens on the size of informality across countries. They show that while a heavier burden of regulations correlates positively with the size of the informal sector in countries with a weak rule of law, such an effect may not happen in countries with better legal quality. In addition,

Thi Bich Tran and Hai Anh La, *Why Do Household Businesses Stay Informal?* In: *Micro, Small, and Medium Enterprises in Vietnam*. Edited by: John Rand and Finn Tarp, Oxford University Press (2020).
DOI: 10.1093/oso/9780198851189.003.0007

De Andrade et al. (2014) reveal that firms are forced to register by government interventions in countries with a weak rule of law.

Our research is motivated by these legal system-related findings and the literature on the 'exit' view that recognizes an informal firm as a decision-maker considering net benefits of formalization. For these firms, the evasion of tax and social security costs for labour are perceived as benefits. They will persist in the informal sector as long as these benefits are higher than the costs that they pay for their illegal action (Rand and Tarp 2012). In addition, in Vietnam, collusion corruption, or a handshake, between household businesses and government tax officials for personal gains at the expenses of the state is very common (Giang et al. 2016). It may provide one of many explanations why a household prefers to stay informal given its profit maximization function.

In this chapter, we look at determinants explaining why household businesses, with a particular focus on those in the top tiers, stay informal. There are two reasons for paying more attention to thetop tier. First, only these households can consider costs and benefits of formalization whereas businesses in the lower tier are too weak to afford the cost of formalization (Cling et al. 2012). Second, while empirical evidence (Demenet et al. 2016) and our descriptive statistics show that formalized businesses often belong to the upper tier, a significant proportion of businesses in this spectrum of the informal sector remains informal. We contribute to the literature by focusing on the legal system-related reasons, especially regarding tax evasion and government controls, and their effects on formalization in Vietnam. It should be noted that in this research the division of household businesses into lower and upper tiers is based on households' revenues. This classification is closely related to the entrepreneurs' ability, as empirical evidence shows that businesses with higher value added and profits are run by more educated owners and have more workers (Rand and Torm 2012a; Nguyen et al. 2013; Boly 2018).

Because most of the informal firms in Vietnam are household businesses, we limit our study to the household sector. According to Vietnamese laws, all non-farm household businesses which employ up to ten employees and have one establishment have to register for a business licence and a tax code. The exemption is for households which earn less than a certain amount and mobile street vendors including motorbike taxis (xe om) (Decree 88/2006/ND-CP). However, because only very few household businesses have an income less than this threshold, they generally should be registered (Cling et al. 2012). Nevertheless, in practice the informal sector in Vietnam is prevalent, not only among the lower but also in the upper tiers.

The remainder of our chapter is organized as follows. Section 7.2 overviews the existing literature on the heterogeneity of the informal sector and its associated factors. In Section 7.3 we describe the dataset and discuss the analytical approach. Section 7.4 presents the main empirical results and Section 7.5 concludes.

7.2 Literature Review

Since the work of Maloney (2004), the literature has converged into unanimous consensus on the heterogeneity of informality in developing countries. Accordingly, informal workers are classified from the lower to the upper tiers of the informal labour market spectrum, and their existence is observed as the last resort and as the preference of workers. The last resort view considers informal workers as those in the lower tiers who could not find a job in the formal sector, then escape unemployment by working involuntarily in the informal sector (Harris and Todaro 1970; Lewis 1954). The preference view argues that informal employment is the choice of workers in the upper tiers given their profit and utility maximization (Hart 1973; Levenson and Maloney 1998).

Empirical evidence on the issue of heterogeneity of informality can be found for the case of Mexico (Cunningham and Maloney 2001), Côte d'Ivoire (Günther and Launov 2012), and Vietnam (Cling et al. 2012; T. Nguyen et al. 2014). Often, the literature finds at the lowest level of the informal labour market segmentation poorly educated, unskilled, and vulnerable employees. For these people, entry barriers to the formal sector do not matter given their inability (Cunningham and Maloney 2001). They are not generally able to afford the costs of formalization (Cling et al. 2012; Demenet et al. 2016; Nelson and De Bruijn 2005). They have no choice but to stay informal for surviving. Therefore, instead of losing constraints, development policies need to identify disadvantages that they face and focus on helping these people for the objective of inclusive growth.

Within this lower tier of informal employment, Roubaud (1994) and Bacchetta et al. (2009) present two approaches that segment the informal labour market into further detail. The 'dualist' approach considers the informal sector as the residual component of the market, which is entirely unrelated to the formal economy. On the other hand, the 'structuralist' approach focuses on the interdependencies between the informal and the formal sector (Moser 1978, Portes et al. 1989). According to the 'structuralist' approach, when young people start up as small informal businesses, they might have interaction with the formal sector and are eager to transform into the formal status. Moreno-Monroy (2012) argues that when formal and informal firms take part in the value chain through backward and forward linkages, and if informal enterprises undertake part of the production process of formal enterprises through sub-contracting, benefits such as productivity and wages could occur. This more detailed classification implies that regulatory burdens may impede firms in the higher end of the lower tiers to formalize.

In the heterogeneous informal labour market, the upper tier of informal employment comprises successful and voluntary entrepreneurs. As indicated in the literature, those people select the informal sector as their preferences and their earnings are as high as salaried workers in the formal sector (Cross 2000; Rand and Torm 2012b; Snyder 2004). Despite empirical evidence on the benefits of formalization such as increases in profits and investment (Rand and Torm 2012), customer base (McKensie and Sakho 2010), access to information and protection from corruption (Cling et al 2012), government assistance (Nguyet et al. 2013), and the cost of informality (Tenev et al. 2003), these entrepreneurs stay informal. Regulation burdens are often cited as the main reasons for the existence of informal households in these upper tiers. Rauch (1991), Loayza (1996), Marcouiller and Young (1995), and Azuma and Grosman (2002) show that high tax and regulation burdens are the determinants of informality while entry costs (Auriol and Warlters 2005), labour regulations (Friedman et al. 2000; Johnson et al. 1997; Botero et al. 2004), and financial constraints (Straub 2005) are identified as obstacles for formalization.

As informality is partly seen as a weakness in economic development (Loayza 1996; C. Nguyen et al. 2013) with tax erosion (Dabla-Norris et al. 2008), the unequal playing field for firms which comply with regulations (Tenev et al. 2003), and the disadvantages of employees working with no social security, identifying factors associated with informality and formalizing the sector is a desirable policy goal. However, formalization mainly belongs to the upper tiers of the informal labour market segmentation, and the degree of transition depends on several factors including businesses' characteristics and the macroeconomic environment. For instance, Tenev et al. (2003) and Dabla-Norris et al. (2008) find that the quality of the legal system is a critical determinant of informality while Demenet et al. (2016) reveal that micro-enterprises decide to operate in a more competitive environment.

In Vietnam, heterogeneity in informal household businesses is very common. The majority of the sector comprises of small and weak informal businesses. Households in this lower tier tend to be run by old entrepreneurs, with low levels of education and technical skills. They also have weak social capital and productivity. Household businesses in this group have no incentive to register their businesses. Their informal status can be explained by either their lack of knowledge of laws or lack of control from the government. Most of small informal businesses feel they are ignored by the government (Cling et al. 2012).

The upper tiers of the informal sector include younger and higher educated employers. Households belonging to this group are more modern with high electronic access. They achieve the highest level of productivity and efficiency and have more opportunities to grow (C. Nguyen et al. 2013). Formalization mostly happens among household businesses at the upper tiers (Demenet et al. 2016; C. Nguyen et al. 2013). Tax and regulation burdens, as well as the level of access to resources, affect the firm informality (Tenev et al. 2003). Cling et al. (2011; 2012) find that a business size, income, and professional premises, access to information, large customer base, and protection from corruption are positively and significantly correlated with its registration decision. Moreover, the education level of entrepreneurs influences their behaviour when working under regulations.

In this chapter, we will unveil factors associated with the formal/informal status of micro firms in Vietnam. According to qualitative studies from Cling et al. (2012) and Rand and Torm (2012a), there are two types of registered households. The first is composed of households that are encouraged by their perception of benefits of formalization such as an increase in the probability of accessing formal credits and public facilities (Rand and Torm 2012a). The second type includes businesses which want to avoid harassment and bribes from state officials (Cling et al. 2012). Therefore, in addition to the characteristics of households and household owners, we examine the quality of the legal system, tax evasion, corruption behaviours, and government controls on informality in Vietnam.

The recent literature has focused on the link between corruption and firm informality. Dabla-Norris et al. (2008) investigate this correlation using cross-country micro-firm data from China, India, Brazil, Indonesia, and Russia. They find that informality is positively correlated with corruption. Similar results are found for the case of Vietnam (Tenev et al. 2003). On the other hand, Rand and Tarp (2012) discover that informality is negatively associated with bribe incidence. They then argue that the informal status helps firms easily hide their visibility. Nevertheless, none of these above studies distinguish between two types of corruptions: extortion (corrupt practices which household businesses are exposed to) and collusion (corrupt acts they actively engage in) and the reason may be lack of data.

Giang et al. (2016) are amongst the first persons who separate two types of corruption while investigating corruption in the formal household businesses in relationship to business formalization, tax compliance, and access to information and capital in Vietnam. They find that while extortion in the form of requests for bribes seemed to be low, hidden extortion is quite widespread, especially in the tax area. It is quite common in the business sector that business owners have incentives to collude with state officials for personal gains at the expenses of the state. Using cross-sectional household data in the two biggest cities in Vietnam, Hanoi, and Ho Chi Minh City in 2007, Cling et al. (2012: 649) reveal that while household businesses express their incentives of registration to avoid corruption, they are in fact the hardest hit by corruption.

These above findings from the literature for the case of Vietnam induce us to hypothesize that collusion corruption is one of the factors that cause self-employed entrepreneurs in the upper tiers of informal employment to stay informal even if they are subject to being registered. If informal households can collude with tax officials for personal benefits, they will not formalize. Although we do not have information to evaluate whether tax evasion arises from collusion or extortion corruption, we can evaluate whether benefits from tax payment are correlated with the size of informality in Vietnam.

7.3 Data and the Analytical Framework

In this chapter, we use panel dataset from the Small and Medium Enterprise (SME) surveys conducted every two years by the Central Institute for Economic Management of Vietnam and the University of Copenhagen in 2005, 2007, 2009, 2011, 2013, and 2015. The SME surveys use a stratified sampling approach to sample formal enterprises and registered households in ten cities and provinces of Vietnam. The sampling frame for formal enterprises and registered households is selected from the enterprise censuses of the General Statistics Office of Vietnam. Informal household businesses, which were included in the SME surveys, were sampled randomly by the enumerator in surveyed districts. Therefore, it is worth noting that the sample of informal household businesses may not be entirely representative of the informal sector in Vietnam (see Rand and Torm (2012a) for more details about the surveys).

As mentioned above, most of the informal firms in Vietnam have household status, and we limit our study to the household sector. The 15th International Conference of Labour Statisticians defines an 'informal household business' as a household which sells parts of its products, has no business registration certificate, and has a small size regarding the number of employees (Hussmanns 2004b). The size varies across countries (Hussmanns 2004a). In Vietnam, this threshold is set up to ten workers. Households using more than ten workers have to register under the Enterprise Law (Decree 88/ND-CP). According to Vietnamese laws, all non-farm household businesses which employ up to ten employees and have one establishment need to register with the exemption of two types: (i) those who earn less than a certain amount set at district level (usually the minimum wage stipulated by the law)[1] and (ii) mobile street vendors including motorbike taxis (xe om) (Decree 88/2006/ND-CP). Moreover, within ten days since it has obtained a Business Registration Certificate (BRC), a household needs to register for a tax code at the local tax office (Article 22, Tax management law).

Under the first criteria (that households with an income above the minimum wages need to register), and using data from representative informal households surveys in Hanoi and Ho Chi Minh City in 2007–2009, Cling et al. (2012) show that 95 per cent of Informal Household Businesses (IHBs) should register in both cities. If adding the second criteria (that a household business should have a fixed premise), the share of informal households drops to 70 per cent. This result implies that almost all IHBs in Vietnam should register under the laws.

[1] Before 2015, the threshold above which a household had to pay taxes is set up by the local government at the district level, and this threshold cannot be below the minimum wage stipulated by the law. Therefore, this limit depends on the discretion of the local government. Since 2015, the amendment of the Tax Law has set up taxes of households on revenue and families do not have to pay taxes if their revenue is below 100 million VND per year (Tax Law number 71/2014/QH13).

Nevertheless, IHBs account for 81.5 per cent of the total household businesses in 2007 (Cling et al. 2011).[2]

Among household businesses which are registered, many households have a business registration certificate but do not have a tax code (Rand and Torm 2012a). On the other hand, some have a tax code but do not have a business registration certificate (Demenet et al. 2016). This is because the tax office still provides a household with a tax code for the purpose of tax collection even when a household does not have a business registration certificate (Cling et al. 2012). This fact is understandable because a household business applies for a business registration certificate at the district registration office while their request for a tax code is submitted to the tax office. Until now, these two systems of registration have been separated in Vietnam. Therefore, under regulations, a firm is formal if it has either a business registration certificate or a tax code. In this chapter, we define formal household businesses as those who have a tax code.[3]

Our unbalanced panel sample for the descriptive section includes all household businesses with at least two observations during the studying period. This sample covers always-formal businesses (976 or 41.8 per cent of the total), switched firms (933 or 39.9 per cent of the total) and always-informal firms (427 or 18.3 per cent of the total). We limit the sample to only informal and switching businesses for the shake of identifying the reasons behind formalization within the informal sector. It means that the final sample only covers firms that were under informal status at the start of the interviews. These 1,360 informal businesses at the starting points form a panel of 5,424 observations. Out of these businesses, 28.2 per cent have observations in all six surveys, 10.4 per cent have five observations, 15.7 per cent have four observations, 22 per cent have three observations, and 23.5 per cent have two observations.

Our purpose in this chapter is to examine factors associated with the status of informality in Vietnam. As indicated in Section 7.2, households remain informal if either they are too weak or they can evade taxes. Furthermore, formalized households may include businesses that can perceive the benefits of formalization such as an increase in the household performance, or may include businesses which want to escape bribes and harassment. For the first type of formalization, we investigate the impacts of formalization on households' performance and tax payment. For the

[2] Using data on informal household businesses from the Vietnam Establishment Census carried out by the General Statistics Office of Vietnam in 2012 (the census covers all fixed location businesses (household businesses), production establishments (enterprises), administrative organizations, and political and non-profit associations (GSO 2013)), we calculate the proportion of informal household businesses in the household sector. The share is 63 per cent. We think that this drop is not mainly related to changes over time but may be due to different ways of defining informal household businesses. In our data, an informal household business needs to match both the criteria: not registering and having fixed premise, while we think Cling et al. (2011) use only the first criteria.

[3] In the SME data, the number of households having only a business registration certificate is almost the same as those having a tax code.

second type of formalization, we use the probit model to examine the effects of government controls and bribes on the household decision of registering.

To examine the impacts of formalization on household performance and tax payment, we follow the method proposed by Boly (2018). The benefits of formalization on household performance and tax payment can be estimated using the following equation:

$$y_{it} = \beta_0 + \beta_1 F_{it} + \beta_2 NS_i + \beta_3 X_{it} + \lambda_i + \gamma_t + \epsilon_{it}, \tag{7.1}$$

where the dependent y_{it} represents revenue (in logarithm form), taxes and fees (in logarithm form) and ratio of taxes to revenue of firm i at time t. To take into account the time and provincial differences in prices and living costs, both revenue and taxes are converted into values of year 2015 using the spatial cost of living index (SCOLI). The main variable F_{it} is a dummy which is equal to 1 if the household is identified as formal at any point of time on the panel and 0 otherwise. Similar to Boly's (2018) method, we create a non-switcher variable NS_i which equals to 1 for all years if the businesses remained informal through these surveys, and 0 if an informal business has become formalized at any time during the study period. With the construction method as above, NS_i can capture firm-type time-invariant unobservable differences between non-switchers and switchers while F_{it} captures the net effect of formalization. We apply the random effects model for this equation due to the time-constant nature of the non-switcher variable. We run this model over the whole panel sample and among top tier informal households. The top tier informal household businesses are identified as the top 10 per cent among all household businesses at any time before formalization during the survey period.

The literature which studies the benefits of formalization can be split into two types: experimental and non-experimental approaches. Experimental studies involve the use of randomized control trials and often show that the costs of formalization outweigh the benefits (Boly 2018; McCaig and Nanowski 2017). On the other hand, almost all non-experimental studies which use either cross-sectional analysis (Fajnzylber et al. 2009, 2011; McKenzie and Sakho 2010; Monteiro and Assunção 2012) or panel data (Boly 2018; Demenet et al. 2016; Rand and Torm 2012a) reveal the benefits of formalization. For instance, Rand and Torm (2012a) report an increase in profits of 12 to 16 per cent, Demenet et al. (2016) show a growth of 20 per cent in value added while Boly (2018) report an increase in profit and value added of 9 to 11 per cent due to formalization in Vietnam. The only exceptional case is the study of McCaig and Nanowski (2017) who use double-difference methods and data from Vietnam Household Living Standards Surveys. They find that registering is not accompanied by an increase in profits and other performance outcomes. They therefore suggest that controlling for the trend of pre-formalization period is crucial to unveil the 'de facto' effects of formalization.

The reason for controversial results from the non-experimental approach may come from the fact that the decision to formalize is endogenous. Formalized or switched firms may not be comparable to non-switchers due to unobserved heterogeneity. As indicated by McCaig and Nanowski (2017), while household fixed-effects in panel data can control for unobserved time-invariant heterogeneity, unobserved time-variant heterogeneity may remain, such as firm-specific time trends, and these trends may be correlated with changes in business performance and the decision to formalize. Thus, controlling for the pre-formalization trend is important to estimate the correct impacts of formalization. It is fortunate that each year, the SME survey collects information on firms' revenue in two previous consecutive years. Therefore, instead of using double-difference methods, we control for household-specific time trend effects before formalization by utilizing the growth rate of revenue. The revenue growth rate is calculated based on the financial reports of two continuous years in the same survey (e.g, revenue recorded in 2012 and 2011 for the 2013 survey).

Control variables are also incorporated in the model. They consist of observable firm characteristics variables X_{it} such as the gender, age, and education level of the owner/manager; the number of regular full-time employees (in logarithm form), the share of production and service workers, the percentage of female workers, and owning a Certificate of Land Use Right (CLUR). Other time-invariant control variables (λ_i) include industry dummy variable, location dummies (rural/urban and central cities/smaller provinces) to capture variations in local governances. Year dummies (γ_t) are also included to control for potential time effects.

To identity factors (including government control and bribes) associated with the household decision to formalize, we use the probit model as presented below:

$$F_{it} = 1[\alpha_1 Z_i + \alpha_2 X_{it} + \lambda_i + \gamma_t + \epsilon_{it}], \tag{7.2}$$

where $1[.]$ is the binary indicator function; Z_i, the leading independent variable, is a dummy variable which equals 1 (i) if a business paid at least one informal payment during the last financial year, or (ii) if a household had to spend time dealing with business issues with government officials, or (iii) if a business has poor knowledge of or is not interested in tax laws. The first two variables are used as proxy for government control and the level of harassment. All these dummy variables, Z_i, are identified before a firm is formalized to test the hypothesis that firms will formalize to avoid harassment. These dummies are unchanged over time.

7.4 Empirical Results

First, we analyse the characteristics of the informal sector in Vietnam and then discuss the reason behind formalization using results from the analytical model presented in Section 7.3.

7.4.1 Characteristics of the Informal Sector in Vietnam

Considering solely the informal sector, our sample shows that 31 per cent of households are always informal and the majority of them are in the bottom 90 per cent (394 observations in Table 7.1a). Formalization happens more frequently among the top 10 per cent than the bottom 90 per cent groups (73 per cent versus 68 per cent). However, when we exclude the data of the six rounds of this survey in 2015 due to its irrationally high formalization rate among the household business group (96 per cent) when panelled with the 2013 survey, IHBs are predominant in the sample, accounting for 72 per cent. Moreover, the percentage of formalized households in the top 10 per cent is much lower (only 44 per cent in Table 7.1b).

To shed light on the reasons why some households stay informal but others do not, we provide descriptive statistics on the characteristics of households and household owners for the whole sample (Table 7.2) and for the top 10 per cent (Table 7.3). Results from Table 7.2 show that switchers are stronger than non-switchers in terms of economic performance. However, they experience lower revenue growth rate after formalization, especially for the top 10 per cent (8.9 per cent compared to 1 per cent before and after switching; Table 7.3).

Table 7.1a Frequency of business types

	Bottom 90%	Top 10%	Total
Non-switcher	394	33	427
(%)	*31.85*	*26.83*	*31.40*
Switcher	843	90	933
(%)	*68.15*	*73.17*	*68.60*
Total	1237	123	1360
	100	*100*	*100*

Source: Authors' calculation using SME data 2005–15.

Table 7.1b Frequency of business types during 2005–13

	Bottom 90%	Top 10%	Total
Non-switcher	773	57	830
(%)	*71.44*	*51.82*	*69.63*
Switcher	309	53	362
(%)	*28.56*	*48.18*	*30.37*
Total	1082	110	1192
	100	*100*	*100*

Source: Authors' calculation using SME data 2005–13.

Furthermore, formalized businesses pay much more taxes than before switching and they have to be controlled more by government officials after formalization (Tables 9.2 and 9.3). On the other hand, the non-switcher group pays the least taxes and informal fees. Households in this group spend less time to deal with

Table 7.2 Income, tax, and bribe by business types: all sample

	Non-switcher	Pre-switching	After-switching	Total
Revenue (mil VND)	552.8	862.0	1172.1	2425.5
	(772.0)	(2775.8)	(5728.8)	(7988.3)
Revenue growth rate (%)	5.723	6.437	4.117	5.722
	(20.44)	(19.05)	(30.30)	(24.35)
Taxes and fees (mil VND)	1.452	4.252	7.740	43.40
	(3.484)	(15.48)	(31.34)	(153.8)
Tax/Revenue (%)	0.388	0.631	0.679	2.544
	(0.868)	(1.378)	(1.199)	(2.486)
% paid at least one informal payment	12.42	19.59	22.88	37.48
	(24.01)	(33.36)	(36.69)	(33.48)
% spend time to deal with government officials	47.22	61.38	80.92	92.23
	(35.37)	(38.41)	(36.40)	(18.32)
% with poor knowledge/no interest in tax law	82.86	78.58	83.50	57.38
	(26.66)	(33.81)	(31.69)	(34.41)

Notes: Figures in parentheses are standard deviation. We first take average each variable of each firm, and then calculate the mean of each group.

Source: Authors' calculation using SME data 2005–15.

Table 7.3 Income, tax, and bribe by business types: top 10%

	Non-switcher	Pre-switching	After-switching	Total
Revenue (mil VND)	2321.4	3832.0	3346.4	3402.0
	(1488.3)	(7902.7)	(4468.5)	(6018.0)
Revenue growth rate (%)	7.186	8.906	1.044	5.524
	(19.44)	(16.85)	(17.36)	(17.78)
Taxes and fees (mil VND)	4.032	13.39	17.62	13.59
	(6.754)	(40.11)	(47.28)	(40.27)
Tax/revenue (%)	0.383	0.400	0.631	0.488
	(0.805)	(1.048)	(1.271)	(1.112)
% paid at least one informal payment	28.60	29.41	46.36	35.99
	(32.87)	(35.00)	(43.33)	(38.98)
% spent time to deal with government officials	61.26	75.05	92.71	79.87
	(35.13)	(32.86)	(22.24)	(31.54)
% with poor knowledge/no interest in tax law	73.60	71.22	72.89	72.26
	(29.51)	(35.97)	(36.45)	(35.11)

Notes: Figures in parentheses are standard deviation. We first take average each variable of each firm, and then calculate the mean of each group.

Source: Authors' calculation using SME data 2005–15.

Table 7.4 Owner and household business characteristics by business types: all sample

	Non-switcher	Switcher	Total
Male owner (%)	67.25	69.22	63.27
	(40.75)	(38.57)	(41.61)
Age of owner	46.81	46.17	46.37
	(10.33)	(8.634)	(9.382)
Owner completed higher secondary school (%)	38.74	46.76	56.37
	(41.61)	(41.38)	(41.12)
No. of dependent household members	1.320	1.372	1.453
	(1.037)	(0.985)	(1.105)
Total labour force (people)	4.649	5.447	8.848
	(4.663)	(7.570)	(17.02)
Share of female workers (%)	38.80	39.13	34.47
	(26.99)	(25.12)	(22.86)
Share of production and service workers (%)	63.91	59.15	67.30
	(18.11)	(20.40)	(15.27)
Have a CLUR (%)	68.27	74.54	67.93
	(37.74)	(35.59)	(39.59)
Urban areas (%)	27.10	35.90	67.91
	(44.49)	(47.99)	(46.71)
Ha Noi, Hai Phong, and HCM city (%)	12.26	18.52	56.94
	(32.83)	(38.86)	(49.54)
Medium, high-tech sector (%)	28.41	23.58	38.47
	(43.79)	(41.82)	(47.08)

Note: We first take average each variable of each firm, and then calculate the mean of each group.
Source: Authors' calculation using SME data 2005–15.

government officials than switchers. Overall, the results indicate that strong firms can formalize whereas weaker households retain their informal status. In Section 7.5, we investigate whether these factors are associated with the household decision to formalize.

Tables 9.4 and 9.5 present the characteristics of household owners by types. As can be seen from Table 7.4, while the age of owners/managers of households is similar across groups, the percentage of owners who complete higher secondary school is higher in the switcher group compared to that of the non-switcher counterparts. While the result for the whole sample is in line with the literature which shows that informal households are operated by persons with a low level of education, a different story is found for the top 10 per cent. The education level of the households in the switcher group is lower than that of the non-switcher businesses (Table 7.5). Furthermore, knowledge on tax law is similar between non-switchers and formalized households before they register. Results from Tables 9.4 and 9.5 also show that household businesses in urban areas are more likely to be formalized than those in rural places.

Table 7.5 Owner and household business characteristics by business types: top 10%

	Non-switcher	Switcher	Total
Male owner (%)	77.03	78.19	77.90
	(37.70)	(32.05)	(33.45)
Age of owner	41.71	45.48	44.52
	(8.540)	(8.623)	(8.730)
Owner completed higher secondary school (%)	51.44	44.89	46.56
	(41.97)	(38.96)	(39.70)
No. of dependent household members	1.656	1.519	1.554
	(1.215)	(1.053)	(1.094)
Total labour force (people)	9.718	12.70	11.94
	(7.398)	(17.43)	(15.53)
Share of female workers (%)	33.35	37.77	36.64
	(25.33)	(23.66)	(24.08)
Share of production and service workers (%)	75.98	75.21	75.41
	(14.30)	(13.15)	(13.41)
Have a CLUR (%)	74.46	74.91	74.79
	(37.56)	(33.90)	(34.74)
Urban areas (%)	21.62	25.93	24.83
	(41.73)	(44.03)	(43.35)
Ha Noi, Hai Phong, and HCM city (%)	16.22	24.07	22.07
	(37.37)	(42.95)	(41.61)
Medium, high-tech sector (%)	29.73	14.66	18.51
	(46.34)	(34.69)	(38.40)

Note: We first take average each variable of each firm, and then calculate the mean of each group.
Source: Authors' calculation using SME data 2005–15.

7.4.2 Which Households Are More Likely to Formalize?

In this section, we test the most common hypotheses that firms will register either when they perceive benefits of formalization or they want to avoid bribes and harassment. As indicated in the analytical framework, the estimation of the first should consider the issues of endogeneity carefully because firm heterogeneity may be both time-invariant and variant. On the other hand, the estimation of the second type of formalization is straightforward by using the probit model.

Staying in the informal sector because benefits outweigh the costs

Households will consider to register or stay in the informal sector based on their perceived benefits and costs of formalization. Household businesses may compare the benefits such as the increase in their revenues and profits with the costs including taxes and labour regulations. In this chapter, only taxes will be considered because household businesses are not required to register for the use of labour (Rand and Torm 2012a) in Vietnam. We will evaluate the benefits of formalization covering the increase in the household revenue and the cost of paying taxes. Revenue is chosen as an indicator of household performance because it allows us to quickly match them with the tax indicator. The reason is that although before 2015 households had to pay taxes based on their value added (Law on Tax management, 78/2006/QH11), tax officials use households' revenues to compute an amount of tax payment for households. This is because almost all informal households in the sample do not have accounting books (Tables 9.4 and 9.5).

Similar to Boly's (2018) study, we firstly use the random effect (RE) model to examine whether household businesses switch to the formal status because of their expected revenue increase. As indicated in Section 3, random effect models are applied because the non-switcher variable is time-constant. The benefits of formalization on a business revenue and its growth are documented in Table 7.6. In this table, the dummy variable *'non-switcher'* (1 for non-switcher and 0 otherwise) reflects the differentials in revenues of informal households and their formalized counterpart. As the way to construct this variable explained in Section 7.3, it should be noted that the sub-sample 'non-switcher' may include the informal status of formalized businesses before they register. Therefore, the variable 'switcher' *(after formalization)* reflects the net effects of formalization on a switched firm. That means it reflects the revenue that a household gains after formalization.

Model 1 in Table 7.6 shows our estimation for the whole sample. As indicated in the literature and shown in our descriptive section that formalization mostly happens among top tier informal firms, we divide our sample into two groups based on their revenues before they switch from informal to formal status. Model 2 in Table 7.6 indicates the estimates for the top 10 per cent.

Results from model 1 reveals that non-switchers have lower revenues than formalized ones (Table 7.6). The coefficient of this variable in model 1 indicates that overall the revenues of informal household businesses (non-switchers) is about 20 per cent less than their formalized counterparts. The coefficient of variable *'switcher' (after formalization)* indicates that formalization increases a firm's revenue by approximately 15 per cent on average, holding other constant. Rand and Torm (2012a) find a similar rate of profit gains for formalized households using the same SME surveys in 2007 and 2009.

The estimation for the top 10 per cent reveals an interesting story. While formalized households are much stronger than informal businesses, formalization does not bring them any benefit. The coefficient of the variable *'switcher' (after formalization)* is insignificant (model 2, Table 7.6). Furthermore, when we control for pre-formalization trend by using the dependent variable as the growth of revenue, the variable *'switcher' (after formalization)* becomes negative and significant at 10 per cent as shown in model 3, Table 7.6. This indicates that non-switchers have no disadvantages over their formalized counterparts. McCaig and Nanowski (2017) also show that formalization does not bring any benefit for

Table 7.6 Random effect model: Ln(Rev) and ⊿Ln(Rev)

	Ln(Revenue) All (1)	Ln(Revenue)Top 10% (2)	Revenue growth rate: Top 10% (3)
Switcher (after formalization)	0.152***	−0.064	−0.059*
	(0.033)	(0.112)	(0.031)
Non-switcher	−0.197***	−0.237*	−0.014
	(0.042)	(0.127)	(0.030)
Male owner	0.084***	−0.021	−0.005
	(0.028)	(0.101)	(0.027)
Ln(Age of owner)	−0.400***	−0.183	−0.045
	(0.064)	(0.213)	(0.055)
Owner completed higher secondary school	0.075***	0.141*	0.032
	(0.025)	(0.086)	(0.023)
No. of dependent household members	−0.001	−0.008	0.001
	(0.010)	(0.033)	(0.009)
Ln(Total labour force)	0.773***	0.509***	0.007
	(0.021)	(0.057)	(0.015)
Share of female workers	−0.279***	−0.353*	−0.099**
	(0.050)	(0.182)	(0.048)
Share of production and service workers	0.152***	−0.162	0.100
	(0.053)	(0.247)	(0.069)
Have a CLUR	0.029	0.029	−0.029
	(0.027)	(0.092)	(0.025)
Urban areas	0.094**	−0.026	0.013
	(0.041)	(0.146)	(0.034)
Ha Noi, Hai Phong, and HCM city	0.337***	−0.175	−0.049
	(0.056)	(0.162)	(0.036)
Medium, high-tech sector	−0.043	−0.251*	−0.011
	(0.042)	(0.149)	(0.035)
Year 2007	0.075**	−0.110	0.129***
	(0.033)	(0.116)	(0.035)
Year 2009	0.239***	0.133	−0.052
	(0.034)	(0.117)	(0.035)
Year 2011	0.323***	0.405***	0.136***
	(0.037)	(0.126)	(0.037)
Year 2013	0.367***	0.323**	−0.034
	(0.038)	(0.136)	(0.040)
Year 2015	0.323***	0.038	0.024
	(0.052)	(0.168)	(0.048)
Constant	13.019***	14.367***	0.189
	(0.248)	(0.824)	(0.213)
Observations	5,424	516	516
Chi2-Statistics	2,580	140	74
p-value	0.000	0.000	0.000
R2	0.481	0.205	0.126

Note: Standard errors in parentheses; * $p < 0.10$, ** $p < 0.05$, *** $p < 0.01$.

Source: Authors' calculation using SME data 2005–15.

formalized firms if controlling pre-formalization trend using the double-difference method. The result may be one of the reasons explaining why some firms in thetop tiers do not register.

We now turn to evaluate the cost of formalization by considering whether households have to pay higher taxes if they register or benefit from tax evasion if they stay in the informal sector. Table 7.7 documents the random effects of formalization on a firm's percentage of taxes to revenues. As can be seen from this table, household businesses pay higher taxes after formalization and the results are robust in all specifications. Specifically, a formalized household in the top 10 per cent has to pay around two times more taxes than before registering (model 3, Table 7.7). On the other hand, staying in the informal sector saves households' costs. An informal household can preserve 0.002 percentage points of taxes over revenue compared to formalized businesses in the whole sample. Therefore, households do not formalize because they benefit from tax evasion.

As indicated by Giang et al. (2016), it is quite common in the business sector that business owners have incentives to collude with state officials for personal gains at the expenses of the state. Although we do not have information to indicate whether tax gains come from collusion or distortion, our evidence shows that informal households benefit from not paying taxes. For the top 10 per cent, we cling to the assumption that those households cannot benefit from tax evasion without the help from tax officials. Our assumption rests on the fact that the bigger the household is, the more 'visibility' it has (Rand and Tarp 2012). It is also shown in our descriptive statistics (Tables 9.4 and 9.5) that households with higher revenues, for example the top 10 per cent, have the size in terms of labour workforce which is almost double that of small businesses. Therefore, IHBs might deal with tax officials to stay informal for the benefits of tax evasion.

Do government controls promote formalization?

As indicated in the literature, firms are more likely to register in countries with a better quality of the legal system (Dabla-Norris et al. 2008) or they are forced to register by government interventions in countries with a weak rule of law (De Andrade et al. 2014). We add one more reason for the case of Vietnam where informal households formalize to avoid harassment and bribes from state officials (Cling et al. 2012). In order to investigate effects of these factors on the probability of staying in the informal sector, we estimate random effect probit model where the dependent variable is a dummy which takes the value one if a household is formalized and zero if a business is informal. The results are documented in Table 7.8.

To examine how government controls and households' knowledge on the legal system, especially on the tax law, are associated with the probability of being

Table 7.7 Random effect model: ratio of taxes to VA

	Tax/Rev: All (1)	Tax/Rev: Top 10% (2)	Ln(Tax): Top 10% (3)
Switcher (after formalization)	0.005***	0.004***	2.064***
	(0.001)	(0.001)	(0.356)
Non-switcher	−0.002***	0.001	−0.571
	(0.001)	(0.002)	(0.417)
Male owner	−0.000	−0.000	−0.461
	(0.000)	(0.001)	(0.322)
Ln(Age of owner)	0.001	0.000	1.350**
	(0.001)	(0.003)	(0.687)
Owner completed higher secondary school	−0.000	−0.001	0.277
	(0.000)	(0.001)	(0.274)
No. of dependent household members	0.000	−0.000	0.129
	(0.000)	(0.000)	(0.105)
Ln(Total labour force)	0.001***	0.001	0.856***
	(0.000)	(0.001)	(0.183)
Share of female workers	0.001	−0.001	0.284
	(0.001)	(0.002)	(0.585)
Share of production and service workers	−0.004***	0.003	−0.486
	(0.001)	(0.003)	(0.790)
Have a CLUR	0.000	0.003**	0.569*
	(0.000)	(0.001)	(0.294)
Urban areas	0.001**	0.004**	0.731
	(0.001)	(0.002)	(0.477)
Ha Noi, Hai Phong, and HCM city	0.007***	0.010***	1.316**
	(0.001)	(0.002)	(0.533)
Medium, high-tech sector	0.002***	0.000	0.465
	(0.001)	(0.002)	(0.489)
Year 2007	−0.003***	0.001	−0.373
	(0.001)	(0.001)	(0.367)
Year 2009	−0.005***	0.000	−0.775**
	(0.001)	(0.001)	(0.371)
Year 2011	−0.005***	−0.001	−0.497
	(0.001)	(0.002)	(0.401)
Year 2013	−0.006***	−0.002	−0.197
	(0.001)	(0.002)	(0.432)
Year 2015	−0.009***	−0.003	−1.370**
	(0.001)	(0.002)	(0.535)
Constant	0.003	−0.006	−0.943
	(0.004)	(0.011)	(2.659)
Observations	5,424	516	516
Chi2-Statistics	422	78	136
p-value	0.000	0.000	0.000
R2	0.119	0.218	0.274

Note: Standard errors in parentheses; * $p < 0.10$, ** $p < 0.05$, *** $p < 0.01$.

Source: Authors' calculation using SME data 2005–15.

Table 7.8 Random effect probit model of formalization: all sample

	(1)	(2)	(3)
Paid at least one informal payment	−0.126***		
	(0.014)		
Spend time to deal with government officials		−0.162***	
		(0.011)	
Poor knowledge/no interest in tax law			−0.307***
			(0.011)
Male owner	−0.019*	−0.023**	−0.022**
	(0.011)	(0.011)	(0.010)
Ln(Age of owner)	0.024	0.041*	0.054***
	(0.023)	(0.023)	(0.020)
Owner completed higher secondary school	0.038***	0.039***	0.030***
	(0.010)	(0.009)	(0.009)
No. of dependent household members	−0.004	−0.004	−0.004
	(0.004)	(0.004)	(0.003)
Ln(Total labour force)	0.069***	0.069***	0.044***
	(0.008)	(0.008)	(0.007)
Share of female workers	−0.067***	−0.065***	−0.051***
	(0.019)	(0.019)	(0.017)
Share of production and service workers	0.096***	0.085***	0.090***
	(0.022)	(0.022)	(0.022)
Have a CLUR	0.019*	0.021**	0.019*
	(0.011)	(0.010)	(0.010)
Urban areas	0.058***	0.049***	0.046***
	(0.013)	(0.013)	(0.011)
Ha Noi, Hai Phong, and HCM city	0.089***	0.062***	0.002
	(0.017)	(0.017)	(0.014)
Medium, high-tech sector	0.044***	0.044***	0.022*
	(0.014)	(0.013)	(0.011)
Year 2007	0.145***	0.141***	0.143***
	(0.014)	(0.014)	(0.014)
Year 2009	0.214***	0.208***	0.214***
	(0.014)	(0.014)	(0.014)
Year 2011	0.314***	0.305***	0.304***
	(0.015)	(0.015)	(0.015)
Year 2013	0.342***	0.326***	0.299***
	(0.015)	(0.015)	(0.015)
Year 2015	1.027***	1.008***	0.980***
	(0.016)	(0.016)	(0.016)
Observations	5,424	5,424	5,424
Chi2-Statistics	6,325	6,486	7,205
p-value	0.000	0.000	0.000
R2	0.503	0.524	0.571

Notes: Marginal effects; Standard errors in parentheses. * $p < 0.10$, ** $p < 0.05$, *** $p < 0.01$

Source: Authors' calculation using SME data 2005–15.

Table 7.9 Random effect probit model of formalization: top 10%

	(1)	(2)	(3)
Paid at least one informal payment	−0.027		
	(0.040)		
Spend time to deal with government officials		−0.194***	
		(0.042)	
Poor knowledge/no interest in tax law			−0.268***
			(0.043)
Male owner	−0.049	−0.059	−0.063
	(0.041)	(0.039)	(0.039)
Ln(Age of owner)	0.040	0.079	0.070
	(0.085)	(0.081)	(0.079)
Owner completed higher secondary school	0.047	0.043	0.030
	(0.034)	(0.033)	(0.033)
No. of dependent household members	−0.034***	−0.026**	−0.024**
	(0.013)	(0.013)	(0.012)
Ln(Total labour force)	0.029	0.024	0.013
	(0.023)	(0.022)	(0.022)
Share of female workers	0.019	0.010	0.012
	(0.073)	(0.070)	(0.069)
Share of production and service workers	−0.010	−0.009	0.018
	(0.101)	(0.099)	(0.098)
Have a CLUR	−0.014	−0.013	−0.013
	(0.037)	(0.036)	(0.036)
Urban areas	0.013	−0.045	−0.051
	(0.057)	(0.054)	(0.052)
Ha Noi, Hai Phong, and HCM city	0.112*	0.128**	0.054
	(0.061)	(0.056)	(0.055)
Medium, high-tech sector	−0.031	−0.022	−0.029
	(0.058)	(0.054)	(0.052)
Year 2007	0.099**	0.099**	0.101**
	(0.048)	(0.048)	(0.048)
Year 2009	0.159***	0.161***	0.168***
	(0.048)	(0.048)	(0.048)
Year 2011	0.353***	0.350***	0.360***
	(0.050)	(0.050)	(0.049)
Year 2013	0.494***	0.480***	0.485***
	(0.051)	(0.051)	(0.050)
Year 2015	0.955***	0.937***	0.945***
	(0.054)	(0.053)	(0.053)
Observations	516	516	516
Chi2-Statistics	482	504	532
p-value	0.000	0.000	0.000
R2	0.456	0.487	0.509

Notes: Marginal effects; Standard errors in parentheses. * $p < 0.10$, ** $p < 0.05$, *** $p < 0.01$
Source: Authors' calculation using SME data 2005–15.

registered, we separate the impacts of '*paying at least one informal payment*' (1 if paid and 0 if did not pay anything), '*spend management time to deal with government officials*' (1 if spent time and 0 if did not), and '*poor knowledge or no interest in tax law*' (1 if the household has poor knowledge of tax law and 0 otherwise) in three specifications in Table 7.8. These variables are taken in the pre-formalization period, based on the assumption that firms are more likely to register if they were more inspected or had a good knowledge of tax law.

Our results show that paying the informal payment and dealing with government officials in the past do not increase the likelihood of formalization (Tables 9.8 and 9.9). Moreover, the coefficient of variable '*poor knowledge or no interest in tax law*' indicates that households, which have poor knowledge of tax law, are less likely to register (model 3, Table 7.8). For the top 10 per cent, households are indifferent with formalization regardless of involving informal payment or not. In addition, the likelihood of formalization in thistop tier business reduces when households spend more time to '*deal with government officials*' and '*have poor knowledge or no interest in tax law*' (models 2 and 3, Table 7.9). As indicated by Giang et al. (2016: 413), the majority of household businesses are subject to be checked at least once a year and businesses often give informal payment each time they are inspected. Furthermore, business owners often do not understand how the tax level is calculated and have to pay what they are told. It seems that household businesses deal with government officials to stay informal and therefore, they do not need to acquire good knowledge on the tax law.

The above results do not support findings from Cling et al. (2012)'s qualitative study that households register to avoid bribes and harassment. Instead, the results might support our assumption in the previous section that there may be a handshake between informal households, especially those in the top tiers, and tax officials. Although our findings lack evidence to examine whether there is a potential collusion between informal households and tax officials, these are worthy for future qualitative and quantitative studies to investigate the collusion corruption as determinants of informality in developing countries.

7.5 Conclusion

The informal sector remains large in poor and developing countries. Since the existence of the sector has been seen as a weakness of the economy, identifying determinants of informality to promote the process of formalization is an ideal policy goal for any country. In this chapter, we investigate factors associated with the informality of household businesses in Vietnam using the unbalanced panel data from the SME surveys in Vietnam in 2005, 2007, 2009, 2011, 2013, and 2015.

The chapter finds that most of the informal households are in the bottom of 90 per cent. They are run by lower educated owners and have lower revenue than formalized and formal households. On the other hand, informal household businesses in the top 10 per cent have no disadvantages in terms of human capital over their formal counterparts. In line with the literature, our results reveal that only strong firms can formalize whereas weaker households stay informal. Furthermore, household businesses in urban areas are more likely to be formalized than those in rural places. Although we find that formalization happens more frequently among the top than the lower tiers, results from the chapter show that not all stronger firms formalize.

Using the random effect method, we find that while switchers in the whole sample benefit from an increase in revenues, formalized households in the top 10 per cent do not benefit or even experience a negative revenue growth rate when controlling for pre-formalization trend. Whereas staying informal reduces business costs from tax evasion and this gain is higher if a household is in the top tiers. Results from the chapter may explain why a proportion of households in the top-tiers remains informal.

The chapter also examines whether government controls and household knowledge on tax law help to promote formalization. The results reveal that being more inspected by government officials and paying the informal payment in the past do not promote the likelihood of formalization, especially among the top 10 per cent. This, coupled with tax benefits from staying informal, raise a suspicion on the handshake between informal households in the top tiers and government tax officials for personal gains. This opens room for future qualitative and quantitative studies to investigate the collusion corruption as a determinant of informality in developing countries.

References

Auriol, Emmanuelle, and Michael Warlters. 2005. Taxation base in developing countries. *Journal of Public Economics* 89(4): 625–46.

Azuma, Y., and H. I. Grossman (2002). A Theory of the Informal Sector. NBER Working Paper no. 8823. Cambridge, MA: National Bureau of Economic Research. (Available at: http://www.nber.org/papers/w8823.pdf).

Bacchetta, M., E. Ernst, and J. P. Bustamante (2009). *Globalization and Informal Jobs in Developing Countries*. Geneva: ILO and WTO.

Boly, A. (2018). On the short-and medium-term effects of formalisation: Panel evidence from Vietnam, *Journal of Development Studies* 54(4): 641–56.

Botero, J., S. Djankov, R. La Porta, F. Lopez-de-Silanes, and A. Shleifer (2004). The regulation of labor, *Quarterly Journal of Economics*, 119(4): 1339–82.

Cling, J.-P., M. Razafindrakoto, and F. Roubaud (2011). *The Informal Economy in Vietnam*. Hanoi: International Labour Organization.

Cling, J.-P., M. Razafindrakoto, and F. Roubaud (2012). To be or not to be registered? Explanatory factors behind formalizing non-farm household businesses in Vietnam, *Journal of the Asia Pacific Economy*, 17(4): 632–52.

Cross, J. (2000). Street vendors, and postmodernity: Conflict and compromise in the global economy, *International Journal of Sociology and Social Policy*, 20(1/2): 29–51.

Cunningham, W. V., and W. F. Maloney (2001). Heterogeneity among Mexico's microenterprises: An application of factor and cluster analysis, *Economic Development and Cultural Change*, 50(1): 131–56.

Dabla-Norris, E., M. Gradstein, and G. Inchauste (2008). What causes firms to hide output? The determinants of informality, *Journal of Development Economics*, 85(1): 1–27.

De Andrade, G. H., M. Bruhn, and D. McKenzie (2014). A helping hand or the long arm of the law? Experimental evidence on what governments can do to formalize firms, *The World Bank Economic Review*, 30(1): 24–54.

Demenet, A., M. Razafindrakoto, and F. Roubaud (2016). Do informal businesses gain from registration and how? Panel data evidence from Vietnam, *World Development*, 84: 326–41.

Fajnzylber, P., W. F. Maloney, and G. V. Montes-Rojas (2009). Releasing constraints to growth or pushing on a string? Policies and performance of Mexican micro-firms, *The Journal of Development Studies*, 45(7): 1027–47.

Fajnzylber, P., W. F. Maloney, and G. V. Montes-Rojas (2011). Does formality improve micro-firm performance? Evidence from the Brazilian simples program, *Journal of Development Economics*, 94(2): 262–76.

Friedman, E., S. Johnson, D. Kaufman, and P. Zoido-Lobatón (2000). Dodging the grabbing hand: The determinants of unofficial activity in 69 countries, *Journal of Public Economics*, 76(3): 459–92.

General Statistics Office of Vietnam (2013). *Results of the 2012 Establishment Census*. Hanoi: Statistical Publishing House.

Giang, D. H., P. T. Xuan, and N. Q. Hai (2016). Corruption risks in Vietnam? A household business sector, *Crime, Law and Social Change*, 65(4–5): 395–422.

Günther, I., and A. Launov (2012). Informal employment in developing countries: Opportunity or last resort?, *Journal of Development Economics*, 97(1): 88–98.

Harris, J. R., and M. P. Todaro (1970). Migration, unemployment and development: A two-sector analysis, *The American Economic Review*, 60(1): 126–42.

Hart, K. (1973). Informal income opportunities and urban employment in Ghana, *Journal of Modern African Studies*, 11(1): 61–89.

Hussmanns, R. (2004a). *Measuring the Informal Economy: From Employment in the Informal Sector to Informal Employment*. Geneva: Policy Integration Department, Bureau of Statistics, International Labour Office.

Hussmanns, R. (2004b). Statistical definition of informal employment: Guidelines endorsed by the Seventeenth International Conference of Labour Statisticians

(2003). In *7th Meeting of the Expert Group on Informal Sector Statistics (Delhi Group)* (pp. 2–4). Bureau of Statistics International Labour Office CH-1211, Geneva 22, Switzerland.

Johnson, S., D. Kaufmann, and A. Shleifer (1997). The unofficial economy in transition, *Brookings Papers on Economic Activity*, 27(2): 159–239. Washington DC: Brookings Institution.

La Porta, R., and A. Shleifer (2014). Informality and development, *The Journal of Economic Perspectives*, 28(3): 109–26.

Levenson, A. R., and W. Maloney (1998). *The Informal Sector, Firm Dynamics, and Institutional Participation*. Washington, DC: World Bank.

Lewis, W. A. (1954). Economic development with unlimited supplies of labour, *The Manchester School*, 22(2): 139–91.

Loayza, N. V. (1996). The economics of the informal sector: A simple model and some empirical evidence from Latin America. In *Carnegie-Rochester Conference Series on Public Policy* (Vol. 45, pp. 129–62). Amsterdam: Elsevier.

Maloney, W. F. (2004). Informality revisited, *World Development*, 32(7): 1159–78.

Marcouiller, D., and L. Young (1995). The black hole of graft: The predatory state and the informal economy, *American Economic Review*, 85(3): 630–46.

McCaig, B., and J. Nanowski (2017). Business Formalization in Vietnam. LCERPA Working Paper No. 2018-7. Waterloo, ON: Laurier Centre for Economic Research & Policy Analysis. Available at: http://www.lcerpa.org/public/papers/LCERPA_2018_7.pdf

McKenzie, D., and Y. S. Sakho (2010). Does it pay firms to register for taxes? The impact of formality on firm profitability, *Journal of Development Economics*, 91(1): 15–24.

Monteiro, J. C., and J. J. Assunção (2012). Coming out of the shadows? Estimating the impact of bureaucracy simplification and tax cut on formality in Brazilian micro-enterprises, *Journal of Development Economics*, 99(1): 105–15.

Moreno-Monroy, A. (2012). Critical commentary. Informality in space: Understanding agglomeration economies during economic development, *Urban Studies*, 49(10): 2019–30. doi:10.1177/0042098012448554

Moser, C. N. (1978). Informal sector or petty commodity production: dualism or independence in urban development, *World Development*, 6 (9–10): 1041–64.

Nelson, E. G., and E. J. De Bruijn (2005). The voluntary formalization of enterprises in a developing economy? The case of Tanzania, *Journal of International Development*, 17(4): 575–93.

Nguyen, C., T. B. Tran, and H. A. La (2013). The Dynamics of Vietnam Informal Sector: Which Policy Should Be the Best?' DEPOCEN Working Paper No. 18. Hanoi: Development and Policies Research Center. Retrieved from https://EconPapers.repec.org/RePEc:dpc:wpaper:1813 (accessed 18 December 2017).

Nguyen, T., M.-L. Verreynne, and J. Steen (2014). Drivers of firm formalization in Vietnam: An attention theory explanation, *Entrepreneurship and Regional Development*, 26(7–8): 574–93.

Portes, A., M. Castells, and L. A. Benton (1989). *The Informal Economy: Studies in Advanced and Less Developed Countries*. Baltimore: John Hopkins University Press.

Rand, J., and F. Tarp (2012). Firm-level corruption in Vietnam, *Economic Development and Cultural Change*, 60(3): 571–95.

Rand, J., and N. Torm (2012a). The benefits of formalization: Evidence from Vietnamese manufacturing SMEs, *World Development*, 40(5): 983–98.

Rand, J., and N. Torm (2012b). The informal sector wage gap among Vietnamese micro-firms, *Journal of the Asia Pacific Economy*, 17(4): 560–77.

Rauch, James E. 1991. Modelling the informal sector formally. *Journal of Development Economics*, 35(1): 33–47.

Roubaud, François. 1994. *L'économie Informelle Au Mexique: De La Sphère Domestique à La Dynamique Macro-économique*. KARTHALA Editions.

Snyder, K. A. (2004). Routes to the informal economy in New York's East Village: Crisis, economics, and identity, *Sociological Perspectives*, 47(2): 215–40.

Soto, H. de. (1989). *The Other Path: The Invisible Revolution in the Third World*. New York: Harper and Row.

Straub, Stéphane. 2005. Informal sector: The credit market channel, *Journal of Development Economics*, 78(2): 299–321.

Tenev, S., A. Carlier, O. Chaudry, and Q.-T. Nguyen (2003). *Informality and the Playing Field in Vietnam's Business Sector*. Washington, DC: World Bank.

Williams, C. C., M. S. Shahid, and A. Martínez (2016). Determinants of the level of informality of informal micro-enterprises: Some evidence from the city of Lahore, Pakistan, *World Development*, 84: 312–25.

8

Slack Resources and Innovation in Vietnamese SMEs

A Behavioural, Stewardship, and Institutional Perspective

Tam Thanh Nguyen and Chieu Duc Trinh

8.1 Introduction

Small and medium enterprises (SMEs) play an important role in socioeconomic development.* These firms provide a growth engine for the economies through creating jobs and supplying goods and services that are not provided by larger counterparts (Acs and Audretsch 1990, 1993; Cunningham 2011; Honjo and Harada 2006; Storey 1994). This sector accounts for more than 95 per cent of all firms and 60 per cent of employment in developed countries (OECD 2000). They also contribute between half and three-quarters of the value added in the OECD enterprise sector (Mazzarol 2014). Especially in developing economies, the development of SMEs is crucial for society stabilization and poverty alleviation (Smallbone and Welter 2001). The development of SMEs provides solutions for poor people to escape from poverty through attracting them to work or even to start an enterprise themselves (Beck et al. 2005; Bauchet and Morduch 2013). Additionally, the SME sector helps to absorb economic shocks and natural and social disasters (Smallbone and Welter 2001). In Vietnam, according to the General Statistics Office (GSO 2017), 98.7 per cent of operating enterprises are SMEs in terms of the number of employees and they hire around 60 per cent of the total labour force in the enterprise sector.

Despite their important role in economies and society, SMEs are now facing many challenges during their development that may prevent them from profitable operation, such as limited access to markets and customers, and difficulties in sustaining growth. The facts show that innovation provides an efficient tool for these firms to overcome these shortcomings (Cefis and Marsili 2006).

* The authors thank John Rand for his invaluable comments, and Thinh Nguyen for his assistance in preliminary data analysis.

Tam Thanh Nguyen and Chieu Duc Trinh, *Slack Resources and Innovation in Vietnamese SMEs: A Behavioural, Stewardship, and Institutional Perspective* In: *Micro, Small, and Medium Enterprises in Vietnam*. Edited by: John Rand and Finn Tarp, Oxford University Press (2020). © United Nations University World Institute for Development Economics Research (UNU-WIDER).
DOI: 10.1093/oso/9780198851189.003.0008

Through introducing new products, firms have advantages in the access to new markets and new customers (Hausman and Johnston 2014). Meanwhile, the application of new business processes allows firms to reduce production costs and enrich the specifications of current products that enable firms to gain market share and sustain growth (Hall et al. 2009). However, common constraints for the innovation of SMEs-such as shortage of capital and lack of qualified staff-prevent firms from investing in innovation activities that are as such risky and costly (Hadjimanolis 1999; Madrid-Guijarro et al. 2009; Sandberg and Aarikka-Stenroos 2014). The presence of slack resources might provide an efficient solution for firms to innovate.

There is extensive research on the role of slack resources on performance and innovation. Slack resources would equip firms with a buffer from resource shortages which provides sufficient capital for innovation activities (Cyert and March 1963). The existence of slack resources also motivates firm owners/managers to search for business opportunities to fully utilize those unused resources, resulting in the introduction of new products, new processes or new markets (Penrose 1959). However, possessing resource slack is not always associated with innovation (Nohria and Gulati 1996). The possible interest difference/conflict between owners and managers drives managers to maintain excessive resources in the operation of firms, thus causing a resource waste in low-risk investments (Fama 1980). Consequently, this discourages firms to innovate. In addition, too much slack occupies the required resources for innovation thus restricting the efforts of introducing new products (Tan and Peng 2003).

A first possible explanation for the different influences of slack is the difference in business types. In family-run businesses where the benefits of the business are strongly connected with the welfare of family members, one of the owners/managers' priorities is to ensure the longevity of the firm, which in the long run benefits various family members (Gomez-Mejia et al. 2007). Consequently, this may prevent firms from using slack to finance firms' activities including innovation. This is different in large firms with well-organized structures where the managers are willing to deploy those excessive resources to meet the demands of the firm.

Second, different types of slack have different impacts on innovation. Slack is different in terms of divisibility, tangibility, and mobility (Mishina et al. 2004). Those differences in turn affect the ability of firms to exploit and deploy the slack for innovation activities (Wang et al. 2016). For instance, divisible slack is more easily mobilized to meet the resource demand of innovation activities, thus positively influencing the innovation of firms.

Another reason for the different directions and influences on firms' innovation is that slack resources do not work in isolation. The impact of slack resources depends on the combination with other external and internal innovation support factors that have been less understood (Marlin and Geiger 2015). Extant research explores this relationship focusing on firms in developed countries, whereas in developing countries, the impact of slack resources may be more pronounced due to the less mature nature of both the capital and the labour market (ILO 2016). Taken together, the heterogeneity across firms in different business environments/circumstances and the differences among types of slack challenge the impact of slack resources on innovation.

Therefore, in order to respond to these speculations, we ask two connected research questions. The first question is whether different types of slack resources improve innovation and the second question is how the institutional context strengthens or hinders the impact of slack resources on the innovation of firms. We investigate these two research questions through an exploration of a longitudinal dataset for Vietnamese SMEs. To do this, we first provide a brief literature review of innovation and slack resources, culminating in a research model and hypotheses. We then explain our data collection and methods and conclude with a discussion of our findings and possible theoretical and practical contributions.

8.2 Conceptual Background and Hypothesis Development

8.2.1 Innovation

Innovation is well studied under the theme of economics and management (Schumpeter 1939; Peters et al. 2017). Innovation involves a range of activities such as Research and Development (R&D) and product delivery and occupies a large amount of financial and human resources with the final aim of introducing something new that potentially benefits the firm's operations and performance (Hogan et al. 2011). This includes the introduction of a new product/service, production technology, and organizational management method (OECD 2005, 2010). Although the induction of innovation may be either new to the world, new to the market or new to firms, it all shows the importance for the survival/existence and development of firms through the retention and widening of the customer base, opening of new markets, reduction of production costs, and allowing more efficient management (Agarwal et al. 2003; Hausman and Johnston 2014). Consequently, innovation attracts lots of efforts from scholars to examine its nature, determinants and driving forces which again provides insights for managers/owners and governmental agencies into the promotion of innovation in firms (Acs and Audretsch 1988; Freeman 1982; Hall and Rosenberg 2010).

Extant research on innovation literature has investigated a range of different determinants of innovation arising from both external and internal factors. The external factors include components outside firms that have an influence on the innovation activities such as the dynamic business environment, technological development trends, preference changes of customers and suppliers and also the industrial and economic structure (Capaldo et al. 2003; De Jong and Vermeulen

2004; Romijn and Albaladejo 2002). Meanwhile, the internal factors comprise of the resource availability, the capability to sense, seize and transform business opportunities into real innovation output, and the characteristics of managers/owners such as risk-taking (Mel et al. 2009). Furthermore, recent scholars argue that not one single factor influences the innovation output, but the combination of both internal and external factors benefits innovation of firms, of which the internal ones play a crucial role in those innovative activities (Hogan et al. 2011; Ngo and O'Cass 2009). Among those factors, slack resources are a key ingredient that promote firms' innovation.

8.2.2 Slack Resources

Slack resources are well explored in their role for firm performance. Slack resources are defined as the overabundance of resources that exceed the required amount to ensure the normal production of firms (Bourgeois 1981; Geiger and Cashen 2002; Nohria and Gulati 1997). It is the unused resources that exist within firms and can be mobilized to serve particular needs of firms (Child 1972; Cohen et al. 1972). Slack resources are also considered as the non-fully utilized resources that firms can further fully utilize through appropriate strategies and actions. The existence of slack resources is obviously due to the nature of indivisibility of resources (Penrose 1959). Because 'resources are only obtainable in discrete amounts', thus, if a resource is demanded for a single activity or service, it would not be fully utilized for the need of that demand (Penrose 1959: 67). Consequently, this non-fully deployed resource creates an excess of resource within the firm. In addition, the knowledge created through business operations further generates the resource excess through more efficient resource deployment methods (Cyert and March 1963). In other words, the knowledge creation allows firms to reduce the execution time required for normal activities, thus generating slack (Pitelis 2007).

The importance of slack resources in innovation is well understood. Prior research has shown that slack is considered as the determinant and also driving force for firms to innovate (Cyert et al. 1959; Damanpour 1991). The presence of slack provides a buffer against shortage of resources for innovation activities which is common among SMEs (Mishina etal. 2004). Slack resources also motivate firms to search for business opportunities to deploy that slack, resulting in a new product a business process. The presence of slack encourages owners/managers to invest in innovative business activities that may lead to the introduction of a new product (Penrose 1959). In addition, the excess resource not only provides an endogenous incentive to innovate but also enables firms to recombine available resources in more creative ways (Nason and Wiklund 2015). However, notwithstanding the extensive theoretical and empirical studies, the relationship between resource slack and innovation remains ambiguous. Some scholars argue that too much slack creates struggles for firms in mobilizing resources for innovation activities as the necessary resource is locked within such slack (Fama 1980; Katila and Shane 2005). As a result, this prevents firms from investing resources in innovative activities. Furthermore, the high level of slack indicates the lower risk-taking levels of the owner/managers, thus, does not encourage them to look for business opportunities to fully deploy that slack (Singh 1986).

A first possible explanation for the controversial results is that the impact depends on the slack types and firms' characteristics. First, slack differs among firms. For example, in small firms, slack rarity is worse than in larger counterparts. Slack is also found to have different impact mechanisms in privately held firms than in public firms (George 2005). Second, slack resources are different in terms of availability, fungibility, absorbability, and recoverability (Voss et al. 2008). For example, there is absorbed and unabsorbed slack, genetic and rare slack. These differences influence the role of slack in supporting innovation. For instance, there is slack that is more fixed in certain business activities, therefore, is not easily allocated to other tasks. This slack is supposed to have less impacts on innovation. Among those types, financial and human resource slack are typical in organizations (Voss et al. 2008). These forms of slack are also important for SMEs to overcome the common financial and human capital constraints in their survival and development as will be explained next.

Financial slack typically refers to the excessive financial resources for the normal operation of an organization (Ang and Straub 1998; Voss et al. 2008). These financial resources are also not currently allocated for certain business activities (Bizzi 2017; Yanadori and Cui 2013). Extant research has proven the positive influence of financial slack on innovation of firms. For instance, Natividad (2013) argued that the presence of a high level of financial slack provides a resource buffer for innovation activities and thus enables firms to innovate. However, in small-scaled family-run businesses, the impact directions may differ. According to the stewardship theorists, in family business, the owners/managers have the responsibility to look after dependants (Davis *et al.* 1997). They act not only on behalf of the business but also of their family. Consequently, they first have to ensure the benefits of the whole family (Corbetta and Salvato 2004; Donaldson and Davis 1991). In other words, the well-being of family is strongly connected with the successful performance of the family's business. Therefore, if the unused financial resources are used to develop innovation, it may lead to constraints in the family's living standard due to the risky nature of innovation activities. Instead, the owners/managers prefer to use this financial slack in less risky activities.

Moreover, in these small-scaled family businesses, there is a blurred line between firm and family operational activities, especially in less developed countries. The underemployed financial resource can be used to meet the demand of family rather than firm activities. In addition to that, financial slack is completely divisible across multiple activities (Greve 2003). Thus, any available financial slack will be deployed for currently demanded activities, which are typically constrained by limited internal resources in small firms, rather than be invested in innovation that requires long-term commitment (Parida and Örtqvist 2015). Consequently, possessing a high level of financial slack reduces the likelihood of introducing a new product or business process. Therefore, it is theorized that:

Hypothesis 1 (H1): Financial slack negatively influences the probability of having innovation

Human resource slack is defined as the human resources in excess of that required for the efficient operation of an organization (Williamson 1963). The presence of this excessive staff enables firms to allocate the required human resources to additional tasks without interfering daily operational activities (Welbourne et al. 1998). From the stewardship theory perspective, because the firm and family interests are guaranteed, the owners are more open to invest this human resource slack to prepare for future growth. Moreover, human resource slack is less flexible than financial slack. It is also an absorbed slack which is not easily redeployed into variety use (Mishina et al. 2004). Therefore, it is not easy for the owner to use that unused resource to meet the resource demands of family activities. Instead, the human resource slack is preferred to be exploited within firms.

The presence of high levels of human resource slack means that the productivity of the workforce is not currently maximized. In other words, the workforce does not work at maximum capacity. This encourages the owner to further deploy the underemployed staff by allocating this excessive human resource to additional tasks. The reallocation of human resources allows firms to effectively respond to emerging business opportunities and achieve higher growth. In other words, human resource slack stimulates firms to search and transfer business opportunities, resulting in the introduction of a new product or a new market (Chang et al. 2012). Additionally, excess human resources also motivate firms to reconfigure the current production technology to maximize the capacity of the current workforce. For instance, introducing a new business process is also a way to improve the productivity in terms of human resource utilization. Therefore, we posit that:

Hypothesis 2 (H2): The human resource slack positively influences the probability of having innovation

8.2.3 The Moderation Role of Institutional Context

For SMEs that are typically facing resource constraints, the availability of slack resources is essential to engage in innovation activities and offer new products or business processes. However, slack resources do not act in isolation. Though slack equips firms with additional resources or motivates them to find business opportunities, the innovation outcome results from a range of connected activities. Thus, firms still require other factors in addition to slack. Among those factors, the institutional context plays an important role in enhancing the impact of slack resources on innovation as will be explained next.

Institutions are 'social structures that have attained a high degree of resilience' (Scott 1995: 33). They include different cognitive, normative, and regulative elements that operate at different levels of jurisdiction in the interpersonal, organizational, national, and global system. Institutions contribute to the formation of a business environment for firms, thus having influence on the operation and development of businesses (North 1991). The importance of institutions in firm's performance can be illustrated through the facilitating or hindering role. For instance, institutions can help alter the constraints and the structure of incentives in a society to direct self-interested behaviour towards either more or less economically productive activities (Baumol 1990; Nee 1996). Institutions also have an impact on the innovation of firms in both direct and indirect ways (Wang 2013). The direct effect is reducing uncertainty in the business environment through a stable legislation framework (World Bank 2013). Meanwhile, creating favourable conditions for firms to innovate such as developed inputs and outputs market is an example of the indirect impact of institutions on innovation (Mokyr 2007).

As noted, high levels of financial slack hinder the effort of introducing innovation in the firm. Though the excessiveness of financial resources provides a financial buffer for firms, the stewardship role does not encourage owners to invest the excess resources in new activities. The fungibility of that type of slack instead allows owners to easily allocate the financial excessiveness to activities that ensure the welfare of family rather than innovation activities. However, operating in different institutional levels may lead to different results in the impact of financial slack on innovation. For instance, in a region with a stable legal framework, the business environment is less uncertain, thus, reducing the perceived risk of owners and transaction costs when implementing innovation activities (Williamson 2005). Consequently, they are more open to invest the financial slack in developing new products or acquiring a new production technology. More importantly, the development of institutions may remove the owners' burden of ensuring family benefits. In a region with a developed financial market, the access to financial resources is more favourable, allowing the owners to have more alternative choices to ensure family welfare rather than using the firm's financial slack (Brown et al. 2012; Hsu et al. 2014). Additionally, firms have more access to other necessary resources to combine with financial slack in developing a new product or improve current products.

Taken together, high levels of institutional development may help to exit the family wellbeing trap, thus liberating the unused financial resources. Therefore, it is hypothesized that:

Hypothesis 3 (H3): The negative impact of financial slack is lessened in firms located in areas with a more favourable business environment

Human resource slack improves innovation. The excess of this slack type encourages owners to first search for business opportunities and second reconfigure business operations to fully deploy the underemployed staff. First, high levels of institutional development allow firms to have favourable conditions in accessing financial and other resources such as premises, information and technology to supplement for human resource slack. Firms also have more advantages to develop their capabilities in a stable policy condition. These are crucial for the successful development of a new product because innovation requires the combination of a range of resources and capabilities (Hogan et al. 2011). Second, the development of institutions contributes to the removal of barriers to market entrance and creates an equal playing field among businesses. Firms have less constraints when entering/opening new markets with new products or expanding the current market with improved products as a result of consuming human resource slack. Consequently, this enriches the impact of human resource slack on innovation. Therefore, it is hypothesized that:

Hypothesis 4 (H4): The positive impact of human resource slack is stronger in firms located in areas with a more favourable business environment

8.3 Methodology

8.3.1 Sample

This study explores the longitudinal Vietnamese SME dataset collected biennially from 2005 to 2015. The surveys were conducted under the collaboration of Central Institute for Economic Management (Vietnam), Institute for Labour and Social Affairs (Vietnam), and University of Copenhagen with sponsoring by the Danish Development Agency and UNU-WIDER. The surveys cover around 2,500 small and medium manufacturing firms in ten provinces of Vietnam namely Hanoi, Ha Tay (ex), Hai Phong, Phu Tho, Nghe An, Quang Nam, Lam Dong, Khanh Hoa, Ho Chi Minh city, and Long An (CIEM 2007). The sample selection is implemented with the aim to ensure the correct representation of the manufacturing sector development in Vietnam.

8.3.2 Measurements

Dependent variables

In the study, we investigated three binary innovation dependent variables, namely radical, incremental product and process innovation. In the survey, firms were asked whether they introduced the following types of innovation: a new product, a major improvement to a current product or a new technology/production process (OECD 2005). The radical product innovation is determined by whether firm introduced a new product to the market. Some authors argued that the radical product innovation relates to the introduction of a product that is totally new to the market. However, in our sample, the radical product innovation is only new to firms but demonstrates a huge effort from these small firms to introduce this new product (Slater et al. 2014). Thus, our sample could be a reasonable proxy for radical product innovation. The second dependent variable is incremental product innovation which is defined by the introduction of a major improvement to current products. Meanwhile, process innovation is determined by the application of a new product process or technology. These three dependent variables were coded as binary variables that assigned value 1 if introducing innovation and 0 otherwise.

Explanatory variables

We measured financial slack as the difference between the ratio of total sale to total assets of firms and the mean ratio for all firms operating in the same two-digit industry (Bourgeois 1981). Meanwhile, human resource slack was calculated by subtracting the number of full-time equivalent employees from the total sales of firms and the mean ratio of the industry (Vanacker et al. 2017). These two measures present the physical and human capital excess that firms use to generate specific amount of sales as compared with other counterparts.

For institutional context, the Provincial Competitiveness Index (PCI) is employed to represent the level of business favourability. The PCI was first introduced in 2005 in Vietnam and conducted annually (Malesky 2017). The overall PCI comprises ten sub-indices, reflecting economic governance areas that affect private sector development. A province that is considered to perform well on the PCI is the one that has: (i) low entry costs for business start-up; (ii) easy access to land and security of business premises; (iii) a transparent business environment and equitable business information; (iv) minimal informal charges; (v) limited time requirements for bureaucratic procedures and inspections; (vi) limited crowding out of private activity from policy biases toward state, foreign, or connected firms; (vii) proactive and creative provincial leadership in solving problems for enterprises; (viii) developed and high-quality business support services; (ix) sound labour training policies; and (x) fair and effective legal procedures for dispute resolution. The PCI is the weighted mean of the ten sub-indices with a maximum score of 100 points.

Control variables

Four control variables that are important for firm-level analyses—namely firm size, firm age, industry, and legal form—were included. Firm size was measured by the number of the total regular workforce (log). Firm age was measured by the number of years a firm was in business (log). Firm industries were classified based on the Vietnamese Standard Industrial Classification that complies with the International Standard Industrial Classification (OECD 2009). Legal form was classified as household and non-household firms (Romijn and Albaladejo 2002). The variables are summarized in Table 8.1.

Table 8.1 Independent variables in the innovation models

Variables	Explanation of variables
Financial slack	Financial slack calculated by comparison between the firm's ratio of total sale over total assets and the mean ratio of firms in the same industry (2-digit industrial code)
Human resource slack	Human resource slack calculated by comparison between the firm's ratio of total employees over total sale and the mean ratio of firms in the same industry (2-digit industrial code)
PCI	Provincial Competitiveness Index calculated by taking weighted mean of ten sub-indices with a maximum score of 100 points
Firm size	The total number of full-time employees (Log)
Firm age	Number of years in business (Log)
Household	Dummy variable. If firms are household, Legal form=1, otherwise Legal form=0
Low industry	Dummy variable. If firms's industry is low technology, thus, Low_industry=1, otherwise, Low_industry=0
Medium-low industry (Ind_MedLow)	Dummy variable. If firms' industry is medium-low technology, thus, Medium_Low_industry=1, otherwise, Medium_Low_industry=0
Medium-high industry (Ind_MedHigh)	Dummy variable. If firms' industry is medium-high technology, thus, Medium_High_industry=1, otherwise, Medium_High_industry=0
High industry (Ind_High)	Dummy variable. If firms' industry is high technology, thus, High_industry=1, otherwise, High_industry=0

Source: Authors' calculation based on the 2005–15 Vietnamese SMEs data.

8.3.3 Bias Testing

We conducted a number of tests and techniques to ensure the avoidance of bias in the estimation. First, the survey followed a random sampling procedure to assure the representation of different types of firms in our sample, thus, sample selection bias does not appear to be a problem (Pannucci and Wilkins 2010). Second, the high response rate of typical governmental surveys indicates that non-response bias is not an issue (Armstrong and Overton 1977). Third, we also performed a Harman's single factor test to find out whether there is a presence of common method bias. The results show that the first factor did not account more than 50 per cent of variance of other factors; therefore, common method bias seems not to be a main issue on our estimation (Podsakoff et al. 2003). Finally, together with the inclusion of PCI data from the Vietnam Chamber of Commerce and Industry, the application of direct interviews with firm's owner/managers who have outstanding knowledge about the operation of firms helps us to limit the bias arising from using a single data source.

8.3.4 Research Method

As the dependent variables are binary, we apply binary probit regression as a method to test our hypotheses (Wooldridge 2010). The specific model is described as:

$$E(y|x) = \exp(x\beta)/[1 + \exp(x\beta)],$$

where $E(y|x)$ is a binary probit function and x is a set of explanatory and control variables.

A firm would initially be better endowed with innovation, thus raising concerns about endogeneity leading to estimation bias. Therefore, statistical techniques such as adding control variables and/or using robust standard errors will be applied to control for endogeneity problem.

8.4 Results and Discussion

8.4.1 Results

Table 8.2 presents the descriptive statistics and correlation matrix on the variables used in the study. There was 65 per cent of our sample operating as household firms, indicating a high proportion of informal firms in the Vietnamese manufacturing industry. In our sample, as we keep track firms during a 10-year period since

Table 8.2 Descriptive statistics and correlation matrix

		Mean	SD	1	2	3	4	5	6	7	8	9	10	11
1	Radical product innovation	0.128	0.334											
2	Incremental product innovation	0.324	0.468	0.256***										
3	Process innovation	0.130	0.336	0.254***	0.372***									
4	Financial slack	0.656	3.184	−0.004	−0.025**	−0.013								
5	Human resource slack	0.001	0.009	0.026**	0.014	0.026**	−0.003							
6	PCI	56.224	5.040	0.101***	−0.108***	−0.056***	−0.002	−0.194***						
7	Firm size	14.106	27.462	0.083***	0.155***	0.197***	0.056***	0.027**	0.031**					
8	Firm age	14.242	9.522	−0.032**	−0.099***	−0.078***	−0.056***	0.001	−0.019**	−0.094***				
9	Legal form	0.654	0.476	−0.066***	−0.138***	−0.164***	−0.004	−0.013	−0.097***	−0.449***	0.187***			
10	Medium- low-technology industry	0.241	0.427	0.025**	0.048***	−0.016**	0.019**	−0.006	0.015	−0.033***	−0.024**	0.002		
11	Medium- high-technology industry	0.087	0.282	0.036***	0.084***	−0.006	−0.013	−0.003	−0.037***	−0.023**	−0.018**	0.032***	−0.174***	
12	High- technology industry	0.022	0.148	0.086***	0.053***	0.062***	−0.012	−0.001	0.013	0.041***	−0.025**	−0.056***	−0.085***	−0.047***

Note: Spearman correlation. *$p < 0.05$; **$p<0.01$; and ***$p < 0.001$.

Source: Authors' calculation based on the 2005-15 Vietnamese SMEs data.

2005, firms were quite mature with the average age of more than 14 years in business which is typical in manufacturing industries. The average size of firms was 14 regular full-time employees. The majority of firms operated in low and medium-low-technology industries such as food and beverage, garments and textiles. Only 9 per cent of firms are in medium-high-technology industries while 2 per cent in high tech. This is the case of Vietnamese manufacturing industries which is confirmed in the industrialization policy during the last 20 years (Anh et al. 2014).

The results also show the proportion of firms that introduced radical, incremental product and process innovation. While 32 per cent of firms had major improvements to current products, there was only 13.8 per cent launching a new production process. The percentage of firms offering new products to the market was 12.8 per cent. Table 8.2 also illustrates significant correlations between the financial and human resource slack, firm size, firm age, legal form, and business environment favourability.

Table 8.3 exhibits the results of our estimation on the impact of financial slack on the three mentioned innovation types. The results show that the financial slack is statistically significantly negatively related to incremental product ($p<0.001$) and process innovation ($p<0.05$) (see Model 4 and 6). In other words, firms encountering financial slack are less likely to make improvement to the current product, and to engage in a new technology/production process. However, the results do not demonstrate a statistically significant impact of financial slack on the introduction of a new product (Model 1). Therefore, H1 was partly confirmed.

Table 8.4 demonstrates the estimation results of the impact of human resource slack on the three mentioned innovation types. The estimation results show that human resource slack has a positive impact on all three mentioned innovation types at any considered statistical significance levels (Models 8, 10, and 12). In other words, firms encountering human resource slack are more likely to introduce new products, to make improvement to the current product, and engage in a new technology/production process. Therefore, H2 was confirmed.

The estimation for the moderation impact of institutional context on the relationship between financial slack and human resource slack and innovation is illustrated in Tables 8.5 and 8.6. As expected, a location in regions with higher levels of institutions reduces the negative impact of financial slack on incremental product and process innovation (Models 14 and 15). However, this location does not statistically impact on the relationship between financial slack and radical product innovation (Model 13). Therefore, H3 was partially confirmed. The results in Models 17 and 18 present the negative moderation of institutional context on the relationship between human resource slack and incremental product and process innovation. In other words, firms located in a more favourable business environment will gain less positive impact from human resource slack. Therefore, H4 was rejected.

Table 8.3 The impact of financial slack on innovation

	Radical product innovation	Incremental product innovation	Process innovation			
	Model 1	Model 2	Model 3	Model 4	Model 5	Model 6
Explanatory variable						
Financial slack		−0.004		−0.021***		−0.014*
Control variables						
Firm size (log)	0.118***	0.119***	0.261***	0.264***	0.282***	0.284***
Firm age (log)	0.057**	0.056**	0.019	0.013	−0.011	−0.015
Medium-low- technology industry	0.204***	0.204***	0.230***	0.233***	−0.057	−0.056
Medium-high- technology industry	0.301***	0.301***	0.477***	0.476***	−0.065	−0.068
High-technology industry	0.290***	0.289***	0.127	0.120	0.091	0.086
Legal form	−0.184***	−0.173***	−0.095**	−0.090**	−0.147***	−0.144***
Year 2007	−1.395***	−1.395***	−0.396***	−0.396***	−0.488***	−0.487***
Year 2009	−1.672***	−1.673***	−0.463***	−0.463***	−0.548***	−0.548***
Year 2011	−2.259***	−2.259***	−1.192***	−1.196***	−0.951***	−0.951***
Year 2013	−2.274***	−2.227***	−1.202***	−1.204***	−0.943***	−0.942***
Year 2015	−0.425***	−0.425***	−1.336***	−1.338***	−1.106***	−1.105***
Constant	−0.603***	−0.600***	−0.366***	−0.341***	−1.014***	−1.002***
Observations	15,589	15,589	15,589	15,589	15,589	15,589
χ^2	2240.924***	2240.40***	2717.92***	2770.08**	1412.91***	1414.77***
Pseudo R2	0.2808	0.2808	0.1638	0.1653	0.1462	0.1470

Note: Probit regression. Based: Low technologyindustry, year 2005. *p < 0.05; **p<0.01; and ***p < 0.001.

Source: Authors' calculation based on the 2005–15 Vietnamese SMEs data.

Table 8.4 The impact of human resource slack on innovation

	Radical product innovation	Incremental product innovation	Process innovation			
	Model 7	Model 8	Model 9	Model 10	Model 11	Model 12
Explanatory variable						
Human resource slack		7.925***		4.522**		7.622***
Control variables						
Firm size (log)	0.118***	0.118***	0.261***	0.261***	0.282***	0.282***
Firm age (log)	0.057**	0.056*	0.019	0.019	−0.011	−0.011
Medium-low- technology industry	0.204***	0.204***	0.230***	0.231***	−0.057	−0.056
Medium-high- technology industry	0.301***	0.302***	0.477***	0.477***	−0.065	−0.065
High-technology industry	0.290***	0.291***	0.127	0.127	0.091	0.092
Legal form	−0.184***	−0.174***	−0.095**	−0.095**	−0.147***	−0.147***
Year 2007	−1.395***	−1.393***	−0.396***	−0.395***	−0.488***	−0.487***
Year 2009	−1.672***	−1.671***	−0.463***	−0.462***	−0.548***	−0.547***
Year 2011	−2.259***	−2.258***	−1.192***	−1.193***	−0.951***	−0.95***
Year 2013	−2.274***	−2.273***	−1.202***	−1.202***	−0.943***	−0.942***
Year 2015	−0.425***	−0.424***	−1.336***	−1.336***	−1.106***	−1.104***
Constant	−0.603***	−0.603***	−0.366***	−0.362***	−1.014***	−1.014***
Observations	15,589	15,589	15,589	15,589	15,589	15,589
χ^2	2240.924***	2293.92***	2717.92***	2735.05***	1412.91***	1458.49***
Pseudo R2	0.2808	0.2810	0.1638	0.1639	0.1462	0.1464

Note: Probit regression. Based: Low technology industry, year 2005. *p < 0.05; **p<0.01; and ***p < 0.001.

Source: Authors' calculation based on the 2005–15 Vietnamese SMEs data.

Table 8.5 The moderation impact of institutional context on the relationship between financial slack and innovation

	Radical product innovation	Incremental product innovation	Process innovation
	Model 13	**Model 14**	**Model 15**
Explanatory variable			
Financial slack	0.043	−0.177**	−0.206*
PCI	−0.010*	−0.006*	−0.007*
Financial slack *PCI	−0.001	0.003*	0.003*
Control variables			
Firm size (log)	0.054*	0.267***	0.280***
Firm age (log)	0.135***	−0.008	−0.017
Medium-low-technology industry	0.151**	0.215***	−0.087*
Medium-high-technology industry	0.126	0.387***	−0.115
High-technology industry	0.154	−0.016	0.049
Legal form	−0.169**	−0.057	−0.085
Year 2009	−0.267***	−0.058	−0.048
Year 2011	−0.835***	−0.777***	−0.437***
Year 2013	−0.862***	−0.782***	−0.429***
Year 2015	0.981***	−0.9***	−0.568***
Constant	−1.482***	−0.385*	−1.099***
Observations	12,787	12,787	12,787
χ^2	1165.27***	1701.53***	690.09
Pseudo R2	0.2213	0.1300	0.1038

Note: Probit regression. Based: Low technology industry, year 2005. *p < 0.05; **p < 0.01; and ***p < 0.001.

Source: Authors' calculation based on the 2005–15 Vietnamese SMEs data.

8.4.2 Discussion

Around more than 80 per cent of Vietnamese SMEs experienced some constraints (CIEM et al. 2016), including financial shortage, limited demand, and fierce competition. Therefore, taking use of slack resources should be one of the important solutions for dealing with their main constraints. The data analysis revealed the impact of both financial and human resource slack on innovation but in reverse directions. Financial slack shows the negative impact on innovation in terms of incremental product and process innovation, meaning that firms encountering financial slack are less likely to make improvement to the current product, and to engage in a new technology/production process. This confirms the firm owners' stewardship role in managing the family welfare (Donaldson and Davis 1991). The flexibility of financial slack allows firm owners to direct the use of those excessive resources to meet the family demands rather than to invest in the firm's activities such as translating business opportunities into a new product or business

Table 8.6 The moderation impact of institutional context on the relationship between human resource slack and innovation

	Radical product innovation	Incremental product innovation	Process innovation
	Model 16	Model 17	Model 18
Explanatory variable			
Human resource slack	−70.981	30475.89***	35621***
PCI	−0.011*	−0.002	−0.003
Human resource slack *PCI	−31.853	−785.135***	−870.813***
Control variables			
Firm size (log)	0.051*	0.258***	0.276***
Firm age (log)	0.138***	0.007	−0.007
Medium-low-technology industry	0.147**	0.201***	−0.092*
Medium-high-technology industry	0.120	0.366***	−0.129*
High-technology industry	0.150	−0.038	0.029
Legal form	−0.162**	−0.016	−0.046
Year 2009	−0.274***	−0.101**	−0.073
Year 2011	−0.847***	−0.852***	−0.491***
Year 2013	−0.875***	−0.858***	−0.483***
Year 2015	0.970***	−0.978***	−0.624***
Constant	−1.428***	−0.519**	−1.295***
Observations	12,787	12,787	12,787
χ^2	1171.94***	1713.03***	719.15***
Pseudo R2	0.2214	0.1367	0.1088

Note: Probit regression. Based: Low technology industry, year 2005. *p < 0.05; **p < 0.01; and ***p < 0.001.

Source: Authors' calculation based on the 2005–15 Vietnamese SMEs data.

process. In contrast, human resource slack illustrates a strong positive impact on all mentioned innovation types in the data analysis, meaning that firms experiencing human resource slack are more likely to introduce new products, make improvements to the current product, and to engage in a new technology/production process. Unlike the financial slack, the human resource slack is more fixed in firms (Voss et al. 2008). Workers employed by firms have specific knowledge and skills to meet the requirements of the firm's business activities, which means that it is not easy for owners/managers to relocate this type of slack to family activities rather than to the firm. Consequently, owners/managers are more likely to deploy that underemployed resource to meet the demands of new business opportunities that lead to the introduction of innovation.

The results also illustrate that the impact of financial slack resources on innovation is also influenced by the institutional context, where a higher level of business favourability causes smaller negative impact on incremental product and process innovation. One possible explanation for this fact may be that the firms operating in better business circumstances usually have more business opportunities, including the expansion into a new market. Thus, it is easier for them to make use of resource slack for their production compared to those firms operating in more difficult business circumstances. Considering the fact that financial shortage is usually the biggest constraint for SME development (CIEM et al. 2016), this finding may imply that improvement of business conditions should suggest a better use of financial slack for SME innovation in Vietnam. More importantly, the presence of high levels of institutions associated with the development of the financial market expedites the access to financial sources, thus giving firm owners more choice in sustaining their family's financial capabilities instead of using financial slack. On the other hand, financial slack now can be used to serve the demands of growth of firms, resulting in the induction of new products or technologies.

In the case of human resource slack and its impact on innovation, the findings show that operating in more favourable business environment does not enhance the impact. In contrast, it reduces the positive effect of human resource slack on innovation. One possible explanation for this unexpected consequence is the employee turnover. The high level of development of labour market in favourable business environment allows the excessive employee easier to move to other firms. This employee movement creates a loss in human capital and knowledge of firms (Eriksson et al. 2014). Though firms might have chance in exploring business opportunities in a favourable business environment, the presence of a loss of knowledge does not at least allow firms to transfer these business opportunities into real new product or business process. Consequently, it reduces the impact of human resource slack on innovation.

As expected, firms operating in higher level of technology industries are more likely to innovation than those in low technology counterparts in terms of introducing new products and improving existing products. However, the results do not show the significant difference amongst three considered levels of technology industries regarding to the process innovation. In addition, the results also strongly indicate that larger firms are more likely to engage in innovation than smaller firms at all three types of innovation. Finally, informal firms (household businesses) are less likely to engage in innovation probability than formal firms.

8.5 Conclusions

In this chapter, the study deepens the understanding of the role of slack resources in promoting innovation. By exploring a dataset from the Vietnamese SMEs survey, the study offers a number of theoretical and managerial contributions. First, the research expands the boundary conditions of the impact of slack resources on family business innovation. This contributes to the explanation for the different impact of slack resource types on innovation. While in public firms, there is a clear line between firms and owners'/managers' family operational activities, the blurred line in family business together with the stewardship role motivates owners to direct the underemployed resource to first guarantee their family benefits (Donaldson and Davis 1991, 1993). This leads to the negative consequence of slack on innovation. This is more pronounced for slack resources that are less fixed such as financial slack. Meanwhile, for more fixed slack, the owners have no other choices but to invest in firm's activities, thus explaining the positive effect.

Second, the study sheds light on the relationship between slack resources and innovation through the influence of institutional context in emerging economies. The findings show that slack does not work in isolation in supporting innovation. It requires an interaction with other external factors embedded in the institutions. The constitution of business environment conditions thereby can hinder or facilitate the impact of slack on innovation. In other words, it further confirms the orchestra of resources in sustaining growth and competitive advantages.

The findings also suggest a number of managerial and economic policy implications. First, a clear direction in the deployment of different slack resource types is crucial for the introduction of a new product or business process. While financial slack is fungible across inner and outer business activities, the high levels of that type of slack may not always be associated with innovation. Meanwhile, the more fixed human resource slack is an important source of innovation support. Second, ensuring the retention of human resources is supportive for the impact of human resource slack on innovation. Third, the findings suggest that the facilitation of the business environment, such as developing financial markets, will motivate firms to more fully deploy their slack resources.

Although our study has advanced the understanding of the role of slack resources on innovation, it is important to highlight some limitations. First, we are unable to create continuous variables for innovation, thus the possibility of measurement bias exists. We reduced the likelihood of that error by testing the regressions with an assumed substitute variable of a continuous innovation slack resource change level. The consistent results indicate a high degree of robustness.

References

Acs, Z. J. and D. B. Audretsch (1988). Innovation and firm size in manufacturing, *Technovation*, 7: 197–210.

Acs, Z. J. and D. B. Audretsch. (1990). *Innovation and Small Firms.* Cambridge MA: MIT Press.

Acs, Z. J. and D. B. Audretsch (1993). *Small Firms and Entrepreneurship: An East-West Perspective.* Cambridge: Cambridge University Press.

Agarwal, S., M. K. Erramilli, and C. S. Dev (2003). Market orientation and performance in service firms: role of innovation, *Journal of Service Marketing*, 17(1): 68–82.

Ang, S., and D. W. Straub (1998). Production and transaction economics in information systems outsourcing: A study of the U.S. banking industry, *MIS Quarterly*, 22(4): 535–52.

Anh, N. T. T, M. D. Luu, and D. C. Trinh (2014). The Evolution of Vietnamese Industry. WIDER Working Paper 76/2014. Helsinki: UNU-WIDER.

Armstrong, J. S., and T. S. Overton (1977). Estimating non-response bias in mail surveys, *Journal of Marketing Research*, 14: 396–402.

Bauchet, J., and J. Morduch (2013). Is micro too small? Microcredit vs. SME finance. *World Development*, 3: 288–97.

Baumol, W. (1990). Entrepreneurship: productive, unproductive and destructive, *Journal of Political Economy*, 98, 893–921.

Beck, T., A. Demirgüç-Kunt, and R. Levine (2005). SMEs, growth and poverty: Cross-country evidence, *Journal of Economic Growth*, 10: 197–227.

Bizzi, L. (2017). The strategic role of financial slack on alliance formation, *Management Decision*, 55(2): 383–99.

Bourgeois, L. J. III. (1981). On the measurement of organizational slack, *Academy of Management Review*, 6: 29–40.

Brown, J., G. Martinsson, and B. Petersen (2012). Laws, stock markets, and innovation, *Journal of Finance*, 68: 1517–49.

Capaldo, G., L. Iandoli, M. Raffa, and G. Zollo (2003). The evaluation of innovation capabilities in small software firms: A methodological approach, *Small Business Economics*, 21, 343–54.

Cefis, E., and O. Marsili (2006). Survivor: the role of innovation in firm's survival, *Research Policy*, 35, 626–41.

Chang, S., Y. Jaw, and H. Chiu (2012). A behavioral perspective of international new ventures: Slack, early internationalization, and performance, *The Journal of Global Business Management*, 8(2): 200–11.

Child, J. (1972). Organizational structure, environment, and performance: The role of strategic choice, *Sociology*, 6(1): 1–22.

CIEM. (2007). *Characteristics of the Vietnamese Business Environment: Evidence from a SME Survey in 2005.* Hanoi: Labour and Social Affairs Publishing House.

CIEM, DoE, ILSSA and UNU-WIDER (2016). Characteristics of the Vietnamese business environment: Evidence from a SME Survey in 2015. Available at: https://www.wider.unu.edu/sites/default/files/SME2015-report-English.pdf (accessed on 10 January 2018).

Cohen, W. M., J. G. March, and J. P. Olsen (1972). A garbage can model of organizational choice, *Administrative Science Quarterly*, 17(1): 1–25.

Corbetta, G., and C. Salvato (2004). Self-serving or self-actualizing? Models of man and agency costs in different types of family firms: A commentary on comparing the agency costs of family and non-family firms: Conceptual issues and exploratory evidence, *Entrepreneurship Theory and Practice,* 28(4): 355–62.

Cunningham, L. X. (2011). SMEs as motor of growth: A review of China's SMEs development in thirty years (1978–2008), *Human Systems Management,* 30(1): 39–54.

Cyert, R. M., E. A. Feigenbaum, and J. G. March (1959). Models in a behavioral theory of the firm, *Behavioral Science,* 4(2): 81–95.

Cyert, R. M., and J. G. March (1963). *A Behavioral Theory of the Firm.* Englewood Cliffs: Prentice Hall.

Damanpour, F. (1991). Organizational innovation: A meta-analysis of effect of determinants and moderators, *Academy Management Journal,* 34(3): 555–90.

Davis, J. H., F. D. Schoorman, and L. Donaldson (1997). Toward a stewardship theory of management, *Academy of Management Review,* 22: 20–47.

De Jong, J. P. J., and P. A. M. Vermeulen (2004). *Determinants of Product Innovation in Small Firms: A Comparison across Industries.* Zoetermeer, Netherlands: Scientific Analysis of Entrepreneurship and SMEs.

Donaldson, L., and Davis, J. H. (1991). Stewardship theory or agency theory: CEO governance and shareholder returns, *Australian Journal of Management,* 16: 49–65.

Donaldson, L., and Davis, J. H. (1993). The need for theoretical coherence and intellectual rigour in corporate governance research: Reply to critics of Donaldson and Davis, *Australian Journal of Management,* 18: 213–25.

Eriksson, T., Qin, Z., and Wang, W. (2014). Firm-level innovation activity, employee turnover and HRM practices—Evidence from Chinese firms, *China Economic Review,* 30: 583–97.

Fama, E. F. (1980). Agency problems and theory of the firm, *Journal of Political Economy,* 88(2): 288–307.

Freeman, C. (1982). *The Economics of Industrial Innovation,* (2nd ed.), London: Frances Printer.

Geiger, S. W., and Cashen, L. H. (2002). A multidimensional examination of slack and its impact on innovation, *Journal of Management Issues,* XIV(I): 68–84.

George, G. (2005). Slack resources and the performance of privately held firms, *Academy of Management Journal,* 48: 661–76.

Gomez-Mejia, L. R., Haynes, K., Nuñez-Nickel, M., Jacobson, K. J. L., and Moyano-Fuentes, J. (2007). Socioemotional wealth and business risks in family-controlled firms: Evidence from Spanish olive oil mills, *Administrative Science Quarterly,* 52: 106–37.

Greve, H. (2003). A behavioral theory of RandD expenditures and innovations: Evidence from shipbuilding, *Academy of Management Journal,* 46: 685–702.

GSO (2017). *Statistical Year Book.* Hanoi: Statistical Publishing House.

Hadjimanolis, A. (1999). Barriers to innovation for SME in a small less developed country (Cyprus), *Technovation,* 19: 561–70.

Hall, B. and Rosenberg, N. (2010). *Handbook of Economics of Innovation,* vol. 1. Amsterdam: North-Holland.

Hall, B. H., Lotti, F., and Mairesse, J. (2009). Innovation and productivity in SMEs: Empirical evidence for Italy, *Small Business Economics*, 33(1): 13–33.

Hausman, A., and Johnston, W. J. (2014). The role of innovation in driving the economy: Lessons from the global financial crisis, *Journal of Business Research*, 67(1): 2720–6.

Hogan, S. J., Soutar, G. N., McColl-Kennedy, J. R., and Sweeney, J. C. (2011). Reconceptualizing professional service firm innovation capability: Scale development, *Industrial Marketing Management*, 40(8): 1264–73.

Honjo, Y., and N. Harada (2006). SME policy, financial structure and firm growth: Evidence from Japan, *Small Business Economics*, 27: 289–300.

Hsu, P., X. Tian, and Y. Xu (2014). Financial market development and innovation: Cross country evidence, *Journal of Financial Economics*, 112: 116–35.

ILO (2016). *Key Indicators of the Labour Market* (Ninth edition). Geneva: International Labour Office.

Katila, R., and Shane, S. (2005). When does the lack of resources make new firms innovative?, *Academy Management Journal*, 48(5): 814–29.

Madrid-Guijarro, A., Garcia, D., and Van Auken, H. (2009). Barriers to innovation among Spanish manufacturing SMEs, *Journal of Small Business Management*, 47(4): 465–88.

Malesky, E. (2017). *The Vietnam Provincial Competitiveness Index: Measuring Economic Governance for Private Sector Development, 2016. Final Report.* Ha Noi: Vietnam Chamber of Commerce and Industry and United States Agency for International Development.

Marlin, D. R. and Geiger, S. (2015). A reexamination of the organizational slack and innovation relationship, *Journal of Business Research*, 68(12): 2683–90.

Mazzarol, T. (2014). *Growing and Sustaining Entrepreneurial Ecosystems: What They Are and the Role of Government Policy,* White Paper WP01-2014. Fremantle: Small Enterprise Association of Australia and New Zealand (SEAANZ), www.seaanz.org.

Mel, S. D., McKenzie, D., and Woodruff, C. (2009). Innovative Firms or Innovative Owners? Determinants of Innovation in Micro, Small, and Medium Enterprises. Policy Research Working Paper No. WPS4934. Washington, DC: The World Bank.

Mishina, Y., Pollock, T. G., and Porac, J. F. (2004). Are more resources always better for growth? Resource stickiness in market and product expansion, *Strategic Management Journal*, 25, 1179–97.

Mokyr, J. (2007). 'Technology, Institutions, and Economic Growth, collected essays, Richard R. Nelson', *Research Policy*, 36(10): 1668–72.

Nason, R. S., and Wiklund, J. (2015). An assessment of resource-based theorizing on firm growth and suggestions for the future, *Journal of Management*, 20(10): 1–29.

Natividad, G. (2013). Financial slack, strategy, and competition in movie distribution, *Organization Science*, 24(3): 846–64.

Nee, V. (1996). The emergence of a market society: Changing mechanisms of stratification in China, *The American Journal of Sociology*, 101: 908–49.

Ngo, L. V. and O'Cass, A. (2009). Creating value offerings via operant resource-based capabilities, *Industrial Marketing Management*, 38(1): 45–9.

Nohria, N., and Gulati, R. (1996). Is slack good or bad for innovation?, *Academy of Management Journal*, 39(5): 1245–64.

Nohria, N., and Gulati, R. (1997). What is the optimum amount of organizational slack?, *European Management Journal*, 15, 603–11.

North, D. C. (1991). Institutions, *Journal of Economic Perspectives*, 5(1): 97–112.

OECD (2000). Small and medium-sized enterprises: Local strength, global reach. OECD Policy Brief, June 2000. Paris: OECD.

OECD (2005). *Proposed Guidelines for Collecting and Interpreting Innovation Data: Oslo Manual.* Paris: OECD Publishing.

OECD (2009). *OECD Science, Technology and Industry Scoreboard 2009*, Paris: OECD Publishing.

OECD (2010). *Measuring Innovation: A New Perspective,* Paris: OECD Publishing.

Pannucci, C. J., and Wilkins, E. G. (2010). Identifying and avoiding bias in research, *Plastic and Reconstructive Surgery*, 126(2): 619–25.

Parida, V., and Örtqvist, D. (2015). Interactive effects of network capability, ICT capability, and financial slack on technology-based small firm innovation performance, *Journal of Small Business Management,* 53(S1): 278–98.

Penrose, E. T. (1959). *The Theory of the Growth of the Firm*. Oxford: Oxford University Press.

Peters, B., Roberts, M. J., Vuong, V. A. and Fryges, H. (2017). Estimating dynamic R&D choice: An analysis of costs and long-run benefits. *The R&D Journal of Economics,* 48, 409–37.

Pitelis, C. N. (2007). A behavioral resource-based view of the firm: The synergy of Cyert and March (1963) and Penrose (1959). *Organization Science,*18(3): 478–90.

Podsakoff, P. M., MacKenzie, S. B., Lee, J.-B., and Podsakoff, N. P. (2003). Common method biases in behavioral research: A critical review of the literature and recommended remedies. *Journal of Applied Psychology,* 88, 879–903.

Romijn, H. and Albaladejo, M. (2002). Determinants of innovation capability in small electronics and software firms in southeast England. *Research Policy,* 31(7): 1053–67.

Sandberg, B., and Aarikka-Stenroos, L. (2014). What makes it so difficult? A systematic review on barriers to radical innovation. *Industrial Marketing Management,* 43(8): 1293–1305.

Schumpeter, J. A. (1939). *Business Cycles.* New York: McGraw-Hill.

Scott, W. R. (1995). *Institutions and Organizations.* Thousand Oaks, CA: Sage.

Singh, J. (1986). Performance, slack, and risk taking in organizational decision making, *Academy of Management Journal*, 29, 562–85.

Smallbone, D., and Welter, F. (2001). The role of government in SME development in transition economies, *International Small Business Journal*, 19, 63–77.

Slater, S. F., Mohr, J. J., and Sengupta, S. (2014). Radical product innovation capability: Literature review, synthesis, and illustrative research propositions, *Journal of Product Innovation Management*, 31(3): 552–66.

Storey, D. J. (1994). *Understanding the Small Business Sector.* London: Thomson Learning.

Tan, J., and M. W. Peng (2003). Organizational slack and firm performance during economic transitions: Two studies from an emerging economy, *Strategic Management Journal*, 24, 1249–63.

Vanacker, T., V. Collewaert, and S. A. Zahra (2017). Slack resources, firm performance, and the institutional context: Evidence from privately held European firms, *Strategic Management Journal*, 38(6): 1305–26.

Voss, G. B., D. Sirdeshmukh, and Z. G. Voss (2008). The effects of slack resources and environmental threat on product exploration and exploitation, *Academy of Management Journal*, 51(1): 147–64.

Wang, C. (2013). Can institutions explain cross country differences in innovative activity?, *Journal of Macroeconomics*, 37: 128–45.

Wang, H., J. Choi, G. Wan, and J. Q. Dong (2016). Slack resources and the rent-generating potential of firm-specific knowledge, *Journal of Management*, 42(2): 500–23.

Welbourne, T. M., Johnson, D. E., and Erez, A. (1998). The role-based performance scale: Validity analysis of a theory-based measure, *Academy of Management Journal*, 41: 540–55.

Williamson, O. E. (1963). Managerial discretion and business behavior, *American Economic Review*, 53: 1032–57.

Williamson, O. E. (2005). Transaction cost economics. In C. Menard and M. M. Shirley (eds.), *Handbook of New Institutional Economics*, 41–6. Amsterdam: Springer.

Wooldridge, J. (2010). *Econometric Analysis of Cross Section and Panel Data.* Cambridge, MA: MIT Press

World Bank (2013). *World Development Report 2014: Risk and Opportunity—Managing Risk for Development.* Washington DC: World Bank.

Yanadori, Y., and Cui, V. (2013). Creating incentives for innovation? The relationship between pay dispersion in R&D groups and firm innovation performance, *Strategic Management Journal*, 34(12): 1502–11.

PART III

CERTIFICATION, WORKING CONDITIONS, AND UNION MEMBERSHIP

9
Certification and Business Risk

Neda Trifković

9.1 Introduction

This chapter investigates the scope for international private standards to play a role in reducing business risk. Standards are measures by which products, processes and producers are judged (Hatanaka et al. 2005). Different products are subject to information asymmetry problems, because consumers cannot easily verify all the quality characteristics before the purchase. It is, for example, difficult to ascertain by looking at the product, whether it is grown organically or whether responsible labour, trade, environmental, or animal welfare practices have been followed (Lee et al. 2010). Trade globalization is making the communication about product attributes even more complex, as the consumption and demand for more product information take place in high-income countries, while the production takes place in developing countries with usually different levels of public regulation stringency. Standards and certification schemes address the need for more information by signalling specific attributes of, for example, product quality and safety or social and environmental aspects of production processes. Signalling is usually a part of a firm's strategy to raise its credentials in the marketplace, indicate reliability, and increase consumers' trust (Fulponi 2006; Henson and Jaffee 2006; Terlaak and King 2006).

The literature on standards in the context of transition economies and developing economies has mainly analysed the emergence of international standards for safety, quality, and sustainability as a new global regulation mode (Hatanaka et al. 2005; Henson and Reardon 2005). Even though the results are still ambiguous, this stream of research highlights the trade-facilitating effects of international standards (Beghin et al. 2015). Standards give an opportunity for firms in emerging economies to increase access to international markets and to raise their productivity and sales performance (Calza et al. 2019; Goedhuys and Sleuwaegen 2013; Henson et al. 2011; Masakure et al. 2009; Trifković 2016). The ability of standards to increase firm productivity comes from modifications in internal practices, streamlining procedures, and improving workplace conditions (Calza et al. 2019; Delmas and Pekovic 2013; Levine and Toffel 2010; Trifković 2017). These processes can also reduce uncertainty and the risk of supplying

Neda Trifković, *Certification and Business Risk* In: *Micro, Small, and Medium Enterprises in Vietnam.* Edited by: John Rand and Finn Tarp, Oxford University Press (2020).
DOI: 10.1093/oso/9780198851189.003.0009

inferior goods to the market. This argument has been put forward in several studies (Antle 1996; Terlaak and King 2006; Henson and Reardon 2005), but the possibility of risk-reducing benefits of standards have not been empirically tested.

Risk is defined as the potential for financial loss or physical damage associated with a business activity (Chapman and Cooper 1983). Future financial returns can be subject to unpredictable processes, but they can also depend directly on the firm's activities, such as investment decisions. The primary measure of business risk in this chapter is variability in revenue from three main products over time. The choice of the measure is consistent with earlier empirical work (Gomez-Mejia et al. 2001; Henkel 2009; Ruefli et al. 1999). If one part of the firm's revenue variability comes from a low ability to assure product quality and safety, then standards can stabilize year-to-year revenue by reducing cases of malfunctioning and discarded or contaminated products. Additional measures of business risk include customer risk, based on the variability in the customer base, informal payments, and temporary business closure.

The results based on a sample of small- and medium-sized enterprises from Vietnam show lower levels of business risk among certified firms. Heterogeneity analysis confirms the result for middle deciles of the risk distribution and location differences in favour of firms located in rural areas and northern provinces. Certification is also a useful risk-reduction tool for technologically advanced firms. The overall conclusion of benefits from standards also holds for alternative risk measures, namely customer risk, informal payments, and temporary business closure. Certification is found to correlate negatively with customer risk, informal payments, and temporary business closure. Estimations account for bias from unobservable time-invariant heterogeneity, suggesting that firms could find protection from business downsides by investing in activities that go beyond minimal regulatory compliance.

9.2 Key Concepts and Literature

The literature distinguished three ways of obtaining information about products and therefore three types of goods (Darby and Karni 1973; Nelson 1970). Search goods are those for which consumers have perfect information before purchase (such as colour, shape, or size), but for other goods it may be difficult to have full information beforehand. Products whose attributes are revealed only after the consumption (such as taste) are called experience goods, and products whose quality can be determined only with necessary expert knowledge are credence goods. For example, pathogens that present food safety hazards or cancer-causing toxins cannot be identified prior to the purchase. Instead, consumers may become aware of them at the onset of illness. As a consequence, the imperfect information in product markets will lead to an inefficient level of food quality and safety, and lower quality products will dominate (Akerlof 1970). Under these conditions of asymmetric information, sellers know the product quality and they can signal higher product quality with higher price. However, as the higher price strategy undermines the price competition (Antle 1996), sellers are increasingly aiming to remove the uncertainty about product attributes by making the information available to consumers, most commonly through product labelling or certification in accordance with international standards.

Standards are an increasingly important governance mechanism in global production and trade between developed and developing countries (Ponte and Gibbon 2005). They were traditionally devised and enacted by individual governments, with the intention to shape the market environment and influence the behaviour of the concerned actors (Blind et al. 2017). With the increasing trade globalization—where production occurs in various locations and under different sets of rules and conditions—the standard-setting role of governments is taken over by various non-governmental, international, and private regulatory bodies. Private standards are thus developed by coalitions of private sector actors (Henson and Humphrey 2010) and enforced by third-party certification (Hatanaka et al. 2005). Focusing on a variety of quality attributes that are not stipulated by public regulation, private standards are deemed more stringent and more comprehensive than public regulation (Farina et al. 2005; Reardon and Berdegué 2002).

Since the early 1990s, standards have been a way of responding to the requests for specific product attributes, commonly transferred from consumers to producers. ISO 9001 is the most commonly used international standard. The International Organization for Standardization (ISO) published the ISO 9001 standard in 1987, as a framework for quality management from manufacturing to delivery. Many firms have adopted the ISO 9001 standard as a way of meeting the demands of global competition (Manders et al. 2016). The process of implementing the ISO 9001 standard and certification can be quite expensive, but the cost seems justifiable to many firms across the globe. The ISO Survey (ISO 2016) shows that more than one million organizations in 187 countries have ISO 9001 standard certification. The second most commonly applied standard is ISO 14001, implemented to improve environmental management practices of firms. ISO 22000 is implemented for the purpose of managing food safety risks, which is particularly relevant for the food industry.

Standards and certification schemes assure credibility of the production process and inform about product quality and safety, as well as about the social and environmental conditions of the production process. This illustrates the signalling role of standard certificates, which are used strategically to raise the firm's credentials in the marketplace by indicating to external parties that the firm is a reliable supplier and partner (Goedhuys and Sleuwaegen 2013; Henson and Jaffee 2006; Potoski and Prakash 2009; Terlaak and King 2006). One of the signalling benefits is the reduction in transaction and search costs, that is, the time and resources customers need to identify eligible suppliers. Another benefit is the ability of certified firms to address competitive pressures by shifting from price-based competition to quality-based competition and from undifferentiated commodities to value-added differentiated goods (Henson and Reardon 2005). Such product differentiation can increase profits (e.g. Spence 1976; Tirole 1988). A particularly relevant aspect of quality-based competition for producers from developing countries is using certificates as a way to differentiate themselves from informal sector producers (Jaffee and Masakure 2005).

Apart from the signalling effect, standard certification could lead to internal benefits for firm performance. Implementation of private standards such as ISO 9001 usually requires putting in place a set of planning, controlling, and corrective activities, such as, for example, (i) examining adequacy of work processes and methods for meeting product specifications; (ii) documenting work processes, work instructions, and quality assurance procedures; (iii) internal auditing to verify that activities comply with the procedures; and (iv) designing preventive and applying corrective actions in response to audits (Naveh and Erez 2004). Studies link certification with process and product upgrading, better managed production procedures and business practices, increased monitoring, increased efficiency in the use of resources, and reduction of waste and pollution, as evidenced in a number of studies (González et al. 2008; Iraldo et al. 2011; Goedhuys and Sleuwaegen 2013). Improved control and increased efficiency can, in turn, create competitive advantage (Caswell et al. 1998; Henson and Caswell 1999).

The internal benefits can also be generated through an effect on human resources. Successful standard implementation is difficult without investments in human capital. Building employee skills and capabilities through training and improving workplace safety and satisfaction may contribute to better working conditions and consequently to higher productivity (Delmas and Pekovic 2013; Levine and Toffel 2010; Trifković 2017).

Enterprises face several types of risk. For example, strategic risk affects the implementation of a particular business strategy, operational risk disrupts core processing capabilities, customer risk affects the likelihood of customers placing orders, financial risk arises from changing financial markets or debtor defaults, while reputation risk erodes the value of the whole business due to loss of confidence (Harland et al. 2003; Simons 1999; Smallman 1996). The sources of risk can be direct and indirect. Human, organizational, and technological activities can directly cause business crises, while regulatory, infrastructural, and political factors can contribute indirectly (Smallman 1996). Conditions of the natural environment can also be counted as indirect risk factors as they are beyond the organization's and individuals' influence. Risks affect businesses negatively, causing financial, performance, physical, psychological, social, or time loss (Harland et al. 2003). Risks should be managed, when doing so improves the expected value of outcomes or if the potential damage of events exceeds what the firm finds acceptable (Bromiley et al. 2016).

While risk can refer to the firm's preferences, behaviour, or actions, the focus here is on the outcomes of risk.[1] Literature is far from unified in providing guidance on how to measure risk, but one of the proposed ways is to use information on variability in actual firm performance, which reflects uncertainty about the firm's income stream due to its particular decisions or activities.[2] If one part of the firm's revenue variability comes from a lack or limited ability to assure product quality and safety, standards could serve as a risk-reducing tool and stabilize revenue levels over time. This effect could come from obtaining better insight into the firm's processes and preventing undesired events such as cases of malfunctioning and discarded or contaminated products.

9.3 Data

The analysis is based on the data from the biannual small- and medium-sized enterprise (SME) survey for Vietnam. This survey has been conducted in 10 provinces in Vietnam: Ho Chi Minh City (HCMC), Hanoi, Hai Phong, Long An, Ha Tay, Quang Nam, Phu Tho, Nghe An, Khanh Hoa, and Lam Dong. The sampling frame comprises a consolidated list of formal enterprises obtained from the Establishment Census from 2002 (GSO 2004) and the Industrial Survey 2004–06 (GSO 2007). Firms are randomly drawn from this list, accounting for ownership type to obtain representative data on household-owned, private, cooperative, limited liability and joint stock enterprises. Apart from the officially registered firms, the survey also includes informal firms that were identified randomly on-site.[3] As the survey traces the same firms over the years, it is able to capture legal structure changes and formalization of unregistered businesses. Firms who stop operating are randomly replaced based on the need to maintain a constant level of household firms based on the information in GSO (2004) and the new 2014 population of firms registered under the Law on Enterprises obtained from GSO (2015).

The analysis in this chapter is based on the data from the 2011, 2013, and 2015 survey rounds, because the question about the compliance with internationally recognized standards was introduced in 2011. The survey targets non-state manufacturing enterprises from different sectors. Informal businesses are unlikely to obtain a certificate of compliance with standards, as the main information on the

[1] Bromiley et al. (2017) offer a summary of different connotations of risk.

[2] Other empirical measures of firm-level risk include: stock price, variability in stock analyst forecasts and discretionary firm activity, such as investment in research and development (Bromiley et al. 2017; Chatterjee and Lubatkin 1990).

[3] More details about sampling are available in CIEM et al. (2014, 2016).

certificate is precisely the firm registration number. That is why informal firms are excluded from the analysis. The total sample used in the analysis thus comprises 4,728 firms; 1,377 firms in 2011, 1,363 in 2013, and 1,988 in 2015.

The main questionnaire includes information on enterprise characteristics and practices. All questions refer to the situation in the previous calendar year, namely 2010, 2012, and 2014, while the economic accounts contain information on two consecutive years prior to the survey. The questionnaire has stayed almost the same over the years, with the exception that the questionnaire from 2015 separately asks about international and domestic standards. The 2011 and 2013 survey rounds only contain an indicator for whether firms have applied for any of the internationally recognized standards, while the 2015 round reveals exactly which standards are certified.

9.3.1 Descriptive Statistics

Summary statistics in Table 9.1 show average values and standard deviations of key dependent and control variables. The first three rows show average values of annual revenue in million Vietnamese Dong for three main products. The values are deflated for spatial and temporal differences in the cost of living in different areas of Vietnam. Firms were asked in the interviews to identify the most important products in value terms. As the majority of firms are micro or small, only 65 per cent produce more than one product. The consequence is that the first most important product contributes the most to the value of the business risk variable, whose average value has been steadily increasing in the observed six-year period. Informal payments and the incidence of temporary closures have in contrast decreased in the observed period. Customer risk, measured as variation in the customer base, has not changed much between 2011 and 2015, indicating on average a fairly stable customer portfolio.

The proportion of firms with internationally recognized private standards in the sample is 7.7 per cent. This average masks a large drop between 2013 and 2015, where the proportion of certified firms declined from 10 to 4.6 per cent. This is similar to the observed twofold decline in the total number of ISO 9001 certificates in Vietnam that decreased from 6,164 in 2012 to 3,786 in 2014 (ISO 2016).[4] The most commonly certified standards among the Vietnamese SMEs are ISO 9001,

[4] In addition to the general declining trend of certification in Vietnam, there is a small possibility that the drop in the number of certified firms in 2015 could be due to the change in the questionnaire. Whereas the 2011 and 2013 survey rounds asked about certification against internationally recognized standards, the 2015 round asked in addition about domestic standards. The wording of the question about internationally recognized standards has remained the same, but it has perhaps offered a possibility for some respondents to more carefully reflect on the type of the certification they have. Another reason could be that companies reached a point when they needed to re-certify and could not fulfil stricter conditions of re-certification.

Table 9.1 Summary statistics of key variables

	All years		2011		2013		2015	
	Mean	SD	Mean	SD	Mean	SD	Mean	SD
Revenue 1st product	0.192	7.72	0.037	0.63	0.534	14.01	0.049	0.32
Revenue 2nd product	0.716	2.15	0.129	0.66	1.008	2.55	0.932	2.43
Revenue 3rd product	0.310	1.02	0.048	0.28	0.460	1.21	0.392	1.18
Business risk (ln)	1.074	0.35	1.102	0.34	1.041	0.36	1.078	0.35
Customer risk (ln)	1.310	0.46	1.322	0.46	1.263	0.46	1.338	0.46
Informal payments (%)	49.73	50.00	52.25	49.96	52.89	49.93	45.50	49.81
Temporary closure (%)	12.21	32.75	12.59	33.18	12.82	33.44	11.48	31.89
Certification (%)	7.67	26.62	9.34	29.11	10.10	30.15	4.61	20.98
Firm size	17.50	31.02	19.88	32.79	18.01	29.61	15.36	30.58
Capital–labour ratio	0.476	0.80	0.544	1.05	0.493	0.66	0.413	0.66
Export (%)	7.64	26.56	7.74	26.73	7.91	27.00	7.35	26.10
Post-secondary education (%)	74.91	43.36	71.63	45.09	78.29	41.24	74.77	43.44
Female owner or manager (%)	40.63	49.12	39.18	48.83	41.80	49.34	40.80	49.16
Household establishment (%)	54.01	49.84	50.89	50.01	49.77	50.01	59.50	49.10
Private/sole proprietorship (%)	9.49	29.31	11.17	31.51	11.03	31.33	7.09	25.67
Partnership/collective/ cooperative (%)	2.94	16.88	3.72	18.94	3.06	17.23	2.26	14.87
Limited liability company (%)	28.29	45.04	28.90	45.34	30.31	45.97	26.32	44.04
Joint stock company (%)	5.28	22.36	5.32	22.45	5.83	23.44	4.83	21.44
Observations	5,723		1,692		1,732		2,299	

Note: Real revenue and capital values are in million Vietnamese Dong (VND). 1 USD ≈ 20,000 VND. The number of firms with revenue information for two products is 2,183 (3,770 observations) and the number of firms with revenue information for three products is 1,591 (2,583 observations).

Source: Author's calculation based on SME data.

ISO 14001, and ISO 22000. Figure 9.1 shows how important different contacts were for deciding whether to adopt standards. The most important input in the certification decision comes from customers and surprisingly also from suppliers. The former case indicates that certification works through signalling desirables attributes of a product or a production process and it is well-described in the literature (Henson and Humphrey 2010; Fouayzi et al. 2006). The latter case is likely to occur for more technically advanced products or vertically integrated value chains, where quality needs to be assured in downstream operations, such as, for example, in the case of different assembly activities.

Table 9.1 also shows that the average firm size is about 17 employees. Micro firms, defined as those with less than 10 employees, comprise 60 per cent of the sample. One half of that fraction are small firms and the rest are medium firms, employing between 50 and 300 employees. The average firm size has declined between 2011 and 2015, which is in line with the general trend of declining firm size in Vietnam (CIEM et al. 2014). Table 9.1 also shows a declining value of the

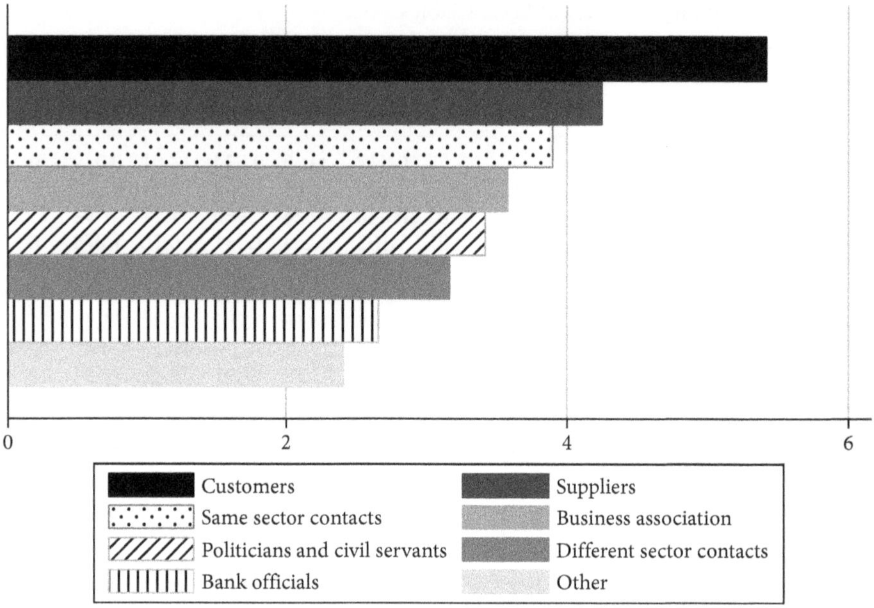

Figure 9.1 How important were the following contacts for your decision to implement standards? (scale 0–7)
Source: Author's illustration based on SME data.

capital-labour ratio. About 8 per cent of firms from the sample export and this proportion has remained unchanged over time.

In terms of owner or manager characteristics, about three-quarters have completed at least upper secondary school. About 41 per cent of firms are owned or managed by women. The proportion of women in this role has been declining since 2011. Around 40 per cent of enterprises belong to sectors characterized by low intensity of technology: food and beverages, textiles, apparel, leather, wood processing and recycling. Slightly more than half of the sample are enterprises from rural areas, defined as locations different from Hanoi, Ho Chi Minh City, and Hai Phong.

Comparing the enterprises from the sample by certification, the first aspect to observe is a significant difference in revenue between certified and non-certified firms, as shown in Figure 9.2. The Kolmogorov-Smirnov test statistic is 0.43, indicating that the distributions of revenue in certified and non-certified firms are statistically different ($p = 0.00$). Moreover, certified firms have significantly lower business and customer risk value, as shown in Table 9.2. These firms have much lower incidence of temporary firm closure, but higher incidence of informal payments, perhaps due to higher visibility. Certified firms have a higher capital value, indicating that they could be more technologically advanced than non-certified firms. These firms are also much more likely to export than non-certified

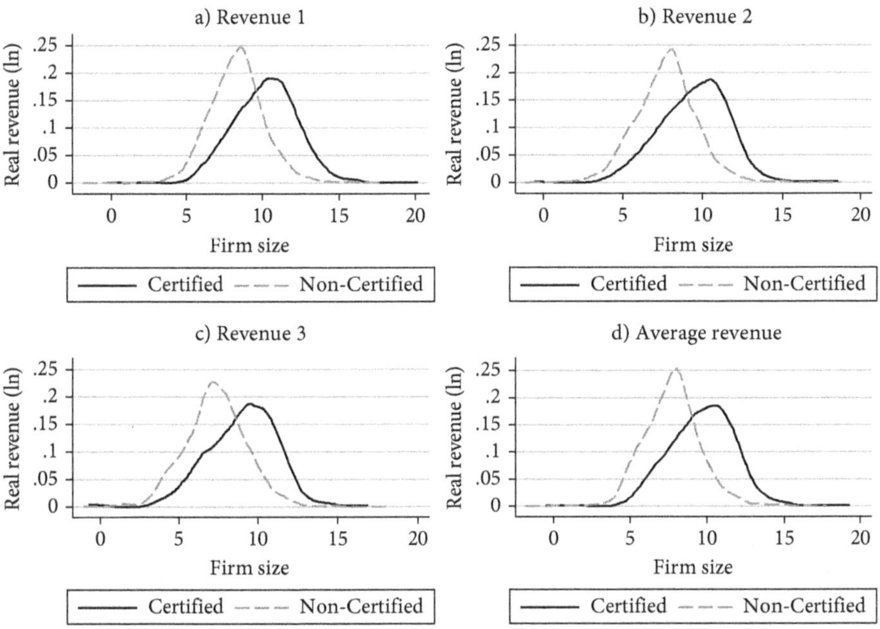

Figure 9.2 Differences in revenue for the three most important products by certification

Source: Author's calculation based on SME data.

Table 9.2 Differences between firms by certification (t-test)

	(1) Non-certified	(2) Certified	(3) Difference (N-C)	(4) t-value	(5) Observations
Business risk (ln)	1.08	0.97	0.11	6.63***	5,723
Customer risk (ln)	1.33	1.06	0.27	11.91***	5,723
Informal payments (%)	48.69	62.19	−13.49	−5.45***	5,723
Temporary closure (%)	12.74	5.92	6.81	4.20***	5,723
Firm size	14.12	58.13	−44.01	-30.84***	5,723
Capital–labour ratio	0.47	0.61	−0.14	−3.57***	5,723
Export	4.96	39.86	−34.90	−28.24***	5,723
Post-secondary education	73.05	97.27	−24.22	−11.37***	5,723
Female owner or manager	39.53	53.76	−14.22	−5.85***	5,723

Source: Author's calculation based on the SME data

firms and to be managed by women who tend to be better educated than owners or managers of non-certified firms.

9.4 Estimation

The main goal is to estimate the effect of certification on business risk over the period 2011–15. The estimation follows the form specified in the following equation:

$$y_{ijt} = \alpha_i + \beta_i C_{it} + \delta X_{it} + \rho_j + \tau_t + e_{ijt}$$

where i denotes firm, j denotes location and t denotes time period. α_i, are firm fixed effects and e_{ijt} is the statistical noise term. The dependent variable, y_{ijt} is business risk. Following Ruefli et al. (1999) and Gomez-Mejia et al. (2001), it is defined as performance variance relative to performance level, where performance is measured as revenue. The revenue values are spatially and temporally deflated using spatial cost of living indices for different years and provinces of Vietnam. The risk is calculated as the logarithm of the ratio of the variance in revenue for the three most important products, $k = 1, 2, 3$ divided by a term consisting of the average revenue minus the minimum revenue squared:

$$y_{ijt} = \ln\left(\frac{r_{\text{var},ikt}}{\left(r_{\text{av},ikt} - r_{\text{min},ikt}\right)^2}\right)$$

Other things being equal, the more the average revenue for a given period exceeds the minimum revenue, the term in the denominator increases, and business risk decreases accordingly. Conversely, as the variance in the revenue (the numerator) increases, business risk increases accordingly. This index is similar to the coefficient of variation, which is positively related to the variance of performance outcomes over time and negatively related to the mean of the distribution, implying a lower risk for higher mean performance outcomes (Miller and Reuer 1996).

Following the same procedure, I obtain an alternative measure of business risk based on the customer base structure, which measures the performance based on the proportion of goods sold to individual households, tourists, non-commercial government authorities, domestic non-state enterprises, state enterprises, foreign invested companies or to export. Additional measures of business risk used in the estimation are informal payments and temporary business closure.

The variable of interest, C_{it}, takes value 1 if a firm owns any internationally recognized certification and 0 otherwise. X_{it} are time-varying firm-specific and owner/manager control variables, such as firm size, ratio of capital to labour, export behaviour, gender of the owner or manager, and education level of the owner or manager. Firm size category is determined from the total number of regular full-time employees. It is a necessary control as larger firms have an advantage in complying with standards. A positive size effect on the adoption of standards was found in previous studies (Herath et al. 2007; Masakure et al. 2011; Nakamura et al. 2001). One explanation could be that fixed costs that are bound to be incurred in relation to implementation of standards are less significant for larger firms. Ratio of capital and labour is also included in the estimation to proxy for the cost and the nature of technology. This is measured as the deflated value of the total assets of the firm divided by the total number of full-time employees. Firms in contact with foreign markets are more likely to obtain certifications, so the estimation controls for exporting. Managerial characteristics are important for firm performance (Bloom and Van Reenen 2007), so the estimation controls for gender and education level of the owner or manager. Due to relatively high levels of completion of primary and secondary school in Vietnam, the control variable for education is a dummy variable taking value one if the owner or manager have completed any post-secondary education, which captures a potential premium for higher education. The estimation also controls for industry, province, and legal ownership form to account for common factors affecting all firms within industries, provinces, and particular legal ownership forms. All monetary variables are corrected for spatial cost of living between different provinces.

The key variable for certification is potentially endogenous, as there could be unobserved firm characteristics that influence the firm's certification decision that are also correlated with risk performance. For example, a manager of a firm may have access to specific information or experience, which could both lead to the adoption of standards and better risk performance. Including firm-fixed effects addresses this issue to some extent, given that it allows controlling directly for all time-invariant unobserved firm-specific factors, such as manager preferences and characteristics that do not change over time. In addition, time dummies, τ_t, control for general trends that affect all firms, while location dummies control for policy changes that may differentially impact firm performance in different geographical areas.

The estimation could be biased by omitted time-varying unobservable factors that impact both business risk and certification decisions, such as, for example, a change in management. The bias due to time-varying unobservable factors could be both positive and negative. For example, a change in management could be such as to increase business risk and reduce investment in certification, in which case the least squares effect size will be overestimated. It may also be that a new management is more favourable of certification due to a change in regulations or buyers' preferences, which could reduce business risk and lead to underestimated least squares effect size. These examples illustrate that the direction of causality may be difficult to disentangle, so the results are correlations without assigning a causal interpretation.

9.5 Results

To see which firms decide to certify against international standards, the adoption of standards is estimated as a function of observable firm characteristics, such as size, asset ownership, production of final goods, ownership type, and location, as described in the previous section. The results using pooled least squares and fixed-effect estimations on the unbalanced and balanced panel, respectively, are shown in Table 9.3. All least squares and probit specifications control for firm location, technology type of the sector in which it operates, legal ownership form, and survey year. Time-invariant sector and location controls, as well as the owner's gender are excluded from the fixed-effect model in column (6).

Table 9.3 shows the determinants of certification. We see from column (1) that firm size is a strong predictor of the adoption of standards. The subsequent columns show that other firm characteristics also contribute to the decision to adopt standards, confirmed by a decrease of the firm size coefficient. Enterprises that are endowed with more capital are, as expected, more likely to adopt standards. Exporting firms are also more likely to decide in favour of certification. The relationship is positive and significant across all specifications.

Table 9.4 shows the relationship between certification and business risk. Columns (1)–(4) show least square estimation results. The first three columns show the results for the unbalanced and column (4) shows the results for the balanced panel. The final column shows the results with firm–fixed effects, which, as described in the previous section, account for bias due to time-invariant unobservable heterogeneity. All specifications show a negative association between certification and business risk. A decision to certify an internationally recognized standard for managing the quality, safety, or environmental impact of the production, associates with a 5.6 per cent lower business risk. Fixed-effects estimates are slightly higher than the least squares estimates, indicating that the unobserved heterogeneity correlates negatively with certification incidence. This suggests that less productive firms are more likely to self-select into certification of international standards and that fixed-effects correct for the downward bias in least square estimation.

Control variables—such as firm size and having a female owner or manager—also correlate negatively with business risk. Assets also show a negative association with business risk and exporting shows a positive association, but the relationship is imprecisely determined in all specifications.

Table 9.5 shows the relationship between certification and additional measures of business risk, such as customer risk, temporary closure and informal payments.

Table 9.3 Determinants of international standard certification

Dep. var. Certification	**OLS**	**OLS**	**OLS, balanced**	**Probit marginal effects**	**Probit, balanced**	**FE, balanced**
	(1)	(2)	(3)	(4)	(5)	(6)
Firm size (ln)	0.092***	0.059***	0.068***	0.044***	0.049***	0.079***
	(0.004)	(0.005)	(0.006)	(0.003)	(0.004)	(0.006)
Capital/labour (ln)		0.016***	0.021***	0.019***	0.021***	0.024***
		(0.003)	(0.004)	(0.003)	(0.003)	(0.004)
Export		0.011*	0.010	0.010*	0.010	
		(0.007)	(0.008)	(0.006)	(0.007)	
Post-secondary education		0.000	0.000	0.000	0.000	0.000***
		(0.000)	(0.000)	(0.000)	(0.000)	(0.000)
Female owner or manager		0.241***	0.253***	0.078***	0.086***	0.229***
		(0.023)	(0.026)	(0.007)	(0.009)	(0.030)
Constant	-0.120***	-0.273***	−0.342***			−0.426***
	(0.009)	(0.043)	(0.053)			(0.053)
Year dummies	Yes	Yes	Yes	Yes	Yes	Yes
Sector FE	No	Yes	Yes	Yes	Yes	No
Legal FE	No	Yes	Yes	Yes	Yes	No
Location FE	No	Yes	Yes	Yes	Yes	No
R^2	0.16	0.24	0.26			
Observations	5,803	5,792	4,448	5,792	4,448	4, 448

Note: OLS stands for ordinary least squares. Robust standard errors in parentheses. * $p < 0.10$, ** $p < 0.05$, *** $p < 0.01$.

Source: Author's calculation based on SME data.

Table 9.4 The relationship between certification and business risk

Dep. var. Business risk	OLS	OLS	OLS	OLS, balanced	FE, balanced
	(1)	(2)	(3)	(4)	(5)
Certification	−0.113***	−0.033*	−0.035*	−0.047**	−0.057**
	(0.018)	(0.020)	(0.020)	(0.021)	(0.028)
Firm size (ln)		−0.048***	−0.049***	−0.046***	−0.068***
		(0.005)	(0.006)	(0.007)	(0.015)
Capital/Labour (ln)		−0.006	−0.002	0.002	−0.005
		(0.004)	(0.004)	(0.005)	(0.008)
Export		0.016	0.018	0.016	−0.005
		(0.020)	(0.020)	(0.022)	(0.046)
Post-secondary education		−0.000***	−0.000	−0.000	0.000
		(0.000)	(0.000)	(0.000)	(0.000)
Female owner or manager		0.006	−0.019**	−0.019*	
		(0.009)	(0.009)	(0.011)	
Constant	1.112***	1.314***	1.320***	1.255***	1.292***
	(0.008)	(0.051)	(0.058)	(0.069)	(0.121)
Year dummies	Yes	Yes	Yes	Yes	Yes
Sector FE	No	No	Yes	Yes	No
Legal FE	No	No	Yes	Yes	No
Location FE	No	No	Yes	Yes	No
R^2	0.01	0.04	0.12	0.11	0.02
Observations	5,723	5,723	5,723	4,419	4,419
Number of firms	2,969	2,969	2,969	1,671	1,671

Note: OLS stands for ordinary least squares. Columns (1)–(3) show results from unbalanced panel. Robust standard errors in parentheses. * $p<0.10$, ** $p<0.05$, *** $p<0.01$.

Source: Author's calculation based on SME data.

Table 9.5 The relationship between certification and business risk: additional risk measures

Dep. var.:	Customer risk		Informal payments		Temporary closure	
	OLS	FE, balanced	OLS	FE, balanced	OLS	FE, balanced
	(1)	(2)	(3)	(4)	(5)	(6)
Certification	−0.091***	−0.103**	−0.088***	−0.123***	−0.017	−0.041*
	(0.025)	(0.042)	(0.027)	(0.045)	(0.015)	(0.023)
Firm size (ln)	−0.069***	−0.080***	0.067***	0.002	−0.020***	−0.081***
	(0.008)	(0.022)	(0.008)	(0.025)	(0.005)	(0.018)
Capital/labour (ln)	−0.030***	−0.020	0.037***	0.040***	0.008*	−0.008
	(0.006)	(0.013)	(0.006)	(0.015)	(0.004)	(0.010)
Export	0.047*	−0.097*	0.034	0.055	0.036**	0.016
	(0.025)	(0.052)	(0.027)	(0.064)	(0.017)	(0.031)
Post-secondary education	−0.000	−0.000	−0.000	−0.001	−0.000**	−0.000**
	(0.000)	(0.000)	(0.000)	(0.000)	(0.000)	(0.000)
Female owner or manager	−0.017		−0.002		−0.023**	
	(0.012)		(0.013)		(0.009)	
Constant	1.941***	1.797***	−0.069	0.077	0.069	0.433***
	(0.079)	(0.191)	(0.082)	(0.215)	(0.056)	(0.144)
Year dummies	Yes	Yes	Yes	Yes	Yes	Yes
Sector FE	Yes	No	Yes	No	Yes	No
Legal FE	Yes	No	Yes	No	Yes	No
Location FE	Yes	No	Yes	No	Yes	No
R^2	0.12	0.01	0.10	0.01	0.04	0.02
Observations	5,792	4,448	5,792	4,448	5,792	4,448
Number of firms	2,986	1,671	2,986	1,671	2,986	1,671

Note: OLS stands for ordinary least squares. Robust standard errors in parentheses. * $p<0.10$, ** $p<0.05$, *** $p<0.01$.

Source: Author's calculation based on SME data.

The results show again a negative association between certification and different risk measures.

How does the effect of certification on business risk come about? It is likely that simultaneously different mechanisms are in force that may influence several dimensions of firm performance. The implementation of standards entails incentives for adjusting the production systems towards planning and performance analysis, which could stabilize the revenue streams over time. Standards are also credited with improved working conditions and workplace practices (Levine and Toffel 2010; Trifković 2017), leading to better employee performance, which could lead to more stable revenue streams by reducing the number of instances of product malfunctioning, damage, or contamination. Finally, standards inform customers about higher product reliability, which could result in more stable levels of purchase.

9.5.1 Heterogeneity Analysis

The distributional differences in the relationship between certification and business risk are assessed in a more systematic way by focusing on different deciles of the risk distribution. The specification of the quantile regressions is exactly the same as the least squares regression in column (3) in Table 9.4. Least squares and quantile regressions coefficients are given in Figure 9.3, where the red line presents quantile regression coefficients and the black line shows the least squares coefficients. The dashed part of the least squares line indicates the part of distribution in which least squares and quantile regression coefficients are statistically different, while the full line indicates the area where the coefficients from two types of estimations are not statistically different from each other.

The results in Figure 9.3 show statistically significant and negative association of certification and business risk in 30 to 50 per cent deciles. The point estimates are highest around the median (−0.14). The relationship between certification and risk is not statistically significant in the bottom and the top deciles of the risk distribution. This indicates that the gain from standards is a decline in business risk of about 15 per cent for the middle risk levels. This finding indicates that larger levels of business risk could require other means of risk management than standards.

In Table 9.6, location controls are excluded to investigate if location differences, such as urban–rural and south–north, are associated with different benefits of certification. The south–north differences are particularly relevant due to country's historical division into south and north regions, which nowadays manifests in different modes of operation, behaviour and managerial styles (Ralston et al. 1999). The estimates in column (1) show a negative association between certification and business risk for enterprises located in rural areas. As

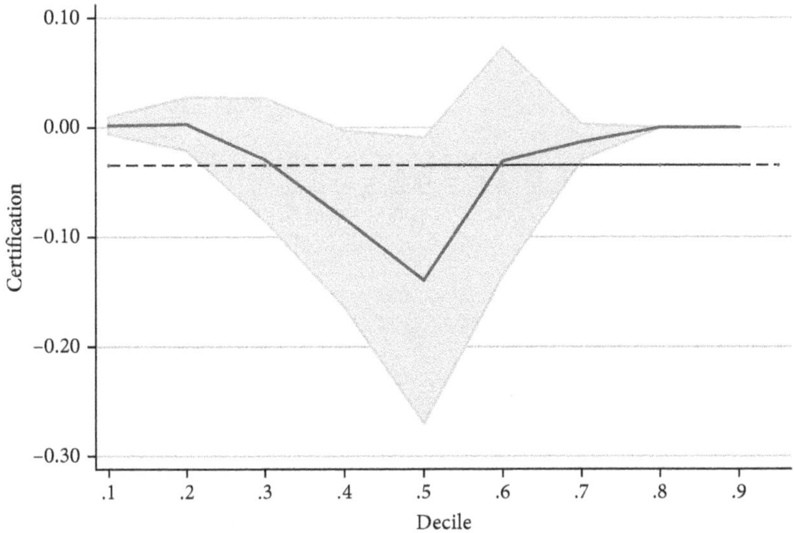

Figure 9.3 Least square and quantile regression coefficients

Notes: The red line presents quantile regression coefficients and the black line shows the least squares coefficients. The dashed part of the least squares line indicates the part of distribution in which least squares and quantile regression coefficients are statistically different, while the full line indicates the area where the coefficients from two types of estimations are not statistically different from each other.

Source: Author's illustration based on the SME data.

shown in column (2), the relationship is also significant and negative among the firms in the north, perhaps a consequence of higher competitive pressures.

The market in which main products are sold can affect certification decisions (Adolph et al. 2017; Newman et al. 2018), so column (3) shows the result for firms from the sample who export at least some part of their output. The estimates show a negative correlation between certification and risk for exporting firms, but the effect is not precisely determined. Similarly, there are no heterogeneous effects by firm owner's gender. Column (5) shows a significantly negative correlation between certification and risk for firms that operate in technologically more advanced industries.

More innovative firms, that is, those that tend to invest in innovative activities, such as introducing new or modifying existing products or technologies, are found to be more likely to adopt standards (Calza et al. 2019; Manders et al. 2016). This relationship is not simple, as standards and innovation can have synergistic benefits, but may also compete for resources, which is why the interplay depends on the importance of signalling in the business model of the firm, firm motivation, the sector and the region in which the firm operates. The results in column (6) show a significantly negative correlation between certification and risk for firms that do not implement product improvements, indicating opposite influence of standards and innovation on business risk.

Table 9.6 Certification and business risk for different sub-samples

Dep. var. Business risk	Rural	North	Export	Female owner	Medium to high technology	No innovation
	(1)	(2)	(3)	(4)	(5)	(6)
Certification	−0.074**	−0.074***	−0.011	−0.008	−0.072***	−0.059**
	(0.030)	(0.028)	(0.053)	(0.028)	(0.025)	(0.026)
Firm size (ln)	−0.051***	−0.051***	−0.019	−0.060***	−0.029***	−0.049***
	(0.009)	(0.009)	(0.028)	(0.010)	(0.009)	(0.008)
Capital/labour (ln)	−0.002	0.002	−0.045**	−0.010	0.008	−0.005
	(0.006)	(0.006)	(0.021)	(0.007)	(0.006)	(0.005)
Export	−0.023	−0.019	−0.059		−0.008	0.013
	(0.015)	(0.015)	(0.048)		(0.015)	(0.012)
Post-secondary education	−0.000***	−0.000	−0.001	−0.000	−0.000	−0.000
	(0.000)	(0.000)	(0.001)	(0.000)	(0.000)	(0.000)
Female owner or manager	0.012	0.005		0.037	−0.004	0.033
	(0.032)	(0.033)		(0.033)	(0.029)	(0.027)
Constant	1.379***	1.355***	1.930***	1.404***	1.022***	1.303***
	(0.081)	(0.081)	(0.339)	(0.101)	(0.086)	(0.072)
Year dummies	Yes	Yes	Yes	Yes	Yes	Yes
Sector FE	Yes	Yes	Yes	Yes	No	No
Legal FE	Yes	Yes	Yes	Yes	Yes	Yes
Location FE	No	No	Yes	Yes	Yes	Yes
R^2	0.11	0.13	0.21	0.13	0.05	0.06
Observations	3,070	2,797	265	2,325	3,467	4,336

Note: OLS (ordinary least squares) regressions on unbalanced panel. Robust standard errors in parentheses. * p<0.10, ** p<0.05, *** p<0.01.

Source: Author's calculation based on SME data.

9.6 Conclusion

This chapter has examined the relationship between certification of international standards and business risk on a sample of manufacturing firms from Vietnam. The results show that certification contributes to a significant reduction in business risk, measured as fluctuation of revenue of firm's three most important products over time. The result is in particular relevant for the middle deciles of the risk distribution. Heterogeneity analysis by location shows risk-reducing benefits of standards for firms located in rural areas and northern provinces, as well as for firms that use technologically advanced production methods. Certification also tends to assure a more stable customer portfolio, reduce informal payments, and prevent temporary business closure.

The results suggest that certification of internationally recognized standards is a strategic decision for firms, illustrating benefits from investing in activities that go beyond minimal regulatory compliance. Policy support for certification could take the form of tax deductions for one part of the implementation expenditures and information campaigns on how to deduct some of the associated costs. This could encourage further adoption of international standards by SMEs from Vietnam, providing a way of sheltering from business downsides.

References

Adolph, C., Quince, V., and Prakash, A. (2017). The Shanghai effect: Do exports to China affect labor practices in Africa?, *World Development*, 89: 1–18.

Akerlof, G. A. (1970). The market for 'lemons': Quality uncertainty and the market mechanism, *The Quarterly Journal of Economics*, 84(3): 488–500.

Antle, J. M. (1996). Efficient food safety regulation in the food manufacturing sector, *American Journal of Agricultural Economics*, 78(5): 1242–7.

Beghin, J. C., Maertens, M., and Swinnen, J. (2015). Nontariff measures and standards in trade and global value chains, *Annual Review of Resource Economics*, 7(1): 425–50.

Blind, K., S. S. Petersen, and C. A. F. Riillo (2017). The impact of standards and regulation on innovation in uncertain markets, *Research Policy*, 46(1): 249–64.

Bloom, N. and J. Van Reenen (2007). Measuring and explaining management practices across firms and countries. *Quarterly Journal of Economics*, 122(4): 1351–408.

Bromiley, P., Rau, D., and McShane, M. K. (2016). Can strategic risk management contribute to enterprise risk management? A strategic management perspective. In T. J. Andersen, ed. *The Routledge Companion to Strategic Risk Management*. New York: Routledge.

Bromiley, P., Rau, D., and Zhang, Y. (2017). Is R&D risky? *Strategic Management Journal*, 38(4): 876–91.

Calza, E., Goedhuys, M., and Trifković, N. (2019). Drivers of productivity in Vietnamese SMEs: The role of management standards and innovation, *Economics of Innovation and New Technology*, 28(1): 23–44.

Caswell, J. A., Bredahl, M. E., and Hooker, N. H. (1998). How quality management metasystems are affecting the food industry, *Applied Economic Perspectives and Policy*, 20(2): 547–57.

Chapman, C. B. and Cooper, D. F. (1983). Risk engineering: Basic controlled interval and memory models, *The Journal of the Operational Research Society*, 34(1): 51–60.

Chatterjee, S. and Lubatkin, M. (1990). Corporate mergers, stockholder diversification, and changes in systematic risk, *Strategic Management Journal*, 11(4): 255–68.

CIEM, DoE, ILSSA and UNU-WIDER (2014). *Characteristics of the Vietnamese Business Environment: Evidence from a SME Survey in 2013*. Hanoi: Central Institute of Economic Management (CIEM).

CIEM, DoE, ILSSA and UNU-WIDER (2016). *Characteristics of the Vietnamese Business Environment: Evidence from a SME Survey in 2015*. Hanoi: Central Institute of Economic Management (CIEM).

Darby, M. R. and Karni, E. (1973). Free competition and the optimal amount of fraud, *Journal of Law and Economics*, 16(1): 67–88.

Delmas, M. and Pekovic, S. (2013). Environmental standards and labor productivity: Understanding the mechanisms that sustain sustainability, *Journal of Organizational Behavior*, 34(2): 230–52.

Farina, E. M. M. Q. et al. (2005). Private and public milk standards in Argentina and Brazil, *Food Policy*, 30(3): 302–15.

Fouayzi, H., Caswell, J. A., and Hooker, N. H. (2006). Motivations of fresh-cut produce firms to implement quality management systems, *Applied Economic Perspectives and Policy*, 28(1): 132–46.

Fulponi, L. (2006). Private voluntary standards in the food system: The perspective of major food retailers in OECD countries, *Food Policy*, 31(1): 1–13.

Goedhuys, M. and Sleuwaegen, L. (2013). The impact of international standards certification on the performance of firms in less developed countries, *World Development*, 47: 87–101.

Gomez-Mejia, L. R., Nuñez-Nickel, M., and Gutierrez, I. (2001). The role of family ties in agency contracts, *Academy of Management Journal*, 44(1): 81–95.

González, P., Sarkis, J., and Adenso-Díaz, B. (2008). Environmental management system certification and its influence on corporate practices: Evidence from the automotive industry, *International Journal of Operations & Production Management*, 28(11): 1021–41.

GSO (2015). *Results of a Survey on Non-farm Individual Business Establishments 2014*. Hanoi: General Statistics Office of Vietnam.

GSO (2004). *Results of Establishment Census of Vietnam 2002: Volume 2 – Business Establishments*. Ha Noi: Statistical Publishing House.

GSO (2007). *The Real Situation of Enterprises: Through the Results of Surveys Conducted in 2004, 2005, 2006*. Ha Noi: Statistical Publishing House.

Harland, C., Brenchley, R., and Walker, H. (2003). Risk in supply networks, *Journal of Purchasing and Supply Management*, 9(2): 51–62.

Hatanaka, M., Bain, C., and Busch, L. (2005). Third-party certification in the global agrifood system, *Food Policy*, 30(3): 354–69.

Henkel, J. (2009). The risk–return paradox for strategic management: Disentangling true and spurious effects, *Strategic Management Journal*, 30(3): 287–303.

Henson, S. and Caswell, J. A. (1999). Food safety regulation: An overview of contemporary issues, *Food Policy*, 24(6): 589–603.

Henson, S. and Humphrey, J. (2010). Understanding the complexities of private standards in global agri-food chains as they impact developing countries, *Journal of Development Studies*, 46(9): 1628–46.

Henson, S. and Jaffee, S. (2006). Food safety standards and trade: Enhancing competitiveness and avoiding exclusion of developing countries, *European Journal of Development Research*, 18(4): 593–621.

Henson, S., Masakure, O., and Cranfield, J. (2011). Do fresh produce exporters in sub-Saharan Africa benefit from GlobalGAP certification?, *World Development*, 39(3): 375–86.

Henson, S. and T. Reardon (2005). Private agri-food standards: Implications for food policy and the agri-food system. *Food Policy*, 30(3): 241–53.

Herath, D., Z. Hassan, and S. Henson (2007). Adoption of food safety and quality controls: Do firm characteristics matter? Evidence from the Canadian food processing sector, *Canadian Journal of Agricultural Economics/Revue canadienne d'agroeconomie*, 55(3): 299–314.

Iraldo, F., F. Testa, and M. Frey (2011). Is an environmental management system able to influence environmental and competitive performance? The case of the eco-management and audit scheme (EMAS) in the European Union, *Journal of Cleaner Production*, 17(16): 1444–52.

ISO (2016). The ISO Survey. Geneva: International Organization for Standardization. Available from: http://www.iso.org/iso/home/standards/certification/iso-survey.htm?certificate= ISO%209001&countrycode=VN#countrypick (accessed 4 March 2016).

Jaffee, S. and Masakure, O. (2005). Strategic use of private standards to enhance international competitiveness: Vegetable exports from Kenya and elsewhere, *Food Policy*, 30(3): 316–33.

Lee, J., Gereffi, G., and Beauvais, J. (2010). Global value chains and agrifood standards: Challenges and possibilities for smallholders in developing countries, *Proceedings of the National Academy of Sciences of the United States of America*, 109(31): 1–6.

Levine, D. I. and Toffel, M. W. (2010). Quality management and job quality: How the ISO 9001 standard for quality management systems affects employees and employers, *Management Science*, 56(6): 978–96.

Manders, B., de Vries, H. J., and Blind, K. (2016). ISO 9001 and product innovation: A literature review and research framework, *Technovation*, 48–9: 41–55.

Masakure, O., Cranfield, J., and Henson, S. (2011). Factors affecting the incidence and intensity of standards certification evidence from exporting firms in Pakistan, *Applied Economics*, 43(8): 901–15.

Masakure, O., Henson, S., and Cranfield, J. (2009). Standards and export performance in developing countries: Evidence from Pakistan, *The Journal of International Trade & Economic Development*, 18(3): 395–419.

Miller, K. D. and Reuer, J. J. (1996). Measuring organizational downside risk, *Strategic Management Journal*, 17(9): 671–91.

Nakamura, M., Takahashi, T., and Vertinsky, I. (2001). Why Japanese firms choose to certify: A study of managerial responses to environmental issues, *Journal of Environmental Economics and Management*, 42(1): 23–52.

Naveh, E. and Erez, M. (2004). Innovation and attention to detail in the quality improvement paradigm, *Management Science*, 50(11): 1576–86.

Nelson, P. (1970). Information and consumer behavior, *Journal of Political Economy*, 78(2): 311–29.

Newman, C., Rand, J., Tarp, F. and Trifković, N. (2018). The transmission of socially responsible behaviour through international trade. *European Economic Review*, 101: 250–67.

Ponte, S. and Gibbon, P. (2005). Quality standards, conventions and the governance of global value chains, *Economy and Society*, 34(1): 1–31.

Potoski, M. and Prakash, A. (2009). Information asymmetries as trade barriers: ISO 9000 increases international commerce, *Journal of Policy Analysis and Management*, 28(2): 221–38.

Ralston, D. A., Thang, N. V., and Napier, N. K. (1999). A comparative study of the work values of North and South Vietnamese managers, *Journal of International Business Studies*, 30(4): 655–72.

Reardon, T. and Berdegué, J. A. (2002). The rapid rise of supermarkets in Latin America: Challenges and opportunities for development, *Development Policy Review*, 20(4): 371–88.

Ruefli, T. W., Collins, J. M., and Lacugna, J. R. (1999). Risk measures in strategic management research: Auld Lang Syne?, *Strategic Management Journal*, 20(2): 167–94.

Simons, R. (1999). How risky is your company?, *Harvard Business Review*, 77(3): 85–95.

Smallman, C. (1996). Risk and organizational behaviour: A research model, *Disaster Prevention and Management: An International Journal*, 5(2): 12–26.

Spence, M. (1976). Product differentiation and welfare, *The American Economic Review*, 66(2): 407–14.

Terlaak, A. and A. A. King (2006). The effect of certification with the ISO 9000 quality management standard: A signaling approach, *Journal of Economic Behavior & Organization*, 60(4): 579–602.

Tirole, J. (1988). *The Theory of Industrial Organization*. Cambridge, MA: MIT Press.

Trifković, N. (2016). Private standards and labour productivity in the food sector in Vietnam. WIDER Working Paper 2016/163. Helsinki: UNU-WIDER.

Trifković, N. (2017). Spillover effects of international standards: Working conditions in the Vietnamese SMEs, *World Development*, 97: 79–101.

10
Pecuniary Returns to Working Conditions

Christophe J. Nordman and Smriti Sharma

10.1 Introduction

Working environments can vary in terms of hazards that workers are exposed to (e.g. noise, heat, asbestos, lead, and pesticides), poor ergonomics (heavy lifting, repetitive tasks, sedentary work), unfavourable working times (working day length, overtime incidence), and workplace discrimination and harassment. Most studies in economics tend to focus on wages, wage growth, and occupational attainment as indicators of labour market success, while paying little attention to the quality of the work environment. This is especially important in developing countries in which manufacturing sectors have generated jobs in the face of rapid industrialization, but we have little knowledge about the working conditions being offered.[1] However, growing evidence shows that working conditions and job quality can have long-lasting effects on workers' physical and mental health, worker absenteeism, and more generally on life satisfaction (for overviews, see Pouliakas and Theodossiou 2013; and Barnay 2016).[2] For instance—using data from the European Community Household Panel—Datta Gupta and Kristensen (2008) find that a satisfactory work environment promotes employee health. Buhai et al. (2017) find that improvements in occupational health and safety lead to an increase in performance among Danish manufacturing firms. Somanathan et al. (2015), using high-frequency worker data spanning a variety of manufacturing sectors in India, find that higher ambient temperatures in the workplace have economically significant negative effects on worker productivity and attendance. In a related vein, Adhvaryu et al. (2018) show that adoption of LED lighting, an energy-saving technology that emits less heat, increases productivity among garment factory workers in India.[3]

[1] The deadly collapse in 2013 of the Rana Plaza building in Bangladesh that housed five garment factories producing for major apparel retailers is an infamous example of unsafe and poor-quality work conditions.

[2] The International Labour Organisation (ILO) estimates show that work-related diseases and accidents account for economic losses as high as 4 per cent of worldwide gross domestic product (ILO 2003).

[3] Dell et al. (2014) provide an overview of impacts on productivity arising from pollution and high indoor/outdoor ambient temperatures.

Christophe J. Nordman and Smriti Sharma, *Pecuniary Returns to Working Conditions* In: *Micro, Small, and Medium Enterprises in Vietnam*. Edited by: John Rand and Finn Tarp, Oxford University Press (2020).
DOI: 10.1093/oso/9780198851189.003.0010

In this chapter, we first document working conditions in Vietnamese small and medium enterprises (SMEs), and then examine the existence of compensating wage differentials for vulnerable jobs and unfavourable working conditions. The theory of compensating differentials which was formalized in the 1980s (Brown 1980; Rosen 1986; Murphy and Topel 1987) states that workers should receive higher wages to compensate for the strenuous or hazardous nature of their jobs or adverse working conditions.[4] In developed countries, for example, it has been observed that physically onerous and risky jobs are often better paid (e.g. French and Dunlap 1998; Groot and Maassen van den Brink 1998; Lanfranchi et al. 2002), while the existence of compensating mechanisms mostly depends on the workers' labour market segment and their relative position in the wage distribution (Poggi 2007; Fernández and Nordman 2009). Despite the abundant explanations and the strength of the theoretical predictions regarding compensating wage differentials, the lack of appropriate data on job matches (including the workplace, the employee, and the attributes of the job) has been an impediment to empirically testing the theoretical predictions in developing countries. Using rich data on working conditions faced by workers in Vietnamese SMEs, our aim is to contribute to this discussion. This is salient given the scope of SMEs in Vietna they contribute to approximately 45 per cent of the country's GDP and 60 per cent of its employment.

In the UK, Fernández and Nordman (2009) assess the relative contribution of working conditions to wages with an emphasis on differences along the earnings distribution. They find that adverse working conditions—such as doing repetitive tasks, working under tight deadlines or facing health risks on the job—are associated with significant premiums, but sometimes also penalties. Quantile regressions confirm the presence of penalties to poor working conditions that are significant in the middle section of the earnings distribution. Böckerman et al. (2011) also confirm the presence of compensating differentials using data from Finland where they show that workers are compensated in terms of wages for uncertainty arising from establishment-level worker turnover. Ose (2005) finds that private sector manufacturing workers in Norway are not fully compensated for working in noisy environments. Furthermore, his theoretical model shows that only partial compensation for such disamenities can result in higher worker absenteeism. Using data on gender-specific injury incidence in the United States, Hersch (1998) finds that females are well compensated for occupational risk, while for males in white-collar jobs, there is a negative relationship between job risk and earnings. In contrast, there is scant empirical evidence to support the existence of such risk premiums and penalties in developing countries. For West Africa,

[4] The theory assumes that once job characteristics other than the wage become part of the labour market decisions of workers and firms, the resulting equilibrium will equalize utilities, rather than wages across individuals.

Bocquier et al. (2010) shed light on the link between vulnerability and incomes for wage workers and self-employed workers. They test whether workers in vulnerable jobs are paid better than workers in less strenuous jobs. They also adopt a distributional approach with the idea that vulnerability can have a different effect on income depending on the worker's relative position in the income distribution. Their results show that a vulnerability-compensating mechanism is mainly observed in the informal sector, and in the upper tail of the earnings distribution. Employment vulnerability is not compensated for the poorest workers in the private sector. They argue that long job queues and weak institutional protection of workers may have reduced bargaining power in the formal sector.

The existence of compensating mechanisms—or lack thereof—at different points of the earnings distribution can be due to bargaining power differences and labour market imbalances. For instance, workers in the upper tail of the earnings distribution may have greater bargaining power to demand and secure higher compensation for the stress that their jobs entail. The employer's capacity to provide financial compensation for undesirable working conditions might also differ depending on the type of imbalances found in certain market segments. For example, in segments where labour supply far outstrips demand, employers are reluctant to compensate workers for adverse working conditions. Like in Fernández and Nordman (2009), this justifies looking at the existence of compensating mechanisms across the wage distribution, and not only at the mean.

We use the Vietnam Small and Medium Enterprise data in which the employee survey has information on contract type, duration of work, provision of a range of workplace benefits, and working conditions. Based on this, we construct indicators of job vulnerability and working conditions. We first present descriptive statistics on working conditions and job quality for three rounds of data—2011, 2013, 2015—as well as by the formality status of the enterprise. Multivariate regression analyses at the employee level explore the existence of compensating wage differentials. We estimate unconditional quantile regressions at the employee level to discern whether the wage differential attributable to working conditions changes along the conditional wage distribution when we consider other wage shifters. One possible mechanism that can shift workers' bargaining power within the firm is the channel through which they were hired: formally or informally through social networks (Berardi 2013). Hence, we also investigate whether the hiring channel of the workers may differentially affect the relationship between working conditions and wages. Finally, we estimate a mean decomposition of wage gaps based on working conditions. This splits the wage gap between workers in poor working conditions and workers in non-poor working conditions into two parts: the first is due to differences in socioeconomic characteristics between workers, and the second part is attributable to different valuations of the workers' characteristics in different jobs (the differences in returns to characteristics).

This chapter is organized as follows. Section 10.2 provides a background on the Vietnamese context. In Section 10.3 we describe the data and methodology, and report descriptive statistics. Section 10.4 presents results from regressions and decomposition analyses. In Section 10.5, we provide concluding comments.

10.2 Background

Analysing the wage consequences of employment vulnerability and working conditions in Vietnam is particularly interesting since the country has experienced spectacular social, economic, and political changes in the recent period. On the labour market front, there are two striking features in recent years. First, the increasing rate of wage and non-agricultural employment; and second, a sharp rise in real wages and labour incomes (Cling et al. 2010). Wage dynamics have been higher for the semi-skilled and highly skilled workers than for unskilled workers. Although the formal sector of the economy has grown progressively, informal employment, especially that in SMEs, represents an important part of the Vietnamese labour market. Despite this, little is known about employment risks and working conditions that workers in SMEs face, and that is the gap this chapter intends to fill.

We now turn to a description of the landscape in Vietnam with respect to laws on working conditions, social insurance as well as on occupational safety and health. The Labour Code of 2012 is currently operational in Vietnam. As compared to the Labour Code of 1994 which it superseded, it has introduced significant changes that are potentially beneficial from the employees' perspective. For instance, it stipulates that the employer and the employee are required to sign a contract *before* the start of employment to ensure that employers honour their statutory obligations towards employees. The new Labour Code also requires a 15-day termination notice period to be served to employees on definite-term contracts of 12–36 months duration. The Code also dictates limits on working hours as well as overtime work. The first Law on Social Insurance was introduced in 2006 with the aim of improving social protection. The law applies to employees who work under a definite-term labour contract or a contract exceeding three months. Compulsory social insurance, which both employers and employees are obliged to join, includes sickness leave, maternity leave, employment injury and occupational and disease benefit, old-age benefit, and survivors' benefit. It also stipulates unemployment insurance that came into effect in 2009. The 2015 Law on Occupational Safety and Health applies to both contract and non-contract workers in all enterprises. The Law states that employers are obliged to provide training in matters related to occupational safety and health. They are also to compensate workers in case of occupational accidents or disease. Workers have the right to demand and work in safe working environments where they are provided information on hazardous factors as well as on preventive measures.

Despite the existence of a comprehensive social protection that is legally mandated, compliance and implementation remain a policy challenge. In a 2015–16 survey of 257 garment factories, ILO (2015) found that while there has been improvement over time, non-compliance with the above-mentioned laws remains high. For example, 40 per cent of factories were underpaying for overtime work and 62 per cent of employers failed to specify all terms and conditions of employment in the contract. Furthermore, in around 40 per cent of factories, inadequate fire detection and alarm systems were observed. Trifković (2017) examines the effect of internationally recognized management standards on firm working conditions in Vietnam to find that firms that have adopted standards are also more likely to offer formal contracts to their employees, although there is no systematic effect on financial benefits such as sick leave, unemployment insurance, accident insurance, etc.

10.3 Data and Methodology

10.3.1 Data

We rely on the 2011, 2013, and 2015 waves of the Vietnam Small and Medium Enterprises data, that is collected jointly by Central Institute for Economic Management (CIEM) of the Ministry of Planning and Investment (MPI) of Vietnam, the Institute of Labour Science and Social Affairs (ILSSA) of the Ministry of Labour, Invalids and Social Affairs (MoLISA) of Vietnam, the Development Economics Research Group (DERG) at the University of Copenhagen, and UNU-WIDER, Helsinki.

The enterprise-level surveys, administered to the owners or managers, are longitudinal in nature and have been conducted biennially since 2005. In about a quarter of randomly selected enterprises that are part of the enterprise surveys, a random subset of employees is interviewed for the employee survey. However, it should be noted that it is not possible to construct a panel dataset at the level of the employee. For this chapter, we primarily use data from the 'employee module'. Through this, we have access to variables such as wages earned by these employees, their demographic and socioeconomic characteristics such as gender, marital status, educational attainment, prior experience (in years), tenure in the current enterprise (in years), and occupation.[5] In addition, the survey asks questions

[5] Our analysis is limited to employees who report earning a monthly wage. This is about 88 per cent of the sample. Due to concern about quality of wage data where workers report being paid per hour, per day, and per week, we do not include those observations in our analysis.

related to availability and type of contract, provision of social security benefits and occupational safety and health and training, and areas in which employees consider working conditions to be most adversely affected.

Our main variables of interest are those capturing vulnerable terms of employment and working conditions. To that end, we create a binary variable for *informal contract* (takes value 1 if there is no formal written contract, 0 otherwise). We construct a variable called *financial benefits* that sums up whether the following nine financial benefits are provided: sick leave, maternity leave, retirement pay, severance pay, survival benefit, health insurance, annual paid leave, unemployment insurance, and compensation for accidents/illness.[6] For working conditions, we create a binary variable that takes value 1 if the employee reports receiving no occupational safety and health (OSH) training. We also create binary variables that take the value 1 if the employee responds in the affirmative to each of the following working conditions being adversely affected, 0 otherwise: air quality, fire hazards, heat, lighting, waste disposal, and water pollution. We create an additive index that sums up the binary variables corresponding to the unfavourable working conditions and OSH training. All employees facing higher than the median number of adverse working conditions are assigned a value 1 indicating *poor working conditions*, 0 otherwise.[7]

10.3.2 Methodology

We begin with estimating ordinary least squares (OLS) regressions of the following type where *i* represents the employee and *j* represents the fir

$$
\begin{aligned}
Y_{ij} = \beta_0 + \beta_1 \, \textit{Informal Contract}_i + \beta_2 \, \textit{Financial Benefits}_i \\
+ \beta_3 \, \textit{Poor Working Conditions}_i + X_i\alpha + \delta_j + \epsilon_i,
\end{aligned}
\tag{10.1}
$$

Where *Y* is the log of real hourly wages of employee i in firm j. In addition to variables capturing vulnerable employment (*Informal Contract, Financial Benefits*) and working conditions (*Poor Working Conditions*), we include a vector X of dimension K, controlling for employee characteristics such as gender (takes value 1 if female, 0 if male), marital status (takes value 1 if married; 0 otherwise), years of experience prior to joining the firm and its quadratic term, tenure in the current firm and its quadratic term (in years), dummy variables for highest level of

[6] The question on maternity leave is answered by male and female employees.

[7] We considered using principal components analysis to reduce the dimensionality of the vector of working conditions. However, due to the low pair-wise correlations, five factors appeared to explain a large part of the variance (i.e., eigenvalues exceeding 1). As this was not helpful, we resorted to creating a binary variable based on an underlying additive index. The median number of adverse working conditions is 3 (for the pooled sample as well as for individual years).

educational attainment such as secondary, high school, vocational, and college (with no education or primary being the omitted category) as well as dummy variables for occupation such as manager, professional worker, office worker, sales worker, and service worker (with production worker being the omitted category). We include firm-fixed effects (δ_j) that control for all time-invariant firm-level characteristics. As we pool the survey years in the regression analyses, we finally include dummies for survey years. To account for correlation in the error terms between employees in the same firm, we cluster standard errors at the firm level.

In the estimates, varying effects of working conditions and terms of employment on wages may result from worker selection by firms and vice versa. For example, firms with poor working conditions could only select workers that accept lower pay and are not inclined to bargain over wages. It may also be that some observed firms with unsavoury work environments select or attract workers that are more motivated or less reluctant to working in unfavourable situations. Moreover, firms may decide to compensate for the bad working conditions of the employees they seek to retain, i.e., those with greater unobserved productivity. All these selectivity effects may then affect estimates of working conditions and terms of employment in individual wage equations if one does not control for firm and worker matching processes. Since it is impossible to fully control for these phenomena with our data, we have little choice but to assume that selectivity and matching effects are well accounted for by the inclusion of workers' and firms' controls, in particular the firm-fixed effects, and that residual effects may be overlooked. However, due to the rigidity of the Vietnamese formal labour market (with sluggish administrative procedures, and little public information on jobs and workers), it is plausible that selection effects are less intensive than in developed countries in general.

Furthermore, as the OLS regressions only capture the average relationship between working conditions and hourly wages, we also conduct a distributional analysis by estimating unconditional quantile regressions (UQR) à la Firpo et al. (2009). This allows us to comment on how employment vulnerability and poor working conditions matter at different points of the wage distribution. The main advantage of this method over conditional quantile regressions is that the estimated marginal effects do not depend on the set of explanatory variables in the model. UQR is based on extending the concept of Influence Function to what has been termed the Recentered Influence Function (RIF). The RIF for the quantile θ of log wage (Y) is given by:

$$RIF(Y, Q_\theta) = Q_\theta + [Y - d_\theta]/f_Y(Q_\theta), \tag{10.2}$$

where $f_Y(Q_\theta)$ is the density distribution function of Y at Q_θ and d_θ is a binary variable taking value 1 if $Y \leq Q_\theta$ and 0 otherwise.

After recalculating the variables of interest, the following is estimated by OLS:

$$RIF(Y, Q_\theta) = X\beta^{UQR} + \epsilon. \tag{10.3}$$

Finally, we conduct wage decompositions that allow us to discern how much of the 'working conditions wage gap' may be due to differences in workers' characteristics across jobs, and how much of it is due to the price the market pays for these workers' attributes in these different jobs (i.e., the differences in returns to characteristics). The most common approach for identifying sources of wage gaps is the Oaxaca-Blinder decomposition (Blinder 1973; Oaxaca 1973). The issue with these traditional approaches is how to determine the reference wage structure. This choice poses the so-called index number problem, given that either the poor working conditions group or the non-poor working conditions group structure can be used as the reference benchmark. While there is a priori no preferable alternative, the decomposition can be quite sensitive to the selection made. The literature has proposed different weighting schemes to deal with this index problem.

In this chapter, we rely on the general decomposition proposed by Neumark (1988). This decomposition can be reduced to Oaxaca-Blinder's two special cases if it is assumed that the poor working conditions group structure is the benchmark (the non-poor working conditions group would be underpaid), or if it is assumed that the benchmark is that of the non-poor working conditions group (hence the poor working conditions group would be overpaid). This benchmark is then estimated using the weighted average of the wage structures of these two groups using the pooled sample. Neumark's approach usually provides estimates that lie between the two opposing assumptions of the Oaxaca-Blinder decompositions. This is also true in these data.

10.3.3 Descriptive Statistics

In Table 10.1, we present summary statistics for each of the three survey years for the variables included in this study. We first discuss the demographic and socio-economic characteristics of the study sample. Approximately 40 per cent of the employees are female, and over three-quarters are married. On average across the three years, 4–5 per cent are uneducated, 30–32 per cent have completed secondary education, and 21–24 per cent reached a college or higher degree level. The share of employees reporting high-school education declined from 41 per cent in 2011 to 29 per cent in 2015. This was accompanied by an increase in those with vocational education from 3 per cent in 2011 to 9–10 per cent in 2013 and 2015. The average years of experience prior to joining the firm range between 6 and 7 years, and most employees have been at the current firm for around 6 years. In terms of occupational structure, 60 per cent of employees are in the production

Table 10.1 Descriptive statistics

	2011	2013	2015
	Mean (SD)	Mean (SD)	Mean (SD)
Employment and working conditions			
Informal contract	0.446 (0.497)	0.409 (0.492)	0.382 (0.486)
Financial benefits	3.418 (3.585)	4.115 (3.722)	4.076 (3.503)
No occupational safety and health training	0.445 (0.497)	0.569 (0.495)	0.682 (0.466)
Problem: air quality	0.393 (0.489)	0.540 (0.499)	0.461 (0.499)
Problem: fire hazard	0.339 (0.474)	0.471 (0.499)	0.411 (0.492)
Problem: heat	0.582 (0.494)	0.633 (0.482)	0.617 (0.486)
Problem: lighting	0.221 (0.415)	0.278 (0.448)	0.293 (0.456)
Problem: noise	0.452 (0.498)	0.505 (0.500)	0.461 (0.499)
Problem: waste disposal	0.121 (0.327)	0.155 (0.362)	0.130 (0.336)
Problem: water pollution	0.0919 (0.289)	0.0499 (0.218)	0.0439 (0.205)
Poor working conditions	0.300 (0.459)	0.448 (0.498)	0.486 (0.500)
Employee characteristics			
Female	0.397 (0.490)	0.408 (0.492)	0.404 (0.491)
Married	0.796 (0.403)	0.838 (0.368)	0.785 (0.411)
No education/primary	0.0483 (0.215)	0.0456 (0.209)	0.0355 (0.185)
Secondary education	0.298 (0.458)	0.309 (0.462)	0.329 (0.470)
High school education	0.411 (0.492)	0.328 (0.470)	0.295 (0.456)
Vocational education	0.0306 (0.172)	0.104 (0.306)	0.0944 (0.293)
College education	0.212 (0.409)	0.214 (0.410)	0.246 (0.431)
Prior experience	6.723 (6.716)	6.388 (6.190)	6.811 (6.195)
Tenure	5.583 (4.595)	6.005 (4.982)	6.889 (5.329)
Manager	0.0836 (0.277)	0.103 (0.304)	0.0738 (0.262)
Professional worker	0.101 (0.302)	0.111 (0.314)	0.0953 (0.294)
Office worker	0.0860 (0.281)	0.0987 (0.298)	0.107 (0.310)

Sales worker	0.0777	0.0727	0.0720
	(0.268)	(0.260)	(0.259)
Service worker	0.0377	0.0456	0.0346
	(0.191)	(0.209)	(0.183)
Production worker	0.614	0.569	0.617
	(0.487)	(0.495)	(0.486)
Observations	849	922	1070

Notes: This table reports means and standard deviations in parentheses for each year of data included in the study. The sample is limited to employees who report earning a monthly wage. The minimum and maximum values for the *financial benefits* variable are 0 and 9 respectively. *Poor working conditions* takes a value 1 if the sum of the adverse working conditions is higher than the pooled sample median, 0 otherwise.

Source: Authors' calculations using Vietnam Small and Medium Enterprises Survey for 2011–15.

worker category, with managers, professional workers, office workers, and sales workers each making up about 7–11 per cent of the sample. Service workers are about 3–4 per cent of the sample.

In terms of employment and working conditions, we find that between 2011 and 2015 there has been a significant drop in the share of employees with an informal contract from approximately 45 per cent to 38 per cent (two-sided test of proportions, p-value = 0.004), and a significant increase in the number of financial benefits offered by employers (two-tailed t-test, p-value < 0.001). There is also significant increase in the share of employees reporting overall poor working conditions (i.e., those facing higher than the median number of adverse working conditions) from 30 per cent in 2011 to 49 per cent in 2015 (two-sided test of proportions, p-value < 0.001). In terms of individual components of working conditions, we observe that, while in 2011 about 45 per cent of employees reported receiving no OSH training at the workplace, this jumped to over two-thirds in 2015. There was also an increase in the share of employees reporting fire hazard, heat problems, lighting, and poor air quality. On the other hand, there was a decline in water pollution reported as a problem. There were no meaningful changes in problems reported regarding noise and waste disposal.

In Table 10.2, we shed light on variation in employment terms and working conditions based on the formality or registration status of the firm. On the one hand, as per the compensating wage differential theory, informal firms might compensate workers for not being covered by social security and for facing generally poorer working conditions. On the other hand, according to efficiency wage theory, formal firms may voluntarily pay higher wages to attract high quality workers, to improve worker retention, and to elicit higher effort levels. Firms are defined as being formal if they have an Enterprise Code Number (ECN) or if they have a Business Registration Certificate (BRC) and a tax code. The share of workers reporting informal contracts is significantly lower in the formally registered firms, as expected (two-sided test of proportions, p-value < 0.001).

Table 10.2 Employment and working conditions: formal and informal firms

	Informal firms	Formalfirms
Informal contract	0.916	0.381
	(0.279)	(0.486)
Financial benefits	0.487	4.087
	(1.305)	(3.605)
No occupational safety and health training	0.649	0.571
	(0.479)	(0.495)
Problem: air quality	0.519	0.463
	(0.501)	(0.499)
Problem: fire hazard	0.331	0.413
	(0.472)	(0.493)
Problem: heat	0.513	0.617
	(0.501)	(0.486)
Problem: lighting	0.182	0.272
	(0.387)	(0.445)
Problem: noise	0.448	0.474
	(0.499)	(0.499)
Problem: waste disposal	0.0909	0.138
	(0.288)	(0.345)
Problem: water pollution	0.0325	0.0618
	(0.178)	(0.241)
Poor working conditions	0.481	0.415
	(0.501)	(0.493)
Observations	154	2687

Notes: This table reports means and standard deviations in parentheses. The sample is limited to employees who report earning a monthly wage. The minimum and maximum values for the *financial benefits* variable are 0 and 9 respectively. *Poor working conditions* takes a value 1 if the sum of the adverse working conditions is higher than the sample median, 0 otherwise. Firms are defined as being formal if they have an Enterprise Code Number (ECN) or if they have a Business Registration Certificate (BRC) and a tax code.

Source: Authors' calculations using Vietnam Small and Medium Enterprises Survey for 2011–15.

On average, less than one financial benefit is provided in unregistered firms as compared to approximately four benefits in registered firms (two-tailed t-test, p-value < 0.001). There is about a 7-percentage point gap between the shares of workers in formal and informal firms reporting poor working conditions, and this just fails to reach significance at conventional levels (two-sided test of proportions, p-value = 0.106). Looking at individual components, 57 per cent of workers in registered firms report no OSH training as compared to 65 per cent in unregistered firms (two-sided test of proportions, p-value = 0.05). Significantly higher shares of employees in the formal firms report problems related to fire hazards, heat, light, and waste (two-sided test of proportions, all p-values < 0.1). This suggests that poor conditions are not specific to informal firms only, as unfavourable work environments seem to be prevalent in formal sector enterprises as well.

10.4 Results

10.4.1 Regression Analyses

In Table 10.3, we present results from an OLS regression wherein the outcome variable is the log of real hourly wages. In Column 1, we only include worker characteristics such as gender, marital status, educational attainment dummies, experience, and tenure and their respective quadratic terms, occupation, province, and survey year dummies. In line with existing literature, we find that female employees earn 10 per cent less than male employees, and this result is robust to alternative specifications in columns 2 and 3. In accordance with previous studies that have estimated wage returns to education in Vietnam (Liu 2006; Pham and Reilly 2007; Nguyen et al. 2013; Oostendorp and Quang 2013), we find returns to education to be increasing with the level of education attained. In column 2, we proceed to adding the right-hand side variables measuring employment terms and working conditions, and we add each as a separate variable. We find some evidence that those reporting poor air quality earn higher wages, and those reporting poor lighting, earn lower wages (although both these coefficients are weakly significant at the 10 per cent level). Note, however, that jointly these variables are statistically significant (F-statistic = 1.82; p-value = 0.05). In column 3, we use the dummy for poor working conditions instead of the separate variables, and from this point on, this remains our preferred measure. We indeed believe that what would matter the most in order to observe wage compensations for poor working conditions (i.e., when the worker is able to bargain for such compensation) is the cumulative nature of adverse job conditions, rather than one specific unfavourable situation on the job. We find however that those facing poor working conditions earn about 3.7 per cent lower hourly wages, indicating that compensating differentials are not at work here. Finally, in column 4, we add the firm-fixed effects. Upon adding these, we find that the association between wages and working conditions is negative but ceases to be significant. This indicates the existence of working condition-based sorting across firms such that poor working condition jobs are mostly found in firms that tend to also offer low wages.

In Table 10.4, we estimate unconditional quantile regressions—with the full specification of right-hand side variables as in column 4 of Table 10.3—at the following points of the wage distribution: 10th, 25th, 50th, 75th, and 90th. We find that the number of financial benefits is positively correlated with wages at the 25th percentile of the wage distribution. On the other hand, those facing poor working conditions earn lower wages at the median and higher points of the distribution, but the coefficients are significant at the 75th and 90th percentiles only. Furthermore, throughout the distribution, those with informal contracts earn lower wages but the coefficients are not statistically significant. Our results on financial benefits and poor working conditions seem to suggest that workers at the

Table 10.3 Mean wage regressions (pooled sample)

	(1)	(2)	(3)	(4)
Female	−0.104***	−0.103***	−0.109***	−0.042*
	(0.017)	(0.017)	(0.017)	(0.022)
Married	0.064***	0.059***	0.063***	0.028
	(0.021)	(0.020)	(0.021)	(0.023)
Secondary education	0.051	0.043	0.040	0.094*
	(0.034)	(0.034)	(0.035)	(0.054)
High school education	0.094***	0.078**	0.073**	0.111**
	(0.035)	(0.036)	(0.036)	(0.049)
Vocational education	0.128***	0.107**	0.100**	0.131**
	(0.044)	(0.045)	(0.045)	(0.062)
College education	0.239***	0.213***	0.206***	0.208***
	(0.044)	(0.044)	(0.044)	(0.057)
Prior experience	−0.000	0.000	−0.000	0.004
	(0.004)	(0.004)	(0.004)	(0.005)
Prior experience squared	0.000	0.000	0.000	−0.000
	(0.000)	(0.000)	(0.000)	(0.000)
Tenure	0.010*	0.009*	0.009*	0.013**
	(0.005)	(0.005)	(0.005)	(0.006)
Tenure squared	−0.000	−0.000	−0.000	−0.000
	(0.000)	(0.000)	(0.000)	(0.000)
Informal contract		−0.015	−0.016	−0.024
		(0.027)	(0.027)	(0.042)
Financial benefits		0.005	0.005	0.004
		(0.004)	(0.004)	(0.008)
No OSH training		−0.037		
		(0.024)		
Problem: air quality		0.030*		
		(0.018)		
Problem: fire hazard		−0.003		
		(0.019)		
Problem: heat		0.008		
		(0.020)		
Problem: lighting		−0.045*		
		(0.024)		
Problem: noise		−0.009		
		(0.019)		
Problem: waste disposal		−0.008		
		(0.026)		
Problem: water pollution		−0.066		
		(0.042)		
Poor working conditions			−0.037*	−0.033
			(0.022)	(0.033)
Observations	2847	2841	2841	2841
R^2	0.237	0.247	0.242	0.600
Firm fixed effects	No	No	No	Yes

Notes: This table reports marginal effects from an OLS regression on the pooled sample for 2011, 2013 and 2015. The dependent variable is log of real hourly wage. Standard errors in parentheses clustered at the firm level. The sample is limited to employees who report earning a monthly wage. All regressions include year and occupation dummies. * $p < 0.10$, ** $p < 0.05$, *** $p < 0.01$.

Source: Authors' calculations using Vietnam Small and Medium Enterprises Survey for 2011–15.

Table 10.4 Unconditional quantile regressions (with firm fixed effects)

	Q10	Q25	Q50	Q75	Q90
Female	0.009	−0.044**	−0.043**	−0.073***	−0.130***
	(0.035)	(0.020)	(0.017)	(0.023)	(0.038)
Married	0.122**	0.032	0.001	−0.001	0.048
	(0.051)	(0.024)	(0.022)	(0.029)	(0.038)
Secondary education	0.121	0.065	0.083*	−0.002	−0.008
	(0.131)	(0.055)	(0.046)	(0.061)	(0.072)
High school education	0.144	0.088	0.101**	0.010	−0.028
	(0.134)	(0.056)	(0.047)	(0.060)	(0.071)
Vocational education	0.111	0.106*	0.122**	0.065	−0.060
	(0.146)	(0.063)	(0.054)	(0.071)	(0.092)
College education	0.131	0.123**	0.207***	0.147**	0.131
	(0.143)	(0.061)	(0.055)	(0.071)	(0.092)
Prior experience	−0.000	0.004	0.007**	0.010*	0.005
	(0.008)	(0.004)	(0.004)	(0.005)	(0.008)
Prior experience squared	0.000	−0.000	−0.000	−0.000*	−0.000
	(0.000)	(0.000)	(0.000)	(0.000)	(0.000)
Tenure	0.019**	0.011**	0.014***	0.010*	0.009
	(0.009)	(0.005)	(0.004)	(0.006)	(0.010)
Tenure squared	−0.001**	−0.000*	−0.000**	−0.000	−0.000
	(0.000)	(0.000)	(0.000)	(0.000)	(0.000)
Informal contract	−0.085	−0.044	−0.028	−0.045	−0.010
	(0.064)	(0.037)	(0.033)	(0.042)	(0.063)
Financial benefits	0.013	0.010*	0.008	−0.002	−0.009
	(0.009)	(0.005)	(0.005)	(0.007)	(0.009)
Poor working conditions	0.011	0.017	−0.003	−0.092***	−0.077*
	(0.044)	(0.022)	(0.021)	(0.032)	(0.042)
Observations	2841	2841	2841	2841	2841

Notes: This table reports marginal effects from unconditional quantile regressions. Dependent variable is log of real hourly wage. Bootstrapped standard errors based on 500 replications are reported in parentheses. * $p < 0.10$, ** $p < 0.05$, *** $p < 0.01$. The sample is limited to employees who report earning a monthly wage. All regressions include firm fixed effects, year dummies and occupation dummies.

Source: Authors' calculations using Vietnam Small and Medium Enterprises Survey for 2011–15.

bottom of the wage distribution are able to obtain some premium for unfavourable work conditions while for those at the higher wage percentiles, lower financial benefits and poor working conditions are also detrimental to wages. In terms of other controls included in the regression, we find that women are disadvantaged across the wage distribution and the gender wage gap is larger at higher percentiles. This phenomenon, known as the 'glass ceiling' effect, is often obtained in emerging and developing countries, including using matched worker-firm data (Chi and Li 2008; Nordman and Wolff 2009; Cardoso et al. 2016). There are generally positive and significant returns to college education, except at the 10th and 90th percentiles, while the reverse is observed for high school education that is positively and significantly valued from the 10th to the median percentiles.

Table 10.5 Mean wage regressions, by hiring channels

	(1)	(2)
Informal contract	0.018	−0.164**
	(0.047)	(0.064)
Financial benefits	0.008	−0.007
	(0.008)	(0.011)
Poor working conditions	−0.023	−0.049
	(0.032)	(0.056)
Formal hire	0.133*	
	(0.080)	
Formal hire*Informal contract	−0.181**	
	(0.073)	
Formal hire*Financial benefits	−0.014	
	(0.010)	
Formal hire*Poor working conditions	−0.027	
	(0.051)	
Manager tie		−0.151*
		(0.086)
Worker tie		−0.121
		(0.084)
Manager tie*Informal contract		0.164**
		(0.080)
Manager tie*Financial benefits		0.019
		(0.012)
Manager tie*Poor working conditions		0.060
		(0.059)
Worker tie*Informal contract		0.192**
		(0.078)
Worker tie*Financial benefits		0.012
		(0.010)
Worker tie*Poor working conditions		0.007
		(0.054)
Observations	2833	2833
R^2	0.602	0.603

Notes: This table reports marginal effects from OLS regressions. Dependent variable is log of real hourly wage. Standard errors in parentheses clustered at the firm level. * $p < 0.10$, ** $p < 0.05$, *** $p < 0.01$. The sample is limited to employees who report earning a monthly wage. All regressions include worker characteristics (gender, marital status, education dummies, experience and tenure), firm fixed effects, year dummies and occupation dummies.

Source: Authors' calculations using Vietnam Small and Medium Enterprises Survey for 2011–15.

In Table 10.5, we explore the avenue of the channel through which the worker was hired, with the idea that the hiring channel may differentially affect the relationship between working conditions and wages. We do this by creating two variables. The first is whether the employee was hired through formal channels: a variable *formal hire* takes a value 1 if the job was obtained through an employment agency, door to door visits, responding to job advertisements, and 0 otherwise. The second is whether the worker got the job through a connection to the owner/

manager or another worker within the firm. Using the formulation of Larsen et al. (2011), we create a variable called *manager tie* that takes a value 1 if the worker got a job through the owner/manager whom they are related to or friends with, and 0 otherwise. Similarly, we create *worker tie* that takes a value 1 if the worker got a job through a relative, friend, or acquaintance who was also an employee at the firm, and 0 otherwise. Pooling data from the three survey rounds, we find that 27 per cent of employees found the job through a manager tie and 45 per cent through a worker tie.

In Column 1 of Table 10.5, we interact *formal hire* with the vector of employment terms and poor working conditions. We find that formally hired employees with an informal contract earn less than informally hired employees. In column 2, we interact *manager tie* and *worker tie* with working conditions variables. Upon doing so, we find that those employed based on their connection to the manager as well to a worker earn more on an informal contract than those without such ties. This is consistent with column 1 wherein formally hired workers fared worse with an informal contract. This is in contrast to the findings of Larsen et al. (2011) who find that the manager tie is more important than the worker tie in wage determination. Here, we observe that both worker and manager ties are able to possibly provide workers with some additional wage bargaining power when they are informally hired.

10.4.2 Decomposition Analyses

Up till now, we relied on the potentially restrictive assumption that the returns to covariates are the same in 'poor' and 'non-poor' working conditions jobs since we estimated wage equations on samples of workers working in both types of jobs. We now relax this assumption and observe the determinants of wages across jobs defined by the dummy for *poor working conditions*. Using a wage decomposition allows us to discern how much of the mean 'working conditions wage gap' may be due to differences in workers' characteristics across jobs, and how much of it is due to the price the market pays for workers' attributes in these different jobs. We use the decomposition proposed by Neumark (1988). *The* decompositions are performed on the pooled years' sample, and also on year-wise samples. We rely on nominal wages instead of real wages when we turn to the three specific years.

Before discussing the decompositions, we describe the distribution of workers across the two types of jobs. In the four panels of Figure 10.1, we present kernel density graphs of log hourly wages across workers facing 'poor' or 'non-poor' working conditions (WC) for the pooled sample, and then for each year separately. Kolmogorov-Smirnov tests for the equality of distributions cannot reject the null for the 2011 sample (p-value = 0.8) but for the pooled sample and for years 2013 and 2015, the density functions are not equal (Kolmogorov–Smirnov tests

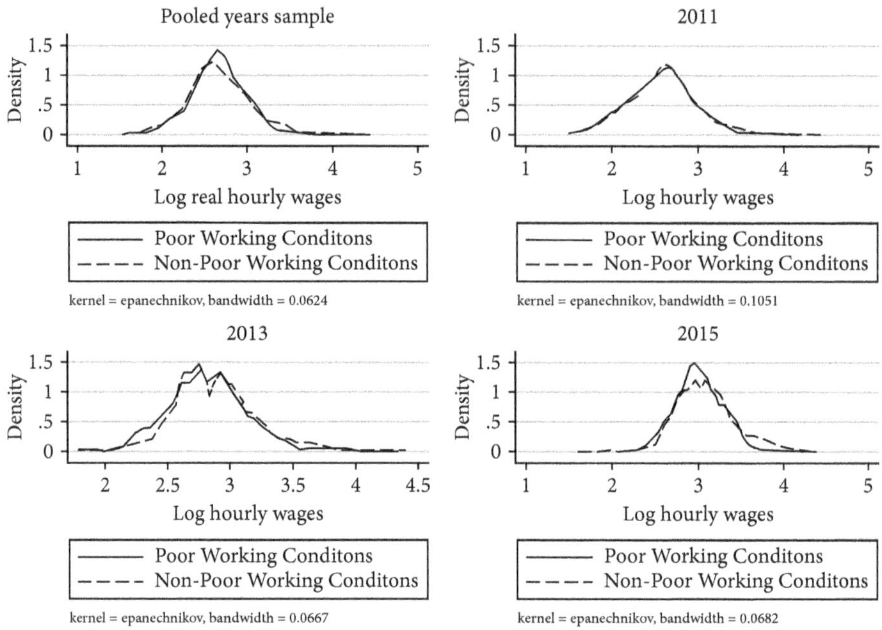

Figure 10.1 Density of log hourly wages across workers facing 'poor' or 'non-poor' working conditions

Notes: *Poor working conditions* takes a value 1 if the sum of the adverse working conditions is higher than the pooled or yearly sample median, 0 otherwise. For year-specific graphs, we use log of nominal hourly wages and for the pooled years graph, we use the log of real hourly wages.

Source: Authors' calculations using Vietnam Small and Medium Enterprises Survey for 2011–15.

with p-values = 0.003, 0.093, and 0.002, in the pooled sample, 2013 and 2015 respectively). This justifies looking at yearly decompositions.

The results of the decompositions for 2013 and 2015 are reported in Table 10.6. The raw wage differential is negligible in the pooled sample, and insignificantly different from zero in 2011. There is then virtually nothing to be decomposed in these two samples. The raw differentials are in contrast somewhat sizable and significant in 2013 and 2015, respectively 6.1 and 7.6 per cent, in favour of non-poor WC job workers. For these two years, we then proceed with decomposing the raw gaps using as explanatory variables the employees' characteristics and terms of employment, and then we add the firm-fixed effects.

Interestingly, while the explained share of the gap (the differences in workers' characteristics and terms of employment) is dominant in 2013 (65 per cent), this explained share is much smaller in 2015 (40 per cent). We then conclude that most (if not all) of the increase in the WC wage gap between 2013 and 2015 (from 6.1 to 7.6 per cent) might be attributed to unobserved characteristics of the workers and/or of their jobs. Adding the firm-fixed effects to the decompositions further dramatically reduces the unexplained portion of the WC gap in 2015 from

Table 10.6 Neumark decompositions of log hourly wage gaps by working conditions (WC) (difference between 'poor' WC and 'non-poor' WC)

	(1) Raw differential	(2) Unexplained	(3) Explained	(4) % unexplained	(5) % explained
Pooled years	0.006				
2011	0.017				
2013	0.061**				
Employee characteristics and employment terms		0.021	0.040	34.4	65.6
Adding firm fixed effects		0.022	0.039	36.5	63.5
2015	0.076***				
Employee characteristics and employment terms		0.046	0.031	59.8	40.2
Adding firm-fixed effects		0.013	0.064	16.6	83.4

Notes: Year-wise Neumark decompositions stem from log hourly *nominal* wage equations shown in Columns 3 and 4 of Table 3 but without the poor working condition dummy. The sample is limited to employees who report earning a monthly wage. All regressions include employee characteristics (gender, marital status, education level, experience and tenure), year dummies, and occupation dummies. * $p < 0.10$, ** $p < 0.05$, *** $p < 0.01$.

Source: Authors' calculations using Vietnam Small and Medium Enterprises Survey for 2011–15.

60 per cent to 16.6 per cent, leading us to explain over 80 per cent of the WC wage gap. By contrast, adding firm-fixed effects does not increase the explained component of the gap in 2013, in fact it leads to a marginal drop in the explained share. This further reveals that most of the heterogeneity that was potentially increasing the WC gap between 2013 and 2015 was that of the firms, and much less that of the workers, perhaps reflecting changing firm wage policies between the two years.

10.5 Concluding Comments

In this chapter, our objective was to examine the existence of compensating wage differentials for workers in vulnerable jobs and those facing undesirable working conditions in SMEs in Vietnam. Descriptive statistics first show that there is some heterogeneity in terms of the prevalence of vulnerable and unfavourable working conditions across the survey years. We find a decline over time in the share of employees with an informal contract, and an increase in the number of financial benefits offered by employers. There is also significant increase in the share of employees reporting overall poor working conditions. Looking at the formality divide at the firm level, an interesting finding is that adverse work environments seem to be largely widespread in both formal and informal enterprises.

Wage regressions show that there are no clear compensating mechanisms for poor working conditions in terms of wages in these Vietnamese SMEs, thus rejecting the compensating differentials theory. In fact, evidence from quantile regressions shows that employees above median wage levels are not compensated for unfavourable working conditions and even suffer a wage penalty. This result of varying effects across the wage distribution appears puzzling at first sight. Indeed, one may expect to observe the reverse pattern assuming that workers at the upper tail of the wage distribution are usually better positioned than their low-wage counterparts to negotiate for higher wages when their work environment is unfavourable. But the firm's ability to compensate the worker for bearing poor working conditions also depends on the degree of competition in the market for labour (Fernández and Nordman 2009). If labour supply outstrips demand, which might only be the case in some parts of the pay ladder, the employer may not need to pay a premium for exposure to bad working conditions. This is one of the interpretations we could make here: highly qualified workers willing to enter the labour market may in fact be largely queuing for a formal sector job, perhaps creating a mismatch between qualifications and offered jobs if labour demand is weak and decreasing reservation wages of high ability workers. In such cases, poor working conditions jobs at the higher ends of the formal sector would largely correspond to poorly paid jobs, all else being equal. Finally, another interpretation of the absence of penalty at the bottom of the wage distribution relies on the existence of some wage rigidity in the lower formal labour market segment. There, subsistence wages would prevent employers from paying poorly even in unfavourable work environment compared to jobs without such attributes. The new Labour Code and Trade Union law of 2012–13, being part of the ongoing efforts in Vietnam to modernize labour market governance in line with international standards, may have provided a better environment for workers to negotiate their own terms and conditions of employment through collective bargaining (ILO 2015).

Upon estimating mean decompositions of wage gaps based on working conditions, we find that the explained share of the gap is dominant in 2013 (65 per cent) and is much weaker in 2015 (40 per cent). Once firm-fixed effects are added in these decompositions, due to the matched worker-firm structure of the data, the working conditions wage gap is almost entirely explained by the conjunction of worker, job and firm characteristics in 2015 (83 per cent), in contrast to the previous survey year of 2013 where the explained share remained almost constant upon adding firm controls (63 per cent). Hence, we conclude that most of the increase in the working conditions wage gap between 2013 and 2015 is on account of increased unobserved firm heterogeneity in 2015. This then opens the door for additional interpretations, possibly changes over time in firm wage policies, perhaps due to the implementation of the new Labour Code in 2013. This chapter does not consider these aspects, but this is an avenue for further research.

References

Adhvaryu, A., N. Kala, and A. Nyshadham (2018). The Light and the Heat: Productivity Co-benefits of Energy-Saving Technology. NBER Working Paper No. 24314. Cambridge MA: National Bureau of Economic Research.

Barnay, T. (2016). Health, work, and working conditions: A review of the European economic literature, *European Journal of Health Economics*, 17: 693–709.

Berardi, N. (2013). Social networks and wages in Senegal's labor market, *IZA Journal of Labor and Development*, 2: 3.

Blinder, A. S. (1973). Wage discrimination: Reduced form and structural estimates, *Journal of Human Resources*, 8(4): 436–55.

Böckerman, P., P. Ilmakunnas, and E. Johansson (2011). Job security and employee well-being: Evidence from matched survey and register data, *Labour Economics*, 18: 547–54.

Bocquier, P., C. J. Nordman, and A. Vescovo (2010). Employment vulnerability and earnings in urban West Africa, *World Development*, 38(9): 1297–314.

Brown, C. (1980). Equalizing differences in the labor market, *The Quarterly Journal of Economics*, 94(1): 113–34.

Buhai, I. S., C. Cottini, and N. Westergaard-Nielsen (2017). How productive is workplace health and safety?, *Scandinavian Journal of Economics*, 1 19(4): 1086–1104.

Cardoso, A. R., Guimaraes, P., and Portugal, P. (2016). What drives the gender wage gap? A look at the role of firm and job-title heterogeneity, *Oxford Economic Papers*, 68(2): 506–24.

Chi, W., and Li, B. (2008). Glass ceiling or sticky poor? Examining the gender earnings differential across the earnings distribution in urban China, 1987–2004, *Journal of Comparative Economics*, 36(2): 243–63.

Cling, J.-P., Razafindrakoto, M., and Roubaud, F. (2010). Assessing the potential impact of the global crisis on the labour market and the informal sector in Vietnam, *Journal of Economics & Development*, 38: 16–25.

Datta Gupta, N., and Kristensen, N. (2008). Work environment satisfaction and employee health: Panel evidence from Denmark, France and Spain, 1994–2001, *European Journal of Health Economics*, 9(1): 51–61.

Dell, M., Jones, B. F., and Olken, B. A. (2014). What do we learn from the weather? The new climate-economy literature, *Journal of Economic Literature*, 52(3): 740–98.

Fernández, R. M., and Nordman, C. J. (2009). Are there pecuniary compensations for working conditions?, *Labour Economics*, 16: 194–207.

Firpo, S., Fortin, N. M., and Lemieux, T. (2009). Unconditional quantile regressions, *Econometrica*, 77(3): 953–73.

French, M. T., and Dunlap, L. J. (1998). Compensating wage differentials for job stress, *Applied Economics*, 30(8): 1067–75.

Groot, W., and Maassen van den Brink, H. (1998). The price of stress, *Journal of Economic Psychology*, 20: 83–103.

Hersch, J. (1998). Compensating differentials for gender-specific job injury risks, *American Economic Review*, 88(3): 598–607.

ILO (2003). *Safety in Numbers: Pointers for a Global Safety Culture at Work.* Geneva: International Labour Office.

ILO (2015). *Better Work Vietna Garment Industry.* 8th compliance synthesis report. Geneva: International Labour Office.

Lanfranchi, J., Ohlsson, H., and Skalli, A. H. (2002). Compensating wage differentials and shift work preferences, *Economics Letters*, 74, 393–8.

Larsen, A. F., Rand, J., and Torm, N. (2011). Do recruitment ties affect wages? An analysis using matched employer-employee data from Vietnam, *Review of Development Economics*, 15(3): 541–55.

Liu, A. Y. C. (2006). Changing wage structure and education in Vietnam 1993–1998: The roles of demand. *Economics of Transition,* 14(4): 681–706.

Murphy, K. M., and R. H. Topel (1987). Unemployment, risk, and earnings: Testing for equalizing wage differences in the labor market. In K. Lang and J. S. Leonard (eds), *Unemployment and the Structure of the Labor Market*, 103–40. New York and Oxford: Basil Blackwell.

Neumark, D. (1988). Employers' discriminatory behavior and the estimation of wage discrimination, *Journal of Human Resources*, 23: 279–95.

Nguyen, H. C., Nordman, C. J., and Roubaud, F. (2013). Who suffers the penalty? A panel data analysis of earnings gaps in Vietnam, *Journal of Development Studies*, 49(12): 1694–1710.

Nordman, C. J., and Wolff, F.-C. (2009). Is there a glass ceiling in Morocco? Evidence from matched worker-firm data, *Journal of African Economies*, 18(4): 592–633.

Oaxaca, R. (1973). Male–female wage differentials in urban labor markets, *International Economic Review*, 14(3): 693–709.

Oostendorp, R. H., and Doan Hong, Q. (2013). Have the returns to education really increased in Vietnam? Wage versus employment effect, *Journal of Comparative Economics*, 41, 923–38.

Ose, S. O. (2005). Working conditions, compensation and absenteeism, *Journal of Health Economics*, 24, 161–88.

Pham, H., and Reilly, B. (2007). The gender pay gap in Vietnam, 1993–2002: A quintile regression approach, *Journal of Asian Economics*, 185(5): 775–806.

Poggi, A. (2007). Do satisfactory working conditions contribute to explaining earning differentials in Italy? A panel data approach, *Labour*, 21(4/5): 713–33.

Pouliakas, K., and I. Theodissou (2013). The economics of health and safety and work: An interdisciplinary review of the theory and policy, *Journal of Economic Surveys*, 27(1): 167–208.

Rosen, S. (1986). The theory of equalising differences. In O. Ashenfelter and R. Layard (eds), *Handbook of Labor Economics, Vol. 1*. Amsterda Elsevier.

Somanathan, E., R. Somanathan, A. Sudarshan, and M. Tewari (2015). The Impact of Temperature on Productivity and Labour Supply: Evidence from Indian Manufacturing. CDE-DSE Working Paper 244. Delhi: Delhi School of Economics.

Trifković, N. (2017). Spillover effects of international standards: Working conditions in the Vietnamese SMEs, *World Development*, 97: 79–101.

11

Does Union Membership Pay Off? Evidence from Vietnamese SMEs

Nina Torm

11.1 Introduction

In developed economies, trade unions are generally associated with a positive work environment, including higher wages, increased benefits, reduced wage negotiation costs, and lower wage inequality and worker turnover (Freeman 1980; Standing 1992). In developing and transition countries characterized by different employment structures, including the presence of large informal and unorganized sectors, evidence remains more scarce.[1] However, precisely in such contexts of low wage levels, inadequate institutional support, and limited provision of public sector goods and services, trade unions represent a potentially important collective 'voice' for the promotion of worker benefits and welfare.

In the case of Vietnam, the transition to a market economy has, along with a growing private sector and the parallel equitization of state-owned enterprises (SOEs), led to the formation of new employment relationships and bases for the establishment of local trade unions. Moreover, in recent years, several changes have been made to the regulatory framework, including the Labour Code and the Trade Union Law, which together provide the impetus for formalizing and strengthening the role of unions. Yet the effectiveness of workplace trade unions remains questionable due partly to their marginal independence, employer dominance, and the generally low incidence of collective agreements.

It is within this context that the current chapter analyses whether trade unions are associated with higher wage outcomes, using firm-level survey data on small and medium-sized (non-state) manufacturing firms in Vietnam over 2013–15 (Rand et al. 2014). The firm panel has been matched with employee data from a subsample of workers in each year. The survey covers micro-, small, and medium-sized firms, and I use the World Bank's classification in terms of the number of employees. One key advantage of using matched employer–employee data is that

[1] See Eaton et al. (2017) and Schurman and Eaton (2012) for reviews of the growing literature on trade unions and worker organizing in the informal economy.

Nina Torm, *Does Union Membership Pay Off? Evidence from Vietnamese SMEs* In: *Micro, Small, and Medium Enterprises in Vietnam.* Edited by: John Rand and Finn Tarp, Oxford University Press (2020).
DOI: 10.1093/oso/9780198851189.003.0011

it allows for disentangling worker from firm heterogeneity by controlling for firm *and* worker characteristics which could affect both union status and wage outcomes. Second, in being able to construct a balanced panel of workers some of whom change union status over time, I am able to control for determining factors and selected *observed* time-varying factors that may simultaneously influence the decision to unionize and subsequent wage outcomes. Third, the availability of numerous firm-level variables allows for identifying valid instruments so as to capture time-varying *unobserved* characteristics which, if left unaccounted for, could bias the results. In line with similar studies, the analysis shows a union member wage premium of around 9–22 per cent, depending on the econometric approach. An earlier version of this study undertakes some further robustness checks revealing considerable variation along the conditional wage distribution, with the union wage differential being substantially higher for the top quantiles (Torm 2018). This in turn calls into question the ability of unions to promote the rights and interests of all workers and their accountability for doing so. Moreover, Torm (2018) shows that the union-related wage gain is individual, arising directly from being a union member, rather than a spill-over effect from the presence of unions.

In Section 11.2 I provide a selective overview of the existing literature and theoretical background. Section 11.3 discusses the Vietnamese context, while Section 11.4 describes the data, the methodology and the variables included in the empirical analysis. Section 11.5 presents the main results and Section 11.6 concludes.

11.2 Literature and Theory

Unions provide workers with a mechanism through which to shape their employment relationship and working environment, by, for instance, improving workplace communication, increasing wages and benefits, and reducing labour turnover (Freeman and Medoff 1984). Thus, through serving as an agent for a firm's employees, a union can take on many different roles and be associated with numerous outcomes, as evidenced by the vast number of trade union studies, covering mostly the US, the UK, and other OECD (Organisation for Economic Co-operation and Development) countries.[2] The literature generally portrays unions as operating along at least three dimensions: their wage-making practices; their participatory role in terms of negotiating and administering labour rules related to hiring, training, promoting, and laying off workers; and their activities as a pressure group on government (Pencavel 2005). Rather than attempting to

[2] See Betcherman (2012) for a review of the literature on labour market institutions in general.

cover the enormous trade union literature as a whole, in this section I address the wage dimension, which is the focus of this chapter, by providing a brief theoretical discussion followed by a concise summary of the most relevant studies.

11.2.1 Theoretical Considerations

From a theoretical perspective, the trade union wage gap arises from trade unions introducing a wedge between the reservation wage of the worker and the value of a job, or in other words between labour supply and demand.[3] The ability of the union to achieve a wage rate that is higher than the non-union level depends on various factors, including the power of the union to act as a monopolist in the supply of labour, and the existence of economic rent or surplus in the product market. In a bargaining model where all union members have the same preferences, wages will be higher the stronger the bargaining power of unions, and the lower the responsiveness of labour demand (and profits) to wages. These relations in turn depend on the competitiveness of the product market. In a perfectly competitive market the union-imposed wedge is reduced, since a firm facing an infinite elasticity of demand is unable to pass any union wage differential on to prices. Thus, unions might be able to capture quasi-rents from capital in the short run, but in the long run the firm would leave the market in search of a higher return on capital, or be forced out by non-union firms with lower costs. In addition to the economic factors, the extent of the union wage gap also depends on the degree of coordination and centralization of wage determination activities and the competitiveness of the labour market (Boeri and van Ours 2008).

In addition to the direct individual union wage premium, spill-over effects to non-union members may occur in the presence of industry-level collective agreements, and in most OECD countries union coverage (the share of workers covered by a collective agreement) exceeds union density (union members as a percentage of the workforce). Since collective agreements ensure that non-members, whether firms or workers, are covered by the union-negotiated wage rate, union coverage is often considered a more accurate measure of the bargaining power of unions than density. The latter has been declining in many OECD countries since the 1980s, and the option to free-ride on union-provided services and benefits is cited as one of the reasons for this (Booth and Chatterji 1995; Boeri and van Ours 2008). In the absence of extension rules, the wages of non-union workers are still likely to be affected by the presence of unions—for instance through the 'threat effect' of unionism, whereby non-union employers will pay wages that are comparable to

[3] Booth and Chatterji (1995) and Boeri and van Ours (2008) provide comprehensive reviews of trade union theory. See Lewis (1963, 1986) for earlier work on the union-related wage effect.

those of unionized workers (Pencavel 2005). Alternatively, in the absence of such a threat effect (but in the presence of unions), workers disemployed from union firms due to a wage push will seek employment in non-union firms, shifting the labour supply right and reducing wages in this sector below what they would be in the absence of unions. Therefore, whether a threat effect exists or not, wage levels are likely to be affected by the presence of unions.

11.2.2 Recent Empirical Evidence

Empirical work on the union–wage relationship has been based mostly on either firm-level *or* individual data, yet since the 1990s a growing number of studies using matched employer–employee data have emerged.[4] For instance, Lalonde et al. (1996) use American firm data to examine the effects of newly formed unions on total output, employment, material purchases, wage rates, and productivity. They find reductions in the first three, yet firms do not experience higher wage rates. By contrast, in the UK, Hildreth and Pudney (1997) find higher wages among unionized firms, and especially for individuals covered by a collective agreement but who are not necessarily union members. Using matched employer–employee data from Spain, Card and De La Rica (2006) find that firm-level contracting is associated with a 5–10 per cent individual wage premium. Moreover, the wage gain is larger for more highly paid workers, which is in contrast to UK and US studies—where unions have tended to 'flatten' wages across skill groups (Lewis 1986). This difference could, however, be related to the fact that in the UK and US the comparison group is the non-union sector, whereas in Spain it is the prevailing sectoral agreement.

As mentioned earlier, union studies covering the Global South are more limited, and the findings are also more varied. For instance, Rama (2000) states that in developing countries, unionized workers usually earn between 5 and 30 per cent more than non-unionized workers. In the same study, which summarizes findings from Senegal and Cameroon, Rama (2000) shows union membership to be associated with wages that are 8–12 per cent *lower*. This atypical finding is attributed partly to the 'subordinate' nature of the labour movement in these countries and the distortive labour market policies of the 1980s. This work then points to the importance of the nature of the links with the government and political parties when it comes to how labour movements affect wages. In the case of South Africa, Schultz and Mwabu (1998) show that the union wage gap is as high as 145 per cent at the bottom decile of the wage distribution,

[4] See Abowd and Kramarz (1999) for a review of methods and results using matched employer–employee data. In their comprehensive review of studies on developed countries, Aidt and Tzannatos (2002) find the union wage effect to be between 5% and 15%.

whereas at the top decile there is flattening so that the difference is 11 per cent. This study, however, is unable to account for important firm attributes, such as size, which are likely to explain much of the union wage gap.

Among the few studies on the union wage premium in Asia, Korean estimates suggest very small positive impacts in the 5–6 per cent range (Fields and Yoo 2000; Park 1991). In a case study of ten Vietnamese firms, Clarke et al. (2007) document that trade unions are able to negotiate wages that are 5 per cent higher than those in non-union firms. Moreover, Edwards and Phan (2008) argue that since trade unions in Vietnam are involved in the central wage decision-making processes, wages would be lower were it not for their presence and influence. However, the study provides no evidence of this.

Methodologically, the above studies are based on either qualitative assessments or cross-sections of individual worker data, and are thus unable to account for workplace characteristics or time-invariant factors. Seeking to fill this gap, an earlier study based on matched firm–worker data from 2007 and 2009 (Torm 2014) found that union membership in Vietnamese small and medium-sized enterprises (SMEs) was associated with higher wages and the provision of social benefits. The current study builds upon and extends this earlier work by constructing a balanced worker panel, allowing for a more comprehensive analysis. Moreover, since 2014 a number of regulatory changes, as examined below, have been implemented which could influence the results. To set the scene, the next section provides an overview of Vietnamese trade unions and the context in which they operate.

11.3 Trade Unions in the Vietnamese Context

Under central planning, trade unions functioned mostly as a 'transmission belt' for the ruling Communist Party, as described in Zhu and Fahey (2000). With Vietnam's transition to a market economy, a rights-based system for the regulation of industrial relations has been established, allocating a more prominent role to trade unions. As for most developing countries, data on union coverage and membership is generally limited. The Vietnam General Confederation of Labour (VGCL) provides the most reliable and recent statistics, as summarized in Torm (2018). According to these figures, in 2011 the total number of unions in Vietnam was just under 110,000, the majority of which were located in the state sector. In the non-state sector, unions were found mostly within domestic enterprises (77 per cent), whereas union incidence among foreign direct investment (FDI) enterprises remains relatively low (13 per cent). In terms of union density, this was 26 per cent across the enterprise sector as a whole in 2011, compared with 16 per cent at the national level (including public servants and armed forces). Total union membership was 7.3 million in 2011, with a slightly higher share in the state sector, yet considering that this sector accounts for two-thirds of unions, the membership ratio appears to be higher in the private sector, as also evidenced by the density figures. More recent figures from 2014 estimate total union membership to be 8.6 million (not reported), thus, assuming a stable wage-earner population, this indicates an increase in union membership over time.[5] Regarding collective bargaining agreements (CBAs), as indicated in Torm (2018), national coverage in 2011 was 28 per cent, and was highest in the state sector, at 71 per cent, followed by foreign firms at 54 per cent and domestic firms at 31 per cent. Among unionized establishments the rate was around 67 per cent.[6]

11.3.1 The Legal Framework

The Amended Labor Code (ALC) and the new Union Law (NUL) both became effective in early 2013.[7] In the ALC chapter XIII, on trade unions, the purpose of firm-based unions is clearly stated as follows: 'trade unions serve to represent and protect the lawful and legitimate rights and interests of trade union members and workers; participate in negotiating, signing, and monitoring the implementation of CBAs, wage scales and wage tables, work norms, wage payment regulations, and bonus regulations among others'. The ALC further stipulates that labour contracts are deemed invalid if, among other circumstances, 'the contract contains an agreement that prohibits or obstructs the employee from forming or joining a trade union'. In addition to protecting the rights and interests of their members, trade union representatives are involved in compliance procedures as stipulated in the NUL, including the implementation of regimes and policies for the employees, such as compliance with minimum wage provisions. The NUL does not, however, set out specific requirements for wages to be above the minimum or average wage in a particular industry, and thus the wage level depends on the bargaining power of the involved parties. However, the employer must consult the executive committee of the enterprise trade union on the formulation of wage scales and labour rates.

The NUL also outlines the functions, tasks, and participation of trade unions in inspecting, supervising, and monitoring the activities of agencies, organizations, and enterprises, and confirms the rights of employees to establish and join trade unions and to participate in trade union activities. Although enterprise trade

[5] The VGCL had set a target of recruiting around 600,000 new union members every year between 2013 and 2018 (VGCL 2015).

[6] To the extent that the figures are comparable this indicates an increase over time, as Clarke et al. (2007) estimated only 20% of unionised private sector firms to have collective agreements (although in Ho Chi Minh City the figure is around 65%).

[7] See Decree No. 10/2012/QH13, and No. 12/2012/QH13, for details on the ALC and the NUL respectively.

unions are free to independently represent workers' rights and interests, all trade unions in Vietnam are required to affiliate with the VGCL—the higher-level trade union which is the only legal trade union for Vietnamese workers. The VGCL collaborates closely with the local labour department under the supervision of the relevant (Communist) Party body, and this subordination of the trade union to the Party means that workplace trade unions have limited independence and ability to act as a pressure group on government. Moreover, given that trade unions are generally headed by management rather than senior staff members, they are characterized also by weak representational capacity in that dimension.

Compared with the earlier Trade Union Law (1994), the NUL incorporates some major changes, including the requirement for all companies, whether foreign-invested or local, to pay a mandatory union fee of 2 per cent of the total payroll as a social insurance contribution, even if the enterprise has no trade union. The 2 per cent levy is to be used for activities at all levels of trade unions, including the upper-level trade union, which will collect the payment and subsequently distribute part of the fund to the enterprise trade union. Thus, this points to an increased centralization of the ownership of all trade union assets under the VGCL. Another new dimension of the NUL, as also outlined in the ALC, is that the immediate upper-level trade union (usually at the district level) has the right and obligation to represent and protect the legitimate and lawful rights and interests of workers in situations where a grassroots (local) trade union has not been established. Previously, this was only based on employees' requests, with no automatic default protection for workers in non-union firms. In fact, the ALC lays out a number of provisions, including six months' maternity leave, a two-year work permit, and revised working and rest times, which appear to strengthen the position of employees and decrease management flexibility. The impacts of these amendments on employers and the economy as a whole remain to be seen.

11.3.2 Collective Bargaining

The ALC has sought to strengthen collective bargaining by extending the right of workers in non-unionized enterprises to be covered by a relevant collective agreement. The negotiation and monitoring of collective agreements provides an important 'test' of the effectiveness of firm trade unions in representing the interests of their members, and collective agreements should in principle include agreed wage and bonus scales.[8] Aside from the fact that one-third of unionized

[8] Note that on 5 July 2019, Vietnam deposited the instrument of ratification of the Right to Organise and Collective Bargaining Convention, set out by the International Labour Organization (ILO), but has not yet ratified the international convention on Freedom of Association and Protection of the Right to Organise.

firms do not have such agreements (Torm 2018), the actual substance of collective agreements is questionable, since they offer few benefits for covered workers beyond conditions provided for by law. For example, a 2009 joint review between the International Labour Organization (ILO) and trade unions found that most agreements in Vietnam were initiated by employers to fulfil corporate social responsibility requirements rather than as a consequence of genuine labour–management negotiations (Grimshaw and de Bustillo 2016), demonstrating employers' unwillingness to bargain effectively. Furthermore, collective bargaining rules purposely exclude many categories of workers, such as public sector workers, foreign enterprise workers, subcontracted workers, etc., which is not very conducive to achieving labour market inclusion.

The combination of weaknesses in collective bargaining mechanisms and enterprise unions' weak representation capacity as discussed above have meant that workers have resorted to 'collective bargaining by riots'. Such wildcat strikes, in which workers—without the leadership of union officials—have demanded wages higher than the minimum levels and better working conditions, peaked in 2008 and again in 2011, years during which inflation levels were also high and therefore real wages low. In fact, over 70 per cent of around 5,000 strikes which happened between 1995 and 2011 were on the basis of interests rather than rights only (Chi and Torm 2015). The garment industry, characterized by a combination of low wages and poor working conditions, is the most strike-prone sector in Vietnam, accounting for 34 per cent of all nationwide strikes recorded during 1995–2014 (VGCL 2015). However, since 2010, when the first sectoral agreement for the garment industry was signed, efforts have been underway to construct the foundations for more effective and resilient sector-level bargaining. There are no official statistics on CBA coverage in the garment industry, yet the Ministry of Labour, Invalids and Social Affairs estimates the CBA coverage to be 50 per cent of unionized companies in 2012 (Chi and Torm 2015). This is below the average coverage rate of 67 per cent among unionized establishments, as shown in Torm (2018).

The pressure of labour activism has made a growing number of employers adjust their authoritarian approach to wage fixing by allowing for more participation of rank-and-file workers, and their representatives, in de facto wage negotiations. Nevertheless, as long as the representation capacity of enterprise unions remains weak, such models of de facto wage negotiations do not provide a realistic alternative to collective bargaining. Given this combination of weak union leadership, absence of specific requirements on wage levels, and ineffective collective bargaining, the extent to which unions are associated with higher wages becomes an empirical question. Against this background, I now turn to analysing the union wage premium among Vietnamese SMEs.

11.4 Data and Econometric Approach

11.4.1 Data

The chapter is based on matched employer–employee data from two SME surveys, carried out during 2013–15 (Rand et al. 2014). In both years, the surveys included a separate employee module consisting of randomly sampled employees from a random subsample of firms stratified by location. Between one and seven workers were interviewed in each firm, representing different categories. In Vietnam, household firms are not officially registered by the central authorities under the different enterprise laws (although they are listed by local officials), and as such are not covered by the Trade Union Law.[9] In other words establishing a trade union is only mandatory for firms with more than ten workers and therefore not for household firms. This is evidenced in the data, where only non-household firms report having established firm-level unions and there are no union members observed among household firms. For these reasons, I exclude household firms, and focus solely on firms categorized as private enterprises, cooperatives/collectives/partnerships (CCPs), and limited liability and joint stock companies. After applying this selection criterion and undertaking a thorough data cleaning, including checking the consistency of time-invariant variables between the two survey rounds, I was left with an unbalanced panel of 1,594 permanent workers: 885 in 2013, and 709 in 2015, corresponding to 301 firms. Through identifying repeatedly surveyed employees, I construct a balanced employee panel consisting of 758 individual observations (379 in each year), corresponding to 152 repeated firms.[10]

11.4.2 Econometric Approach

In order to analyse the union–wage relationship, I estimate an equation where individual wages depend on both worker attributes and the characteristics of the firm where the worker is employed. Building on the basic model of Abowd and Kramarz (1999), the specification takes the following for

$$\ln Y_{ijt} = \alpha + X_{ijt}\beta + Z_{jt}\gamma + U_{ijt}\delta + \epsilon_{ijt}. \tag{11.1}$$

Where the log of (real) individual wages for worker *i* in firm *j* at time *t* depends on a set of individual worker characteristics (X_{ijt}) and a vector of firm-level covariates for the firm where worker *i* is employed (Z_{jt}). Our main variable of interest (U_{ijt})

[9] For more detail on coverage see NUL No. 12/2012/QH13, article 3.

[10] The reason for restricting the analysis to two survey rounds is to be able to construct a balanced panel of workers. Since the employee module was not intended to capture repeat workers, adding an additional year would reduce the balanced panel substantially, or even make it impossible to construct one.

is an indicator for whether the individual is a member of a firm-level trade union. Finally, there is the worker-specific error term (ϵ_{ijt}).

In estimating Equation (11.1), several potential biases are taken into account. First, in order to address the possibility of autocorrelation arising from repeated observations over time, the standard errors are clustered at the firm level. This allows for intragroup (within-firm) correlation over time and between workers, while maintaining the assumption that the observations are independent across firms. Second, bias may arise from the presence of unobserved individual heterogeneity, such as worker ability, which influences both wages and union membership. For example, an observed wage differential between unionized and non-unionized workers may arise simply because the workers who are most likely to become union members are also the ones with the highest unobserved abilities. In order to account for such worker fixed effects (FE), e.g. ability, in the wage specification, we estimate Equation (11.1) using the balanced panel. Third, bias may arise if changes in union-related policies (for instance as result of the new Trade Union Law which came into effect 1 January 2013) that influence membership are also correlated with changes in wages. To overcome these potential sources of endogeneity bias, I use standard matching techniques to control for determining factors and selected observed time-varying factors that may simultaneously influence the decision to unionize and subsequent wage outcomes. More specifically, I compare differences in wages between workers who unionized in the period 2013–15 and similar workers who remained non-unionized in the 2015 survey.

Finally, I use IV (instrumental variable) identification in order to control for time-varying *unobserved* characteristics, e.g. if the decision to unionize is a function of the perceived wage increase, beyond what is captured by unobserved fixed effects (ability) or observed changes in firm/worker attributes. To instrument for union membership (the endogenous variable), I use the share of firms that have unions, by district and four-digit sector. In order to be able to assess the validity of the instrument (test for overidentifying restrictions), I use a second instrument—the share of firms reporting having good knowledge of the Labour Code, again by district and four-digit sector. The key assumptions of this identification strategy are that (a) the IVs are strongly correlated with the individual union membership, and (b) after adding the full set of worker and firm controls, the selected instruments have no independent influence on individual wage outcomes. If the IV assumptions hold, any observed relationship between union status and wages has a causal interpretation for workers whose union membership status is affected by the instrument (Angrist et al. 1996).

11.4.3 Descriptive Statistics

Table 11.1 presents the descriptive statistics for the unbalanced panel. First, the main variable of interest is union membership, taking the value 1 if the worker is a member of a union and 0 otherwise. Union membership averages 29 per cent and increased from 27 per cent to 32 per cent over 2013–15. Next, the outcome variable is the logged monthly real basic wage, which in nominal terms increased from 3.7 to 4.6 million Vietnamese dong (VND) over 2013–15. The increase in the real wage is less steep, from 3.2 to 3.7 VND million over 2013–15.[11]

In terms of worker attributes, I control for gender, age, and education and training of the worker, as well as job function, hiring method, and reasons for choosing current job. The justifications for the selection of these covariates and their summary statistics are as follows. First, previous studies on Vietnam (Bjerge et al. 2016; Torm 2014) have shown substantial gender wage gaps, which are also commonly found in other developing country studies (Jones 2001). Thus, I incorporate a gender dummy and Table 11.1 shows that 55 per cent of the sample are male workers. Second, I control for the age of the worker as a proxy for experience—a key variable in the standard human capital earnings function (Mincer 1974)—and include age squared to allow for a diminishing marginal effect. The average worker age is 36 years. Third, I include a series of education indicator variables, since educational attainment explains a large share of the variation in earnings across individuals (Mincer 1974; Spence 1973). Moreover, this also removes some of the bias arising from the possibility that unionized firms may hire better-quality workers. Around 64 per cent of the sample have finished secondary education, while the share of workers with a higher education is 34 per cent, and this has risen over time. Fourth, the different job functions are included as dummy variables on the basis that both wages and union membership are likely to vary substantially across occupation categories, beyond what is accounted for by education. The largest share is production workers, at 48 per cent—a share that has increased over time, whereas managers and professional and service workers have seen declining shares over 2013–15. Fifth, I include a dummy variable for whether the worker found their job through an informal contact (knowing the owner or someone who works in the firm) as opposed to via a formal contact (advertisement, employment agency, etc.), as this has been shown to be associated with higher individual wages (Larsen et al. 2011). Informal hiring remains the most common recruitment mechanism, at 67 per cent of workers, yet with a slight decrease over time—an indication of increased formalization of the Vietnamese labour market. Sixth, training incidence is added since this has been shown to have an impact on workers' wages in Vietnam (Bjerge et al. 2016). In addition, theoretical models have predicted that union workers receive more training and higher returns to training than non-union workers.[12] Seventh, based on the reasoning that job choice preferences may be related to both union status and wages, two indicator variables are included

[11] Real wages are deflated using province-level deflators, where the base is Hanoi, year 2010.

[12] See for instance, Booth and Chatterji (1995).

Table 11.1 Summary statistics

	2013		2015		All	
	Mean	SD	Mean	SD	Mean	SD
Member of a trade union	0.27	0.44	0.32	0.47	0.29	0.45
Nominal monthly wage VND1,000	3,733.50	1,306.09	4,643.70	2,213.03	4,138.35	1,824.29
Real monthly wage VND1,000	3,178.79	1,073.89	3,652.00	1,758.40	3,389.27	1,438.58
Gender (male = 1)	0.55	0.50	0.55	0.50	0.55	0.50
Worker age	34.14	9.35	38.65	9.32	36.15	9.60
None	0.01	0.09	0.00	0.04	0.01	0.07
Primary school	0.01	0.11	0.02	0.13	0.01	0.12
Secondary school	0.66	0.47	0.62	0.49	0.64	0.48
College and higher	0.32	0.47	0.36	0.48	0.34	0.47
Manager	0.12	0.32	0.09	0.28	0.10	0.31
Professional worker	0.15	0.35	0.13	0.33	0.14	0.35
Office worker	0.13	0.34	0.14	0.35	0.14	0.34
Sales worker	0.09	0.29	0.09	0.28	0.09	0.29
Service worker	0.06	0.23	0.04	0.20	0.05	0.22
Production worker	0.45	0.50	0.51	0.50	0.48	0.50
Informally hired	0.69	0.46	0.65	0.48	0.67	0.47
Training	0.18	0.38	0.27	0.45	0.22	0.41
Job choice conditions	0.21	0.41	0.26	0.44	0.23	0.42
Job choice salary	0.24	0.43	0.27	0.45	0.26	0.44
Firm size	34.22	39.73	41.64	48.66	37.52	44.07
Private	0.23	0.42	0.17	0.38	0.20	0.40
Collective	0.06	0.23	0.06	0.24	0.06	0.23
Limited liability	0.57	0.50	0.63	0.48	0.60	0.49
Joint stock	0.15	0.35	0.14	0.34	0.14	0.35
Urban	0.57	0.50	0.59	0.49	0.58	0.49
Sector low value added	0.29	0.46	0.27	0.44	0.28	0.45
Sector medium value added	0.43	0.50	0.46	0.50	0.44	0.50
Sector high value added	0.25	0.43	0.25	0.43	0.25	0.43
Wage negotiations	0.32	0.47	0.34	0.47	0.33	0.47
Owner is male	0.50	0.50	0.44	0.50	0.48	0.50
Owner has higher education	0.95	0.22	0.97	0.17	0.96	0.20
Share of women in labour force	0.41	0.22	0.41	0.23	0.41	0.22
Share of professionals	0.10	0.09	0.09	0.10	0.09	0.09
Share of casual workers	0.07	0.15	0.05	0.14	0.06	0.15
Observations	885		709		1,594	

Note: Summary statistics are for the unbalanced panel. Real wages are deflated using province-level deflators. VND20,500 is around US$1.

Source: Author's elaboration based on SME data (Rand et al. 2014).

representing whether the worker chose their current job due to working conditions or for salary reasons. Table 11.1 shows that 23 per cent indicate having selected their job due to better working conditions and 26 per cent due to a higher salary—both have risen over time, indicating that workers are having more influence on the kinds of jobs they attain.

Turning to firm characteristics, I include firm size, legal status, location, sector, wage determination method, owners' gender and education, and the share of professional workers, casual workers, and women. First, firm size (logged) is to account for the commonly found firm-size wage premium (Oi and Idson 1999; Söderbom et al. 2005), and the possibility that larger firms may be more likely to be unionized. The average firm has 38 workers, and this has increased over time. Second, due to the substantial variation in wages and unionization across firm ownership types, I incorporate dummies for the different legal categories. In fact, ownership form has been shown to be a critical factor influencing human resource practices, including in relation to trade unions (Zhu et al. 2008). Limited liability companies comprise the largest category at 60 per cent, followed by private firms at 20 per cent, joint stock companies at 14 per cent, and finally CCPs at 6 per cent. The share of limited liability companies has increased over time, while the share of private firms has fallen, in line also with the overall rise in firm size. Third, I also control for firm location, as wages and human resource initiatives differ across provinces (Zhu et al. 2008), possibly due to the relative autonomy of provinces in the implementation of centrally planned initiatives (Nguyen et al. 2007). Table 11.1 shows that 58 per cent of firms are located in urban areas (Ho Chi Minh City, Hanoi, and Hai Phong). Fourth, wage returns and human resource practices may vary across sectors of production (Zhu et al. 2008), and thus I control for the different sectors. The majority of firms fall into the medium-value-added category, and this is increasing over time. Fifth, around 33 per cent of firms respond that individual wage negotiation, which is likely to be associated with both individual wages and union membership, was the most important determinant of wages.

Sixth, the gender of the owner has been shown to be important in terms of compensation, with female owners being more generous in the provision of non-wage benefits (Rand and Tarp 2011). Between 2013 and 2015, female-owned firms became more dominant, as indicated by the fall in male-owned firms from 50 to 44 per cent. Seventh, as well-educated managers are more likely to hire well-educated workers (Rosenbaum et al. 1999), I include a dummy indicating whether the owner has at least high school education. The share is very high, at 96 per cent, and increasing over time. Eighth, the share of female workers is included because this is likely to be correlated with lower overall wage outcomes, given the gender wage gap (Croson and Gneezy 2009). Ninth, the share of professional workers acts as a proxy for the general skills level of the workforce, which could be (positively) correlated with unobserved worker-specific ability. Moreover, if, as a result of unionization, firms choose to hire better-quality workers such that productivity increases are commensurate with the union-imposed higher wage (Lewis 1986), average worker quality would eliminates the bias that might arise from a positive correlation between union status and worker quality. Professionals make up around 9 per cent of the workforce, and the share is stable over time. Tenth, the casual workforce share (measured as the average number of casual workers relative to the average number of full-time regular workers in a year) is included as a measure of the stability of employment contracts, as this could be related to both union and wage outcomes. Given that the sample considers only formal firms, it is not surprising to see a relatively low share of casual workers, at around 6 per cent.

The appendix in Torm (2018) shows differences in firm and worker characteristics by union membership status. As expected, (raw) wages are higher for union members, and women are more likely to be union members. Union members are slightly older than non-union members, but this is not significant. Union members are well educated and are significantly more likely to have a college education compared with non-union workers, who are more likely to have stopped studying after secondary school. In line with the education figures, managers, office workers, sales workers, and service workers are significantly more likely to be union members (professionals also, but not significantly), whereas among production workers non-unionization is more common. Union members are less likely to have been hired informally, and training incidence is substantially higher among unionized workers—as would be expected given that unions have a longer time horizon and promote the value of training, and as also predicted by theory (Booth and Chatterji 1995). The incidence of workers who chose their current job due to the salary is lower among union members, indicating that higher wages are not a driver of unionization. As expected, union members tend to work in larger limited liability companies (and CCP firms), located in Ho Chi Minh City and Quang Nam, whereas private, more rurally based firms have a higher share of non-union members. Moreover, union workers are found in firms with highly educated female owners, and a higher share of professional workers. Finally, in terms of sectors, the ratio of union members is significantly higher in wood, chemical products, and fabricated metal products.

11.5 Results

Table 11.2 shows the relation between union membership and individual wages. In column 1, when employee attributes only are included, the union wage gap is 13 per cent, yet when the first set of firm-level characteristics (size, legal status, sector, and location) are added in column 2, the wage premium falls to 10 per cent, although this is still highly significant. In column 3, the second set of firm-level

Table 11.2 Wages and union membership

	(1)	(2)	(3)	(4)
	OLS	OLS	OLS	FE bal.
Member of a trade union	0.133***	0.101***	0.105***	0.091*
	(0.027)	(0.026)	(0.025)	(0.055)
Gender (male = 1)	0.105***	0.107***	0.097***	
	(0.019)	(0.019)	(0.019)	
Worker age	0.027***	0.024***	0.024***	
	(0.006)	(0.005)	(0.005)	
Age squared	−0.306***	−0.266***	−0.261***	
	(0.078)	(0.066)	(0.066)	
Manager	0.308***	0.304***	0.305***	0.191**
	(0.033)	(0.032)	(0.032)	(0.082)
Professional worker	0.120***	0.121***	0.120***	0.101
	(0.028)	(0.028)	(0.027)	(0.071)
Office worker	0.091***	0.092***	0.089***	−0.007
	(0.028)	(0.028)	(0.028)	(0.055)
Sales worker	0.087***	0.082***	0.082***	0.067
	(0.030)	(0.029)	(0.029)	(0.073)
Service worker	−0.042	−0.054**	−0.062**	−0.067
	(0.028)	(0.027)	(0.027)	(0.080)
Informally hired	−0.023	−0.007	−0.007	−0.038
	(0.022)	(0.025)	(0.025)	(0.037)
Training	−0.016	0.005	0.004	−0.008
	(0.027)	(0.024)	(0.023)	(0.051)
Job choice conditions	0.000	−0.015	−0.020	−0.027
	(0.021)	(0.019)	(0.019)	(0.041)
Job choice salary	0.058***	0.042**	0.032	0.013
	(0.021)	(0.020)	(0.020)	(0.040)
Firm size and education controls	Yes	Yes	Yes	Yes
Legal ownership, sector and location controls	No	Yes	Yes	Yes
Owner gender and education	No	No	Yes	Yes
Workforce shares and wage determinant	No	No	Yes	Yes
R2	0.22	0.29	0.30	0.21
Number of groups				379
Observations	1,594	1,594	1,594	758

Notes: OLS are based on the unbalanced panel. Year dummy included in all specifications. Standard errors (in parentheses) are clustered at the firm level. *p<0.10; **p<0.05; ***p<0.01.

Source: Author's elaboration based on SME data (Rand et al. 2014).

characteristics are added (owner gender and education, workforce shares, and wage determinant), and the union coefficient remains just over 10 per cent. In order to account for the possibility that unobserved worker heterogeneity is driving the results, I use the balanced panel of workers to control for worker fixed effects (i.e. ability or motivation). Column 4 shows that the union wage gap remains when worker fixed effects are accounted for, yet the size of the coefficient drops slightly, to 9 per cent, indicating that unobserved heterogeneity is *positively* correlated with union membership. This suggests that higher-ability workers are more likely to be unionized. This is in line with Torm (2018), which showed that among union members the education category that comprises the highest union member share is college education, whereas among non-union workers the share falls as education levels rise. Also as shown in Torm (2018), non-production workers are more likely to be in unions than production workers. The small difference in the OLS and FE union coefficient is reassuring and indicates that the numerous controls account for a large share of ability/other unobserved heterogeneity. Assuming that the union membership contribution, which amounts to 2 per cent of wages (and which, as outlined earlier, is now a mandatory fee imposed on the employer), has not been deducted in the reported wage, the real wage gain would be slightly lower. The results are in accordance with Clarke et al. (2007) and Torm (2014).[13]

As for the individual worker attributes, these generally conform to human capital theory. First, there is a substantial gender wage gap, with male earnings being around 10 per cent higher than those of women, depending on the exact specification. This is in line with similar studies (Bjerge et al. 2016) and appears to have fallen slightly over time (Liu 2004; Torm 2014). Second, the age of the worker is also highly significant and has the expected concave effect, with a maximum at around 40 years of age. Third, the different occupation categories indicate a substantial wage premium compared with production workers, especially for managers, who earn around 30 per cent more—although this falls to 19 per cent when ability is accounted for in the fixed effects specification. Fourth, as expected, wages are higher if the worker has chosen their job based on the salary. With regard to education (not reported), the results show positive and increasing returns, with a college graduate having a wage that is 19 per cent higher than that of a worker with no education. Yet when the firm-level control variables are added the significance disappears.

For presentational purposes, firm-level variables are not reported, yet larger firms pay significantly higher wages (Söderbom et al. 2005) and individuals working in a CCP have significantly lower wages compared with private-firm employees. Education and gender of the firm owner are not well determined, yet the share of women in the workforce is significantly negative and indicates that shifting from a 0 to a 100 per cent female worker share is associated with approximately a 13 per cent lower wage bill, which is in line with similar studies (Card and De La Rica 2006). Both the temporary worker and professional

[13] Similarly, in the case of Spain, Card and De La Rica (2006) showed that unions were associated with a 5–10% individual wage premium.

worker shares are insignificant, the latter possibly due to being accounted for by the individual education variables. The location controls (not reported) show that workers in urban areas (Ho Chi Minh City and Hanoi) earn more than those based in rural areas. This is most likely because firms in urban areas pay an efficiency wage in order to attract more productive workers. This is in line with the Vietnam Provincial Competitiveness Index (Malesky 2009), according to which Hanoi and Ho Chi Minh City ranked no. 1 and no. 4 respectively in the 2014 labour policy sub-index, which among other components includes a measure of labour quality (PCI 2015). High-value-added sectors (especially transport equipment and furniture) generally pay higher wages than low-value-added sectors, yet medium-value-added sectors (in particular rubber and refined petroleum) generally pay lower wages than low-value-added sectors. Further, the year dummy shows an increase in real wages of about 6 per cent over 2013–15.

In Table 11.3 I zoom in on those workers who became union members between 2013–15 and compare the difference in their wages to that of similar workers who remained non-unionized in 2015. This matching approach is applied to take account of determining factors and selected *observed* time-varying factors that may simultaneously influence the decision to unionize and subsequent wage outcomes. In terms of control variables, column 1 corresponds to the first column of Table 11.2, column 2 to the second, and column 3 to the third. In column 1, when only employee characteristics (all lagged) are included, the union coefficient is just below 15 per cent, which is reasonably in line with Table 11.2. However, once firm controls are added, becoming a union member increases wages by between 22–28 per cent, depending on the number and type of firm-level controls.

Table 11.3 Impact of union membership on wages, matching estimates

	(1)	(2)	(3)
	ATET	ATET	ATET
Becoming union member	0.147**	0.277**	0.222**
	(0.066)	(0.119)	(0.103)
Treated	38	38	38
Observations	275	275	275

Notes: Average treatment effect of the treated (ATET) using bias-corrected nearest-neighbour matching (four matches per observation). Estimations done using the 'teffects nnmatch' command in Stata (Abadie and Imbens 2006, 2011). Matching is based on initial 2013 observed characteristics as documented in the corresponding columns in Table 11.5. Standard errors (in parentheses) are independent and identically distributed (iid). Matched difference-in-difference (DD) estimates are comparable, yet the coefficients are slightly smaller in magnitude (results available upon request). *p<0.10; **p<0.05; ***p<0.01.

Source: Author's elaboration based on SME data (Rand et al. 2014).

The matched results, however, do not consider the endogeneity bias arising from the possibility of workers self-selecting into unions due to *unobserved* time-varying factors that also simultaneously influence individual wages.[14]

Thus, in order to deal with potential *unobserved* time-varying factors, in Table 11.4 I present the instrumental variables estimation (2SLS), using the instruments as described earlier, and the results confirm the positive effect of union membership on wages of workers. Columns 1a and 1b are based on the unbalanced panel, showing a union wage gap of 12 per cent—which, reassuringly, is in line with the earlier results in Tables 10.2 and 10.3. As seen in the first-stage estimation in column 1b, the chosen instruments are significantly related to union membership. In column 2b, based on the balanced panel, the union coefficient is higher (21 per cent) than the FE in Table 11.2, but comparable to the matching estimate in Table 11.3. As reported in the bottom rows of Table 11.4, the joint test of significance (F-stat) indicates that the instruments are jointly statistically significant at the 1 per cent level. Moreover, the validity of the instruments is confirmed by the Sargan and Basmann tests of overidentifying restrictions (OID), whereby I am unable to reject that the instruments are valid. All in all, this suggest that the chosen instruments influence wages only through their effect on union membership.

The preceding results are all based on the mean distribution of wages, yet in Torm (2018) the possibility that the effects of union membership vary over different parts of the conditional wage distribution is analysed using a set of (semi-parametric) quantile regressions. Interestingly, the results reveal that the union membership gain increases considerably as we move up the wage distribution. Thus, unions in Vietnam do not seem to be bargaining as effectively on behalf of those at the lower end of the wage distribution, and this bias towards the more skilled segment of the workforce is in part related to the management structure and political subordination of unions, as discussed earlier. This differs from previous similar studies. For instance, Schultz and Mwabu (1998) find that in South Africa there are large union effects at the lower part of the wage distribution and that these decrease towards the top. In the case of Ghana, Blunch and Verner (2004) show a union membership premium which is significant only for the tenth quantile. Similarly, in the US, Chamberlain (1994) demonstrates that union membership has a larger effect on the lower quantiles than on the higher quantiles of the conditional distribution of wages, and in the case of the UK public sector, Manquilef-Bächler et al. (2009) find a higher union wage return at the bottom of the distribution among males, while for females the premium is constant across the wage distribution.

[14] In addition to nearest-neighbour matching I also use double-difference matching, and the results are qualitatively the same, yet the coefficients are smaller in magnitude in all columns (result available upon request).

Table 11.4 Wages and union membership, IV estimates

	(1a)	(1b)	(2a)	(2b)
	First stage	Wages	First stage	Wages
Member of a trade union		0.116***		0.211***
		(0.035)		(0.044)
Trade union—share of firms	0.706***		0.756***	
	(0.033)		(0.045)	
Labour code knowledge	0.052**		0.040	
	(0.026)		(0.046)	
r2	0.30		0.29	
Observations	1,594		758	
F-stat (instrument relevance)	258.72***		152.89***	
OID	0.85		0.84	

Note: 2SLS estimations on the unbalanced sample (columns 1a and 1b) and the balanced panel (columns 2a and 2b). Control variables are the same as in Table 11.5, column 3. Standard errors (in parentheses) are heteroskedasticity-robust. *p<0.10; **p<0.05; ***p<0.01.

Source: Author's elaboration based on SME data (Rand et al. 2014).

The current analysis compares the wages between union members (in unionized firms) and non-union members (in union and non-union firms). However, these two groups may not be directly comparable, because the latter have not been faced with the choice of becoming union members, unless they purposely chose to work in a non-unionized firm. Thus, the observed wage difference may simply reflect the differential between being employed in a unionized versus a non-unionized firm, rather than the individual wage gain associated with union membership. In Torm (2018) the fact that that about 20 per cent of workers in unionized firms are not union members, is exploited to test the wage gap *within* unionized firms only. The results show that within unionized firms, the wage gain from being a union member remains significant, and close to the estimates presented in Table 11.2. Thus, what is observed throughout the current analysis is the *direct* union membership premium—rather than spill-over effects from there being a union at the firm, allowing non-union members to free-ride on union members. This finding is not surprising given the low prevalence of collective agreements and lack of effective bargaining in general.

11.6 Conclusion

This chapter has examined the union wage premium among Vietnamese manufacturing SMEs using matched employer–employee survey data over 2013–15. In contrast to the situation in many developed countries, union membership is on the rise in Vietnam, and recent regulatory changes are said to have strengthened the position of employees vis-à-vis management. At the same time, however, the NUL contains elements which imply increased centralization of trade union assets, in turn adding to already limited union autonomy and representative power. These aspects, coupled with the transitional environment in which unions operate, make Vietnam an interesting case study.

Methodologically, the main contribution of the chapter, compared with similar studies, is that the data set allows for the construction of a balanced worker panel, making it possible to account for observed and unobserved time-varying factors which may influence both union status and wage outcomes. The results show that union membership is associated with higher individual earnings when both firm and employee characteristics are controlled for, and that this effect holds when using an IV approach to take account of unobserved time-varying factors. Depending on the analytical approaches adopted, the union wage premium ranges from 9 to 21 per cent.

The variation in the union-wage gap arises from the fact that union membership gains are particularly high for workers in higher-level positions, in turn implying a widening of the wage-skill differential, which is somewhat concerning. Potentially, this could be countered by local trade unions more adequately representing all workers' rights equally, as well as playing an imperative role in ensuring that compliance with labour regulations is upheld. The fact that the incidence of firm-based trade unions is on the rise is positive, yet their ability to act in the interests of their members depends to a large extent on the existence and extension of collective agreements based on effective and inclusive bargaining. In this area, Vietnam still has work to do.

References

Abadie, A., and G. W. Imbens (2006). Large sample properties of matching estimators for average treatment effects, *Econometrica*, 74: 235–67.

Abadie, A., and G. W. Imbens (2011). Bias-corrected matching estimators for average treatment effects, *Journal of Business and Economic Statistics*, 29: 1–11.

Abowd, J. M., and F. Kramarz (1999). The analysis of labor markets using matched employer–employee data, *Handbook of Labor Economics*, 3(2): 2629–2710.

Aidt, T., and Z. Tzannatos (2002). *Unions and Collective Bargaining: Economic Effects in a Global Environment*. Washington, DC: World Bank.

Angrist, J. D., G. W. Imbens, and D. B. Rubin (1996). Identification of causal effects using instrumental variables, *Journal of the American Statistical Association*, 91(434): 444–55.

Betcherman, G. (2012). Labor Market Institutions: A Review of the Literature. World Bank Policy Research Working Paper 6276. Washington DC: World Bank.

Bjerge, B., N. Torm, and N. Trifković (2016). Gender Matters: Private Sector Training in Vietnamese SMEs. Working Paper 2016/149. Helsinki: UNU-WIDER.

Blunch, N.-H., and D. Verner (2004). Asymmetries in the union wage premium in Ghana, *The World Bank Economic Review*, 18(2): 237–52.

Boeri, T., and J. van Ours (2008). *The Economics of Imperfect Labor Markets*. Princeton and Oxford: Princeton University Press.

Booth, A. L., and M. Chatterji (1995). Union membership and wage bargaining when membership is not compulsory, *The Economic Journal*, 105(429): 345–60.

Card, D., and S. De La Rica (2006). Firm-level contracting and the structure of wages in Spain, *Industrial and Labor Relations Review*, 59(4): 573–92.

Chamberlain, G. (1994). Quantile regression, censoring and the structure of wages. In C. Sims (ed.), *Advances in Econometrics*. New York: Elsevier.

Chi, D. Q., and N. Torm (2015). Wage Fixing Institutions and Their Impacts in Major Garment-Producing Countries: The Case of Vietnam. Mimeo. Geneva: International Labour Organization.

Clarke, S., C.-H. Lee, and D. Q. Chi (2007). From rights to interests: The challenge of industrial relations in Vietnam, *Journal of Industrial Relations*, 49(4): 545–68.

Croson, R., and U. Gneezy (2009). Gender differences in preferences, *Journal of Economic Literature*, 47(2): 1–27.

Eaton, A., S. Schurman, and M. Chen (eds) (2017). *Informal Workers and Collective Action: A Global Perspective*. Ithaca and London: Cornell University Press.

Edwards, V., and A. Phan (2008). Trade unions in Vietnam: From socialism to market socialism. In J. Benson and Y. Zhu (eds), *Trade Unions in Asia: An Economic and Sociological Analysis*. New York: Routledge.

Fields, G. S., and G. Yoo (2000). Falling labor income inequality in Korea's economic growth: Patterns and underlying causes, *Review of Income and Wealth*, 46(2): 139–59.

Freeman, R. (1980). Unionism and the dispersion of wages, *Industrial and Labor Relations Review*, 34(1): 3–23.

Freeman, R. B., and J. L. Medoff (1984). *What Do Unions Do?* New York: Basic Books.

Grimshaw, D., and R. de Bustillo (2016). *Global Comparative Study on Wage Fixing Institutions and Their Impacts in Major Garment Producing Countries*. Geneva: International Labour Organization.

Hildreth, A. K., and S. E. Pudney (1997). Employers, Workers and Unions: An Analysis of a Firm Worker Panel with Endogenous Sampling, Attrition and Missing Data. Discussion Papers in Economics. Leicester: Department of Economics, University of Leicester.

Jones, P. (2001). Are educated workers really more productive?, *Journal of Development Economics*, 64: 57–79.

Lalonde, R., J. G. Marschke, and K. Troske (1996). Using longitudinal data on establishments to analyse the effects of union organizing campaigns in the United States, *Annales d'economie et de statistique*, 41–2: 155–86.

Larsen, A. F., J. Rand, and N. Torm (2011). Do recruitment ties affect wages? An analysis using matched employer–employee data from Vietnam, *Review of Development Economics*, 15(3): 541–55.

Lewis, H. G. (1986). Union relative wage effects, *Handbook of Labor Economics*, 2: 1139–81.

Lewis, H. G. (1963). *Unionism and Relative Wages in the United States.* Chicago: Chicago University Press.

Liu, A. Y. C. (2004). Changes in gender wage gap in Vietnam, *Journal of Comparative Economics*, 32(3): 586–96.

Malesky, E. (2009). *The Vietnam Provincial Competitiveness Index: Measuring Economic Governance for Private Sector Development.* Hanoi: Vietnam Chamber of Commerce and Industry (VCCI) and Vietnam Competitiveness Initiative (VNCI).

Manquilef-Bächler, A. A., W. Arulampalam, and J. C. Smith (2009). Differences in Decline: Quantile Regression Analysis of Union Wage Differentials in the United Kingdom, 1991–2003. IZA Discussion Papers 4138. Bonn: Institute for the Study of Labor.

Mincer, J. (1974). *Schooling, Experience and Earnings.* New York: National Bureau of Economic Research (NBER) and Columbia University Press.

Nguyen, B. T., J. Albrecht, S. J. Vroman, and D. M. Westbrook (2007). A quantile regression decomposition of urban–rural inequality in Vietnam, *Journal of Development Economics*, 83(2): 466–90.

Oi, W., and T. Idson (1999). Firm size and wages. In O. Aschenfelter and D. Card (eds), *Handbook of Labor Economics*, Vol. 3. Amsterdam: Elsevier.

Park, Y.-B. (1991). Union/nonunion wage differentials in the Korean manufacturing sector, *International Economic Journal*, 5(4): 79–91.

PCI (2015). PCI Data 2015. The Provincial Competitiveness Index. Available at: http://eng.pcivietnam.org/publications/full-report-2015/ (accessed 2 July 2018).

Pencavel, J. (2005). Unionism viewed internationally, *Journal of Labor Research*, 26(1): 65–97.

Rama, M. (2000). Wage misalignment in CFA countries: Were labour market policies to blame?, *Journal of African Economies*, 9(4): 475–511.

Rand, J., and F. Tarp (2011). Does gender influence fringe benefits provision? Evidence from Vietnamese SMEs, *Feminist Economics*, 17(1): 59–87.

Rand, J., F. Tarp, and N. Trifković (2014). Characteristics of the Vietnamese Business Environment: Evidence from a SME Survey in 2013. Hanoi: Central Institute for Economic Management (CIEM).

Rosenbaum, J., S. R. DeLuca Miller, and K. Roy (1999). Pathways into work: Short and long-term effects of personal and institutional ties, *Sociology of Education*, 72: 179–96.

Schultz, P., and G. Mwabu (1998). Labour unions and the distribution of wages and employment in South Africa, *Industrial and Labor Relations Review*, 51: 680–703.

Schurman, S., and A. E. Eaton (2012). *The Transformation of Work: Challenges and Strategies. Trade Union Organizing in the Informal Economy: A Review of the Literature on Organizing in Africa, Asia, Latin America, North America and Western, Central and Eastern Europe.* Report to the American Center for International Labor Solidarity, Rutgers University. Washington DC: Solidarity Center.

Spence, M. (1973). Job market signalling, *Quarterly Journal of Economics*, 87(3): 355–74.

Standing, G. (1992). Do unions impede or accelerate structural adjustment? Industrial versus company unions in an industrialising labour market, *Cambridge Journal of Economics*, 16: 327–54.

Söderbom, M., F. Teal, and A. Wambugu (2005). Unobserved heterogeneity and the relation between earnings and firm size: Evidence from two developing countries, *Economics Letters*, 87(2): 153–9.

Torm, N. (2018). Does Union Membership Pay Off? Evidence from Vietnamese SMEs. WIDER Working Paper 2018/71. Helsinki: UNU-WIDER.

Torm, N. (2014). The role of trade unions in Vietnam: A case study of small and medium enterprises, *Journal of International Development*, 26(2): 207–21.

VGCL (Vietnam General Confederation of Labour) (2015). VGCL Strike Report. Presented at the International Conference on Labour Relations and Dispute Resolution, Ton DucThang University, Vietnam, 26–28 March 2015.

Zhu, Y., N. Collins, M. Webber, and J. Benson (2008). New forms of ownership and human resource practices in Vietnam, *Human Resource Management*, 47(1): 157–75.

Zhu, Y., and S. Fahey (2000). The challenges and opportunities for the trade union movement in the transition era: Two socialist market economies—China and Vietnam, *Asia Pacific Business Review*, 6(3/4): 282–99.

12
Conclusion

John Rand and Finn Tarp

Structural change has been a significant contributor to Vietnam's impressive growth experience over the past three decades. Labour has moved rapidly from agriculture into manufacturing, with important improvements in livelihoods as the result. The private sector has played a key role in this success story, and especially SMEs have shown the necessary dynamism to adapt to an economic policy and institutional reform design, characterized as decentralized experimentalism. This dynamism of private SMEs has played a crucial role for the pace of diffusion of experimental successes—upstream and downstream along the value chain. Whether this success will carry into the future when innovation of new technologies (instead of diffusion of existing technologies) and TFP/productivity growth (instead of structural change) will have to become core drivers of Vietnam's growth prospects (as argued by Dang et al. 2019) stands out as a major challenge for future success.

In this book volume, we addressed this challenge striving to develop a better understanding of what drives SME growth and progress, as well as uncovering insights into the underlying behaviour of SME owners, managers, and employees. Coming to grips with these issues, is essential for both the development profession and policy-making community in figuring out how to address the task of promoting continued and sustainable private sector development. The roots of this volume grew from a time when the first Danida supported SME survey of Vietnamese non-state manufacturing enterprises covering more than 2,500 firms (formal and informal) in ten provinces began in 2005.[1] The success of the 2005 SME survey became an inspiration. It led the Central Institute of Economic Management (CIEM) of the Ministry of Planning and Investment (MPI) in Hanoi, the Institute of Labour Science and Social Affairs (ILSSA) of the Ministry of Labour, Invalids and Social Affairs (MOLISA), the Development Economics Research Group (DERG) of the University of Copenhagen and UNU-WIDER, together with Danida to plan and carry out an ambitious series of SME panel surveys. Since 2005, we have together implemented the survey of these enterprises every two years. It is on this extraordinary foundation the present volume builds.

[1] The original survey drew inspiration from the work in 1991 by Ronnås (1992).

John Rand and Finn Tarp, *Conclusion* In: *Micro, Small, and Medium Enterprises in Vietnam.* Edited by: John Rand and Finn Tarp, Oxford University Press (2020).
DOI: 10.1093/oso/9780198851189.003.0012

Importantly, since the surveys tracked the same SMEs during a decade characterized by significant economic and institutional changes and transformation, the SME panel data is a very strong tool for gaining detailed and policy-relevant information about private sector firm dynamics and enterprise development in Vietnam from 2005 to 2015. Moreover, all chapters in this volume cover owners, managers, and employees in these SMEs. They lived through and experienced a critical period in Vietnam's economic development process while managing their daily private and productive lives. How firms coped and ended up performing (or not performing) in a highly dynamic business environment under a complex set of constraints is key in what the chapters of this volume tried to uncover. In general, understanding the circumstances under which SMEs operate and the constraints and opportunities they face is an indispensable input into sound evidence-based policy-making for the future of the SMEs, the overall economy, and the welfare of the Vietnamese people in both urban and rural areas.

The SME data are exceptionally informative regarding particular themes and mechanisms influencing SME performance and development. This is why this volume was organized in three component parts, including: (i) credit access and management practices; (ii) political connections, institutional quality, and innovation; and (iii) certification, working conditions, and union membership. Throughout, the authors were determined to bring out the underlying dynamics and on identifying associated policy challenges.

What did we learn from following the same Vietnamese SMEs over a decade? A general, crosscutting, and telling insight from the chapters in this volume is that around 10 per cent of SMEs close their business every year. Given the steady increase in the population of SMEs recorded during the period 2005–2015 together with increasing average performance and productivity among survivors and new entrants, this suggests that a process of positive creative destruction forms part of the Vietnamese success story. On the other hand, we also found coherent evidence supporting that there is significant heterogeneity among smaller firms. One group, 'the necessity entrepreneurs', stays informal with low productivity and lacks better opportunities, while 'opportunity entrepreneurs' often seek formality and perform better in terms of both employment growth and productivity in the longer run. Accordingly, a key lesson here is that many of the informal micro firms stay in operation out of 'necessity', not because of 'opportunity'. The policy implication is that entrepreneurs, driven by respectively necessity and opportunity, need different policies to prosper. A one-size-fits-all approach does not work. This is a conclusion that emerges in different ways as well in the more specific findings of the chapters in this volume. They include nine more specific sets of conclusions.

First, resource misallocation reduces aggregate productivity and growth significantly. Several of the chapters in this volume directly or indirectly address this theme. One key result is that SMEs with higher marginal returns to capital are on average less likely to get access to financing, confirming that misallocation of capital is indeed a concern with real economic implications. Moreover, and importantly, rejected credit applications constraining investment activity are especially limiting at the upper end of the investment efficiency distribution. This leads to clear inefficiencies that future reforms of policy must surely address.

Second, one reason for economic inefficiencies is that the capital structure of Vietnamese firms reflects that firms balance between the 'trade-off' and the 'pecking order' theory. Accessing formal debt is extremely difficult for well-performing young (new entrants) and non-state firms. They bootstrap themselves out of financial constraints by stretching and making the most of their internal resources and assets. In contrast, established incumbents with access to formal loans use their influence, and exploit tax benefits in response to financial distress. Another key finding in this context is that informal debt markets are very important for high profitability entrepreneurs, and while human capital encourages entrepreneurs to obtain formal loans, its interaction with institutional quality deters debt financing, and favours other financial sources. We reiterate that this leads to in-optimal loan allocations that policy must address as a key priority.

Third, managerial capabilities are an important determinant for the growth path of SMEs in Vietnam. Utilizing a multidimensional measure of managerial capital, which combines both practices and attitudes of entrepreneurs, we see a clear positive association between managerial capital and productivity. We also see how changes in management practices support firms in becoming more efficient over time. Importantly, 'entrepreneurial attitudes' are more important for success than learning elementary business skills. This result has critical policy implications for the design of entrepreneurial training programmes for SMEs. Furthermore, effects are very heterogeneous across firm size, with improvements in managerial capabilities having significantly more impact on smaller inexperienced SMEs than on larger incumbents. Key insights for effective policy design flow from these observations.

Fourth, having close ties to government officials may not only be beneficial for smaller businesses wanting to stay 'under the radar'. It may also be of importance for SMEs operating at a larger more formal scale. Our data reveal that is very important for formal SMEs to have political connections when it comes to both the access to and the cost-of-credit obtained from formal financial institutions. Having close ties through membership of the Communist Party of Vietnam decreases the likelihood of being credit-constrained by 4 percentage points. Moreover, politically connected SMEs accessing credit face lower cost-of-capital than non-connected SMEs not excluded from formal financial markets. Finally, the data shows that the impact of political connections is most valuable during periods of financial distress, and less prevalent during business cycle upswings. These findings are important. They reinforce the above finding that credit-allocation is not optimal and that policy change would lead to greater economic efficiency. It also suggests that it is wise policy to consider expanding credit in periods of distress as Vietnam did in 2007–08.[2]

Fifth, we have already observed that differential impacts across firm size matter. So do different degrees of formality. Taking into account previous experience with the Vietnamese licencing system, the most productive informal household businesses are not always those that 'switch' into formality. Many of these highly productive informal SMEs do not perceive the potential positive effects of formalization as relevant for their business going forward. Tellingly, they state that the reason for staying informal is that they expect the net costs from increased tax payments to surpass the net benefits from formalization, also in the longer run. We stress though that the data also give rise to an alternative explanation.[3] Government 'push' initiatives towards increased formalization are heterogeneous across informal household businesses, with the upper tier informal entrepreneurs most likely to 'escape' civil servant demands for improved business licensing. Combined with information from bribe incidence data, this raises the possibility and critical policy concern of collusion between upper tier informal SMEs and public officials. This highlights that no single policy can ensure proper balance between the need for generating public revenue and the critical importance of furthering firm efficiency.

Sixth, differences in institutional capacity/quality across the ten provinces covered by the SME survey matter for the innovative capacity of SMEs. The same goes for the interaction with human and financial capital scarcity in these locations. This volume therefore zoomed in on the relationship between the innovative capacity of SMEs and the relative abundance of resources available (slack resources) to the SMEs across different locations. This reveals that in locations with a more favourable business environment the impact (on innovation rates) of relative human resource abundance is lesspronounced than the impact (on innovation rates) of relative abundance of capital. In terms of policy, this calls attention once more to the need for pursuing an effective balance between the allocation of scarce capital and human capital policy—and associated institutions.

Seventh, a promising policy-tool to protect especially mid-sized businesses from downside shocks and minimize risk is the development of internationally recognized quality control systems (i.e., certification). Interpreting business risk as variability in revenue, variability in customer base, a practice of making informal payments, and temporary firm closure, our data document that certified firms experience lower levels of business risk. We once again find significant heterogeneity across provinces with firms located in rural areas and in the northern

[2] See Thurlow et al. (2011).

[3] See also see Rand and Tarp (2012).

provinces of Vietnam as those most likely to benefit from such internationally recognized certifications. The policy implication is that further expansion of such systems is highly recommended both with a view to expanding exports and from the perspective of minimizing business risk in a challenging environment.

Eight, a particular strength of the SME panel data is its employer-employee component. This made it possible in this book volume to add value to the literature on the effect of different labour market conditions on individual earnings. In the absence of adequate institutional mechanisms, trade unions can help promote equity and social justice for workers through higher wages and other worker benefits. The results show that the wages of unionized workers are 9–22 per cent higher than the wages of non-union workers, controlling for both firm and worker characteristics. This point to a potentially important role for trade unions that could bring future advantages if further developed in Vietnam.

Ninth and finally, the employer–employee data makes it possible for analysts to establish whether workers obtain compensation through higher wages for working in vulnerable jobs and in unfavourable working conditions. The results indicate that there are no clear compensating mechanisms for working in poor conditions, for having an informal contract, and for having few financial benefits. In addition, workers in the upper tail of the wage distribution are more likely to suffer due to working in adverse working conditions. Finally, employees recruited through official hiring channels with an informal contract earn less compared to employees, relying on a social network hiring channel. Such differences are clearly a concern and they suggest that decisive policy action is required to address them.

In sum, the need to develop the private sector and the importance of ensuring that the motoring capacity of private initiative and entrepreneurial spirit is mobilized to the maximum in support of sustainable development took a central place in the Sustainable Development Goals (SDGs) approved by the UN General Assembly in September 2015. While the development community across a wide spectrum recognizes the need for private sector dynamism, we know much less about how to ensure this happens in practice, and what is required in concrete terms when it comes to policy action. We put forward the present volume with the ambition to help fill this gap with a series of insights from a dynamic East Asian country that has managed to combine aggregate growth, structural transformation, and poverty reduction. We hope this will help inspire action elsewhere as we believe researchers and policy makers can learn a great deal from this experience. We also hope that our findings and recommendations will help inform Vietnamese policy-making in the continued search of how to promote private sector driven development in the years to come and how to achieve the SDG aspirational goal of leaving no one behind.

References

Dang, T. T. H., F. Tarp, and D. van Seventer (2019). Growth and structural transformation in Vietnam: The real story beneath. In C. Monga and J. Lin (eds), *Handbook of Structural Transformation*. Oxford: Oxford University Press.

Rand, J. and F. Tarp (2012). Firm-level corruption in Vietnam. *Economic Development and Cultural Change*, 60(3): 571–95.

Ronnås, P. (1992): *Employment Generation through Private Entrepreneurship in Vietnam*. Geneva: ILO and SIDA.

Thurlow, J., F. Tarp, S. McCoy, N. M. Hai, C. Breisinger, and C. Arndt (2011). The impact of the global commodity and financial crises on poverty in Vietnam, *Journal of Globalization and Development*, 2(1): 1–31.

Index

Note: Tables and figures are indicated by an italic 't' and 'f', respectively, following the page number.